MW01229680

DEATH BY SOCIALISM

DEATH BY SOCIALISM

J. M. ROCK

Copyright © 2024 by Jonathan Michael Rock

Published by Paradocracy

All rights reserved. No part of this publication may be reproduced, stored in a retrieval system, or transmitted in any form or by any means, electronic, mechanical, photocopying, recording, or otherwise, without written permission of the publisher.

ISBN Paperback: 979-8-218-37228-6
ISBN Hardcover: 979-8-9901552-0-6

For permission to reproduce excerpts, use copyrighted material, translate, or adapt this work, please contact the auhor or publisher.

For my precious girls, Leila and Luna, who have inspired my crusade against tyranny: it is through you that I have a profound interest in the future. For my wife Lara, who has graciously indulged me throughout all of my writings, who has entertained my lectures and encouraged me in my undertakings. For those in search of the truth; those who have fought valiantly for the cause of liberty; and those who will contribute to the cause in the years ahead.

The greatest threat to liberty is the aspiration to define its terms.

CONTENTS

PREFACE

The great deeds of minds and men are soon forgotten. They turn to dust or, as stories on a shelf, collect it. Novel discoveries and cautionary tales live there; words outliving visionaries, patiently awaiting approbation, vindication and the impartial, enlightened verdict of mankind. Their time scarcely comes.

The truest visionaries buck the conventions, speak the unspeakable, and contest the uncontested; they are guided indefatigably by truth, indifferent to its popularity, and willing to defend it at all costs.

The truth and the visionary are ahead of the times. Like poetry, they are as misunderstood as they are unpopular. They are as celebrated in their time as they are for all of time: for them, vindication is only steps away from the people who are always facing the other direction, who are ordered to never look back. They never do.

They never understand the problems. They never understand why they happened or what they can do about them. They never give the visionaries their due, and they never manage to find the truth.

* * *

As fields of study, history, philosophy and economics are matters of perspective, fallible assessments of truth. In reality, they are meager attempts at capturing the essence of life, the product of affection, avarice, preference, passion, and — in their highest forms — love. They are mankind's best effort at seeking to understand, or to otherwise distort, the most fundamental questions before us: what drives human action, and what is our purpose on planet Earth? The first of these questions is easier to answer, at least by approximation; the second, however, is for the individual to determine. That is the cause of this book, and one this author humbly seeks to defend.

INTRODUCTION

Every year, there is a list of the world's top causes of death. The list ordinarily includes heart disease, stroke, pulmonary disease, lung cancer, tuberculosis, and malaria, among others. However, there is one cause of death that is conspicuously absent from this list; one that has claimed more than one hundred million lives over the past century alone, and one that has left countless millions of lives and families in shambles.

You will not find this cause of death listed on any coroner's reports. You will not find any laboratories researching a cure. There are no fundraisers or public awareness campaigns around it. You will not even find a passing mention of it in any of the newspapers. It is the most ruthless of serial killers, and yet it never has its day in court. More than people, this cause of death has claimed entire civilizations.

It is the most silent of killers: it is *Death by Socialism*.

ABOUT THE AUTHOR

Born just north of Detroit, Michigan, Jonathan Michael Rock is an author, economist, historian and philosopher dedicated to the cause of liberty. As the founder and author of Paradocracy.com, Mr. Rock draws on his extensive research and his personal experience in fields both public and private, ranging from the armed forces, subsidized housing, real estate, and social work to financial services, business intelligence, and the mortgage industry. Apart from his career, his endless research and the hundreds of articles he has written, Mr. Rock is an avid adventurer, traveler, musician, athlete, mountaineer, Civil War reenactor, and collector of historical artifacts and Americana. Proud of his American heritage and way of life, he spends his time with his family on his ranch in the shadows of the Sierra Nevada, usually donning a Stetson. In all of his writings, his objectives are clear: to advance the cause of liberty, to resist the tides of tyranny, to discover and deliver the truth, and, above all, to leave his heirs and posterity better prepared to defend and exercise their inalienable rights.

CHAPTER I

WELCOME TO 2030

"Welcome to 2030. I own nothing, have no privacy, and life has never been better". That is the title of an article from the World Economic Forum in November of 2016. The title is essentially socialism in a nutshell: no private property, no self-ownership, and no privacy, but somehow, they contend, life will be better.

This is the budding trend in America, away from freedom and capitalism in favor of government and socialism; and the data bear this out. Decades after the collapse of the Berlin Wall and the dissolution of the Soviet Union, socialism has reemerged as ungracefully as bellbottom jeans, in both the classroom and the collective conscience.

According to a 2015 Reason-Rupe survey, 53 percent of Americans under 30 admit to having a favorable view of socialism. Likewise, a 2016 Gallup poll found that an astounding 69 percent of Millennials say they would be willing to vote for a "socialist" presidential candidate. For comparison's sake, roughly a third of their parents' generation confess positive views toward socialism.

In 2016, national surveys and exit polls revealed that roughly 70 to 80 percent of young Democrats cast their ballots for presidential candidate Bernie Sanders, a self-proclaimed "democratic socialist". Likewise, according to a 2023 Statista Research Department publication, "The popularity of socialism in the United States has been increasing among people who identify as Democrats, rising from 50 percent in 2010 to 65 percent in 2021."

No matter where you stand on today's political, social, and economic issues, you have probably heard about this. And for those unaware of this trend, it is time to heed this warning and learn of the risks. After all, as Dr. Ron Paul has said, "It's the prevailing attitudes of the people that determine the kind of government that *we have.*"

As for the growing approval of socialism in the United States, this is a trend long in the making, a phenomenon with its origins in gullibility, indifference, degeneracy, complacency, and ignorance of both heritage and the value of liberty. Indeed, the story of Leftism has its roots in power and persuasion, envy and greed, empty promises and wishful thinking, the most vile and the most innocent of human traits, the most extreme of vices and sensibilities: among them pity and jealousy, indulgences and instant gratification; personal or political gain, pride in one's subordination to the establishment and its stated causes; arrogance and overconfidence in one's own intelligence, his perceptions and his designs; gullibility and ignorance to the laws of scarcity, human nature and physics; the belief in unlimited abundance, a world with a "solution" to all of life's problems; the belief that society may feasibly be brought into perfect harmony without consequence, that it may be solved formulaically as any academic problem, and that the power necessary to effect the "solution" is a worthwhile compromise.

Of course, another form of ignorance is expressed as incredulity: incredulity to answers, reasons, and explanations that people do not particularly like. Indeed, one critical error committed by many people is that, in not understanding why something is the way that it is (i.e. "I don't understand why..."), many either never consider looking for the answer, never even consider the possibility that there is an answer, never find an answer to their satisfaction, or, most commonly, simply assume that there is no valid answer. This is precisely why so many people, in their incredulity, continually operate from invalid assumptions, rush to unfounded judgments, seek refuge in baseless conclusions, and generally assume that there are better ways and that they have the solutions. This is how so many people have been tempted by the lure of Leftism: they are so consumed by "what should be" that they scarcely consider "what is", let alone the reasons why.

Of course, that is to completely dismiss another driver of socialism: malice. However, this author's assessment is charitable enough to assume the best, to give the Leftists the benefit of the doubt that they are less malicious than ignorant, a dangerous supposition, to be sure. However, as Hanlon's razor puts it, "Never attribute to malice that which can be adequately explained by ignorance." As for Leftism, it is an ideology which, at least intellectually speaking, is fraught with enough ignorance that, so far as logic and reason are concerned, it would seem superfluous to assess the character of its exponents.

For this reason, a study of socialism need not even deal with the subject of malice upon adequately scrutinizing its foundations in ignorance. Of course, as for the theories and the ideas of Leftism, they are indeed the product of both. As for the Leftists themselves, their support can be attributed, with absolute certainty, to ignorance or naïveté; whereas, especially in the ranks of those with vested interests, the rest of the support can be attributed to malice or indifference in service to self-interest. Regardless of the specific causes, regardless of the route taken, the outcome and the destination are the same: the uncompromising wrath of a failed system which simply cannot be made to work; a trend toward, and operating from, progressively more ignorance.

Indeed, it is a trend growing with every passing decade and every subsequent generation, and one which has spread considerably since the Korean War, when the chief of intelligence of the "Chinese People's Volunteer Army" reported in a memorandum to his superiors that American prisoners of war had become easy targets for Leftist indoctrination; targets lacking in their understanding of those differences of principle which distinguish their civilization from the society of their adversaries:

"Based upon our observation of American soldiers and their officers captured in this war, the following facts are evidenced. There is little knowledge or understanding, even among United States university graduates, of American political history and philosophy; of federal, state, and community organizations; of states rights and civil rights; of safeguards to freedom; and of how these things supposedly operate within [their] own system."

Indeed, to paraphrase the author Henry Grady Weaver, Leftism bores from within; it is a program of infiltration and attrition. It is an infection, a disease which, as one American officer has put it, "might well be considered the Number One Social Disease of America." The same officer prophetically cautioned, "Its prevention and its treatment are essential to the continuing survival of our system." It is a contagion which infects and ultimately destroys a civilization; one metastasizing incrementally and surreptitiously within the minds, and often with the approval, of its victims.

This trend is certain to continue, and, perhaps most frightening of all, it will continue with the benefit of the collective conscience. The risks of socialism are incalculable, but they are real. They measure not only in the risks posed to life, but in the risks posed to everything which brings meaning to it. There is simply no metric conceived by man that can even remotely account for all of the risks, but we know this for certain: if we should fail to defend the stake of liberty, these are the costs to be borne by our heirs.

It is therefore essential, in the interest of life, liberty and posterity, to guard against the unwarranted influence of *tyranny by the collective conscience*; we must never allow the weight of this combination to endanger our liberties and God-given rights. After all, socialism threatens liberty in the same way that Satan comes disguised as an angel.

In this treatise, we will uncover the identity of socialism, its various disguises, and the continual threats posed to us and any free society. Finally, we will embark to prescribe the antidote and the lifeblood to our freedom.

At the outset, it is essential to begin with a set of critical definitions; such being the case for any honest and credible assessment. It is especially important to define a few terms which appear repeatedly throughout this book, whose definitions enable the reader to translate this assessment more clearly and correctly. The following definitions are provided by the author in his own words for the express purpose of this assessment. As such, where these terms appear, they appear strictly as they are hereafter defined, not as they may be used elsewhere or otherwise.

Throughout this text, the terms "state" and "government" refer to any number of bodies, agencies, or administrations, namely political, which maintain an exclusive monopoly over the instruments of force and coercion within a given jurisdiction.

The term "establishment" is generally used interchangeably with the term "government", while also referring to the broader networks, the cronies, the enterprises, the syndicates and the affiliates through whom government enjoys support and carries influence.

In the context of this writing, the term "liberty" is to describe a state or condition free from government restraints on the rights of man, each man being free from force, coercion, and aggression; where the individual is entitled to the full enjoyment and use of his own labor and property; where his private property, his associations, and his contracts are respected and negotiated voluntarily; where the individual is secure in his personal property, his person, houses, papers and effects; where the individual is free to enjoy the full scope of his rights, free to express himself and to conduct his affairs, free to think and to operate in accordance with his own will, free to govern his own family, and free to define the purpose of his own life and his own labor, so long as he does not infringe upon the rights of another; where each individual is afforded due process in the remediation of crimes, disputes, damages, and any incursion upon an individual's God-given rights and contractual entitlements.

The term "Leftist" represents those who advocate for the progressive expansion of the power of government, the ever stricter regimentation of society, the development or the mobilization of a standing army, whether at home or abroad. The term thus applies to those advocating for the greater influence of the establishment over the lives and the possessions of the people, namely their persons, their property, their personal effects, their customs, affairs and God-given rights.

Ultimately, the term "socialism" is defined as sharply as possible throughout the remainder of the book. As the text bears out, it is properly defined not by what it is claimed to be, but by what it truly is. It is properly assessed not merely as it has been defined historically, but as it has evolved to influence social affairs, to corrupt families and the minds of men, and to indeed infect the whole of human civilization; as it has served faithfully as the means to communism, to complete and uncompromising control over everything worth holding, just as capitalism, abused politically, and as illustrated throughout this book, has served as the means to the same ends, by way of cronyism and central banking: control over the land and the resources to the very lives and the fate of the people. This is the basic objective of the entire book: to properly define "socialism" by contrasting its various disguises with its true identities, by equating it with its many consequences and insurmountable risks, by exposing its inherent deficiencies, and, finally, by prescribing the most effective antidote to such an insidious disease. Let us begin with a more formal introduction of the term.

CHAPTER II

SOCIALISM DEFINED

S ocialism is traditionally defined as collective ownership over
the means of production. Its admirers regard it as a form
of compassion, moral by definition, virtuous by fiat. Yet this
betrays the truth about socialism, a dynamic despotism that
adapts to its environment and the technologies at its disposal.
It is indeed "a pestilential whore," as a 1925 publication once
described it, "cloaking herself as social virtue and brotherly
love." Whatever its motives, whatever its definition, it amounts
to force and, ultimately, oppression in execution. At its core,
socialism is truly whatever its defenders want it to be, tailored
to suit any hot topic and conveniently aligned with anything
perceived as kind, compassionate, or sensitive to the plight
of the citizenry and the so-called "common good". Whether
it is an ambitious plan to end poverty or world hunger, or
to eliminate inequality in our midst, socialism is merely a
specious device for social control and, invariably, social ruin.

In vying for control, the socialist must pry the people from
their scruples, their time-tested traditions and values to bring
them under the control of the new dominion and the new social
order. Indeed, the socialist must inoculate the public to reason,
convincing some significant fraction of them that, as one
Samuel Clemens may have put it, "what they know ain't so", or
that, alternatively, they can't possibly "know" anything at all;
that truth is rather a function of one's personal feelings or "lived
experience"; that outrage and enthusiasm can, and indeed *must*,
take the place of logical arguments and critical thought. Indeed,
this is why politicians and propagandists so often characterize
their beliefs as "feelings", as the second is generally more difficult
to dispute than the first, and in most cases feelings are far more
persuasive. This kind of subjectivism effectively enables pundits
and politicians to get away with the absurd.

Indeed, this is why some Leftists point to the concept of
relativity, often confusing the concept as license to regard

all things as arbitrary or subjective; this, of course, is not in order to advance scientific understanding, but to aimlessly philosophize and needlessly confuse. However, despite the fact that information and data sets can be tracked relative to others, these relationships do not suggest that all information and all judgments cannot be measured against a fixed standard or benchmark, that they cannot be assessed by an *objective*, common, or realistic standard. This is precisely where the subjectivists go awry: they contend that a universal state of relativity denies the existence of an objective reality. This is particularly dangerous because absurdities are identifiable only "relative" to a constant and immovable standard — one that simply cannot exist in a space where all things are deemed merely relative. It is in this way that the people are stripped of their sense of reality, whereafter their overlords manipulate them like putty to their satisfaction. After all, as Voltaire once proclaimed, "Those who can make you believe absurdities, can make you commit atrocities."

For this reason, the socialists focus their efforts on such campaigns as identity politics, a resort for those who refuse to deal with the facts. In this, the socialists aim to create their own convenient "truths" and doctrines by which people are to be guided and governed, albeit with the popular support of people who have since come to accept this school of thought and, indeed, prefer it over the rigors of reality, logic and reason. As the old phrase goes, "Whom the gods would destroy they first make mad."

It is often said that, between two extremes, the truth is usually found somewhere in the middle. Unrestrained by any standard of ethics, objectivity, or truth, however, there is no limit to the Leftist extreme, as the Leftist can always voyage even further into the absurd. For this reason alone, "the middle" — politically speaking — always favors one extreme:

the one on the Left. The Leftists in power are intimately aware of this, which is why they are constantly becoming more extreme, why they are always introducing more absurdities, and yet so often going undetected as "the middle" continues to migrate to the Left.

Indeed, one vital aspect of socialism, and broadly any form of Leftism, is the art of rendering the world confusing and unintuitive, such that the political elite assume authority as the final arbiter in political as well as social and moral issues. As the state comes to assume the role of the final arbiter on all things, each of its pronouncements and every piece of legislation, and even its silence on any given issue, come to be viewed as moral imperatives, judgments from on high, rulings on *good* versus *evil* and *right* versus *wrong*, instead of the limited extent to which the state is permitted to judge human action.

It is imperative to remember that government is not to be trusted with the power of legislating morality; that government cannot possibly accomplish this task; and that, where it aims or claims to do so, it also seeks (or otherwise manages) to corrupt. Indeed, it is essential that the people remember that, in a state of liberty, they must be free to advocate for and to adhere to their own moral codes, so long as they do not violate the essential rights of their fellow man. To rely on government to enumerate the codes of morality is to entrust government with the greatest of powers in the world: control over the collective conscience of the people.

Where this power is held by government, so too are the people held as putty in its hands, ready to be shaped and hardened, stretched and squashed. Indeed, the constituents, in their attempts to conform or to appear "progressive" and "educated", will heed the instruction voiced from high atop the ivory tower, where judgments, pronouncements and gestures are made daily, weaving one falsehood, embellishment or contradiction into the next. The relative complexity of modern society offers the further benefit of convincing the youth that their parents are idiots, that all of their ancestors were uncivilized morons, and that their heritage is rooted inextricably in primitive and immoral thinking. This encourages the youth to reject their parents, their ancestors, their traditions, and wisdom in favor of the arbitrary demands and assertions of the establishment.

In this way, the more complex a society, and the more confused the people, the more power the establishment is likely to seize over the public. This ultimately witnesses the last gasps of humanity, whereupon the masses, fighting desperately and perilously for their survival, and for the survival of their traditions, descend into social unrest, economic depression, total war and, ultimately, utter ruin in the wake of some fantastical dream.

Henry Grady Weaver eloquently articulated this point in his 1947 work *The Mainspring of Human Progress*:

"The truth of the matter is that the American revolution for human freedom is the only thing that's really new, and it did not end with the surrender of Cornwallis nor with the signing of the Constitution. It's still going on, and the counterrevolutionists — the enemies of freedom — are on the march. Their major attack is not on the open battle field. It is in the fifth-column technique of skillfully boring from within — a program of infiltration and attrition. The principal secret weapon is traceable to Lenin, who allegedly instructed his followers to first confuse the vocabulary. Lenin was smart. He knew that thinking requires words of precise meaning. Confuse the vocabulary, and the unsuspecting majority is at a disadvantage when defending themselves against the small but highly disciplined minority which knows exactly what it wants and which deliberately promotes word- as the first step in its efforts to divide and conquer."

Indeed, one of the great confusions in vocabulary is that around the words "understand" and "sympathize", two words often linked, together threatening not only to excuse poor behavior but to potentially enable it. One need not sympathize in order to gain a proper understanding of someone or something; just as one need not sympathize as a consequence of that proper understanding. Confusion between those two words is particularly dangerous because it causes people to equate *understanding* with *sympathy* and, thus, to conclude that every understandable action is thereby deemed worthy of another's sympathy.

Additionally, the word "sympathy" is often dangerously associated with "acceptance" and "embrace", so in such a case where understanding leads to sympathy, it is likely to also lead to acceptance and embrace; the very types of reception that can make "understanding" dangerous, the types that can penalize people, and consequently society, for their understanding.

Ironically, given enough understanding, virtually *all* of human behavior is understandable, and that is precisely the risk posed by this kind of confusion; that, instead of understanding the wrongs in order to identify the faults or the oversights, or to make the appropriate adjustments, the wrongs become the burden of the honest and the insightful, who are ultimately outnumbered and overwhelmed by those who are neither understanding nor sympathetic, who will happily take advantage of the understanding and the sympathy so generously extended to them.

The advantages enjoyed by the tyrants through word-confusion are twofold: the confusion affords the tyrants exclusive authority as the final arbiters of *truth*, or rather their distorted form of it; and the wordplay enables the tyrants to continually *manufacture* their own convenient *truths*, to condemn their subjects to their alluring fantasies. Ironically, those fantasies enjoy the advantages bestowed upon them by the market economy, and in turn they form the basis for the assault upon it. It is no mere coincidence that so many artists come to sympathize with Leftism: they come to so believe in their intellect, to so indulge their grandiosities, to so believe in their fantasies that they virtually inhabit them.

Indeed, too many artists (i.e. writers, actors, musicians, painters, et cetera) have been artists for too long without any real or relatable experiences on which to draw, without much basis in reality. They therefore operate from and live within their own limited fantasies, with a complete and utter disregard for reality, the laws of nature and physics notwithstanding. After all, their fantasies are far more appealing than the rigid realities of life on planet Earth. Fantastical thinking and word-confusion, and truthfully confusion of all kinds, play perfectly into those fantasies, and the people's curiosities are always ready to be piqued. In the United States, Hollywood and mainstream media are always eager to lead the charge and share in the spoils. As Samuel Adams once put it, "How strangely will the Tools of a Tyrant pervert the plain Meaning of Words!"

In their assault on virtually everything American, Hollywood not only denounces capitalism and traditional family values, but it routinely blacklists people who stand in their way. Actor Kevin Sorbo is one such actor who met this fate as an outspoken conservative Christian. Referring to Hollywood, Sorbo has said that being a conservative Christian is "like being a double leper." In an interview on the subject, he went on to point out some of the blatant contradictions of the Left:

"They're the ones who say, 'We need to be tolerant; we need to have love,' but they're the most anti-tolerant people... Every movie, every TV show... there's always some point, someplace, where they'll pretty much degrade anybody who's conservative or Republican."

This is because Hollywood does not really care about anything or anyone other than that which sells. They do not care about "diversity" or "tolerance" or any number of political buzzwords that have come into vogue just as suddenly as they have been rendered meaningless. They care about selling their stories; and it just so happens that, in the world of cinema, *pretending* to care is just as good for sales as actually caring. Fortunately for Hollywood, pretending is quite akin to acting, so you might say they are fairly well-rehearsed in it.

For Hollywood and the political Left, they are a marriage of convenience: they share a common vision, but only insofar as their ideas intersect with some measure of popularity and control; not just control over the space, but over the minds and matters of the people. They do not care about truth or righteousness, "diversity" or "tolerance". They might celebrate those terms, but only selectively whenever they serve their own specific interests. Indeed, they have no respect for diversity or tolerance where it actually counts, which is to say they have no respect for it at all.

Diversity is entirely irrelevant in the context of gender and ethnicity, which are at the front and center of every Leftist's application of the term. The only relevant forms of diversity are those of skill and character: not the state in which one is born, but the manner in which one conducts himself, the manner in which he presents his ideas and his opinions. Likewise, tolerance is just as irrelevant in the space of agreement. True tolerance is found in the face of dissent, and that is precisely where it is tested.

However, the Left has no patience for this kind of diversity or tolerance, because it cannot rally unthinking political support around it. Indeed, wherever Leftists are found promoting *diversity* or *tolerance*, it is invariably a means to appeal to minorities, who tend to identify strongly with their own minority groups; who embrace virtually any narrative, however nonfactual, which seeks to make them the heroes or the *oppressed*; who are always ready to rally against a common enemy, especially one of their own construction; who are always ready to empower the government to destroy that enemy.

Wherever Leftists are found promoting *diversity* or *tolerance*, it is invariably a means to exploit the sensibilities of their opponents; to make them *tolerant* of forces opposed to truth, virtue, and liberty, and even their way of life; and to make them amenable to *diversity* insofar as it compels them to *tolerate* (then later to accept and embrace) the ideas and allies of Leftism.

True diversity and tolerance are anathema to Leftism, as they threaten its very foundation. They threaten to shatter the entire premise of the Left overnight, by guiding the people to the truth as Ayn Rand once put it: "The smallest minority on earth is the individual." Of course, the plight of the individual is a non-starter in politics, because the concept invariably reaches the conclusion that the best state is the state of liberty; that government is, as Thomas Paine rightly proclaimed, even in its best state, but a necessary evil, and in its worst state, an intolerable one.

Fortunately for Hollywood, the plight of the people is always at their disposal, and so are their minds as clay ready to be shaped and hardened; and wherever that plight fails to meet their ends, Hollywood is happy to embellish or to invent one out of thin air. As it turns out, in a society progressively stripped of its principles and any sense of personal responsibility, there are more willing victims all the more eager to entertain their message. By their designs, the people are left to dream and to fantasize, paying little mind to the truth; after all, it is a costless exercise for those who haven't the gumption nor the liberty to afford much else.

For a people just as poor in resources as in principles, and for a people willing to do just about anything in their lust for money, it is never long until they have abandoned roughly all of their sacred traditions and beliefs, even their Creator. In the case of Christianity, the Leftists seldom hesitate to crucify its believers: they vehemently oppose its teachings, and, even among those who profess the faith, they contradict themselves in virtually every way. On the whole, the Leftists unabashedly reject the Bible or otherwise make hypocrites of themselves, doing this through their denial of both free will and the sovereignty of God; their rejection of personal responsibility, sound money, and the nuclear family; their celebration of sins, among them theft, extortion, false idols, cross-dressing, promiscuity, homosexuality, transgenderism, and overt sexual expression; and through the "liberation" of the people from their Creator and the standards of righteousness. They often fancy themselves *secularists, atheists, anti-theists, progressivists,* faithful believers in *the science,* but it is through arrogance, ignorance, or deceit that they come to embrace, profess, and spread their new religions. In the course of spreading each new religion, they either intentionally or mistakenly neglect to acknowledge its many shortcomings and the grave risks that each poses to civilization.

One of the considerations omitted, underestimated or overlooked by so many atheists, and particularly anti-theists, is whether they can successfully abolish religion without introducing another, whether society can completely abandon traditional religious values in favor of *secularism, enlightenment* or *science* without bringing the people under the rule of a technocracy, a new religion administered by a select class of appointed "experts"; without, over the long run, that ruling class assuming so much control over social affairs as to face no challengers, as to no longer be held accountable to the truth or *the science*; without a major share of the population failing to convert to the new religion but to instead simply depart altogether from universal values, to descend entirely into the relative and the subjective, and to thereby devolve into a society of hedonistic individuals uninterested in natural law, wholly unencumbered by virtue, and increasingly lacking in compassion and the bonds between men which sustain a people, their civilizations, and their species.

Indeed, this is the only case in which the *Leftists* can be properly identified as *liberals*: where they seek to "liberate" the people from virtue, reality, personal responsibility, and truth. Among an infinite number of others, these are some of the most pernicious tenets of Leftism: the "liberation" of the people from traditional gender roles, the celebration of sexuality and deviancy, and the encouragement of promiscuity and sexual expression. The end of all of this is a "liberation" from truth and virtue, purpose and principle, honor and discipline, reality and the responsibilities of observing these and the other standards of honest, honorable and fruitful living.

CHAPTER III

DECEIT AND DENIAL

One such example of the Leftists' denial of reality, things as they naturally and immutably exist, is found in their promotion of the "minimum wage" — or the so-called "living wage" with which the legislation is so often advertised — which is demonstrably destined to fail against their stated objectives. Mind you, their stated objectives may, in fact, belie their true aims, but their denial of reality is essential to their execution nevertheless. Through the subject of the minimum wage, the reader doubtless gains an understanding of the general practice of Leftism.

Indeed, by its very nature, the minimum wage law can never be effective. Where it is too low to influence wages in any industry, it will be moot; whereas, wherever it is theoretically high enough to affect wages, it will invariably cause a surplus of labor supply and a shortage of labor demand. On the whole, the end result will always be a shortage, and one which, as evidenced by history (i.e. the case *Adkins v. Children's Hospital* (1923) and the *National Industrial Recovery Act* of 1933), hinders economic growth by promoting cartels and monopolies, and by disproportionately diminishing the prospects for small businesses, low-skilled workers, and, incidentally, minorities and immigrants.

In the same vein, Leftist regimes also float ideas about price ceilings on the goods regularly consumed by the working class. However, this too would predictably produce the same result through a shortage, whether through quantity, quality, or some combination thereof. Whether a price floor, by the name of a *minimum wage*, or a price ceiling, by way of a maximum sales price, the results are always identical: unintended consequences magnitudes of order beyond the wildest imaginations of the initiatives' unwitting supporters; profound social, legal and economic implications outside the frame of hypnotizing propaganda; and devastating losses disproportionately incurred by those who can least afford them.

Ultimately, great confusion surrounds the minimum wage, principally because of the academics, the politicians and the protestors who preoccupy themselves and others with the nominal wage increases that are anticipated, rather than the real effect that the law has, or is bound to have, on the flesh-and-blood employee who is no longer employable at that wage, or the flesh-and-blood candidate who is deprived of the opportunity that might otherwise exist below that artificial price floor.

As it turns out, any level is too high for a price floor on anything, whether a good or a form of labor, as such a law stubbornly interferes with the manner in which resources are consensually traded for the betterment of those who own the goods or offer the services involved in the exchange.

Ultimately, the lowering of prices has been the most effective means for empowering the greatest numbers of people to gain access to those luxuries once enjoyed by only the wealthiest of society. The lowering of prices means lower prices for goods, services and wages, the latter of which forms one of the bases for all prices.

The academics, the politicians and the protestors all too often get lost in the numbers, where they forget that the numbers are merely representative. It is not important that the mere numbers rise, but that productivity and relative costs improve in order to enhance the purchasing power of the average worker. All else equal, these are costs which are naturally expressed in lower general prices as we learn to produce more with less, and incidentally we enable higher-order employment opportunities with progressively lower measures of risk and wider ranges of benefits. However, a higher *nominal* wage need not imply a higher *real* wage, just as a lower *nominal* wage need not imply a lower *real* wage. The *real* value of compensation follows from the productivity of the worker and the production of real goods, and it can appreciate or depreciate in real terms based on the productivity of the broader market.

Because of the nature of higher-order enterprises, their compensation depends heavily upon the stability of the supporting market structure. In contrast, lower-order enterprises are better equipped to subsist amidst instability, as demand for lower-order goods is less elastic and the final products rely less heavily on commercial trade. Higher-order enterprises, on the other hand, are heavily dependent upon trade. The higher the order of enterprise, the further removed it is from the final product and the inherent state of affairs — or the Robinson Crusoe economy, if you will. So, while there is a lower risk of injury or death, the long-term prospects are not remotely guaranteed, and in many cases compensation may be meager. However, where compensation for any trade or service is meager, those aforesaid risks are generally mitigated or wholly eliminated — or otherwise the compensation is deemed more reliable than the alternative.

These factors are important because low-skilled jobs with relatively meager wages tend to be under-appreciated in the "civilized" world. Whereas the human being could each day combat adversity in order to survive of his own might, economies of scale have largely equipped him for specialized labor in a secure, air-conditioned space to afford to survive the day both unassailed and with near-certainty. However meager the compensation, the willing worker demonstrates by his actions, regardless of his protests after he has clocked out, that his arrangement is an improvement over the alternative.

Unfortunately, the minimum wage law serves only to limit those opportunities over the foregone alternatives. And job losses are not the only cost of the minimum wage law: the law prevents jobs from ever being created below that wage level; a level which is essentially plucked out of thin air. Beyond this, the minimum wage law causes higher prices, but not merely in the manner that one might expect.

Interestingly, wherever the minimum wage law has not conspicuously caused a price increase, it has exacted this cost obscurely upon the economic system in the form of less opportunity and unrealized supply. Like an iceberg, there are far weightier implications than what appears at the surface to readily meet the eye. Wherever the costs of the minimum wage are less conspicuous, the economic system bears those costs through the conveyance of savings into consumption; whereas the nominal wage increase for the employee amounts to a relatively trivial boost to income, it amounts to a potentially sizable loss incurred by the employer on his payroll. Moreover, the loss of savings to consumption, as wage-earners are disproportionately more likely to spend the marginal dollar than to save or invest it, exacts a cost on the economic system through the reduction of capital investment, which drags on productivity and future consumption.

Minimum wage advocates often focus on how much workers could earn instead of appreciating the way in which incentives alter decisions within the market. They also fail to consider an alternative, that they could just as well call for something else in order to achieve the same intended end: they could call for greater measures of productivity, which would then lower the costs of the goods that we buy, thereby boosting the wages of workers in *real* terms. If the minimum-wage advocate were to understand this, or if he were truly interested in improving economic outcomes through labor, he would not embark upon limiting employment opportunities, thus impeding economic mobility, by outlawing them; he would not sentence discouraged or unskilled workers to lives of dependency upon a welfare state, condemned to an unfulfilling life as consumers in lieu of gainful employment and self-sufficiency; in lieu of a lifetime of becoming ever more skilled, productive and fulfilled as they materially improve their lives, and the lives of their families, instead of mindlessly consuming their way to the end.

However, the minimum wage advocate is generally not interested in understanding the issue or effecting real change. He is interested primarily in appearances: the kind of publicity whereby he or his camp stands to benefit in some twisted or calculated way. Whatever you do, whether you attempt to engage or ignore them, do not allow their messaging to hypnotize you, as their college-educated vocabulary serves only to deceive their unsuspecting victims. Like an infant who has just learned profanity, protestors abound chanting catchy phrases that they do not fully understand, and perpetuating fallacious rationalizations for ideas that are not their own. In other words, they are pawns in a game that they have not even studied, and yet they believe that they are in control.

Reject them each time as they attempt to lure you into play. Reject them when they call for *liberation*, for what they offer is not "liberation" at all, but complete abandonment of reason in favor of insanity; a condemnation of the people to confusion and purposelessness, the kind which the establishment is pleased to exploit for its own gain; and the kind for which the politicians claim to offer clarity and purpose. Ultimately, while the signs claim to direct the people to the promised land, it turns out to be far more than they bargained for. It's not that the destination turns out to be a major disappointment, but that it isn't even on the map. It is an endless trip with no sense of direction or understanding of the terrain. In fact, the road doesn't just reach a dead end or take an endless series of detours; it eventually leads the people off a cliff.

As Russian chess grandmaster Garry Kasparov once put it, "Socialism will always be an alluring dream, even in the freest and richest countries in the world." Of course, it is not the dream itself which is so dangerous and deadly, but rather the dastardly attempt to forge it into reality at all costs. As the economist Thomas Sowell once wrote, "The first lesson of economics is scarcity: There is never enough of anything to satisfy all those who want it. The first lesson of politics is to disregard the first lesson of economics." It comes as no surprise, then, that so many dictators, politicians and activists throughout history have been so disinterested in the study of economics.

* * *

The task of economics is to analyze and to understand complex systems, how they function, and what ends they serve; to, through analysis, per the Greek roots of the term, break down complex relationships, systems, and models into simpler elements; to likewise assess the factors, the variables, and their relationships within those systems; and to, through that understanding, predict the effect of any manipulations, distortions or alterations applied to that system. All such analyses, at least the honest and truthful kinds, must account for the relevant assumptions and the guiding principles, and they demand an explication of the conditions under which the given findings and models are useful in the real world.

Applied to politics, among other functions economics uncovers the deceit in government, the complex incoherence within the talking points and the legislation, the clever means by which politicians and their cronies pilfer the public purse and convince the public that they (the bureaucrats, the politicians and their cronies) know what they are doing. In the realm of politics, there are no designs more pernicious than those of socialism. They are as clever as they are bold, becoming progressively bolder in time.

In its more nuanced forms, such as in the United States, socialism lays claim to some fraction of business or property, cleverly leaving the main of business in the hands of those who know better how to manage it. This, however, is not a benefit of socialism but rather a clever disguise by which it cons its subjects into believing that they are free, in effect exploiting some vestige of capitalism for the advantage of the bureaucracy and the furtherance of socialism, albeit in its modern incarnation.

Make no mistake. Excusable usurpations of power have always sown the seeds of social destruction, the most heinous of atrocities through the most virulent of tyrannies. After all, tyranny descends not under clear skies but discreetly through the fog of uncertainty, deceit, and the dark of night. It shows up with a smile and good-sounding intentions, occasionally under the guise of incoherent babble and harmless incompetence, before showing its true colors when the tyrants have finally got the people where they want them: under their thumb, submitting to their every demand. It appears invited until rebuked by those much too late in revoking their invitation.

Always contemporary in their methods, leveraging the most fashionable language and relevant context of the time, the currents beat ceaselessly against liberty as the unthinking masses fail to recognize the parallels to the past. Instead, they term their measures *progressive* or *responsible*, as if their historical counterparts were any less convicted or compelling about theirs. Always cunning, they are sure to first get the camel's nose under the tent, to take their time in dismantling the people's values and traditions, and to maintain the pretense for as long as possible. Out of necessity, as with the American experience, this means that capitalism will fade away, that it will die in just the same manner as the public liberty, and even many of the people themselves: not necessarily by a blow to the head, but instead a death of a thousand cuts.

For its own purposes, therefore, the establishment preserves some semblance of private property, whereby the bureaucracy assumes authority in deciding how much belongs to it; only thereafter does the remainder stay in the hands of the so-called *owners*. Of course, under this arrangement, it is the bureaucracy that truly owns the business and the property, but it cleverly allows for the illusion of private ownership, whereby those so-called "owners" are left to manage the businesses for the benefit of the bureaucrats. After all, the bureaucrats will enjoy a much larger take with this arrangement, as there will be a greater pie for the politicians to enjoy so long as those businessmen still believe they are the rightful owners.

Suffice it to say, the sustainability of this system depends squarely on the maintenance of that illusion and the hope that the people never grow wary of it; as soon they have become aware of the system to truly appreciate their relationship with their government and their society, they will want nothing to do with it. They will have finally awakened to the truth about their enslavement, and they will invariably determine that the effort and the risk of their daily toil are inadequately offset by the limited advantages and future prospects, pecuniary or otherwise, inherent to this kind of arrangement. At this juncture, only force and coercion will stave off the mass exodus, and this can only slow the death of a system destined for its demise, but not before it spills some blood and drags its opponents, and even many of its supporters, down with it. This is precisely where socialism grows violent, either in response to or in anticipation of this exodus, because it cannot possibly endure without the subjects whom it enslaves. For this reason, the masters of deceit are always clever in their methods and their disguises, consistently keeping their subjects at bay as they claim an ever greater share of the pie for themselves; and the state is constantly experimenting with still more ways to expand their share, perhaps epitomized by its control over the common currency.

Indeed, where government monopolizes the supply of money (or currency) through central banking and bills of credit and, as has recently been shown, through social credit scores governed by political priorities, that bureaucracy can get away with choosing winners and losers and taking an ever greater share of the pie, even without raising the official tax rate. This is precisely why Irwin Schiff wrote in his work *The Kingdom of Moltz*, "To write of inflation is to write of people's infinite capacity to be tricked by politicians." As the future will bear out, their con is made even more effective through digital currency (i.e. digital dollars), which will, at the exclusion of physical currency, enable government to tax, track, penalize, manipulate, and expose virtually all of human action on one electronic ledger.

Indeed, through such means as digital currencies and social credit scores, along with its existing suite of powers, the state will establish itself as the absolute authority over all of industry and commerce (that is to say virtually every aspect of meaningful human activity), and as the gatekeeper for market access, for producer and consumer alike. What's more, the state will predictably get away with all of this through the benefit of having secured control only indirectly, not by force, micromanaging the people's lives, or depriving them of their God-given rights, but merely by limiting the public's access to money and credit, albeit for the purposes of "national security" and in the interest of the "common good" — that is according to the state at least. Aware of the serious implications of these powers, this is precisely why Henry Ford once said, "It is well enough that people of the nation do not understand our banking and monetary system, for if they did, I believe there would be a revolution before tomorrow morning."

This is the great paradox in the evolution of the market economy, the progress and plenty equipping government to manipulate that market and to more strictly control the people. The mere introduction of money and currency is one such example, having improved market outcomes but having also expanded the means by which governments can tax the people; the evolution toward digital currencies signifying even further means for governments to accomplish more of the same, and to guarantee enforcement through improved oversight and still stricter controls.

The politicians and their acolytes will doubtless champion the cause, emphasizing the conveniences. They will celebrate the many possibilities: among others, the elimination of payment processing intermediaries, the closure of so-called *tax loopholes*, the improvements to national security, and the simplification of tax collection. However, they will conveniently overlook the distinct threats posed by such a scheme which confers so much power upon government: a scheme which materially threatens the right of the people (per the Fourth Amendment to the US Constitution) *to be secure in their persons, houses, papers, and effects*; which systematically imposes upon their privacy; which grants government virtually unlimited creative license in finding new ways to tax the people; and which essentially disintegrates the family unit while reducing each individual to an entity of the state.

Indeed, the politicians are generally quite clever in their art of deception, always concealing the costs, defraying them in clever ways, convincing the people that the sacrifices are warranted by the "common good", or that — according to the politicians, at least — there is no sacrifice at all, that each program will simply "pay for itself". Even the manner in which taxes are collected and enforced, through withholding taxes in particular, suggests that the government is completely in control of your wealth and your income; that the worker relies on the "generosity" and "mercy" of government to receive or to keep any of it; and that, of the part he receives, the worker is fortunate to even lay claim to — let alone keep — a share of it. This is just the nature of government and politicians: they are always coming up with clever ways to fleece the people while keeping them out of the loop.

CHAPTER IV

THE NATIONAL HEIST

In 1960, Dorchester Productions released their hit film *Ocean's 11*. The film featured an ensemble cast led by four of Hollywood's *Rat Pack*: Frank Sinatra, Dean Martin, Sammy Davis, Jr. and Peter Lawford. A crew of eleven was assembled around one objective: to mastermind an elaborate New Year's Eve heist targeting five casinos on the Las Vegas Strip. As sophisticated as it was, the heist would ultimately fail in the end. Why? It wasn't that the team failed to get their hands on the cash, but that they couldn't dependably store it or keep the people from figuring out that they had been robbed. As impressive a heist as it was, *Ocean's 11* looks like child's play compared to the frauds in government who have masterminded the greatest heist in history: the nationwide heist in the name of the *national bank*.

The concept of a national bank is one of the most insidious political devices ever conceived, not only for its sheer economic influence but for its utter perversion of civilization. Whether owned, operated, or strictly regulated by a nation's government, the consequences are the same: an enforced monopoly over the money supply and, thus, the form, function and fruits of the people's labor. Such a monopoly is destined to assume progressively more control and influence over the kind of civilization that the people are to have, and consequently the kind that the people are to leave behind for their heirs. Indeed, that monopoly quickly comes to control the most significant aspects of life, economic or otherwise.

After all, when the state determines the function of labor, it essentially determines the purpose of life; and where the state usurps this power, it assumes progressively more authority over the people's priorities, their perspectives on principle and virtue, good and evil. As such, the state commands the people accordingly, enforcing and reinforcing, asserting and reasserting those priorities which are in the best interest of the establishment.

When so much of life's purpose is committed to satisfying the establishment, the people are called to betray their own standards and their better instincts in order to prioritize more urgent demands: among them those tasks which will enable the people to pay the taxes and to keep themselves (and their families) alive and out of trouble with the state. The people are thereby swindled out of not only their resources but their traditions and their standards. They are, by force and coercion, gradually stripped of their humanity, their purity and their innocence in order to serve the state and its various interests.

They are the children who grow up with a distinct appreciation for virtue and morality but who later realize that they can, or perhaps must, make concessions or completely abandon those standards in order to survive or to thrive under such irreconcilable conditions. They are the children who become the parents, who in turn, one generation after another, eventually realize the futility of their former traditions and those former standards; who therefore neglect to keep them and thereby fail to pass them on to subsequent generations. It is precisely in this way that standards of righteousness wane as the state usurps progressively more authority over the people, their lives and their endeavors. It is in this way that the people become jaded and confused, depressed and unfulfilled, frustrated and angry about the world and the demands that they have inherited in lieu of the standards, the traditions and the freedoms which once made for more honest and fulfilling living.

It is in this way that civilization decays into such a state of fear, greed and desperation, that the people eventually become indifferent to the lying, stealing and cheating deemed necessary in order to meet those demands. It is in this way that people justify their transgressions and that transgressions become not only commonplace but so ubiquitous that righteous living is eventually regarded as childish or idealistic; that sinful behavior is normalized as part of adult life, part of "doing one's duty".

It is in precisely this way that the establishment seizes control over the people and their affairs. It is precisely for these reasons that the greatest threat to the people is that body which seeks the centralization of power over the people's money, and thus their economic affairs. Indeed, Nathan Mayer Rothschild reportedly put it this way in 1815 after taking control of the Bank of England — whether apocryphal or authentic, the sentiment remains true: "I care not what puppet is placed upon the throne of England to rule the Empire on which the sun never sets. The man who controls Britain's money supply controls the British Empire, and I control the British money supply."

Whether regulated or directly owned and operated by the state, a national bank brings the people under the control and influence of government and political actors. Because those political actors have been so successful in exploiting economic crises, and because they have convinced the public of their political promises, the institution has been met with progressively more embrace; otherwise, because of its relative sophistication and complexity, it has been met with public indifference, left to be questioned and scrutinized only by a select minority who suspect foul play or truly understand its inner workings. Whether through embrace or indifference, the institution of the national bank has come to secure a foothold in the modern market economy.

The institution of the national bank has become so entrenched in modern thought that most students of the subject have come to respect it as a sort of unquestioned tradition, a testament to modern refinement, ingenuity and intellectual progress. One such example of the thoughtless reverence paid to this institution is available on a YouTube channel by the name *Dollars and Debt: The Story of Money*. According to one video titled *Greenbacks and the National Bank Act*, "The US absolutely needed a national bank." Of course, upon making this argument, the presenter proceeds without any further explanation. Whereas a student of logic and reason understands that a rational conclusion must proceed from reason and evidence, that an honest assessment must account for any and all assumptions, and that any cogent argument must enumerate the limitations of the study, as well as the tradeoffs and deficiencies of the conclusion, the presenter in this case allows his argument to stand alone, presuming it self-evident. At minimum, it is essential that an argument of "need" express the assumptions.

In this case, the presenter failed to offer *any* explanation as to why "the US absolutely *needed* a national bank"; moreover, he failed to even define "the US" in this particular context. In this case, does "the US" refer to the government of the United States, select or general commercial interests in the United States, the citizenry of the United States, the territory itself, or something else entirely? Consequently, the presenter failed to describe the methods used to determine the *needs* of any of those various entities. Needless to say, his "argument" is hardly an argument at all, instead sharing the characteristics of conjecture and rhetoric.

Fortunately, this author can fill in the blanks: as stated before, "the US absolutely needed a national bank" only in the interest of government, political actors and their initiatives: namely to finance large war efforts and "internal improvements" in support of select programs, enterprises, industries, persons, and locales. After all, the power of the state resides in its war powers, and select business interests are served through the resources required to support those powers. Indeed, former President Dwight D. Eisenhower warned of this very combination of interests in his 1961 farewell address.

* * *

In his 1961 farewell address, President Dwight D. Eisenhower warned against the establishment of a military-industrial complex:

"This conjunction of an immense military establishment and a large arms industry is new in the American experience. The total influence — economic, political, even spiritual — is felt in every city, every state house, every office of the Federal government. We recognize the imperative need for this development. Yet we must not fail to comprehend its grave implications. Our toil, resources and livelihood are all involved; so is the very structure of our society."

He continued:

"We must guard against the acquisition of unwarranted influence, whether sought or unsought, by the military-industrial complex. The potential for the disastrous rise of misplaced power exists and will persist."

"We must never let the weight of this combination endanger our liberties or democratic processes. We should take nothing for granted. Only an alert and knowledgeable citizenry can compel the proper meshing of the huge industrial and military machinery of defense with our peaceful methods and goals, so that security and liberty may prosper together."

With security and liberty in mind, we must endeavor to estimate the risks of militarization within the United States during the major wars since the Revolution, namely World War II (1941-45) and the War between the States (1861-65). Has American militarization through its various departments, as measured in enhanced scale, presence, power, influence, readiness, and materiel, become so threatening to American liberty, so discouraging to the people in the expression of their grievances and the attempted protection of their rights, as to, so far as they are concerned, (potentially more than) offset the gains of military victory? In this calculus, we must account for the standing armies and the worldwide occupations which have habituated the public to the presence of troops (and the business of war) in their midst, to an extent that would formerly (in the first century of the Republic) have been startling if not offensive. This, combined with the fleeting causes of war and the ever-changing gales of politics, presents an urgent question about whether or when those wars might rightly be said to have been in vain.

This is a question not merely of academic importance but one to be answered with reverence for the sanctity of life: a sacrifice in war to be assessed (before and afterward) to better judge the efficacy of war, the costs of future conflicts, and the standards for just war. This is a question directed at ascertaining the facts and the true ends served by war, to be honest about its causes as well as its outcomes and future implications. As it is often said, the first causality of war is the truth; the same may rightly be said about the compromises made in entangling alliances, or through *any* kind of international institution for that matter.

President Thomas Jefferson spoke of this issue when he summarized his essential principles of government in his first inaugural address on the 4th of March, 1801, when he expounded on "the essential principles of our Government, and consequently those which ought to shape its Administration":

"Equal and exact justice to all men, of whatever state or persuasion, religious or political; peace, commerce, and honest friendship with all nations, entangling alliances with none..."

To engage in an alliance to defeat a common foe is one thing, but to jeopardize the rights of the people or the constitution of government through entanglements is another, and a dangerous affair indeed. Once word of this kind is given to form an entangling alliance, there is the real risk that it will condemn itself to ruin. Whether by the unforeseen or by poor judgment, that ally is best served by dissolving that alliance where it fundamentally threatens its obligations to its own people and their general welfare. Indeed, there are such flagrant errors of judgment and existential threats to life and liberty that must invalidate the alliance for the sake of the republic (and its constitution) and the security and happiness of the people. Above all, especially in America, it is worth remembering that, amid any alliance, there is the stake of liberty: a stake far more important than any other abroad, from Europe to Jerusalem.

The word of a government is not the word of the people, but the word of one particular regime or administration. One regime or administration, forming any entangling alliance in defiance of its constitution or in betrayal of its people, whether intentionally or resultantly, need not to condemn the next administration or regime to the same errors. While it is true that a man ought to honor his words and his commitments, administrations commit wrongs and mistakes that need not transcend their terms or continue to threaten the public, their rights, and their government's constitution; in the same way that a company might renegotiate or redefine its terms of service in order to better serve its customers or to return to (and honor) its original promises. Indeed, this is the most honorable commitment, and an obligation that the general government has to the people of the several states. Just as the Supreme Court has erred in judgment, and has occasionally admitted as much, so too can the righteous administration correct the wrongs of its predecessors, among them the unconstitutional or unreasonable commitments made during their respective terms. From a practical point of view, this must be handled diplomatically to maintain good standing and friendships with foreign nations, but nonetheless it is up to representatives to correct the wrongs, not to continue them just because of a misguided or unjust agreement. As President Eisenhower put it in his farewell address:

"It is the task of statesmanship to mold, to balance, and to integrate these and other forces, new and old, within the principles of our democratic system — ever aiming toward the supreme goals of our free society."

The Constitution is for specified purposes, not one of which pertains to the perpetual security or happiness of its allies. While it may, from time to time, enter into alliances for some mutual advantage in the name of its own defense, it must limit those alliances to the short term for specified and achievable objectives. As Jefferson put it, it should not engage in entangling alliances that, merely for the sake of "honor" or obligation, condemn the people to its mistakes and the whims of politicians abroad. If the general government were truly representative of the people, and if their representatives had not relinquished their war powers, the general government would still lack a sufficient case to condemn all of the people and future generations to the mistakes of a wrongheaded administration.

The effect of treaties was intensely debated in the infancy of the American Republic. On one side, Alexander Hamilton regarded treaties as the unquestioned authority:

"The House of Representatives have no moral power to refuse the execution of a treaty, which is not contrary to the Constitution, because it pledges the public faith, and have no legal power to refuse its execution because it is a law—until at least it ceases to be a law by a regular act of revocation of the competent authority."

Whereas James Madison claimed that each treaty must be deliberated by "[t]he House, in its Legislative capacity, [in the] exercise [of] its reason":

"The House, in its Legislative capacity, must exercise its reason; it must deliberate; for deliberation is implied in legislation. If it must carry all Treaties into effect, . . . it would be the mere instrument of the will of another department, and would have no will of its own."

To that end, William Blount added:

"When a Treaty stipulates regulations on any of the subjects submitted by the Constitution to the power of Congress, it must depend, for its execution, as to such stipulations, on a law or laws to be passed by Congress. And it is the Constitutional right and duty of the House of Representatives, in all such cases, to deliberate on the expediency or inexpediency of carrying such Treaty into effect, and to determine and act thereon, as, in their judgment, may be most conducive to the public good."

Ultimately, from the principles outlined heretofore we shall conclude that Americans and their government are not condemned to the treaties entered into by their predecessors; that, through improved judgment and calculus, we may be able to make more informed determinations on just war; that entangling alliances are entered into on invalid premises and assumptions (or for fleeting objectives) not strictly enumerated, not specifically authorized by the Constitution, and not specifically in the interest of domestic security or the general welfare; that entangling alliances are a distinct form of an alliance threatening to the people, their liberty, and their government's constitution; that entangling alliances are incompatible with the vision for American liberty; that treaties condemning the people to war or economic sacrifice, without their approval through their representatives, is immoral, impractical, and unconstitutional. Of course, government is, generally speaking, clever enough to conceal its means to such control and destruction; the kinds which are strictly opposed not only to reason but to the terms of its own Constitution.

It is not only risky and unconstitutional to engage in entangling alliances, but it is often foolish and impractical to intervene in foreign affairs, especially where they concern disputes not directly pertinent to the "general welfare" of the country and its people. Likewise, it is most foolish to become so entangled and so involved in all of the world's affairs such that a government or its armed forces come to act as the policemen of the world; to intimidate, to threaten, or to command the countries of the world; to respond with force or intimidation to every exigency and every crisis beyond their borders; to so immerse themselves in foreign affairs as to claim a stake in every international dispute, to relinquish discretion and to predetermine political actions and reactions on the basis of those existing entanglements; to unilaterally delineate and enforce worldwide political standards pertaining to the rules, conduct, customs, and relations for all countries, relative to each other and their own respective people; to secure or promote their own political or commercial interests through any of these methods; to ensure that the "rules" are always delineated in favor of the establishment and the status quo, appealing to the public's sensibilities, their sense of humanity and civility, wherever necessary. Through such rules and other such measures of "civility", the members and agencies of the establishment succeed in distinguishing themselves as the *humanitarians*, as opposed to the enemy who are regarded as *barbarians*; some measure of savagery, of course, being necessary to overcome the overwhelming power of the establishment and the inertia of the status quo.

Secretary-General of the United Nations Antonio Guterres evidenced this point in a most abstract and intellectualized statement on the 13th of October, 2023, claiming that, "Even wars have rules." Of course, the establishment *would* stake that claim, as it thereby guarantees its hold over a more peaceful, sensible and scrupulous people; a people more easily controlled and persuaded. What's more, those who control the status quo often have the audacity to preach these standards and expectations to the entire world.

Indeed, as Russian President Vladimir Putin stated on October 5th, 2023, during his annual keynote speech at the Valdai Discussion Club, there is a certain arrogance in telling other countries how to behave, especially when, as Putin describes it, these commands are issued in such an "openly boorish" manner. In his speech, Putin specifically addresses the government of the United States: "All the time, we hear, 'You must', 'You have to', 'We're seriously warning you'." He then poses his questions to the governments of the West: "Who are you anyway? What right do you have to warn anyone? Maybe it's time you yourself got rid of your arrogance and stopped behaving that way towards the world."

In the same speech, Putin goes on to define the Russian understanding of the term "civilization", one he describes as "completely different" from that of the Western world. "Firstly," Putin begins, "there are many civilizations, and none of them is [necessarily] better or worse than the other." He continues: "They have equal rights as exponents of the aspirations of their cultures and traditions, their people. Our interlocutors in the West seem to have completely forgotten that there are such concepts as reasonable self-restraint, compromise, and willingness to give in on something in order to achieve a result acceptable to everyone. No, they are literally obsessed with one thing: to push through, at any cost, their interests here and now."

Of course, the government of the United States, as with the government of any other major empire, is hardly ever short on the means to secure its desired results. Indeed, they are always mobilizing for economic and political advantage, which is to say they are constantly mobilizing for war. As hellish and as costly as war is known to be, governments have, for their own purposes, become more clever in conning the citizenry. Beyond the propaganda and the onerous burdens levied upon the people, no device has perhaps proven more insidious than those less conspicuous means for war: among others, those means at the disposal of the central bank.

* * *

As the twentieth century would later reveal, such endeavors of scale (i.e. the two World Wars and the subsequent proxy wars) were possible only because of central banking. So that is why, as the YouTuber under the name *Dollars and Debt: The Story of Money* claimed, "the US absolutely needed a national bank": that is, to circumvent the approval of the people by usurping authority over their resources. Put another way, the United States "absolutely needed a national bank" like a hole in the head. If by "the US", the presenter is referring to the general government, then he is correct insofar as its own interests are concerned; but "the US" is not the general government, but a union of states and their people, whose interests were not (and are not) served by the continuation of central or national banking.

Next, the presenter doubled down with another claim that is entirely unsupported by the facts. Whereas he claims that "[t]he US needed a central bank... in order to effectively and efficiently carry out governmental actions desired by a majority of the citizenry", there is scarcely any evidence which shows that the majority of the citizenry approved of the institution. More important than majority public opinion, however, are the safeguards instituted within the Constitution, specifically for the purpose of preventing the abuses attending political ambition and public opinion. Ultimately, his opinion on the matter is based not on "effectiveness" or "efficiency" but on the expediency of such institutions enabling the general government to circumvent the difficulties attending the administration of a constitutional federal republic; indeed, difficulties specifically built into the Constitution of the United States in order to safeguard the public liberty against the ambitions of both politicians *and* the majority.

The presenter then proceeds still further from the facts with an indirect reference to the United States Constitution. Instead of outlining a coherent argument based on the Constitution, he leans on the interpretation of a political actor, Salmon Chase, the former Treasury Secretary of the United States in the administration of President Abraham Lincoln: "[Chase] actually had a pretty good argument for it, based on Congress's power to regulate the money supply." The presenter specifically references Chase when, as Chief Justice of the United States, he issued the opinion of the court in the 1869 case *Veazie Bank v. Fenno,* supporting Congress's 1869 act imposing taxes on notes of private pensions, state banks, and state banking associations:

"Congress may restrain, by suitable enactments, the circulation as money of any notes not issued under its own authority. Without this power, indeed, its attempts to secure a sound and uniform currency for the country must be futile."

Not surprisingly, these are still more baseless claims and unfounded opinions.

Here are the facts: Article I, Section 8, of the United States Constitution confers upon Congress the power "To coin Money, regulate the Value thereof." It does not empower Congress (or the general government) to "restrain the circulation of money" or "to secure a sound and uniform currency" at the exclusion or discouragement of others. In fact, there is no enumerated power in the Constitution which authorizes Congress (or the general government) to tax wealth, or to effect any direct tax not apportioned according to population. There is also a distinct lack of authority in Congress (and in the general government) to assume a monopoly over the total money supply or the industry of banking. This is a most essential fact, as a monopoly over one is necessarily a monopoly over the other. This is where it is important to remember the general government's distinct lack of authority *to secure a sound and uniform currency* at the exclusion or discouragement of others.

On the subject of Congress's power to "regulate the Value [of Money]", the term *regulate* appears in this context as it does throughout the document: *to make regular or uniform* in quality, payment of debts, and court of law. In the case of Clause 5, this extends exclusively to the regulation (or uniformity) of weights and measures in the issuance of coined money. Remember, the term appears twice in Article I, Section 8, which affords us clear insight into its meaning.

The first of its appearances applies to the power "To regulate commerce with foreign Nations, and among the several States, and with the Indian Tribes". In this particular context, it is important to note that this clause was never intended to authorize the federal government to regulate business or industry, nor to determine the bounds of allowable production, pricing or trade. This is made plain by the fact that the federal government has no jurisdiction in foreign Nations nor within the Indian Tribes; likewise, the federal government is equally powerless within the several States (inclusive of commerce, industry, and banking within those States, respectively), by the deliberate designs of the US Constitution and the preceding Articles of Confederation.

Those who are desperate to find Constitutional bases for such extraneous regulations, limitations or prohibitions predicate their assertions on the Commerce Clause, which is described above as the power to regulate commerce with foreign Nations, and among the several States, and with the Indian Tribes. It is important to note that this clause was never intended to authorize the federal government to regulate business or industry, or to determine the bounds of allowable production, pricing or trade. As written and as intended, the Commerce Clause applies exclusively to the regulation of commerce; in the language of the period, *regulation* is synonymous with *regularization*. As such, the Commerce Clause serves only to ensure that interstate commerce (commerce among the several States) would be subject to uniform laws, rules and customs, and that no artificial barriers (i.e. taxes, duties or tariffs) nor special privileges in trade or contract enforcement would be implemented between the several States. This means that any related dispute between the several States would not be left to the States independently, but that they would instead be adjudicated by the federal government in accordance with the law.

Remember, government's adjudication or regulation extends not to the industry nor to the enterprise, but explicitly to the commerce among the several States; not to the business of banking nor to the total supply of money, but to the money specifically coined by that government. The lone objective of the Commerce Clause was the interest of free trade between the several States; and that, consistent with the character of free trade, commerce between the several States would enjoy the protection of rights under a uniform rule of law. It is important to note that the term *regulate* has evolved in its contemporary uses; however, where it appears in the Constitution it refers explicitly to the maintenance of the cited associations. In the case of commerce, regulation thereof was meant only to facilitate free trade among the several states by preventing the institution of artificial barriers between them; and to adjudicate interstate disputes through an impartial judicial system. The same rings true for the militias, which were meant, when employed in the Service of the United States, to cooperate with the several states in order to execute the Laws of the Union, suppress Insurrections and repel Invasions. The same rings true for the issue of money.

Regardless of the preferred interpretations, the facts stand on their own, and the Constitution is to speak for itself through the "few and defined" powers enumerated therein. For the government, the Constitution is an exhaustive enumeration of powers, whereby any omitted powers are reserved to the States respectively, or to the people. As for the people, relative to the Bill of Rights, that enumeration in the Constitution was not to be construed in any way to deny or disparage others retained by the people. All of this is to illustrate the point that the Constitution is explicit on the powers of the general government and that there is no allowance for reading between the lines or reimagining any of its clauses. In the case of Congress's coinage power, that power is limited to (1) *coining* money, not monopolizing the total money supply or *securing a sound and uniform currency* at the exclusion or discouragement of others; (2) regulating the value of said coinage, not *restraining the circulation of money*, subjecting its value to political expedience, or interfering in commercial exchanges; and (3) fixing the standard of weights and measures (per ounce, as it were) for coinage, not to set the standards for all forms of money or the whole industry of banking.

In response to these criticisms, the presenter makes an effort to modify a previous opinion, one which is less subjective than misunderstanding of the principles enshrined within the Constitution. On the first part of his revised claim, he then asserts that "The US needed a central bank in order to effectively and efficiently carry out its duties under the US Constitution", but this is patently untrue.

Not only did the United States long function without a central or national bank, history shows that industry actually flourished in its absence. What's more, a proper understanding of the US Constitution invariably exposes the unconstitutionality of national (or central) banking, and a proper understanding of economics reveals its metastasizing and exacerbating effects on business cycles. The first is made clear not only through a proper reading of the Constitution, but by a proper understanding of the Constitutional Conventions and the opinions of such luminaries as James Madison and Thomas Jefferson, both of whom stridently opposed the institution on the fear that such centralization of power was anathema not only to sound money, but to the federal republic as a whole; that the institution would invariably operate to the benefit of select business interests in the North, at the expense of broader agricultural interests in the South; that its effect would be to circumvent the Constitution and, as Jefferson put it, "to exclude popular understanding and inquiry... and [to effect the] corruption of the legislature" for the aggrandizement of the general government. Madison and Jefferson protested vehemently against the institution, regarding such a bank as not only superfluous but destructive to the "general welfare" and any republic.

Not surprisingly, a more political James Madison would eventually become more accepting of the institution, but only (1) upon being elected President; (2) upon, per his 30 January 1815 letter to the Senate, "Waving the question of the Constitutional authority of the Legislature to establish an incorporated Bank"; (3) by appealing to "repeated recognitions, under varied circumstances, of the validity of such an Institution, in acts of the Legislative, Executive, and Judicial branches of the Government"; and (4) admitting to its specific use to government "during the war, the period particularly requiring such a medium and such a resource for loans and advances to the Government". Indeed, concerns about the national bank were numerous, pertaining to both its efficacy *and* its legitimacy. One such admission is found in correspondence with President Madison dated 2 January 1815, in which one James Williams expressed his own concerns that "there may be some doubt of [the national bank's] Constitutionality...".

The chief concern about the national bank is not in its effects on specific interests but in the sweeping consequences of centralized banking; an inconspicuous form of warfare through financial operations which succeeds more easily and more handsomely than battles, with fewer questions, less understanding, and less pushback from the people to boot. Indeed, the issues are manifold: among them, that national banks serve specific interests, Northern industry over Southern agriculture, and select regional and state interests over the "general welfare"; that they are unconstitutional; that they impose upon the viability of state banks; that they not only fail to serve the "general welfare" but in fact undermine it. The value of decentralized banking, on the other hand, is that it affords the people options between competing banks and banknotes, thereby enabling a true market for creditors and issuers, and a true market rate of interest while imposing discipline on the issuers of legal tender.

The final takeaway is this: the Constitution grants no positive authority for the establishment of a national bank, and that, as Jefferson put it, "... banking establishments are more dangerous than standing armies, and that the principle of spending money to be paid by posterity, under the name of funding, is but swindling futurity on a large scale."

This is truly the modern form of socialism, whereby ownership over the means of production has been replaced by ownership over the form of money. This is, by appearances, less invasive, but it is truly more pernicious than the forms which preceded it. As the outspoken legislative aide Harold

Wallace Rosenthal stated in a 1976 interview, "Money power was essential in carrying out our master plan of international conquest through propaganda."

Indeed, under this arrangement, the socialists get away with sounding charitable while convincing the public that their initiatives will impose no additional costs. Moreover, they claim that the additional money, which they merely print off the presses (whether literally or figuratively), makes us richer in the process. Of course, nothing could be further from the truth.

In fact, the printing of money only makes us poorer, transferring purchasing power and real goods and services from those "owners" into the hands of the bureaucrats, or those connected to them. Whereas the bureaucrats contend that society will be richer for it, the truth is that the bureaucrats will have successfully stolen more stuff while leaving society with more paper, or its equivalent. So, while people will predictably feel wealthier, and maybe even more "progressive" upon their government's imposition, they will, on the whole, be worse off because of it, especially those who stand to inherit that arrangement from their fathers and grandfathers who condoned it for their own personal benefit.

Indeed, through the various economic policies and subsidization schemes, society is made to serve ends diametrically opposed to nature, a natural order which otherwise effects true progress operating to the benefit of subsequent generations instead of serving and enriching those preceding generations at the expense of their heirs (i.e. progressively higher taxes, an unsustainable public debt, and the wealth effect sustaining ever higher asset prices, pension funds and old-age programs); instead of, as Jefferson put it, swindling them in futurity, a truly regressive process which runs completely contrary to the values of a family society in favor of an individualistic and self-centered outlook on life. It yields such an individualistic society that it pries man and woman away from the essential ethics and the inherent responsibilities within one's own family: responsibilities not limited to caring for each other and bestowing upon one's heirs the blessing of every advantage, the mutual (including economic) assistance necessary for every benefit to the family, and for, above all, carrying on the legacy and the heritage which together define the family and afford it a sense of purpose and the means to further progress.

This is hardly accidental but rather another demand of Leftism, which, through a vicious cycle, begets progressively more poverty across generations and, in turn, broader support for its empty promises. This induces a kind of circling-the-drain effect, whereby poor people and their sycophants, through their approbation, encourage the implementation of countless *welfare* programs which, in turn, guarantee their further impoverishment; this consequently bolsters their ranks as more people are drawn into poverty and predictably call for more of the same.

Of course, the Leftists are deliberate in their designs, as, apart from those who are so blissfully naive, the shrewd and senior members among them know precisely what they are doing; what's more, they know exactly what they are up against. In a virtuous and practical community or civilization, or broadly any environment where people are competing and endeavoring to survive, the natural course is both intuitive and logical, one generally served by man's instincts: that course is the pursuit of sustained life by all practical (and, for the wise, ethical) means; a natural course which is not only necessary but gratifying as man sees the product of his labor and the ends served. Any arrangement which seeks to modify the natural condition, which seeks to renegotiate man's inherent responsibilities, or to redistribute the product of his labor, presents not only a distortion of incalculable risk but myriad violations of law and ethics; likewise disrupting that relationship between a man and his labor, the gratification of man in the product of his labor and the ends served.

Any such distortion, therefore, presents the distinct threat of decadence, lethargy, discontentment, and even social ruin. For this reason, it is incumbent upon any and all who seek to renegotiate the terms of life, liberty, and property, who intend to defy instinct and nature, to strictly enumerate those impositions and the standards by which success and failure are to be measured (and declared); to determine their risks, limitations and assumptions; to ascertain the possibility of failure and the potential ramifications; to approximate the knowns and the unknowns, the foreseeable and the unforeseeable; and to honestly account for the costs, both quantitative and qualitative, attending their implementation.

As for the theories behind their proposals and the philosophical underpinnings of their judgments, there must be some acknowledgment of the possibility that they may be incorrect; and that, where the theories are to be taken seriously at all, an honest and scientific assessment demands the means or measures by which they may be proven invalid. As Popper's falsifiability principle goes, "For a theory to be considered scientific, it must be falsifiable." As it turns out, however, this level of honesty (and accuracy) is not just inconvenient but entirely inconceivable to the Leftist.

CHAPTER V

THE COSTS OF FAILURE

Human error and personal failure are inherent to the human condition. The question is how the costs shall be defrayed. In the case for liberty, there is certainly some *tolerance* for failure or error, as it is generally suffered by the individual, not brought upon anyone by design. However, wherever anyone seeks to empower government in an effort to meet these ends, one must be absolutely certain of its effects, as there is no margin for error behind the barrel of a gun. As the Sagan standard goes, "Extraordinary claims require extraordinary evidence."

One must remember that government is a monopoly on force and coercion. It is force and coercion not by spirit or intention but in accordance with the letter, the understanding and the conscience of the enforcers in their own time.

As opposed to a state of liberty, where mistakes, failures and crimes are unavoidable and still likely to happen, a state of socialism condemns the people to a guaranteed state of misery, failure and crime *by design* — a design in defiance of genuine freedom in favor of another styled *freedom from want*, one condemning the people to a perpetual slavery for the benefit of political ambitions, elusive and ill-defined ends, and a set of fantastical and unachievable dreams; a system inherently destined for failure, the likes of which are incomprehensible among those still enchanted by the false promises of nirvana.

Against a system so brutal, so uncompromising and violent, the people simply cannot afford any measure of uncertainty. For this reason, the Leftist must, for the sake of humanity, satisfy the highest standard of certainty, so as to erase every doubt as to any potential failures. Judging by their passion and their vitriol, one might think that the Leftists have done their homework, but this could not be further from the truth.

Indeed, for a cult that claims to take these matters so seriously, very few are willing to spend any considerable time on the details. Most are satisfied with sound bites and bumper stickers, unwilling to entertain a thorough examination, especially one which contradicts their preconceptions or requires any measure of patience to properly understand.

Indeed, very few Leftists even do any cursory research before reaching a conclusion or forming an opinion; and, in most cases, there is no budging once they have done so. Once established, all time and effort is spent reinforcing them or otherwise ignoring, harassing and shouting over their critics. Of those who do any research at all, they remain Leftists only disingenuously for personal gain, through cognitive dissonance, or for a distinct lack of literacy, logic, and comprehension.

He would rather pursue his policies and just conduct his experiment to see how it plays out, "learning by doing," as Federal Reserve Chairman Ben Bernanke put it in a speech at Jackson Hole, Wyoming, in August of 2012. Indeed, the Democratic House Minority Leader Nancy Pelosi provided a salient example when speaking on the matter of the Affordable Care Act in 2010: "We [need] to pass the bill in order to find out what [is] in it." Of course, the true Leftist already knows of its major implications. Ultimately, the burden of proof is everywhere, and on every occasion, on the Leftist or, more broadly, any who seeks to undermine or to otherwise threaten or redefine the terms for life, liberty, or property.

Of course, if the Leftist were to theoretically satisfy this standard, and if he were to, by some miracle, have a moment of such insight, honesty and sobriety — perhaps some epiphany through divine intervention or by the Grace of God — he would no longer be a Leftist, but rather a staunch advocate and defender of liberty, a classical *liberal* in the truest sense.

Therefore, there is no Leftist who can satisfy that standard, and there is no rational case at all for Leftism; it is dangerous enough to entertain the thought of it, let alone to condemn the people to its abuses. It is dangerous enough that the Leftists confuse themselves as *liberals*; it is high time that the people deny them that privilege, that they (the people) finally reclaim the cause of liberty for themselves, not for political gain but for the sake of posterity.

The case for Leftism is dubious enough on its own, but especially so where such an alternative as liberty is at our fingertips, specifically because it has been so articulated by our forbears, and the fruits so bountifully produced throughout history.

We needn't commit the mistake of entertaining that which has caused so much grief and misery, which has brought so much pain and suffering, and which has claimed so many lives (countless tens of millions by body count alone), and that which ultimately cannot be made to work. Indeed, the socialist system proves only to distort our lives, our ends, and our entire understanding of the world that we mutually inhabit.

One such example of this kind of distortion is the welfare state, which, through subsidy, redistribution, moral hazard, the transference of risk, and the artifice of non-actuarial contracts and non-economic transactions, supports lives, customs, incentives, habits, and traits not suited for fruitful living, continued survival, or independence. This means that these will, not through their own merit or proven effect, but through artifice, not only preserve those non-viable traits into the future, but incentivize more of the same, and only more extreme; that, in order to sustain this arrangement for any longer, further distortions will inevitably be necessary until the ultimate conclusion of decadence, lethargy, and social ruin.

There are precious few instances of such distortions which are more dangerous than those which seek to renegotiate the terms of survival, the immutable necessities of life, the fixed laws of the land, and the costs and tradeoffs attending each of them. This is why we ought, without exception, to be honest and truthful about the risks and the results. These facts are often not easy to accept, to reconcile, or to swallow, and they often challenge the ambitions of dreamers, designers, and opportunists, but they demand just as much appreciation as the laws of physics. The risks attending acknowledgment of the truth may be high, but the risks of ignoring it are far higher.

As stated, the welfare state presents a whole host of distortions to the human condition and the social order. Its ramifications reverberate indefinitely into the future, inevitably coming into conflict with reality, the truth and those who seek it along with their independence.

Indeed, the costs of living serve not merely as a burden to be carried, but as a representation of reality and the demands to be met in order to survive and succeed; and insofar as those demands are met through one's own merits, his qualities shall endure to ensure the best chance of survival for his heirs. Where these qualities are improperly valued or inadequately rewarded, where the fruits are to be enjoyed not by merit but by circumstances or resourcelessness, the distortion will inevitably discourage production and initiative; it will penalize creativity and innovation; and there will ultimately be less product to enjoy, not only by the few but the many.

In the modern context, it has been through the Marxist maxim, *from each according to his ability, to each according to his need*, that the capitalists and the innovators have been vilified and the destitute and, to a lesser degree, the employees have been celebrated; all because of political ambitions and the defiance of economic truth.

The truth is that it is only through savings and scaled production, accomplished through economic efficiencies and labor-saving devices, that capital increases and new enterprises are possible. Contrary to the socialist myths, insofar as the capitalist increases his absolute share of the total production, the absolute *and* proportional share of the total production going to the laborer will also increase. It turns out that the socialist is so confused that he has it entirely backwards. Indeed, it is the capitalist, not the laborer, who stands to benefit least in proportion to the increase in total production; ironically, it is in the opposite case, where capital is decreased, that the laborer stands to suffer most.

It was the French economist Frédéric Bastiat who so neatly summarized this phenomenon: "In proportion as capital is accumulated, the absolute shares of the total production going to the capitalist increases, and the proportional share going to the capitalist decreases; both the absolute and proportional share of the total production going to the laborer increases. The reverse of this happens when capital is decreased."

It therefore defies not only truth and real progress, but the best interest of the many, to overhaul or to reimagine the natural state of human action. It stands not only to ignore reality and truth but to obscure it from posterity and to leave them unprepared to manage it into the future.

Indeed, any social arrangement (or system) which artificially suppresses the cost of living for any person, or class of persons, is bound to inadvertently yield a measure of undesirables, in the form of unaccountable, deluded takers and psychological, behavioral traits which are thereby increasingly likely to be passed on to subsequent generations of growing numbers of (entitled) expectants. Any shortfall to those expectants will then be characterized as oppressive, inequitable or evil. At the same time, the mechanism that caused this outcome eludes scrutiny to instead increase in size, reach and power.

The most insidious of these effects is the distortion over the organic cost of living, which naturally proves to filter out those non-viable human qualities that are unfit for the given environment at the given time. This is planet Earth's way of communicating what works and what doesn't. It is not an opinion, a value or moral judgment, nor is it an appeal to ethics; it is purely the ante to play on this planet.

Although this may at times appear unfair or cumbersome, the terms of personal responsibility are negotiated at that same level; not on the level of social obligation or what one imagines he deserves, but how one might structure his own life for his own personal betterment. Anything beyond this feedback loop merely obfuscates the deadly serious truth of one's existence, to imagine some fantastical fairy tale which envisions a more abstract form of life.

Indeed, any such distortion relieves the individual, or class, of personal responsibility for his or her own survival, irrevocably confounding the calculus of life by which individuals rank priorities, commit to change or otherwise accept the consequences; consequences in the form of death or self-sabotage at one's own expense. Ultimately, such a distorted social order is tantamount to not only a denial of nature but a futile (and extremely dangerous) effort in suspending or rejecting reality in hopes of manifesting a dream or forcing a failed system to work. That is, of course, to discount the very real possibility of more sinister motives.

This sort of scheme is possible through not only redistribution but market bubbles and economic distortions overvaluing certain activities and investments, signaling a need for skills, traits and qualities that are otherwise excessive, unnecessary, or unsuitable for the future; while, on the other side, undervaluing the investments, activities, skills, traits and qualities that *are* essential, that are indeed lacking and necessary for economic stability into the future. This, of course, results in deficits and deficiencies to be exposed in time.

Indeed, such a scheme also succeeds in reducing (in many cases to near-zero) the real costs of living, enabling the individual and his unsuited traits to survive into a space in time which exists ever starkly at odds with them; whereby some part of posterity is left woefully unequipped for the demands and the difficulties of life. Meanwhile, the impetus for change, or otherwise death or self-sabotage in the alternative case, is displaced by a comfortable standard of living maintained by still others, many of whom are living beneath that standard, assumed responsible for those undesirables: undesirables whose very next breaths are made the responsibility of decent and hard-working people who don't even know them; undesirables who therefore sense no obligation to a faceless entity providing for their survival.

* * *

There is this unproven and unstated assumption that, because the people are of the same species, they are inherently indebted to one another; that they must be forced into order and harmony amongst each other; that they cannot, or must not, be left independent to their own devices as the free-willed possessors of their own destiny. On the contrary, the socialist asserts or operates from the assumption that each member of the human species, upon birth, inherits a whole host of obligations for the mere fact that he is born human.

Indeed, it never occurs to the socialist that such assertions and assumptions might defy nature and the possibilities of spontaneous order. It never occurs to the socialist that man is condemned to life as a slave wherever he is born with obligations to his contemporaries; where — as the socialist sees it — man is not and cannot be born into a state of isolation or independence; where man is forbidden from disassociating or associating to his liking; where man is held responsible not just for his own welfare but for the welfare of others; and where he is expected to do more than respect the life, liberty and property of his fellow man.

As with the under-appreciated fruits of spontaneous order, the Left is either blind to or unwilling to accept its advantages for the common man, or what the Left might regard as the *common good*. Indeed, these are advantages enjoyed in plenty at progressively lower costs, with the benefit of maximal liberty and limited government to boot.

Instead, the Leftists hijack the term *common good* (as they do with so many others) for their own purposes, laying claim to it as their sole possessors, despite their blatant rejection of private property, of course; just one of their many contradictions. It is yet again another classic case of Bastiat's *seen versus the unseen* whereby the measures and the stated intentions of the Leftists are more conspicuous, thereby more marketable and easier to sell, than the possibilities of spontaneous order; whereby the costs of the former are measured in the infinite and the undefined, whereby the promises are likewise limited only by their imaginations; whereby man is condemned to such conditions under which no man is free, under which man has no chance of being free until these bonds are finally broken, until each man survives on his own merits, through which his legacy and his traits are to be carried into the future.

So, instead of allowing nature to take its course, instead of permitting those unfit individuals and their traits to perish as they might, or to survive through charity, the establishment coercively employs measures, resources and other people to sustain them (the undesirables) and their traits; individuals who would otherwise be compelled to adapt or perish, and traits that would otherwise endure with the benefit of adaptation or perish along with the person.

Wherever that person shall succeed only by the grace of others without any reciprocal obligation, wherever that individual would have otherwise failed to survive without continued aid, he and his traits survive unsustainably into the future in the form of his heirs (and those whom he has influenced along the way). This carries into the future individuals predisposed to similar outcomes, lacking the necessary discipline and appreciation for life; assuming little to no responsibility for themselves or their own; and even, in some cases, responding rationally to that system which offers ease and convenience while insulating them from the demands of life on Earth.

Consequently, the infection metastasizes, spawning a vicious cycle of dependency and negligence which replaces genuine charity with a faceless machine of hand-outs, depriving the dependent of that impetus for learning, adapting, and soul-searching which originates from that sense of obligation to the donor. Instead of devoting oneself to ends that might justify the investment or to the mission of paying it forward, the dependent collects benefits through a bureaucracy full of nine-to-five under-performers who have no interest in representing the taxpayers or maintaining accountability. Consequently, the dependent is presented with a figure accompanied by a dollar sign on a balance summary, fully convinced that he is *entitled* to those funds and that he must do everything in his power to defy his better instincts, whatever remains of them, to avoid anything (namely work) which might disqualify him from continued benefits. Indeed, the dependent may even manage to convince himself that he has *earned* that income, and that he is a victim. He does this in order to manage the guilt of being a parasite.

Ultimately, without the personal or tangible feedback loop, that starvation for the necessities of life, the dependent is deprived of the forces which might compel change. Instead, he is coddled into complacency, convinced of that victimhood narrative, and deprived of the skills and the appetite for self-sufficiency and independence. In fact, the dependent is *discouraged* from working in the welfare state. Indeed, where he should endeavor to become productive, that first dollar of earned income could ironically prove to be his most expensive decision, as he would then be disqualified from some or all of those benefits while sacrificing the unlimited vacation time and the other advantages attending a life free of work and responsibility.

In a space where work and wealth are vilified and "victims" are celebrated, and where that life free of work and responsibility has become far more readily attainable, expect always a wide range of support from and for those who endorse that arrangement and stand to personally benefit from it; and expect still greater numbers to pour into these ranks to get their hands on that which (they believe) is *rightfully* theirs.

In the fury of all of this, freedom will yield to *free* stuff, which, of course, comes as no surprise. After all, *free stuff* is always more enticing than the challenges of a free life. And while freedom recedes, the masses will lose their appreciation for it, and they will continue to relinquish it for the benefits *guaranteed* in return.

Inevitably, the expanding bureaucracy will grow beyond control, becoming progressively more oppressive in order to meet its *guarantees*. What's more, it will be met with an increasingly-illiterate electorate, at least as measured by both critical thought and their intolerance for any statements measuring beyond 140 characters or the space on a bumper sticker; an environment in which reason and sanity never stand a chance.

Another particular challenge for reason and sanity is the expectation that reasonable people are to remain silent, to give the benefit of the doubt to the Leftists for their stated intentions; and that the reasonable ones are to never expect the same treatment in return, but rather to appreciate the plea that the Leftists are just too passionate to let their opponents off the hook, too passionate to busy themselves with the details, and too busy to even entertain a counterargument, let alone the possibility of being wrong. Of course, according to the Leftists, it is not that they themselves are prejudiced or intolerant or even unintelligent, but that they are simply passionate; and therefore, as they see it, they must not only be forgiven but praised in the event that passion blinds them to the truth.

Ultimately, the rational being will be left to swim against the currents of the new conventions, to ignore the noise, to overcome the peer pressure, to flee from hypnosis and ultimately escape from tyranny. While the devolution proceeds, it will no doubt continue under the banner of *progress* or some twisted iteration of the motto from *The Three Musketeers*: all for none, and one for all.

The political elite are fully aware of these phenomena, which is why they rally to fill their constituencies with the dregs and the most gullible of society, among them refugees, immigrants, "minorities" and the youth. They are easy to deceive and control, and they will scarcely put up a fight when met with the force of government, especially where that government is full of so many empty promises.

Indeed, the state tends to embrace this strategy for the spoils. During the War between the States, for example, the Union fielded hundreds of thousands of immigrants and sons of immigrants to slaughter Southerners, to raze and occupy their cities and towns in the deadliest war in American history. In fact, the foreign-born represented at least twenty-five percent of the entire Union Army during the war, while an additional eighteen percent of the soldiery were men with at least one foreign-born parent. Meanwhile, more than two million Union solders were under the age of twenty-one, more than one million were under the age of eighteen, and fully one hundred thousand were under the age of fifteen. In total, immigrants and the sons of immigrants constituted roughly forty-three percent of the Union forces.

In one particular pamphlet, Confederate writer and diplomat Edwin De Leon informed French readers that the Puritan North had built its army "in large part of foreign mercenaries" composed of "the refuse of the old world," among which included "the famished revolutionaries and malcontents of Germany, all the Red republicans, and almost all the Irish emigrants to sustain its army."

Then, as now, many of the desperate and unquestioning immigrants, who had not the slightest concept of American values or the new American form of government, welcomed the prospect of enlistment for the opportunities, the stable benefits, and the prospect of adventure. These immigrants were not motivated by codes of morality or ethics, nor by the principles of the Constitution which they had sworn an oath to defend, but by personal interests whose costs, borne by their newfound nation, are scarcely ever high enough to satisfy the state.

Indeed, most immigrants of the time were both illiterate and uneducated on the Constitution, let alone the threatening implications of the aggressive war on which they had embarked; a war which had served explicitly to undermine the sovereignty of the states and the new form of government for which America's Patriots had fought, for which nearly one hundred thousand had died not even a century beforehand.

The Union, under the strict control of the fledgling Republican administration during and after the war, strategically set out to politicize and polarize the United States, to promote the economic and political interests of the North at the expense of the South, and to bolster their voting bloc across the country. Those influences remain just as relevant today.

While the modern Republican Party ingratiates itself with business interests, Christians and older voters, the Democratic Party cozies up with students, minorities, unions, feminists, wage-earners, indigents, eccentrics, immigrants, Catholics and Jews. In fact, research shows that roughly two-thirds of immigrants align with the Democrats, whereas only one-quarter favor the Republicans, with the remainder identifying as independents. Likewise, minorities overwhelmingly support the Democratic Party. In a 2018 Pew Research poll, ninety percent of blacks say that they voted Democratic during the congressional races, compared to seventy-seven percent among Asians and sixty-nine percent among Hispanics.

As for the 2020 presidential election, national exit polls indicate that eighty-seven percent of blacks, sixty-five percent of Latinos, and sixty-three percent of Asians cast their votes in favor of Democrats; in each case women being more likely than their male counterparts. The same rings true for sixty-two percent of unmarried women, sixty percent of urban voters, sixty-nine percent of voters who believe that *climate change is a serious problem*, fifty-two percent of Catholics, seventy-six percent of Jews, and ninety-two percent of voters who cite "racial inequality" as the election's most important issue.

Moreover, immigrants and non-citizens alike still serve the greater military and political agenda just as they did in the United States during the nineteenth century. Indeed, non-citizens today even serve in the United States military as a means to naturalization — roughly eight thousand non-citizens enlist each year. According to the Department of Defense, more than three percent of the entire U.S. Armed Forces is comprised of non-citizens and naturalized citizens, amounting to more than twenty-four thousand troops representing the United States military domestically and abroad. In total, immigrants and the foreign-born still constitute more than thirteen percent of all U.S. veterans.

Meanwhile, according to the latest data, more than sixty-three percent of non-citizen households exploit welfare programs, compared to thirty-five percent of native households. Among non-citizen households that remain in the United States for ten years or longer, that figure climbs to a whopping seventy-two percent; for naturalized-citizen households, that figure is fifty-seven percent.

Incidentally, in the average case, the naturalized citizen and the member of the U.S. Armed Forces share at least one common bond: both have never read the Constitution which they have taken an oath to support and defend *against all enemies, foreign and domestic.* And among those who even venture to skim the Constitution, it is as alien to them as Shakespearean literature, the King James Bible, and the Latin language: in their minds, it is tantamount to poetry. For most, they are just words, and malleable ones at that.

Ultimately, most Americans today merely assume that they know what it means to be an *American*, but they rely exclusively upon a vague conception of the word which they have engineered in their own minds, or that which has been constructed for them through the influence of select media outlets. To them, it is based more on feelings than on a grounded understanding of the principles of liberty as defended in war and as declared by the country's founding documents.

The average American today, let alone the average non-citizen or naturalized citizen, has virtually no connection with the important historical events of America's past, whether by knowledge or lineage. Most Americans today are so deluded, so indoctrinated and historically illiterate, that they have even preemptively abandoned or denounced the values and sacrifices upon which the Union was founded. They would much rather avoid sensitive subjects altogether, peruse their social media feeds, pacify their peers and professors, instead of facing the truth and risking hurt feelings; instead of risking resentment or hostility by sharing the truth with their insecure family and friends, professors and classmates, who might finally stand to learn something.

Indeed, it is so much easier to just go with the flow, to watch a movie on Netflix, to scroll mindlessly through videos on YouTube, to talk about the game, reality TV or all things trivial, instead of daring to engage in even remotely meaningful or honest dialogue.

With the rising tide of immigrants, political correctness and totalitarian policies, there is apparently no limit on what can and will be censored, either socially or politically. And just as the War Between the States witnessed the blurring of lines between states and jurisdictions, so too are Americans today witnessing the blurring of lines between the citizen and non-citizen, between republican government and empire.

What does this all say about the relationship between immigrants and the United States government? As far as the government is concerned, it is a match made in heaven! Where there are people desperate enough to do just about anything to gain citizenship or to pursue financial gain, there is a government that promises it all. And for most, the sweeping costs incurred for their salaries, their *entitlements* or their votes, secured at the expense of other people and their Constitutional rights, which they have neither occasion nor inclination respect, go largely unnoticed and are conveniently rationalized away by those ready to excuse the costs so that they can happily enjoy the spoils.

Principle is a hard sell, which is why, so often throughout history, so many people have been so ready to dispose of it for some perceived, even fleeting, benefit. In the United States, politicians are just as eager to dispose of the wealth and the freedom enjoyed by Americans as unwitting immigrants are welcoming of the prospect of facilitating their campaigns.

Unfortunately, the death of America was secured long ago, probably sooner than the ink had dried at the signing of the Declaration of Independence. Of that which remains, today's politicians will predictably squander every vestige just as soon as they perceive a political or pecuniary advantage, and there is seemingly always a cohort of malcontents naive or greedy enough to do their bidding. If only this practice were entirely unique to twenty-first-century America, the writing would not be nearly as clear on the wall.

Desperate for their survival or otherwise seeking a steady paycheck, the malcontents will dispense with virtually any principle in order to pay their bills and to satisfy their government. In their desperation, they will even collaborate with the government as it subverts the law and subjugates the people. The Leftists endeavor to fill their constituencies so that they will outnumber or drown out the others who remember the laws, the traditions, and the principles which keep the government at bay; this population is the enemy of government, which seeks to dispose of them for further power, influence, and control.

In this way, the people who once fought for their liberty, who once framed their government, and the heirs who thereafter inherited it, are soon replaced by constituents who know nothing of it, who are instead concerned with their mere survival or their own enrichment. Soon enough, the ties are completely severed between the people and their forbears, as they are eventually brought under the spell of Leftism. In this particular case, it is the spell of *diversity* and *multiculturalism*, popular buzzwords used to conceal the government's primary objective: control.

CHAPTER VI

THE METROPOLIS

As part of their program, Leftist politicians make a habit of actively marketing their ideas as *progressive, inclusive,* and indispensable to any humane and civilized society. However, the truth is this: the Leftists in charge understand that this kind of program drives social discord and instability, through which they are the chief beneficiaries.

Ironically, this is yet another complication that is entirely incompatible with the theoretical workings of socialism. That is to say that, even insofar as theory can submit a functioning form of socialism, it cannot overcome this complication; as if socialism is not already doomed from the start, this is yet another complication which preordains its failure and exacerbates its predictable consequences. Of course, the Leftist politicians welcome this instability because they are not actually interested in the ideals of socialism after all, but the power to be assumed along the way, especially where they claim to have still further solutions to the problems they have created.

This is what is truly meant by *social*-ism: a design not for the benefit of *society,* but one whereby *society* is necessary to support the establishment, a government of racketeers aiming to swindle the people out of their resources. This is why they seek to bring their subjects into urban and suburban centers, and of course the state has various ways to accomplish this end.

One of the many ways in which the establishment brings people into urban and suburban centers is through the onerous taxes to be suffered on properties of greater scale. This significantly alters the calculus such that the scales are tipped just a little bit more in favor of urban and suburban living — not out of *preference* for the lifestyle, but out of *necessity* to consistently meet the demands (i.e. the taxes) imposed by the state. These are demands that are more easily met through the industry, economies of scale, and commercial intercourse so characteristic of the metropolis; and, ironically enough, those (the latter) are conveniences and pecuniary advantages constituting a mere fraction of the benefits enjoyed in proportion to the extent of its free enterprise, benefits to be curtailed by the state over time.

Once the people have migrated to the urban and suburban centers, they become progressively more dependent upon the metropolis, the economic advantages and conveniences; so dependent that they are willing to tolerate progressively more encroachments upon their liberty. Indeed, upon migrating to the metropolis, they become but one part of the whole. They are judged by "society" and by a uniform code, one as arbitrary as it is uncompromising.

They are homogenized through a strictly regulated academic curriculum and an unending onslaught of propaganda, in forms subliminal and others less subtle. Their lives and their life purpose are reduced in scope, defined by the uniform demands of the state, and simplified through the kind of specialization which enables them to meet those demands; the kind of specialization which leaves a people significantly more susceptible to economic shocks, and thus more susceptible to the measures, "regulations" and interventions imposed by the establishment under the guise of remedying or mitigating the problems.

After all, where so many people have wagered so much on an unhedged bet, in this case a bet on life in the metropolis, as they see it they are left with virtually no alternatives than to rely on the false promises and guarantees of government, to accommodate each of its demands and expectations; all of which, of course, comes at a cost far in excess of the numbers on a balance sheet.

Over time, of course, and across generations, the people simply adjust such that they hardly even notice just how much they have lost and sacrificed since selling the farm — whether literally or figuratively. Of course, the state pursues this end not as its ultimate goal, but as one of its ultimate means. This is not only for the benefit of stricter control, easier policing, and more taxable activity, but to confine the people, to condemn them to the new order, and to "justify" more power for the state.

This comes under the auspices of a people mired in the difficulties of living so close to one another and coexisting among so many clashing and incompatible cultures, philosophies, and ideologies. It is a result pursued by Leftists (under the banner of "diversity") as part of their crusade to exacerbate the complex problem of living together peaceably and to overcome the shared principles, traditions, and convictions of a people already content in their society and their form of government.

Where political ideology dominates, it not only disturbs a society and exhausts its energies; it reduces the people to the product of governmental systems and practices. It ignores the congenial values, principles and beliefs that first secure a people's order, justice, and freedom, and the convictions that sustain civilization and defend all good things in society.

It claims to offer a roadmap to salvation, to point the way to a perfect society. It readies the people to bear any cost and sacrifice any life along the way; and, thus, it prepares a people to welcome or to tolerate government "solutions" to their conflicts and their problems, all expected by, or otherwise created through the deliberate designs of, the establishment.

Indeed, whether intentionally or incidentally, the United States government accomplished these ends generations ago. The lack of congenial interests notwithstanding, the general government would ultimately succeed in its "manifest destiny", as a nineteenth-century journalist first described it; a "destiny" ultimately realized through westward expansion of the "nation" from the Atlantic to the Pacific, from "sea to shining sea".

Of course, the threat posed by this expansion, by *any* expansion of a nation-state, is, among other threats, the diminished value of the individual and that of each sovereign; and thus the increasing inability of the people to effect meaningful change, to effectively withdraw their consent, to productively express their grievances, or to practically maintain any semblance of accountability within government.

Just imagine the perils posed at such a scale as a one-world government, whereby the individual person is made perfectly inconsequential, whereby government possesses the means, which they are certain to use, to preempt the exercise of any of the foregoing, at least so far as any are permitted to accomplish anything of consequence. This is precisely why, among other reasons, government seeks to expand not only its powers to preempt even the very thought of the foregoing, but the vast territory under its control.

This is precisely why, among other reasons, government seeks to continually bring people into the metropolis, where they are made progressively more inconsequential; where they are more likely to sympathize with the measures introduced by the state; where they are bound to birth children into the same state of affairs, for the same purposes, to expand the state's power and influence through the dead weight and sheer numbers of its obedient subjects, more of whom are born every day. After all, as the adage goes, demographics is destiny, not only for the profile of the population but for the cultures, customs, and politics which are to prevail.

This end is achieved by still other means: by fostering division and economic despair, by encouraging childbearing, not for the sake of quality but quantity; and, as with childbearing, by subsidizing old age in order to bolster the ranks of its obedient subjects, to "justify" even more power to the state; the kind of power which enables the state to seize even more control over the people's wealth, and their lives, under the guise of assisting the needy; the kind of power which, more importantly for the state, ensures that an ever greater share of the population will remain supportive of the establishment, and that they will embrace or acquiesce to its future initiatives.

While bringing more and more of the people into the metropolis and expanding the powers of the state, the establishment succeeds in effecting its own interpretation of "unity", securing its control over the people and subsidizing those activities which are most beneficial to the state. Likewise, it continues to subsidize old age, childbearing, and low-income households in addition to non-work. This is not to promote wellbeing, household stability or family values, but to sabotage society, to breed progressively more instability by enabling opportunists and social dependents, by encouraging them to procreate and underachieve so that they (the opportunists and the social dependents) can get their hands on some easy money; and, ultimately, so that the establishment can "justify" getting their hands on more money, too. Whether intentionally or incidentally, all of this benefits the establishment, serving to further destabilize society, to "justify" more and more of the same, and thus more and more power to the state.

These means and ends are significantly similar to the phenomenon that ethologist John B. Calhoun described as "behavioral sink"; a set of discoveries published upon demonstrating, through his "rat utopias" between 1958 and 1962, the risks posed by unlimited access to food and water and, consequently, unfettered population growth. Among the various other findings, Calhoun determined that these factors corresponded with the failure of female rats to carry pregnancies to full term, or to survive delivery if they did; the failure of female rats to perform maternal functions upon giving birth, and infant mortality rates as high as ninety-six percent among the most disoriented groups within the population. He also discovered that they corresponded consistently with certain behavioral disturbances among males, including sexual deviation, cannibalism, frenetic overactivity, crowding, and, for individuals, even a pathological withdrawal, a kind of anti-social behavior, from which individuals would emerge to eat, drink and move about only when other members of the community were asleep.

The latter behavior appears to have aligned with Calhoun's additional findings where he notes a variety of abnormal, often destructive, behaviors, including their refusal to engage in courtship, and, just as notably, females abandoning their young. Among the most insightful findings is that which suggests that the rats' *involuntary* crowding upon beginning the experiment eventually led to *voluntary* crowding through a strict association between feeding and the company of other rats; a finding with serious implications, suggesting that, so far as human behavior mirrors that of rats, once introduced into a crowd, individuals virtually cease to behave as individuals, instead being relegated to one part of the crowd, operating as one member within a hive mind; the crowd thereafter being considered the fountain of all that is good and beneficial, and thus warranting the compromise of individuality and, by extension, one's liberty.

Of course, these outcomes are surely, in the context of human beings, far too applicable to be mere coincidences; and these findings, demonstrated unequivocally through Calhoun's experiments, appear to have some role in guiding political activity, or they have otherwise been operating incidentally to the establishment's benefit. Of course, the establishment is always prepared with "solutions" for the instability, ones which have the tendency of working in its favor.

* * *

Always eager for more control, and ready with a whole host of measures, the establishment also pursues a policy of *multiculturalism* to ensure that the citizenry will cede progressively more power to the state to resolve the people's disputes. Whereas a people sharing mutually in their culture might otherwise have fewer disputes and more reasonable ways to resolve them, multiculturalism introduces a myriad of challenges, stokes resentment, and keeps the people busy fighting each other, vying for control over government in an effort to solve their problems. It is especially useful in the erasure of any culture and civilization born of liberty and independence; from the government's point of view, any such culture or civilization stands in the way of government and serves as a reminder of its historical record. It is in just this way that chaos is in the interest of government; not too much chaos that the people will unite to overthrow their government, but just enough to keep them busy bickering amongst each other and ready to deploy their government against their enemies.

Multiculturalism is just one of many tricks employed by governments to subvert the public liberty; it is just one of the many devices used to subtly and discreetly control a populace, to keep them begging their government for answers while none the wiser to the ploy. Fortunately for government, they have an ally in *democracy*, which presents the illusion that the majority is winning and that the minority stands a chance at reversing things if only they can rally enough support; but the Leftists are always ahead of them, tilting the scales in their own favor.

After nearly a decade in political operations at levels both state and national, former GOP operative Allen Raymond has the insight to prove the point. Raymond put it this way in his 2008 exposé *How to Rig an Election*: "[J]ust about every... operative was so dizzy with power that if you could find two of us who could still tell the difference between politics and crime, you could probably have rubbed us together for fire as well."

In this confession, we find that the political process, in America under delusions of democracy, maintains only the illusion of consensus, the false impression of participation, and the pretense of representative government. It is, in truth, a voting mechanism devoid of credibility, transparency, righteousness, integrity, and intellectual honesty. It is a process as far from truth as it is from ethics, motivated by and aspiring toward neither. It is as likely to distill the truth as it is, through any other poll, to get the people to admit their faults or confess their sins. It is as likely to reward virtue and valor as it is to encourage honesty and selflessness. Of course, it is not that the people don't value these traits, but that, in politics, they have a hard time distinguishing them and separating themselves from their own self-interest. It is not that all politicians are blind to truth and morality, but that they have no place in a business as dirty as politics. As Raymond put it, "... any compass that doesn't lead a campaigner to victory is utterly useless in American electioneering."

Far from a philosophical treasure, democracy, which enjoys celebrity in theory and popularity by design, serves in practice merely to unite the dregs of urban society: the feckless, the wanderers, the aimless, the lost, the confused, and those living with an inferiority complex, against the independent and industrious folks who would rather think and take responsibility for themselves. Indeed, politicians tend to speak favorably of "democracy" or "self-determination" precisely where the public has already, in great numbers, bought into the establishment's empty promises and false narratives. Indeed, this is precisely the case with the suffrage and civil rights movements of the twentieth century.

Indeed, politically speaking, several subjects in modern America have become icons for the masses, objects worshipped whose merits are considered self-evident and, therefore, beyond reproach. Two of those subjects are women's suffrage and the civil rights movement.

Throughout our adolescence, our well-intentioned teachers prepare us to accept that the political evolution which has transpired within the United States has expressed the manifest destiny of righteousness and divine providence. We are, as students, made to believe that movements and reforms have expressed the undeterred courage of humanity toward progress and the shaping of a better world.

It is easy to think in this way, of course, because we are so desperate to believe it is true; we are so desperate to shut our eyes at night under the warm blanket of blissful ignorance. Unfortunately, the inner mechanics of politics have much more in common with sausage-making than with any stairway to heaven. The results are not nearly as satisfying, let alone sustaining.

From a strictly pragmatic point of view, the women's suffrage and Civil Rights movements together served to mobilize the female and minority demographics to fortify the Democratic Party's voting bloc during the twentieth century, after the Republicans had promptly secured the black vote during the Reconstruction era following the War between the States. Indeed, even before the end of the war, the nascent Republican Party had already begun developing its political strategy; this, in part, consisting of an appeal to the average black voter. The Republicans had managed to curry favor with this particular demographic after championing emancipation and the postbellum Reconstruction Amendments, which were met with strict policing across the southern states to ensure compliance with the new laws; measures conveniently — for the Republican Party — instigating racial tensions that would only further inspire political support for the new sheriff in town: that one nation "under God" and "indivisible".

After an epic losing streak lasting a couple of generations, the Democratic Party finally reformed its strategy to compete with the Republican dynasty: women's suffrage, civil rights and welfare were just the lowest-hanging fruit available for the picking, and it has essentially been a race up the tree since then.

Today, the Democrats continue their deployment of the same strategy by expanding upon the so-called War on Poverty, born principally out of the New Frontier and Great Society epochs, by currying favor among immigrants — and dejected voters — and by subsidizing higher education in order to influence and socialize the impressionable youth, incidentally dismantling the family unit by "empowering" their constituency through the rejection of family values and personal responsibility. Oddly enough, it appears that some measure of the latter, personal responsibility, goes a long way in freeing people from poverty:

In fact, a 2013 Brookings Institution study found that 98 percent of American adults who followed these three simple rules were living free of poverty: finish high school, get a full-time job and wait until age 21 to get married and have children. The study thus indicates that each person's lot in life is, on the whole, a product of his own conduct and commitment; that, far from indicating some sort of "systemic" or "institutional" bias, *bigotry, prejudice, discrimination*, or *racism*, it is rather domestic culture and poor decision-making which are apparently responsible for the bulk of those cases of long-term poverty. Of course, this finding is hardly of any value to the Leftists, whose incredulousness reliably keeps them immune to reason, immune to logical explanations and the very concept of responsible behavior; immunities which consistently keep them from appreciating or acknowledging the value of the former values.

Indeed, there is a great deal of resentment toward traditional customs and gender roles in the modern Western world, and yet that resentment is scarcely ever coupled with any complete understanding or compelling explanation, only a constantly changing set of unsupported value judgments. Indeed, despite the endless chants for the "liberation" of women, there is nothing categorically "wrong" with the conventional household composition of a working husband and a stay-at-home wife who performs housework. As it turns out, this arrangement has merely yielded to another which is admittedly preferable by some but nevertheless destructive to the family unit: a nine-to-five or double-shift workload whereby both parents are absent from the home for extended periods of time each day while working for somebody else or some other company instead.

Meanwhile, domestic responsibilities are regularly left unattended, and the average family is left with an increasingly expensive tax burden to boot. Of course, the rising tax burden's coincidence with the burgeoning female labor force participation rate illustrates what exactly has occurred here: women were not as much *liberated* into the workforce as their participation was *necessitated* by the ever increasing burdens of high taxes and inflation resulting from government largesse.

As a consequence of these social changes, along with the incentivization of broken families through the growing welfare state (and a judicial system favoring single mothers on matters of alimony and child support), the modern baby is lucky to even be born into a life with both of his parents. Indeed, in modern America, more than two-thirds of black children live in single-parent households, while unwed childbearing in the United States has eclipsed 40 percent in total, up from 5 percent before the proclaimed War on Poverty officially began in 1964. In modern America, more than at any time in its history, a child is more likely to grow up without one of his parents in the household.

Not surprisingly, this, too, operates to the benefit of the state, which is always prepared to exploit any crisis. Indeed, the data show that single-parent households are more economically unstable, more receptive to the promises of government, and disproportionately supportive of Democratic candidates. Of course, it is no mere coincidence that the United States is also showing record-low fertility rates, providing further evidence of the shift in cultural priorities and economic welfare; effects which the Democratic Party is fully prepared to exploit. In the words of the Joker from the 2008 thriller *The Dark Knight*, "It's all part of the plan."

The political machine is not entirely stupid, and it is not entirely controlled by complete imbeciles who lack basic insights into statistical analysis, Microsoft Excel or Google Sheets. These are relatively intelligent people who know exactly what they are doing, how to manipulate voters and the minds of future voters, and there is a ton of money to be won by those proficient in the trade.

It is called *propaganda*, and it is not a term reserved for study in your high school history class; it is ongoing and living in the mainstream of the material you read, watch, and later entertain in conversations with those who have done the same, where it is most insidious, operating with what appears to be the certification of your peers whose judgment you mistakenly trust.

In the modern context, propaganda takes the form of repeated utterances and constant impressions upon the people through continued exposure to positive or negative stimuli. So effective is political propaganda that, even when faced with some semblance of the truth, the propaganda overcomes it through the power of fear and peer pressure. As one famed politician once uttered, "Men occasionally stumble over the truth, but most of them pick themselves up and hurry off as if nothing ever happened."

"Truth is treason in the empire of lies," another novelist wrote.

It is simply too difficult to speak the truth when something more agreeable can be entertained in its place, especially while the advantages of wielding the truth are so slim, and especially while your associates will scarcely notice the difference. For example, the political embrace of the female demographic through the former suffrage movements and the continued protests for ill-defined *equality* present an amiable facade for the loaded and destructive package of implications it really contains.

In the pursuit of a form of *equality* that conflicts with nature and science, let alone our limited capacity to even vaguely imagine it, the agenda serves to feminize the public in order to bring it more strictly under the government's control, both materially and psychologically. This primes the populace for further encroachments upon liberty by subtly numbing the public to the costs while consistently inundating them with promises of nirvana.

The propaganda machine accomplishes this end by both virtue-signaling and delegitimizing masculinity in order to condition strong and protective men to relinquish those traits across generations, rendering subsequent generations of men more docile and obedient to the budding power structure. This type of non-threatening populace is easier to govern and enslave, and government agents will have fewer opponents, fewer questions to answer, and servants unquestioningly doing their bidding on their behalf.

Totalitarianism is the ultimate destination, and democracy is nothing more than a fashionable vehicle that will take us there. It is also a brilliant distraction for those who have been convinced that they maintain control through its generous process, which appears to also bear out the concerted will of their neighbors.

How could anyone possibly dare to question that?

The truth is this: while most people have no business voting, democracy has no business existing at all. It is a fool's errand for the public, a guaranteed success for the establishment.

Ultimately, government ought to be kept so small as to render inconsequential every uninformed vote, every ill-equipped candidate, and every electoral circus. It ought to refrain from the kinds of social reconstruction which have brought so many ills upon the public. It ought to be made to return funds to those people who originally *earned* them, where they can be productively invested instead of being squandered on special interests, government boondoggles, and propaganda efforts in pursuit of the massive payout. We can do better with freedom, and truth. We can do better by referring to "civil rights" by a more appropriate title: special privileges. We can do better by referring to "democracy" by its more appropriate name: mob rule.

As a form of mob rule, democracy, advantaged inherently by the scale and sophistication of the economies and the populations it exploits, lulls its unsuspecting constituents into supporting the kinds of transgressions they would never independently dream of committing themselves. Ultimately, tyranny of any kind, regardless of the source from which it ostensibly derives its power, is still tyranny; and wherever democracy is said to have prevailed, it has succeeded merely in subjecting the public to the enterprising ambitions of those as cunning as they are thirsty for power.

As President George Washington stated in his 1796 farewell address, the democrats are particularly dangerous as agents of political parties, "charged," as Washington wrote in his 1799 letter to Jonathan Trumbull, "... with concealed ambition" with "regard [to] neither truth nor decency."

In his farewell address, Washington continued: "However [political parties] may now and then answer popular ends, they are likely in the course of time and things, to become potent engines, by which cunning, ambitious, and unprincipled men will be enabled to subvert the power of the people and to usurp for themselves the reins of government, destroying afterwards the very engines which have lifted them to unjust dominion."

Always cunning in their craft, politicians stand everywhere at the ready to charge public opinion with their fine-tuned rhetoric and silver-tongued stanzas, compensating with enthusiasm wherever lacking in reason. They are not nearly as interested in solving problems, insofar as they can even be solved, as they are in creating them and pretending to have solutions.

One of the reasons that rhetoric is so powerful is that it is not accountable to rigid rules or the demands of logic and evidence; it is generally measured by the confidence and the intonation of the presenter rather than the merits and provability of his arguments. Unlike the sciences of physics and mathematics, for example, speech is relatively malleable and unencumbered, offering enough ambiguity and room for interpretation, and reinterpretation, for the presenter to reach a diverse and impressionable audience, to later "clarify" or further equivocate his statements for maximum effect, and to make a case by saying hardly anything at all; certainly nothing specific or coherent enough to be useful.

Rest assured, this is the tool of all sophists, all of those who have dispensed with the rules of logic as soon as they have found a way around them. Indeed, in the view of the sophists, words can mean whatever they want them to mean; and whether to drown, dazzle, or dizzy, they are useful in a whole variety of circumstances and situations. As they see it, speech is most useful where it replaces the need for proof, where it enables disguises and distortions, and where it allows utterances that sound intelligent, significant and correct even where they lack those qualities altogether.

This is precisely why speech and language can be so dangerous, and thus why it is particularly useful to politicians who have little interest in facts, truth, honesty, or accuracy, who are ultimately interested in power and persuasion. Fortunately for them, rhetoric is readily at their disposal to accomplish these ends, to make a convincing case that they know what they are talking about, that, in their pronouncements, they are adhering to just the same standards, and meeting the same requirements, as those demanded among the true sciences. This is quite a setback for truth and science, but it is quite delightful for the sophists who bask in the babble, and for their audiences who prefer it to the rigors of logic; audiences who are more susceptible to emotion than evidence, who are eager to be excited and entertained, who are ready to form an opinion, to reach a conclusion, and to forget about doing their own homework.

As twentieth-century journalist H. L. Mencken observed in 1918, "Civilization, in fact, grows more and more maudlin and hysterical; especially under democracy it tends to degenerate into a mere combat of crazes; the whole aim of practical politics is to keep the populace alarmed (and hence clamorous to be led to safety) by menacing it with an endless series of hobgoblins, most of them imaginary."

CHAPTER VII

FALSE ALARMS

It is precisely due to "practical politics" that there are so many dimwits who are so keen on and receptive to false alarms; one of those alarms, of course, sounding constantly for the myth of manmade climate change. The author will endeavor to address this particular myth to expose just a few of its critical shortcomings.

As the reader will see, this is not to entirely dismiss the reality of climate change, but to distinguish it from the more popular political variety used to promote specific political interests and economic reforms. Let this also serve as a general lesson on appreciating the finer details, the big picture, and man's limited perspective. Let it also serve as a reminder that there remain phenomena in this world yet beyond explanation, and that it is not only honest but essential to the welfare of civilization that man respect the limits of both technology and human understanding.

First, let it be known that there is good cause behind the phrase *1,000-year flood*. *Climate change* is nothing that you have to prove; it is always happening, and it always *has* happened. To sound the alarm about a natural and cyclical global phenomenon is, to put it delicately, disingenuous. Any focus on the temperature change in one part of the world ignores the fact that the average global temperature has been dropping for decades, even though the concentration of carbon dioxide in the atmosphere has been increasing. This finding is even corroborated by the EPA in a report which clearly contradicts the theory that carbon dioxide emissions cause the temperature to rise.

On the subject of rising sea levels, there is no evidence which strictly relates the phenomenon to human activity. First, the methods for measuring sea level have changed over time, and the task has proven difficult all the while. What's more, those measurements account not distinctly for the changing sea levels but also for the movements of land. In most places, the land makes the greater impact. It is for this reason that we simply do not have a reliable gauge for sea level rise. Indeed, for the last several decades, scientists have relied upon satellite measurements, which are not strictly comparable to prior measurements. Ultimately, there is no evidence that these levels have changed much at all over the past few thousand years.

In fact, those levels have been slowly rising all along over these past few thousand years after their initial rapid acceleration after deglaciation twelve thousand years ago. Given the evolution in instrumentation, the claim that we have witnessed a sudden change to these levels, and that we ought to be alarmed by changes in the making for thousands of years, is simply dishonest. Meanwhile, where natural disasters take place, global warming is one of the least significant contributors. Ultimately, from a truly scientific point of view, "global warming" refers to the kind in the making for many thousands of years, not the political variety which erroneously places the blame on human beings.

For this reason, it is essential that human beings be equipped to defend themselves, at the very least philosophically. It is therefore essential to, at minimum, have some rudimentary appreciation for the subject in order to defend against the political ramifications attending baseless theories — theories abounding in the face of extreme weather, and becoming increasingly popular in the halls of government and academia.

All too often, this subject, as with countless others, is complicated by the introduction of factors or events not properly understood by those who do not specialize or even dabble in those particular fields. Too often, academics, such as the physicist Albert Einstein and the economist John Maynard Keynes, among others, apply methods and concepts where they do not belong; or they simply assume that their intuition, presumably validated by discoveries elsewhere, can serve them anywhere, even in those domains where they have done little more than cursory research (if any at all).

This author believes that it is also essential for people to appreciate the fact that weather is distinctly separate from climate; the one certainly factors into the other, but the other describes a general and predictable pattern derived from the first. Only over long periods of time can we possibly determine whether it is indeed climate (as opposed to weather) that is changing; and, if true, that does not necessarily implicate manmade contributions.

Indeed, these are two claims so often linked yet independently unsupported: (1) whether climate, on the whole, is changing as dramatically as claimed amongst certain political and academic circles; (2) whether manmade contributions are responsible. It is important to note here that the academics are not apolitical; they are not altruists forsaking every self-interest. Where they are not expressly sponsored by the state, they are, as humans, motivated by other powerful factors. Indeed, even well-intentioned academics crave the attention and the credit that come along with a major theoretical discovery, the accolades and the awards that come along with being the hero. This is true even among those in any way attached to the field who enjoy the prestige that comes along with being members of the "enlightened class".

Such is indeed the case with Nobel Prize-winning economist Paul Krugman, who has described himself as "an avid science fiction reader" of "the classic set of novels by Isaac Asimov, the *Foundation* novels." As Krugman put it in a 2011 interview, "[those novels] are about how a group of social scientists save galactic civilization through their understanding of the laws that determine the behavior of societies." According to

Krugman, "[he] wanted to be one of those guys, and the closest you can get at this point, I'm afraid, is being an economist."

*   *   *

While this author is intimately aware of the geological, geographical, and ecological effects on weather (and natural disasters), there appears to be insufficient evidence to indicate that urban development has "significantly" contributed to extreme weather patterns, let alone climate change. Granted, the term "significantly" is rather subjective, but it is worth determining whether it is appropriate in this context.

While it is certainly true that urban development can either exacerbate or mitigate the impact of weather, there is a paucity of hard evidence indicating that, on the whole, natural disasters or extreme weather patterns (beyond moderate differences in wind travel, temperature, or precipitation) are on the rise in those developed areas. On the contrary, data (however reliable) points in the opposite direction: that deaths from natural disasters have declined precipitously over the past century, somewhere on the order of ninety percent. While this is not to say that urban development has not, in specific examples, exacerbated or failed to manage the threat of extreme weather, it is to say that, on balance, it has dramatically improved safety and preparedness for such major events. No doubt, these are separate issues, but worthy considerations nevertheless.

On the topic of extreme weather and natural disasters, it is also worth noting that they are most prevalent in the relatively desolate regions of the country. Now, one might argue that these regions are desolate for that very reason, or that urban development would exacerbate those weather phenomena, and this author would agree. Still, he would suggest that this then becomes a question about the extent of its effect (as explained previously).

One of the considerations is the concept of the so-called urban heat/cold island: that buildings and land surface modifications affect the travel of wind and exposure to sunlight at dusk and dawn, thereby inducing more rainfall downwind and causing temperature differences, notably in summer and winter. However, there are incidental benefits associated with these phenomena, namely longer growing seasons; and these effects are not endemic to all urban areas but more specifically depend on the "background climate" and local environmental conditions.

Ultimately, this particular phenomenon, it must be noted, has not driven climate change but has had a moderate (and variable) effect on localized weather; and remember, rural land still constitutes more than ninety-seven percent of the United States' land area. The risk run by this narrative is that academics will forget the nuance and that they will, as their sponsors and their disciples so often do, simply reduce it to binary absolutes that are far easier to sell to the public.

The planet operates as an organism toward a state of homeostasis, and there is no evidence that these particular factors threaten the Earth as a whole. In fact, the greatest threat, so far as this discussion is concerned, is not weather or climate change, but population change. Now, the problem is not *overpopulation* but the building political and economic headwinds, of which there are too many to exhaustively enumerate here.

On the one hand, it is unlikely (if not downright impossible) that the population could endure any of the political or economic measures introduced to meaningfully change course (as tracked against the aforementioned data). On the other, the impending population decline attending those measures is due to be precipitous; and it appears that this decline will, in time, for better or for worse, resolve the issues so stressed in these times (so far as those issues exist at all).

While the severity and the scope of those issues, as highlighted, are inconclusive, we can rest assured that the academics have not reconciled their proposals with the tradeoffs (in just the same way that the academics failed to assess the economic, psychological and social costs of lockdowns during the COVID-19 pandemic); among them the real possibility of a dramatic population decline, a threat with such grave implications that the entire topic of "climate change" will suddenly seem academic.

As is likely obvious by now, the matter of *climate change*, as with various other political and economic subjects, is a complex one, not only in the matter of each case study but for the proposals that follow from incomplete assumptions and conclusions; studies and proposals often lacking sufficient appreciation for other relevant details, such as those found in the subject's history.

The production of fossil fuel energy, beginning with coal, gained around the middle to the latter half of the nineteenth century; whereas coal production has climbed gradually over the period, oil and gas (in that order) have since surpassed it, rising especially sharply after World War II. Meanwhile, wood has constituted a stable (if not slightly smaller) share over the period, with hydro and other renewables constituting a gradually larger (albeit still relatively minor) share over the past several decades.

Now, the issue is not that these developments have positively no impact, but that their impact, save for the localized variety already discussed, pales in comparison to the prevailing forces which determine climate. Again, this is a matter of scale, degree, and relativity, alien concepts to most who struggle to even grasp smaller models.

Finally, despite all of the alarm bells sounding throughout the halls of government and academia, despite the chatter from the mainstream media and the political activists, there is no evidence at all which suggests that the animal kingdom is greatly at risk or that the planet is destined for a mass extinction event. In fact, something like six percent of the world's species are even classified as "critically endangered", and most of those are not facing imminent extinction; most are expected to survive. Of course, it is worth noting that these figures are based on the list of tracked species (numbering 120,372 as of 2021), not accounting for all of the others (estimated in the millions); so, in all likelihood, that percentage is much lower.

It is worth remembering that the five true mass extinction events of the past were caused by enormous cosmic and geological forces. It is also important to remember that extinctions are a natural part of evolution (averaging, overall, two species per year): as it has been said, extinction is the rule, survival is the exception. Recent extinction rates have hardly been outside the norm for the past hundreds of millions of years; in fact, they would have to be many times higher in order to reach the levels of those prior mass extinction events. What's more, the majority of known extinctions since the year 1500, roughly ninety-five percent, were traced to islands, with only five percent being traced to continents.

Upon assessing a more recent period, from 1993 onward, ten bird species and five mammal species have since gone extinct, averaging half a species per year. Accounting for the conservation efforts which likely "saved" upwards of eighteen species during that period, and assuming (in the worst-case scenario) that those eighteen would have gone extinct, we would be left with an average of one and a half species per year. Remember, the overall average is around two species per year. Interestingly, another report indicates that some species have even evolved to cope with ecological and environmental changes, suggesting that the world's organisms and the planet itself are more resilient than commonly believed.

Ultimately, there is no evidence that we are on the precipice of a mass extinction event. There is scant evidence to show that human activity today is substantially more threatening to animal life than when the aboriginal people from Siberia migrated to North and South America more than eleven thousand years ago and helped to wipe out all of the megafauna on those continents. But even then, the crippling mass extinction event did not happen, probably because nature and our planet are far more resilient than believed by those dead set on selling an agenda.

As it turns out, for those seeking to be alarmed, virtually any extinction is akin to a mass extinction; they do not distinguish between types, and they do not account for the fact that extinction is the norm. There is a whole industry around the alarmism, and "the science", as it is ordinarily regarded, is little more than computer models (as opposed to empirical data) operating from incomplete assumptions or otherwise toward predetermined conclusions.

This lesson in alarmism and "practical politics" has perhaps, in the history of man, never been clearer than in the case of the hysteria and the consequent lockdowns following the outbreak of COVID-19; where the alarms sounded by governments across the world, led specifically by those in the West, allowed so many to get away with using and politicizing "the science" for their own benefit, finding still more ways in which to keep the people alarmed, menaced, bewildered, ready to conform, and prepared to promote the cause. After all, *the science*, as it were, determined for itself that the sacrifices were necessary, that they would be more than offset by the results of society's collective submission, their yielding to the judgment of those in power.

Indeed, it is important to remember that, at the very outset of the reported COVID-19 outbreak, the people purportedly had precious little to sacrifice for the "common good": to be precise, "two weeks to flatten the curve"; an attitude eventually shifting from "flattening the curve" to, as one social media personality put it, "we have to find a cure or everyone's going to die". Of course, those "two weeks" eventually turned into months, with months ultimately turning into years, with social ramifications reverberating into the future indefinitely, unabated and beyond measure.

Years removed from the hysteria and yet further into the breakdown of society, it must be confessed that this was either a blatant lie or a projection based on unrealistic expectations. Years later, it is abundantly evident that, while the people indeed responded with something approximating complete cooperation and total compliance, society was surely destined to never achieve perfection, the kind that would have theoretically satisfied the mandates of those demanding total and unquestioning compliance in the administration of experimental vaccines and boosters, the "universal wearing of masks", and the arbitrary six-foot rule for so-called "social distancing".

These mandates were indeed taken and enforced so seriously that, in many cases, police rushed to cite and arrest those people who failed to comply, people who were relentlessly scolded, harassed, and even assaulted by the commoners who became deeply religious about the mandates; indeed, mandates not only serving to mask ulterior motives, but promoting symbolic protection in the projection of fear, and ultimately politicizing and thereby jeopardizing the credibility of "the science".

* * *

Over the course of the COVID-19 lockdowns, Americans and people worldwide had been encouraged to "trust the experts" and to "trust the science". Well, as we know all too well by now, while it often aids in getting there, "science" does not independently produce facts. It is a process which aims, like an asymptote approaching a limit, to get us as close to the truth as humanly possible.

In this way, the risk in depending on "the science" to determine the facts is found in the public's unquestioning obedience to those who claim to represent "the science", who hold it beyond reproach in order to advance their own selfish objectives. For this reason, it is imperative that the people wielding "the science" do so in good faith, and in such a way as to avoid discrediting it. As it turns out, people will trust in an institution so long as it preserves their faith. Once it has betrayed them, it is difficult to regain their trust.

As much of the public has surely become all too familiar with these themes since the beginning of the COVID-19 lockdowns, it is worth remembering that the vaunted institutions which claimed "the science" for themselves had been just as selfish in their demands for compliance with their ever-changing directives. Whether the Centers for Disease Control and Prevention (CDC) or the Food and Drug Administration (FDA), the people had consequently begun to question their faith in the institutions which claim exclusive authority over matters of public health.

Whereas these institutions had leveraged their control over "the science" to justify their directives, their insistence on changing "the science" and their conclusions by the day had jeopardized the public's trust in both. Meanwhile, whereas neither agency possesses legislative or law-making power, or any Constitutional basis whatsoever to even support their existence, both agencies have grown well beyond their intended scope to threaten much more than the public's trust in the so-called "science".

As it turns out, *science* is merely a method, valuable only insofar as it reliably distills the truth. In this way, *science* is only as reliable as the individuals who apply it. Unfortunately, those individuals are often deceitful in their methods or dishonest in omitting their limits and shortcomings. Granted, we are all, in time, all the more likely to improve our methods and to uncover the truth with the benefits of knowledge and technology; however, it is the responsibility of the "scientist" to reasonably account for the foreseeable shortcomings of his methods. Whether for lack of available information, knowledge or technology, the scientist honors his practice by seeking and conveying the truth; by applying his methods patiently, honestly and carefully, so as to leave little doubt about their veracity.

In the event that "the truth" frequently changes, this reflects on both the integrity of the scientist and the veracity of the science. In this way, upon too many betrayals, as with the ever-changing guidance during the lockdowns, the public loses confidence in the "science" just as they lose faith in the "experts" who present their conclusions. After all, where *science* possesses any merit at all, it is strictly where it is reliable and repeatable over time. Short of this standard, it is anything *but* scientific. This is certainly the case with the institutions which have claimed exclusive authority over the subjects of public health. For them, the "science" changes and is (as they see it) permitted to change more often than the "scientists" change their lab coats.

As implied by both the CDC and the FDA in the issuance of such unreliable guidance during the COVID-19 lockdowns, it had been clear that those wielding "the science" were just as uncertain about the virus as they were ambivalent about the treatment, its risks, and its side effects. By all measures, the tale of the coronavirus outbreak, as reported, has been and will likely continue to be more political than scientific.

As it turns out, even before the outbreak, a few facts were already well understood about the practice of mask-wearing, a practice at the time already appreciated in the medical and biotech industries. As it turns out, though not in accordance with the preferred policies of the day, "the science" had indeed already been "settled" (the Left's word of choice) on the subject. Ironically, it was not "settled" in the way that today's "experts" would have you believe.

Indeed, it appears that surgical masks, and certainly any other mask of inferior quality, are demonstrably worse than useless in "slowing the spread" of the virus transmitted through the aerosols we emit with every breath. While invisible, these aerosols escape around and through the masks that people worldwide have been asked or required to wear. According to the CDC, "The smallest very fine droplets, and aerosol particles formed when the fine particles rapidly dry, are small enough that they can remain suspended in the air for minutes to hours." While people had come to believe that they were doing well to protect themselves, and others, by religiously wearing their masks, they had merely afforded themselves a false sense of control, security, and superiority.

As previously mentioned, the masking policy is worse than useless, not only because it is demonstrably ineffective in "slowing the spread" of the virus, but also due to the risks posed by improper wear and those posed to society in the form of social instability and related health implications in the form of higher incidences of anxiety, depression and even suicidal ideation.

Interestingly enough, the introduction of surgical masks just a century ago followed from the knowledge that open wounds face serious risks of infection. It was then determined that surgeons would use face coverings in an effort to prevent water droplets from contaminating those open wounds.

However, this practice preceded knowledge about the nano- and microscopic scale of viruses contained within our breath.

With the benefit of this knowledge, scientists now know that masks are inadequate in preventing the transmission of viruses. As recently as 2010, the US National Academy of Sciences declared that, in the community setting, "face masks are not designed or certified to protect the wearer from exposure to respiratory hazards."

As for the treatment offered at the time, the drugs made available had remained inadequately tested and had proven to be ineffective in preventing both the spread and the contraction of the virus. In fact, according to the CDC itself, at the time of reporting in August of 2021, three-fourths of all new cases had affected those who had already "taken the jab". So, while the treatment had not yet been proven to "slow the spread" of the virus, it had proven ineffective in defending against it.

Meanwhile, the data available at the time had suggested that, where the treatment was shown to offer any value whatsoever, it was in the mitigation of the symptoms. However, even this had come with an undisclosed risk, namely to those with preexisting health conditions. According to the CDC itself, "Information about the safety of COVID-19 vaccines for people who have weakened immune systems... is not yet available."

Of course, this was to say nothing at all about the risks posed by the people foregoing the treatment, who were then expected to follow suit so they, too, could get the treatment and continue wearing their masks. After all, it was not about returning to *normal* or to some semblance of freedom; it was about conformity and control, the public seeking the former while the politicians continued pursuing the latter.

Likewise, the primary value of the mask comes in the form of optics: as Dr. Shane Neilson wrote in his 2016 article titled *The surgical mask is a bad fit for risk reduction*, "the surgical mask is a symbol that protects from the perception of risk by offering nonprotection to the public while causing behaviours that project risk into the future."

In this way, states Dr. Neilson, "The future pandemic is perceived in the present, but its materiality is not just in our minds, it is literally substantiated by the mask." He continues, "Thus we have the means for a self-perpetuating system: the mask symbolically protects against infection just as it represents fear of that infection."

According to Dr. Neilson, the widespread misconception about the use of surgical masks — that wearing a mask protects against the transmission of any virus — is a problem of the kind theorized by German sociologist Ulrich Beck.

While reporting on the sociological implications, Beck suggested that the cosmetic symbols are themselves manifestations of risk that bear their own risks. In this way, the same mask donned in the present for the common cold at a local clinic forms part of the cosmetic framework of future pandemic risk management. Despite the undeniable evidence of its ineffectuality, it becomes part and parcel of the political playbook, for the benefit of appearances at the grave cost of truth and liberty.

Ultimately, wherever anyone seeks to pressure or to coerce another into compliance, he he cannot afford to guess. He must be absolutely certain: he must be certain of the problem, as well as the risks attending the proposed solution and the plausibility of its success. In the event of its failure, the "experts" stand to compromise not only the faith of the public but, more importantly, the sanctity of truth and liberty.

After all, the onus is on anyone who dares to compromise liberty for any temporary advantage. There is no loss in the human experience which is more regrettable than that measure of freedom which is sacrificed in futility. For this reason, anyone who proposes any measure which stands to curtail the public liberty must first demonstrate certainty, and integrity in demonstrating it. In the absence of certainty and integrity, the costs are simply too great, paid perennially by those who had no say in whether they were prepared to bear them. It is in precisely this way that the people become unwitting participants in the symbolization of protection for the projection and perpetuation of fear; and in the perpetuation of fear, they become pawns at the disposal of those "experts" who come to have little use for the "science" which had ostensibly "justified" their authority.

Ultimately, once they have achieved unquestioned authority over the people, *they* decide what "the science" says and, just as importantly, what it doesn't say. What's worse, they leave "the science" so disfigured that it becomes wholly unrecognizable to those who dare to remember it.

It is in this way that future generations are left ill-equipped to challenge their conventions. Invariably, they are made into symbols for the projection of the ongoing political agenda, and since they are assumed subjects beholden to the "experts" who claim exclusive rights over "the science", they are powerless to resist. For this reason, it is absolutely essential that, where the fight for truth stands any chance of success, it be waged passionately and relentlessly for its own sake and the sake of posterity.

As the philosopher Thomas Paine once wrote, "If trouble must come, let it come in my time, so that my children can live in peace." In this particular case, we must welcome trouble now so that our children may also stand to know truth and liberty. In losing any measure of one, they invariably stand to lose both. Fortunately, while their ranks are undoubtedly shrinking by the day, there are still patriots and truth-seekers who are willing to take a stand in the face of such trouble.

One shining example of individuals taking this message to heart was printed on February 18, 2021, in a news report released out of Santa Cruz, California; just one of many examples suggesting that members of the public had finally become fed up with the ongoing lockdowns, the mask mandates, and the restrictions on daily life. The news report covered a group of Santa Cruz shoppers attempting to patronize local grocery stores without wearing any masks. Asked to leave by employees, the mask-less shoppers reportedly insisted on making their purchases, insisting that they have a right to shop freely at any business open to the public, that the mask mandates are unlawful, and that the public is following orders by officials who do not have the authority to issue them: "There is no law passed by the legislature requiring anyone to wear a mask. Contrary to popular opinion, any store open to the public cannot unlawfully discriminate by requiring customers to wear a mask."

According to the report, in what was called *Operation Cash Drop*, "The group [was] seen picking items, documenting the prices and placing money on the checkout counter, but the store refuse[d] to help or serve them and [took] the items back. After a few minutes of arguing, the group [left]."

According to Santa Cruz Police Chief Andrew Mills, who contends that private stores can refuse service, "This is not acceptable in our community and we're going to take aggressive action when we have the opportunity to do so."

This is a complicated issue, to be sure. While there is no such Constitutional right to patronize or to shop at any establishment, as that would constitute an infringement upon the right of the owner of the establishment to refuse service, political precedent has clearly been set in denying certain rights to business owners under given circumstances. Indeed, where a business owner is deprived of the right to deny service on the basis of ethnic, religious or other differences, those protections should, and can be reasonably assumed to, extend to those peacefully patronizing any business.

Whereas we cannot deny the inherent right of self-ownership, and thus the right to withhold service, we must recognize that precedent has already made a terrible mess for us as a society, one which we will have to reconcile sooner or later. Short of people taking a stand like this in the face of tyranny and ostracism, we stand to lose our society along with the freedoms and the customs which once brought us together, along with the forms of common decency which once made society tolerable.

In addition to this, the political class has fooled the people into unquestioning compliance with unlawful mandates, bringing the political battle to us nearly everywhere we go. In order to remain in compliance, or in some cases in order to contribute to the cause, employers, employees and patrons alike generate the illusion of social consensus.

In the estimation of this author, where private enterprise no longer reserves the power to reject the government's imposition or its arbitrary judgments, it is no longer private property; in effect, the business is already under the ownership of government, acting as agents on its behalf.

In this way, private property rights have already been suspended for the benefit of the political agenda, precisely where they are of little benefit to the people — as evidenced by the present trend. The brilliance in all of this is that the government forces "private enterprise" to comply with its orders, and, as evidenced here, it can convince the public that it is just private enterprise making its own decisions.

Regrettably, we are now living in a world where government has its tentacles in virtually every aspect of life, and yet in this way, government is everywhere yet nowhere at the same time:

in this way, it pulls the strings as it hides sheepishly behind the curtain.

In this way, that which is termed *private enterprise* has become yet another arm of the government, only under the familiar names of businesses. The members of the state can thereby maintain the illusion of private property rights, along with that of free enterprise and the very freedom of the people, but they, in fact, remain intact only so far as they stand to preserve the status quo or to selectively advance the political agenda.

Put another way, private property rights are relevant to the political class only where those rights, in this case exercised privately by virtual agents of the state, stand to threaten or to undermine liberty for some political benefit. Mind you, these agents acting on behalf of government are not explicitly on the government's payroll, but they are penalized for any refusal to obey the state's commands, regardless of the edicts' standing in law.

In this way, they are truly agents of the government and, thus, enemies of both freedom and the public liberty. Remember, the virtue of government, insofar as it claims any virtue whatever, is in the goodness of law, not in the pronouncements of mortal men.

Where the people have yielded or acquiesced to their government because of the illusion, it is incumbent upon us to break ranks in support of the public liberty and that common decency which connects us. In this way, due to the conduct of our interactions as a species, and for the hope of a future of free and peaceful coexistence, it is incumbent upon us to risk upsetting the status quo, to remind our neighbors of what it means to be human, to come together to resist the government's imposition, and to endeavor to restore our way of life. In our further acquiescence, there is only more tyranny and less of humanity, only further calls for compliance by a state becoming ever powerful enough to enforce its every demand.

Of course, man's obedience is never enough for the tyrants and their exponents. They are always seeking out ways to exact further punishment, to swindle the people out of more of their property, and to divide and conquer the people with the help of their "useful idiots" who, in their functional illiteracy and their ill comprehension of history, logic, economics, and even "the science" itself, are none the wiser to the long-term agenda. Indeed, even in the case of total compliance with the ever-changing and uncertain guidance from the so-called "experts" and approved channels, there remains no way to vindicate the public, to convincingly prove their innocence to those who have predetermined their guilt; a most convenient fact for those set on holding the people as neanderthals, or worse.

Additionally, in such a case, as far as the persecutors are concerned, there is always a flaw in execution: whether improper use, inadequate materials, new incoming guidance, or something else entirely, it is a classic case of constantly moving the goalposts.

Bearing this in mind, those seeking to encourage or mandate perfection are always chasing an elusive target, one that they are prepared to chase or to manipulate indefinitely into the future. All too often, of course, the endless chase is emboldened by claims about public safety, that the people are better off for the relinquishment of their freedom and, with it, their dignity, privacy, and their very control over their own lives.

This chase invariably continues with new specters, or "variants" as it were, emerging around every corner as the sophists, the talking heads, and the grandstanders keep the public constantly paranoid, bickering and afraid. As previously stated, the journalist H. L. Mencken put it best when describing "the whole aim of practical politics" as "[keeping] the populace alarmed (and hence clamorous to be led to safety) by menacing it with an endless series of hobgoblins, most of them imaginary."

Upon the predictable failure of peer pressure and social humiliation, compliance is pursued by all means available, not limited to force, coercion, or cunning. After all, as witnessed in this case, by the time peer pressure fails, enough time will have passed such that the peers themselves will have become sufficiently motivated to seek recourse by more serious means and more drastic action; such that the people will widely commend the state for any and all of its measures, however draconian.

By the time the state and its exponents have assumed this course, no doubt in earnest and with the best of intentions, scarcely one of them will disavow the threats of force and coercion: prospects wholly anathema to the jewel of the public liberty. By then, the government and its accessories are prepared to sponsor any and all conceivable initiatives for the achievement of their objectives, which will have since become deeply personal for them.

Formerly a journey undertaken with popular intentions, it devolves into a personal and political crusade of epic proportions: undertaken at all costs, the endeavor consists of a solitary objective at the expense of all else, not least of which is the liberty which the public mistakenly takes for granted.

In the course of pursuing their elusive target, government and its accessories continue to curtail the public liberty with impunity; with the benefit of a "worthwhile", "expedient", or "calculated sacrifice" for the sake of the "common good", based on the gospel of "the science" and certified by a panel of "experts" who apparently stand beyond reproach. In this way, the people are led like cattle to slaughter as their familiar peers, trusted representatives, and so-called experts erect around them the institutions which stand to indefinitely impose upon the public liberty; institutions and impositions whose impacts and whose influence are sure to transcend the original periods and purposes for which they were introduced. As Nobel laureate Milton Friedman aptly cautioned in his 1984 work *Tyranny of the Status Quo*, "Nothing is so permanent as a temporary government program."

To be fair, there are virtually two reasons that modern Americans have been so forgiving of their governments and their accessories, and these reasons were hardly any different in the case of COVID-19. They assumed the best of intentions, and they were swindled into believing that the mandates and the sacrifices would be worthwhile and that they would taper off in short order: in the case of COVID-19, precisely "two weeks". As the refrain went, the public was assured that it would take only "two weeks to flatten the curve".

Regardless of "the science" or the new religion, there are necessary safeguards in place that take precedence, and these are safeguards indispensable to a free people. Despite what the politicians and their accessories might prefer to believe, governments are instituted among men to secure the rights of the people, deriving their just powers from the consent of the governed. For this reason, in the American tradition the powers of government are "few and defined", whereas the rights of the people are "numerous and indefinite". This means that the powers of government are strictly enumerated and that all others are assumed by the people; as such, the government cannot, under any circumstances, without the express consent of the people, unilaterally expand its powers or alter the nature of their compact.

Indeed, the Declaration of Independence advises, "That whenever any Form of Government becomes destructive of these ends, it is the Right of the People to alter or to abolish it." The Supreme Court of the United States has specifically stated as much, affirming that the government is strictly prohibited from undertaking such actions which subvert the rule of law. In the 1866 case *Ex parte Milligan*, the Supreme Court ruled that there are simply no allowances for additional powers, even where they are regarded as "temporary" or "exceptional". The court ruled, "No doctrine, involving more pernicious consequences, was ever invented by the writ of man than that any of its provisions can be suspended during any of the great exigencies of government. Such a doctrine leads directly to anarchy or despotism."

Indeed, government is best limited, and rights and freedoms most indispensable, precisely when that government is prepared to usurp some measure thereof. No doubt, government and its accessories will always have compelling reasons for their usurpations, but that is precisely why government is, by the designs of the American system, encumbered by those limits. That is precisely why the people of the United States have expressly protected their rights by imposing those safeguards against the forces which beat ceaselessly against their liberty. After all, those rights and protections are valuable only insofar as they are dependable in the face of adversity and "the great exigencies" which might otherwise pry them away. If they are considered or made conditional, they are not "rights" at all.

Indeed, if people are assumed free only through the mercy of government, they have not a "government by the people" nor one "deriving [its] just powers from the consent of the governed". On the contrary, they have a soft despotism growing harder and stricter every day. Ultimately, the beating heart of the free and vigilant man pumps the lifeblood of liberty. He is the spirit of America, in whose absence liberty is sure to vanish in the name of some temporary security.

It is his eternal vigilance and doubtless his ceaseless suspicions toward government that keep him and others around him free. As the English philosopher John Stuart Mill once declared, "A man who has nothing for which he is willing to fight, nothing which is more important than his own personal safety, is a miserable creature and has no chance of being free unless made and kept so by the exertions of better men than himself." After all, the greatest threat to liberty is the aspiration to define its terms, in particular by those who have little respect for it, who have no interest in fighting for it but who are perfectly willing to wage or to condone the fight against it; and who conveniently stand to benefit from its loss.

Their indifference to history is all too often matched by their indifference to posterity. Predictably, the people who seek to curtail the public liberty have very little interest in appraising the costs, nor do they do their due diligence to be certain of their justifications; to be fair, they stand to benefit too much to contemplate or to care, while their accessories know little of the risks or, otherwise, fall prey to irreproachable intentions.

They are blinded or otherwise sufficiently incentivized to ignore the costs, the risks, and, in many cases, the legality of their actions. Lo and behold, they stand to personally bear none of the costs, nor any of the legal culpability, in the event that they are wrong, and yet these are the people making the decisions that most impact our lives and our future.

As the economist Thomas Sowell once said, "It is hard to imagine a more stupid or more dangerous way of making decisions than by putting those decisions in the hands of people who pay no price for being wrong." Politically speaking, the decision-making tends to end up in the hands of "experts" who are scarcely ever held accountable for the results, who rarely, if ever, pay any price for their failures as they cement their authority over still more of the people's lives, whether it be the people's medical freedom, their freedom to manage their own private affairs or otherwise.

As with the champions of the mandates and the lockdowns during the COVID-19 pandemic, those "experts" pay no price for their arrogance, for overestimating their intelligence, for underestimating the consequences of their actions, for neglecting to account for the big picture, for even, on the rarest of occasions, confessing all of this — as did Dr. Anthony Fauci, after leading the White House Coronavirus Task Force under President Trump and the White House COVID-19 Response Team as President Biden's chief medical advisor.

As with Dr. Fauci, they pay no price for the joblessness, the suicides, even the deaths and the health complications attributable to coerced medical treatment. They pay no price for the loneliness among the sick and the dying, the mistreatment of patients at hospitals; the setbacks suffered by children in their most formative years; the lost time between loved ones, between family, parents and their newborns at the hospital; the cancelation of special occasions; the social unrest and the economic setbacks felt across the country.

They pay no price for their negligence, for their failed risk analysis, for ignoring or dismissing people's concerns and misgivings about the treatment. They pay no price for their wrongs, whether confessed or exposed. The closest we come to justice is where the people start figuring things out for themselves, where wisdom and honesty prevail through the individual, one such example in this case being Dr. Joseph Ladapo, the surgeon general of Florida who has since called on doctors to stop administering mRNA COVID-19 vaccines: "I am calling for a halt to the use of mRNA COVID-19 vaccines. The U.S. Food and Drug Administration and the Centers for Disease Control and Prevention have always played it fast and loose with COVID-19 vaccine safety, but their failure to test for DNA integration with the human genome — as their own guidelines dictate — when the vaccines are known to be contaminated with foreign DNA is intolerable." The "experts" pay no price for the ultimate effects on DNA, whether the DNA is affected, as Dr. Ladapo puts it, "in a way that makes people sick" or "leaves people to pass on characteristics to their offspring." Indeed, the ones who wield the power seldom pay any price at all, no matter the severity or the scale of their crimes, no matter their bearing on humanity or the rest of time. On the contrary, in many such cases, the more extreme the consequences, the more unlikely that anyone will ever be held accountable.

CHAPTER VIII

DECADENCE

Unfortunately, principle and virtue are often lost to expedience and intemperance. In much the same way that people are more willing to spend than to save, there is scarcely any difference in the way that people treat their liberty. It is yet another classic example of Bastiat's *seen versus the unseen*, whereby the comforts and the expedients of the short term conceal the long-term risks and tradeoffs which accompany their short-lived benefits.

It is no mere coincidence that, as evidenced by the experience of America and much of the West, moral decadence and intemperance have coincided with the gradual decline in both liberty *and* savings. Indeed, debt has swept across civilization, in America and elsewhere, along with their indifference toward liberty. This connection is important because, in the main, an indebted society becomes increasingly immoral, intemperate and willing to part with their liberty; after all, at such a juncture many among them will have little more than liberty to sell, so to them it appears to be a fair deal.

It is in just this way that the public liberty is lost: at the hands of people who know the price of everything but the value of nothing; at the hands of people living in the now with little to no regard for the future; at the hands of those all too accustomed to protocols, guarantees, accommodations, and the lifestyle of spending their way through life. All too often, this means spending other people's money or dispensing with their liberty, even, or in many cases *especially*, when it is not even their own.

In most cases, the sacrifice is not even immediately apparent to those who have had little occasion to appreciate their own liberty by realizing its full potential. On the contrary, they come to envy those who have enjoyed their freedom, and they contend that liberty is dangerous, if not oppressive, a privilege enjoyed only by a select segment of society.

This comes as no surprise, as liberty demands initiative and actual work in order to enjoy its fruits. When faced with the opportunity to forego the work and still enjoy some of the fruit, they leap at the opportunity. After all, it comes at a cost that they never expect to pay, or at a cost too distant in the future to trouble them.

As they dispense with liberty in favor of guarantees and *entitlements*, they come to expect others to foot the bill. In this way, they are just as willing to sacrifice others' liberty as they are pleased to spend other people's money. On virtually every conceivable occasion, they will invariably sacrifice liberty and independence for any number of rewards, whether some temporary safety or security, the promise of a better life, or some fantastical illusion thereof.

In their willingness to part with their savings, just as with their independence and their liberty, they eventually find that they have merely suspended reality for some temporary or illusory advantage at a cost that they can ill afford, and one that future generations are sure to pay, in full *and* with interest. It is no mere coincidence that, where the people dispense with savings and sound money, they also dispense with discipline, independence and, altogether, the bountiful inheritances of liberty. These are not only the consequences of, but the minimum price paid for, their ignorance.

Unfortunately, despite the warnings and the well-documented accounts of their forbears, the people occasionally have to learn from their own experiences and their own sorrows to begin to truly appreciate the value of liberty and independence. It is no surprise that people who know the price of everything and yet the value of nothing, who know Liberty as the name of a statue yet nothing more, who readily dispense with freedom for free stuff, do not appreciate what they are giving up for such precious little in return. As it is written in

Proverbs 21:20, "There is treasure to be desired and oil in the dwelling of the wise; but a foolish man spendeth it up." In other words, a fool and his treasure are soon parted. In this case, much the same could be said about a fool and his liberty.

Oddly enough, the people who all too often fancy themselves *progressive* are progressive only in their imagination and the kind of force that they are willing to impose on the people in order to realize their imaginings, or to otherwise continue their chase. They care little about history and are therefore ill-prepared for the future. They are progressive only in the way that they imagine a world entirely unhinged from the one that they inhabit.

In this way, they progress beyond the terrestrial world to inhabit their own, where they assume total control to live out their visions. In their excitement, however, they neglect to appreciate that they have inhabited a dream governed by neither nature nor the physical laws of the land, but by the wishful thinking of people who have become too comfortable in their own imaginations.

Regrettably, their imaginations, clouded by movie magic, misinformation and science fiction, distract them from the realities of the world, preventing them from ever waking up. For this reason, they seek control over a world that they hardly recognize, one that they fail to even remotely understand. In this way, their appetite for control projects their own inadequacies and insecurities, and their desperate desire to make the world make sense. Make no mistake, this means not that they seek to understand the world as it exists, but that they seek to reform it in keeping with their own visions of what it could or "should" be.

From their perspective, premised in theory on "science" and personally in conviction, they cannot conceive of any plausible opposition or any alternative explanations. In the face of any "hesitation" or disagreement, they assume ignorance or worse. Incredulous to their opponents, they insist on their control in order to force the opposition into their dream. As absurd as this sounds, they succeed in carrying out their objective only because so many have come to share the same visions or to otherwise fear shattering them with the truth.

In the case of masks, lockdowns, and experimental drugs, the state and its accessories have refused to even entertain the opposition, however valid or justified in their positions. As far as they are concerned, there is no sacrifice worth sparing in the course of the "common good". Whatever the cost and whatever the evidence, the means are assumed justified by the ends. Unfortunately, because the ends are so poorly defined and always on the move, the public stands to lose everything as they acquiesce to the means.

After all, as the government and its accessories see it, there is no limit on the sacrifice that the public ought to be willing to accept. As they see it, the jewel of liberty is hardly even an afterthought. After all, it is much easier to dispense with liberty than with cold, hard cash; and, for added reassurance, the state assures the people that it will eventually restore that liberty in the future anyway.

Of course, the state seldom gets around to restoring the public liberty, just as it rarely gets around to proving the efficacy of its programs. Indeed, wherever the state fails, it is said to have failed due to a lack of control or resources, and wherever it is said to have had any success at all, it is only further justification for more of the same. In any event, government and its accessories will always crave more power and greater control, and they will always manage to find cause to "justify" their ends.

Always changing in its objectives as in its forms, history decrees that control always emerges under fresh disguises, preventing the public from easily identifying the patterns. This was doubtless the case with the hysteria around lockdowns, vaccinations, boosters, and the mandated use of masks, all of which proved far more successful in politicizing society and spreading fear than in "slowing the spread" of the virus. In many ways, masks were just another way for governments and their accessories to place another barrier between themselves and their challengers, to more easily identify and humiliate their opponents.

A further benefit for the agents of the establishment is that they could readily shield themselves, their shame, their motives and their insecurities from the people whom they resent and whom they seek to bring under their control.

As a consequence, they manage to repress their opponents through the concealment of personalities, emotions and the humanizing features which otherwise unite the people and make it altogether possible for them to commiserate with one another. As it turns out, the concealment of personality is entirely in keeping with the Marxist playbook, which stresses the sheer mass of the people, using their dead weight to crush the opposition; to likewise crush the individual within society, and, in turn, the genuine bonds between people as individuals, indeed the only manner in which those bonds can be forged and maintained.

Indeed, Leftism has the effect of corrupting not only society and the economy at large, but also the very workplace where the people spend most of their waking hours; where Leftist notions progressively suffocate the people through endless "trainings" and "regulations" and threats of legal repercussions pertaining to the nature of their interpersonal relationships. So suffocating do these constraints become that they suck not only the life out of the workplace but the personalities out of the staff, who come to suppress their humanity in favor of more robotic behavior which is more likely to keep them out of trouble with the company (i.e. human resources) or a court of law; ultimately yielding a people so robotic that they become virtually interchangeable with generally any system serving the same ends, however uncaring and unfeeling (i.e. artificial intelligence).

It is in precisely these ways that the people are progressively stripped of their personalities as to be perfectly dehumanized as unfeeling and unsympathetic agents of the state, faceless factors within a system, mere cogs in a wheel. Indeed, the people become so accustomed to the state assuming control, issuing the "resolutions", and determining the "appropriate" course of action, so fearful of the repercussions of using their own discretion or taking initiative themselves, that they come to regard society as a mere system in which every person is to perform little more than an assigned role.

They come to work for the "common good", but only as defined and instructed. They are thereby gradually relieved of the impetus or the sense of obligation to contribute to society outside of their limited work lives, beyond their defined assignments. They likewise become ignorant or numb to the concepts of charity, etiquette, generosity, and initiative where people are truly in need of help, whereby society is otherwise made hospitable through the relationships and the bonds forged between individual people.

After all, they are instructed to "stay in their lanes", and they are threatened with repercussions where they fail to obey, where they may be (and inevitably *are*) met with penalties through lawsuits filed by their comrades or by the state itself, the latter of which encourages and enables such suits. In this way, the Marxist doctrine, as the former Führer of Germany put it in his 1925 manifesto *Mein Kampf*, "denies the value of personality in man, contests the significance of nationality and race, and thereby withdraws from humanity the premise of its existence and its culture." Indeed, it is in just this manner that the doctrine denies the people their mutual sense of identity, their mutual sense of obligation and belonging, their pride as a people, and thereby their inherent motivations to care, to sympathize, to be generous, and to be grateful.

Indeed, it may rightly be said that this is yet another form of censorship whereby politicians and their peers aim to suppress the greatest ambassador of virtue and freedom: the individual. After all, as the journalist H. L. Mencken once wrote, "The most dangerous man to any government is the man who is able to think things out for himself, without regard to the prevailing superstitions and taboos."

Indeed, the single greatest threat to tyranny is the individual, and he is of the smallest minority on earth. In the erasure of the individual and his features, we are all less human, less connected, and therefore easier to divide and conquer. All the while, the government and its accessories bring progressively more people under their spell, convincing them that they (the persecutors) are the compassionate ones. Of course, this is to say nothing at all about the efficacy of their mandates, which are hardly ever followed up with any conclusive evidence; which scarcely ever require evidence to impose their will; and which, in the case of masks, are as diverse in their styles and materials as they are demonstrably incapable of limiting the spread of microscopic particles emitted through aerosols and vapors with every breath. This is to say nothing about the efficacy of the various experimental drugs which have become available, which have been virtually forced upon guinea pigs who quickly succumb to peer pressure, and still others who fancy themselves "progressive" for erring on the side of "science" or compassion.

Regrettably, these are people who have been unwittingly conned into an experiment still in its infancy, lacking in ethics as well as credibility. Of course, the government and its accessories need not say anything at all about efficacy, because the business of politics is the sale of excuses, exigencies, and intentions for the benefit of power. Everything else is purely incidental, a clever disguise or a convenient vehicle for their only destination: control.

So long as the public is inundated with peer pressure and mandates in lieu of evidence, and so long as they are deprived of their freedom, discretion and dignity as they pertain to their personal, commercial and medical affairs, the courses undertaken by government and its accessories are to be assumed dubious and political at best, tyrannical and murderous at worst.

As the French author Albert Camus once wrote, "The welfare of the people in particular has always been the alibi of tyrants, and it provides the further advantage of giving the servants of tyranny a good conscience." This is precisely the threat posed by democracy, or any system so styled: it is power, met with as much popularity as it is supported by a good conscience, and it is a means to unrealistically reimagining the world.

Indeed, democracy empowers a people to betray their traditions in favor of their imaginations, from the tested to the untested; from difficulty and discipline to ease and expedience; from principles to impulses, reason to hunches, critical thought to wishful thinking; from self-ownership to selfishness, from responsibility to robbery. It is a way for some undisciplined majority to legitimize itself against its forbears, to ignore the laws of economics and the demands of reality, and to flout the conventions of growing up; a way for covetousness, envy and greed to triumph over ambition and industry, to defend force against freedom, and coercion against free association; to promote power over persuasion, to divide the people and to conquer them under the illusion of consensus and the false impression of participation.

So long as the establishment places the people under the impression that a significant number of their contemporaries condone or approve of an initiative, it will face little resistance from the rest: those who are either jaded or indifferent, or who assume that they can't make a difference, that they are outnumbered or under-equipped; those who refuse to get caught up in the morass, and still others who aren't ready to "die on that hill".

Those who would otherwise represent the resistance merely succumb to fear, peer pressure, and the threat of legal consequences and social rejection. Ultimately, once the establishment succeeds in bringing enough people into conformity around a new initiative, it can (and *will*) begin to dig in its heels and defend that initiative with the full force of the bureaucracy and the armed men who are more than willing to have their way with the people.

Through the combination of urbanization and democracy, mankind has realized the single greatest threat to liberty: the political means by which to define its terms, uniquely accompanied by the manpower to enforce them, operating from the benefit of conscience, the perception of equitability, and the pretense of consensus. The noble intention behind any political process is in the pursuit of limited government through any means which reliably produces that result. The intended result is not, in and of itself, a democracy which empowers the political will of the majority; the desired result is rather that form of government which is most limited and most accountable, which yields to liberty in the absence of conferred political authority.

In this sense, where there is the pursuit of limited government, there, too, is the pursuit of maximal liberty. Where government seeks to substitute liberty with democracy, or to conflate the two, it can only be a false face for tyranny, albeit a face with an appealing disguise.

As it turns out, the conflation does not end there. It extends to the false association between consensus and truth, as if the first has any relationship with the second. Indeed, this is a popular tool among grandstanders and politicians: a fallacy known in Latin as *argumentum ad populum*, or otherwise the argument of *appealing to the people*.

Where the citizenry has already been thoroughly groomed to view each of these as interchangeable, they have prepared the fertile grounds for the seeds of their own destruction, albeit democratically; and it is not just that democracy is inherently flawed and ill-fated, which is certainly true in its own right, but that it overlooks the risks posed by the consensus of those of so few years and so little experience that they are destined to condemn their comrades to the failings and weaknesses of their childish convictions and limited understandings.

So naive are those of so few years and such little maturity that their basic philosophies are either certain to change along with their understanding of the world or they will strengthen their misconceptions despite the wealth of evidence which has already so thoroughly discredited them. It is for this reason that democracy is not only destined for failure from the beginning, but that, in practice, it will fail in the details, that it will seldom get anything right, and that it will rely on and empower the judgment of those who have enough trouble exercising sound judgment and managing the dysfunction within their *own* lives.

This is the paradox of democracy, whereby flawed government, which would otherwise be flogged in the public square and utterly banished into the foreseeable future, seduces the constituency into believing that they have assumed control, merely to witness a system progressively warped and brazenly empowered by the illusion of consensus; a theoretical consensus of compromised, immature, uninformed and inexperienced citizens who, in their ignorance, believe, want to believe, or have a stake in promoting the belief that they are governed by consent and consensus.

In that land of "democracy" drifting ever from freedom, the tyrants need only to convince some number of the people of their ends; to appeal to them not merely for their votes, which are essentially immaterial, but for the continued illusion of consensus which suffices to bring about their submission to some agreeable political cause, appraised not for its accuracy but for its appeal, which in turn allows the establishment to continue its siege upon their neighbors and their own liberty.

Without fail, democracy invariably finds its way to tyranny, for it does not take long for polished politicians to convince their constituents to empower their government. It does not take long for them to realize that, with their votes, they can claim a greater share of the public purse. From there, they need only to turn their constituents against each other and brandish the establishment as their weapon. As the journalist H. L. Mencken once put it, at its core "Democracy is [nothing more than] the theory that the common people know what they want, and deserve to get it good and hard."

As the Leftists assume control over the establishment, they invariably set out to change the rules and stack the deck. As they reform the ranks of their constituencies, they enjoy the further benefit of the continued illusion of consensus, ensuring that a growing segment of society will approve of their agendas; in turn, their constituencies will predictably do their bidding, pressuring their peers into silence or conformity, and in most cases condemning their heritage while demanding that their peers do the same. Indeed, part of their agenda is to repeat their big lie, and to repeat it as long and as loudly as it takes to sufficiently displace the truth and discourage the opposition.

Given enough time and tongue-lashing, they succeed in burying the truth along with their opponents, left to be excavated by a strict minority of independent thinkers willing to pay the price; a minority of independent thinkers who are, ironically enough, inspired by the mystery, the deceit and the corruption. Indeed, it turns out that if you suppress or destroy evidence of the controversial, this will only encourage independent thinkers and those who have become suspicious of the conventional narrative — those wondering, "What is there to be found in these ruins of monuments so dangerous to the establishment that they had to be destroyed?"

It is in just this way that a civilization circles the drain. As opposed to gravity, however, it is the lure of Leftism which pulls the people down; and it will pull them down until it has emptied the tub. That is, of course, if the tub does not give out first.

By the time Leftism gets a hold of the people and their imaginations, it turns the people and their lives into the instruments of their own enslavement; and by its own designs, the people are so busy keeping up, so distracted by cheap entertainment and propaganda, so preoccupied in their petty disagreements, and so fearful of bucking the conventions, that they live merely to survive. All the while, little did they know that, in their quest to survive, they were erecting or otherwise condoning the very institutions that would continue their own subjugation. Whatever the means and whatever their guise, their ends are always the same: the achievement of further control through the concealment of their motives.

The rights of the people are like a dam: so long as they are intact, the people are protected. Once the dam begins to crack, it will eventually give way. It is not the *final* crack that is to blame for the failure, but the *series* of cracks that went unnoticed, ignored, and unrepaired. Given enough cracks, there is ultimately nothing left to defend the people from the impending flood. It is in just this way that tyranny takes hold of the people and their property: it is at first gradual and inconspicuous, then ubiquitous and unstoppable.

Gradually, through its clever and convoluted network, the bureaucracy will succeed in influencing every aspect of commerce and daily life, not merely at the hands of the state, but by *private* enterprise genuflecting to false idols, repeating their mantras and pressuring their own peers, customers and employees to comply. This is yet another disguise of socialism, a mutilated form of a market economy and an outgrowth of a government wielding too much power and influence. Of course, this is no coincidence.

As Henry Grady Weaver wrote in 1947, in his *Mainspring of Human Progress*, "[Marx and his followers] believed industrial capitalism to be the natural forerunner of socialism; that to bring about the world millennium they must concentrate, first of all, on highly developed capitalistic countries — using the processes of attrition, boring from within, fomenting dissension and class hatred, and promoting collectivistic measures through existing governmental agencies."

Weaver continued, "This is something like jujitsu, which has been described as the technique of defeating an opponent by turning his own strength against him." Weaver concluded, "In other words, it was a program of inducing capitalism to commit suicide, then stepping in and taking things over."

Capitalism, or any other social or economic system, once corrupted or devoid of virtue, continues in its mutilated form only to hasten the destruction of society; the same is true of the corruption of money, the lust for money merely for the sake of personal wealth and little more, the desperation for wealth for the sake of taxes or tributes. As it is written in *1 Timothy 6:10*, "For the love of money is a root of all kinds of evils. It is through this craving that some have wandered away from the faith and pierced themselves with many pangs."

In order for any social or economic system to prosper in the long run, people must necessarily be guided by virtue, self-ownership, personal responsibility and family values. For this reason, Leftism is destined to fail on every occasion. It incentivizes the relinquishment of virtue and responsibility to the state, and it operates from premises diametrically opposed to the individual, the family, the principles of self-ownership and personal responsibility.

When any country abandons virtue within a market economy, in jujitsu-like fashion the velocity of money will quickly correspond with the decay of that society; a form of decadence and indecency which threatens the integrity of the whole of the people, out of which, as Martin Luther once put it, "the same kind of morality flows into all the world." This is the ultimate and inexorable course of Leftism. While one given example may survive longer than another, while one example may *appear* to have perfected the program, they ultimately end up in the same place: complete and utter ruin.

This does not mean that it cannot flourish or endure at some limited scale or for some limited period of time, but that its prosperity and its shelf life are strictly limited; and that, while the establishment will surely benefit for some period of time, and while the "working class" may even see some benefits in the short run, namely *entitlements* and employment within the growing establishment, it will, on net and over time, ultimately come at the cost of society and posterity, their lives, their property and their liberty.

Indeed, this is yet another in a long list of dirty tricks: the manner in which the state exploits so-called "entitlements".

Siphoning the funds from the workers' paychecks, the state assures the workers that they are "entitled" to those funds (or "benefits") at a specified date (or under specified conditions). When that time finally arrives, and in the event that the state is insolvent or, for any other reason, unable or unwilling to disburse the funds, it will have a whole constituency clamoring for restitution. Conveniently enough, that constituency will be prepared to tolerate or to happily endorse nearly all imaginable measures, just to ensure that the state will be able to satisfy those "entitlements", whatever the costs and whatever the consequences for posterity.

This is why state-managed welfare, insurance, and *entitlements* schemes are so dangerous to the public liberty. They essentially secure the people's allegiance to a regime enabling intergenerational theft, with one generation feeding on the next through a massive apparatus always seeking to strip the people of their rights and to fleece them of still more of their resources; in these cases with the approval of the masses who are simply looking out for themselves, who are not personally responsible for the costs, who are unbothered by (or indifferent to) the consequences suffered by their heirs. Of course, this has the effect of creating animosity between generations, always leaving the later generation to resent their elders who selfishly endorsed, condoned, or presided over this scam.

Conveniently for the state, this animosity makes it much easier for the politicians to dismantle the traditions and to condemn the heritage of the people; to insult their ancestors and propose a more "progressive" alternative. Of course, the only aspect that is truly "progressive" about any of this is the type of theft and enslavement just described. This is yet another example of the insidiousness of big government.

Leftism of any variety, wherever it takes hold of a people, will, without fail, degrade that society. It will systematically pick it apart and ultimately bring about its destruction, but not before filling its citizens with hope and exploiting the benefits and the resources afforded it by capitalists and some measure of capitalism; the latter being indispensable to the endless possibilities being entertained.

Socialism feeds on prosperous capitalist societies not only out of economic necessity — for it could not possibly endure, let alone advance, for any meaningful period of time over any other — but for the advantages enjoyed over the kind of public which has grown comfortable and generally unwilling to risk that comfort by any effort which might cost them; whether financially, a night's rest, or some time behind bars. Ironically enough, the free market has enabled much of the public's complacency and many of the illusions of Leftists. This is a kind of complacency which, along with boredom, feigned self-pride and arrogance, leaves the people endlessly in search of entertainment and humor, particularly the kind which is critical of, or scoffing at, others whom they envy or dislike.

This is a kind of self-pride which keeps the people from intervening or protesting when appropriate; a kind of arrogance which ridicules speech and legitimate grievances; a kind of complacency which negates the power and influence of man through his expression and the exercise of his inalienable rights — rights and powers which must, from time to time, necessarily be exercised in the defense of all things essential to life, in the defense of the people, their liberty, their property, and their pursuit of happiness.

In this environment of growing complacency, certain disparaging terms have emerged to describe the people who dare to make a fuss, who dare to fight for something not specifically aligned with the political status quo. There are also certain popular phrases that have become fashionable, among them the following: "It is what it is"; "Let's hope it resolves itself"; "We'll see how this plays out."

These phrases serve to comfort the people, to end the discussion, to relieve themselves of any personal responsibility, to place complete and total faith in the status quo, the prevailing powers, the judgment and the actions of those powers, and to make a habit of prioritizing safety and avoiding conflict. Over time, the people grow so comfortable with the status quo that they are unable to even imagine a sufficient justification for any disturbance, whether a referendum, a protest, or a physical confrontation. Indeed, they come to resent all who dare to even consider such disturbances, regardless of the cause.

As the American author and poet Ella Wheeler Cox put it in her 1914 poem *Protest*, "To sin by silence, when we should protest, makes cowards out of men. The human race has climbed on protest. Had no voice been raised against injustice, ignorance, and lust, the inquisition yet would serve the law, and guillotines decide our least disputes. The few who dare, must speak and speak again to right the wrongs of many."

Yet, in their complacency, in their self-pride and their arrogance, the people continually commit this sin; they do so regularly without fail or even a second thought. This is a disposition which ultimately infects a society; one whereby more and more people are brought progressively into conformity with the status quo — whether silently through acquiescence or vocally with approval, or otherwise out of fear that, in defending (or standing up for) something, they will become the butt of the next joke.

In this way, the people begin to see politics and humor in all things social, and in all of the worst ways. Consequently, more and more people endeavor to come up with the next great witticism, the next clever comment, as opposed to seeking the next great discovery or actually offering a meaningful contribution;

instead of building something useful, instead of enlightening and empowering their fellow man, or enhancing his perspective on his purpose and the greater meaning of life.

This becomes a perpetual decline, a slow death of society, with the symptoms progressively exacerbating the severity of the disease; a disease which degrades not only the people's quality of life but the courage to fight and the general consensus around their purpose, their very species, and the meaning of life. Indeed, when people have lost all meaning and purpose in their lives, they have little trouble seeing little meaning and purpose in the lives of others. As such, people become progressively less inclined to take seriously those things worthy of seriousness, less inclined to respect those worthy of respect. Instead, people come to make jokes out of virtually everything; that is, everything except for those sensitive matters which they are instructed to take seriously. Indeed, the people otherwise come to make jokes about even the most profound cases of loss, sorrow and grief, perfectly in keeping with what little value they place altogether on human life.

Indeed, they come to view every person and every incident as an opportunity for a joke or a laugh, otherwise an opportunity for shame or ridicule; a pestilence in society which manifests itself not only in the attitudes of the people, but in their dress and appearance, in their manners and decorum in public, and more generally in the way in which they interact and conduct themselves on a daily basis. This is precisely because their own lives have been reduced to such a pathetic state through their own perspectives, the consequence of cowardice, weak-mindedness, and resignation, qualities always begetting more of the same; qualities expressed through condescension, hatred, jealousy, indifference, apathy, remorselessness, and flippancy.

These kinds of people are extremely dangerous to civilization, and in large numbers they so weaken a society that it becomes

ripe for manipulation by the types who know just how to capitalize. Over time, the quality of society declines so far as to be
completely and utterly divided, completely and utterly incompetent where it counts, completely and utterly indefensible. Indeed, the quality of society eventually declines to such a point
that the people eventually lack the strength, the initiative, and
even the slightest interest to concern themselves with anything
other than their own selfish desires, deficiencies that the Leftists
are always prepared to exploit for their own benefit.

Through relative abundance and the appearance of
unlimited resources, and through a division of labor which has
made life simpler, the comforts and conveniences of capitalism
tend to favor the Leftists' false promises and illusions; comforts
and conveniences enjoyed, and illusions entertained, without a
sufficient understanding of the factors and forces which first
enabled them. Despite their many advantages, innovation
and specialization, especially where they are combined
with subsidized higher education, university expansion and
credentialism, have had the incidental effect of convincing
people that they are smarter and more capable than they really
are. They have also afforded people ample time and energy to
waste on pet projects, protests and theories; that is, when they
are not completely engrossed in reality television, social media,
and streaming movies.

This is precisely why virtue, discipline, and family values
are so indispensable to civilization. Where an undisciplined
and virtueless people are afforded so much plenty and so
many advantages, that is a civilization destined for decadence;
it is a society becoming increasingly vulnerable to "justified"
encroachments upon the public liberty.

In becoming comfortable, they are more susceptible to any
soft despotism, for they have more to lose, and they have long
been spared the need to fight.

Ironically, unbeknownst to them, they have everything to lose in their complacency and their unwillingness to take up the mantle in defense of liberty. In one of the great tragedies of the human experience, we find that comfort breeds a form of cowardice that leaves the people unwilling to defend the very principle that gives rise to those unrivaled comforts in the first place: liberty. As Fyodor Dostoevsky famously wrote in his 1866 novel *Crime and Punishment*, "Man has it all in his hands, and it all slips through his fingers from sheer cowardice."

This takeover happens gradually and surreptitiously, under the most clever of disguises, often advertised under the banners of *equality, the common good* and the *the general welfare*. Of course, the socialists are always clever enough to have their unwitting victims celebrating their own sacrifices. Indeed, in many cases their victims encourage or join them as they chisel away at the foundations of their liberty, and, in still other noted cases, as they tear down the monuments to their own heritage and their own ancestors.

The socialists, at least the ones leading the charge, are often shrewd enough to pace themselves in their advance upon the public liberty, as they require the assent, or the acquiescence, of the people as they continue their siege. Conveniently for them, most of their victims are functionally illiterate or even willing to comply. Still others try to ignore the siege up until the point that it affects them directly: the point at which the siege has finally arrived at their front door.

They are often reminded of, and ready to recite, their mantras to excuse their meekness and their fears; on the proverbial battlefield, they are afraid to die on this or that hill, all the while neglecting to pick a hill on which they *are* willing to die. All the while, the people cede progressively more territory and resources to the tyrants, who enjoy proportionately more power and influence, while the people find themselves progressively outnumbered and overpowered, making any attempt at resistance appear even more futile, and, in their estimation, justifying only further inaction. However, wherever the socialists are to encounter any resistance at all, their opponents are generally people of principles, standards, and sensibilities, qualities that the Leftists are sure to use against them.

Unlike their opponents, the Leftists are willing to dispense with virtually every principle and every standard just to get their way. Whether it be the Ten Commandments, the Golden Rule, the laws of physics, or the rules of logic, they don't concern the Leftists. Their double standards let the Leftists off the hook: Leftists who selectively enforce their own rules (fashioned along the way) while conveniently exempting themselves; Leftists who operate with the full understanding that their opponents are law-abiding, respectful of authority, and religious in maintaining their *own* standards, namely truth and morality; Leftists who believe that they can always rewrite the rules as they see fit; who know that they will ultimately succeed in wearing their opponents down, that it is only a matter of time. Having already accepted that their ends justify the means, there is no trick the Leftists will not play, no level to which they will not stoop, as they know that their opponents are called to *love thy enemy*.

Through their efforts at vilifying and lampooning their opponents, they erect straw men representative of no one and defended by nobody. Meanwhile, their followers are either compromised by their own personal interests or vendettas or otherwise none the wiser to the ploy. In any case, the species could not possibly conceive of a more convenient opponent.

So, whereas the Leftists expect the benefit of the doubt, indeed scolding those who don't readily give it to them, their opponents are not afforded any leeway, and they do not expect it. The Leftists eventually succeed in destroying their opposition by cunning or force. Whether by silencing, vilifying or lampooning them, by bringing them under their spell, or by threatening them with force, imprisonment or ostracism, the results are the same: fewer opponents and more subjects who have grown amenable to the program.

In fact, the *socialist* is actually a misnomer, a kind of false advertising which seeks to bring the people under the spell of false promises and visions of the *common good*. In reality, as a group they are not as much *socialists* as they are confused malcontents and sanctimonious opportunists. Indeed, the socialist is typically an anti-social type who has virtually no interest in people other than what he can gain by bringing them into conformity and under his control. This comes as no surprise, given the outlook necessary in order to promote such draconian measures as those demanded through socialism, given the aura of negativity surrounding the socialist in his every protest. Indeed, when the socialists are not directly attempting to promote such negativity, they expose it in their view of things. As the American essayist and philosopher Ralph Waldo Emerson put it, "People do not seem to realize that their opinion of the world is also a confession of character." Likewise, the same may rightly be said about their inherent outlook on all things, including their view of their fellow man.

Contrary to his title, the "socialist" is rather bothered by society, if not completely disgusted by it, and in virtually every case he resents the people, especially those who dare to disagree with him. In virtually every case, the socialist detests his fellow man, managing only on occasion to conceal his hatred and his jealousies; but merely managing his disgust for the people as he seeks to rule over them, as he concocts clever schemes for their enslavement, and eventually succeeds in bringing them into conformity (or "equality") as the property of the state. Gradually stripped of their dignity, their sacred honor, and their humanity, they are reduced in standing to mere factors of production, gears in a machine, or digits in a database.

This is not only a benefit to the state but a necessary condition for its proposed world order. Indeed, the Leftists often point to perceived successes in other lands, amongst *other* civilizations, attributing those "successes" to the factors and influences of their liking; in still other cases pointing to the perceived failures of systems based on the models of their adversaries. In this way, the Leftists are found either erring in judgment or deliberately confounding the matter through non-comparables, attempting to "justify" their measures wherever they can claim successes elsewhere.

Of course, these practices are ordinarily found where the anointed pundits neglect to account for critical differences in climates, customs and attitudes, cultural and demographic compositions, geological and geographical conditions. Of course, the Leftists manage to succeed only *because* of these tricks, through a series of convincing fallacies pitched to willing buyers, investors with conflicts of interest, and the many who are not in the market anyway; then, of course, there are still others who, in making their purchases, so to speak, do not distinguish between the quality of the products.

In every pitch, the Leftists remain true to form, operating from unproven assumptions while reducing virtually every case and every individual to simplistic and more convenient terms. True to form, the Leftists prefer to view as fungible and interchangeable all people and all jurisdictions of the world, so far as they can be assumed to corroborate their models; as they are not only assumed fungible and interchangeable for the use of the state, but, by the very definition of its system, this is considered a necessary condition for it to function as proposed.

They scarcely distinguish between the qualities of the people, just as they disregard their unique circumstances.

They propose a set of one-size-fits-all "solutions" irrespective of the relevant differences, and they assert that their "success" anywhere, however measured or defined, shall suffice to justify its practice in virtually every case; a most unscientific hypothesis, to be sure.

Indeed, in this way the people not only become mere factors of production, but through the conveniences afforded the Leftists by technology (i.e. high-tech devices and appliances), the people are reduced to programmable and thus highly controllable assets to the establishment. They are reduced to unthinking resources incapable of their own discretion, guided and governed by the systems around them. They are reduced to assets that are constantly accessible, traceable, and, like pawns, always at the establishment's disposal in its grand strategy; always prepared to relinquish even more of their rights, discretion, privacy and freedoms for promised comforts and conveniences.

As for the Leftists, their most successful political strategy has been to equate their enemies with easier (often cartoonish) opponents, and to thereby frame the debate to their advantage. This has, time and again, been the case in their wars against fascism, through which they conveniently bury the truth (often literally) while concealing their ulterior motives. It is so convenient that the socialists are so often spared in the denunciation of despots, and where they are *not* spared, they are regarded as "fascists" instead. Of course, the socialists are more than delighted to call *them* their enemies, as they (the "fascists") are far easier to handle than the socialists' real opponents, and they (the "fascists") can take the blame for all of socialism's failures. What's more, this strategy offers the further benefit of neutralizing the traditional and patriotic types who, in the view of the Left, stand in the way of "progress".

CHAPTER IX

ENEMIES

The convenient enemy of the Left, fascism is rather easily conflated with any form of nationalism, thus rendering both non-viable (or unfashionable) where either is decidedly so. In their scapegoating of fascism, the socialists have enjoyed much shelter from blame and reprisal, much shelter from calls for retribution.

Indeed, another reason that the socialists identify the fascists as the enemy is that the annals of history and "progressive" Western thought, as professed and as written, especially following World War II, have vilified enough of them such that the people, in so loathing the fascists as instructed, find comfort with the socialists who claim to offer the better alternative; socialists who have, for a number of reasons, eluded the sort of criticism heaped upon the fascists.

By, over time, assuming progressively more control over the media, as well as political, academic, and economic affairs, the socialists virtually guarantee their influence over the people; an influence which prevents the people from appreciating the grave consequences and the repeated failures of socialism, the social, spiritual and economic decay which is always certain to follow; an influence which hypnotizes the people, effectively blinding them to the qualities shared between socialism and its preferred nemesis; and an influence which convinces the people that their system is so radically different and so obviously superior.

While the truth-seekers are, in fact, their true archenemies, the Left prefers to compete with fascism or any other form of statism under any other name; and the Left does so almost exclusively. The reasons are obvious: relative to truth and liberty, fascism poses less of a threat to the power of the state; it portrays patriotism and national identity in a negative light; and, above all, the two agree politically where it counts.

In truth, fascism is one of the many faces of Leftism, a form of authoritarian rule exploiting only a distinct set of public sensibilities. Ultimately, fascists and communists (Marxists, Leninists, Stalinists, socialists, et al.) seek the same powers, only through slightly different means: the first through nationalism, the second through socialism, each often operating from the pretext of some combination thereof; each occasionally citing a warped form of patriotism, a variety celebrating the state as the most sacred of causes, the fountain of splendor, the beacon for righteousness, and the monument to their greatest achievements.

The two share mutually in their appetite for social control and regimentation, the subordination of the individual to the ill-defined "common good", their silencing and forcible suppression of the opposition, and their histories with dictatorship and militarism "just to get things going". The two campaign so mercilessly for power that, contrary to truth and liberty, it is the state that always wins.

In this way, the two are merely different sides of the same sledgehammer. It is through this false dichotomy, between fascism and Leftism, that the people are left to accept (or even embrace) the lesser of evils. In this way, the state stacks the deck to ensure its victory while maintaining the pretense of legitimacy.

Indeed, the Leftists are always cunning enough to mitigate the risks to the state. By pacing themselves and gradually laying siege upon the people and their liberty, the people hardly take notice of the forces enveloping them, and so the Leftists ultimately stand to encounter very little resistance. In most cases, the people simply get out of the way and keep their heads down to avoid being labeled *fascists*, *bigots*, or *enemies of the state*.

One of the advantages of this strategy, of course, is that it allows the people an opportunity to get out of the way, and it affords them time to adapt to their new circumstances;

circumstances in which the socialists and their *useful idiots,* the *korisne budale,* celebrate a new form of *liberty* or *freedom,* enabling only further usurpations. As the Scottish philosopher David Hume once observed, "It is seldom that liberty of any kind is lost all at once."

Indeed, recent examples of genocide offer significant insight into just how a series of small measures can yield such serious results.

Let us first consider the Holocaust. In the aftermath of World War I, the Allies required that German citizens be disarmed, prompting a revision of German law in order to accomplish this task. When the party rose to power, one of the first agenda items of the Nazi regime was to peruse gun registration lists in order to identify their political opponents and disarm them. In accordance with existing German law requiring citizens to demonstrate competency and need in order to qualify for gun ownership, the Nazis needed only to claim that their opponents, among them the Jewish population, were simply too incompetent to handle firearms, or that they simply had no real need for them.

Finally, in 1935, the Third Reich passed a law specifically banning Jews from acquiring gun permits, but this merely formalized the practice that had already been underway. Three years later, in 1938, the Nazi regime officially denied select groups the right to carry firearms, only to grant the privilege to Nazi sympathizers, who were allowed to carry firearms without a permit.

Another such example comes from the Soviet Union.

On December 12, 1924, the Soviet Union limited civilian gun ownership to smoothbore shotguns, restricting all remaining categories of firearms to use exclusively by those employed by the Soviet state, whereupon all violators were subject to severe punishment: up to five years in prison.

On February 25, 1927, the state in Soviet Russia outlawed all attempts at "overthrowing, undermining or weakening of the power of workers' and peasants' Soviets." All suspected violators were subject to the death penalty.

Between 1932 and 1933, Stalin's "Terror-Famine" would result in upwards of 10 million deaths. Between 1934 and 1939, Stalin would imprison over 1 million "enemies of the working class" and execute more than 700,000 such "enemies" during the "Great Purge", before amassing 23.9 million civilian deaths during WWII, which the Soviet state termed the "Great Patriotic War" in order to swindle the citizenry into joining the fight and obeying orders to relinquish their firearms to the state.

Wherever the state is found to employ the term "patriotic", you can be sure that it is ordinarily a disguise for control.

As American journalist H. L. Mencken once proclaimed, "The urge to save humanity is almost always only a false-face for the urge to rule it. Power is what all messiahs really seek: not the chance to serve. This is true even of the pious brethren who carry the gospel to foreign parts."

For this reason, the people must contest every margin of government. They must remember that, where their political bands have been corrupted, they are the last stand for liberty; they must jealously defend it at all costs.

This means that, in the face of absolute despotism, the public may be thrust into resistance for their own preservation and the preservation of liberty. After all, once a population has been brought under such a despotism, it will have been so corrupted that no mere political process would stand to dismantle it.

The final check against this kind of despotism is the man who is willing to fight, who is ready to throw his body upon the gears in order to finally bring the machine to a halt.

Unsurprisingly, tyrants don't take kindly to resistance, and so they use clever language in their attempts to discredit their opposition.

This comes in handy whenever they are casting aspersions, launching ad hominem attacks, committing character assassination, erecting straw men, and committing any number of fallacies through their rhetoric. Indeed, this is standard operating procedure for the Left. For them, it is not just a habit or a compulsion but a lifestyle. In many ways, it is a matter of ideological survival, a game between predator and prey. In the case of politics, the predators are always stalking the patriots and the messengers of truth; they are always distorting the facts, when they are not avoiding them, and they are always on the prowl for the public and their liberty.

When they are not specifically killing their prey, the Left sets out to smear the character and the reputation of their detractors, casually tossing around such terms as "racist" and "bigot" in hopes of invalidating their opposition and calling the rest of the kingdom to join in the hunt and feast on their enemies. However, these labels are nearly always at odds with the truth; indeed, they are a type of diversion that keeps people from assessing the facts and having important (albeit difficult) and honest conversations.

This is why Leftists go to such great lengths to vilify the truth-seekers and to keep the public from even the remotest affiliation with them. Their campaign is against the truth-seekers and any who dares to even entertain their ideas. This is because the truth horrifies the Left: this is not only because it is inconvenient and difficult to combat, but because it serves to undermine the Left's entire platform.

This is precisely why the Leftists slander their opponents and dismiss them as *right-wingers, extremists, partisans, rebels,* and *fanatics* — that is, when the Leftists are not using more disparaging language to humiliate their foes. Needless to say, one need not be any of these to stand vehemently opposed to Leftism. Neither dogma nor bias must necessarily animate the opposition. Indeed, logic, reason, and evidence invariably justify the same resistance.

The truth is that the *racists* and the *bigots*, as they are often erroneously described, are usually the ones bold enough to stand on principle and defend the truth: they are the ones who are most dangerous to the establishment. As the historian David Irving has put it, what the Left regards as "racism" is, in most cases, more accurately described as patriotism. And what is patriotism other than a profound love for the country we've inherited from our parents and grandparents, and a willingness to defend it?

It comes as no surprise that the Left detests the patriots and the people who love their country. The Left views them as an unnecessary hindrance, one to be overcome or summarily eliminated. Indeed, the Leftists view them as an inconvenient reminder of the country's traditions, which threaten to derail the whole political agenda as soon as the public comes to its senses.

For this reason, the Left sets out to discredit the people's former institutions, to spoil every fond memory attached to their ancestors and their heritage, and to repackage their history. Of course, that assessment of the past is hardly inspired by, or seeking the discovery of, *true* history. On the contrary, each reference is deemed useful wherever it can be framed to the liking of the state, for the benefit of the status quo, and in support of its vision for the future; where the preferred narrative comes to enjoy the benefit of the doubt, the protection of plausible deniability, the collective embrace or indifference of the people, and ultimately protection as the *third rail of politics*.

In many cases, the establishment sets out to so thoroughly dumb down the language as to render nearly impossible any description of the truth, or any honest, meaningful discourse for that matter. The establishment even sets out to pre-program the people with pithy or automatic replies and preconceptions, to reduce the people's vocabulary so as to limit their critical thinking and to strip them of the tools required to distill the truth.

Indeed, the Left manufactures its *own* "truths" through repetition, intimidation, and manipulation, engineering the public's very thinking through a curriculum and a vocabulary of the establishment's own construction; a curriculum which ultimately succeeds through force, intimidation, peer pressure, cunning, and repetition. Whether incidentally or by design, there eventually comes a time when language is so restricted by *political correctness*, so reduced by trite, trivial and repetitive phrases, that scarcely a novel thought or an original idea ever escapes a person's mouth.

Indeed, language can singlehandedly reshape a society and its perspective. Consider the words *sexism, misogyny, mansplaining, codependency, homophobia, transphobia, antisemitism, inclusivity, diversity*, and *racism*, among the countless others fashioned and gaining in popularity over the past half-century; indeed, most of these words did not even exist previously. These are words of unquantifiable consequence, words that mold and occupy people's minds; words that draw maps and concepts for easy reference, for framing and guiding the people's thinking; words that convince people that such phenomena and attitudes exist, that they are to be characterized and condemned accordingly.

Like slogans, jingles, and bumper stickers, they are compelling and they are easy to recite and to commit to memory, and therefore they easily conquer and corrupt the minds of the people, among whom the youth are always the most impressionable: youth whose impressionability renders them susceptible not only to deception and half-truths, propaganda and pseudoscience, peer pressure and the temptation to conform, but particularly so to the sob stories and the victimhood narratives — the romantic, the poetic, and the fantastical — each often exploited, embellished, distorted or otherwise concocted to advance a cause.

Indeed, most youth are instructed by elders who, willfully or through some sense of obligation, perpetuate those narratives in order to conform and to appear sympathetic, to avoid persecution, to virtue-signal, to safely align with the conventional wisdom, or to actively support the cause. As the former Führer of Germany rightly acknowledged in his 1925 manifesto, "For the remarkable fact about the language struggle is that its waves strike hardest perhaps in the school, since it is the seed-bed of the coming generation." The struggle over language, then, is "a struggle for the soul of the child" and the future of civilization.

Indeed, the tyrants use language as a Trojan Horse to corrupt minds and civilizations. It should come as no surprise then that, in pursuit of this end, they seek to make a mockery of the most powerful language and terminology which pose the greatest threat to the establishment. Indeed, even where logic and empirical truth stand in their way, the two are seldom their foe, given the tyrants' ability to reinterpret each case in defense of their preferred narratives.

When they are not outright skewing, slanting, or misrepresenting the data, Leftists are apt to support their positions through every imaginable exception, and to "justify" and strictly enforce sweeping "regulations" and prohibitions through every imaginable exigency and extreme — even regardless of its basis in fact; regardless of whether or not it presents sufficient cause for the proposed action; whether or not the proposal is supported logically or empirically; whether it is warranted relative to its foreseeable costs; and regardless of that proposal's probability of success.

For instance, among others, their universal defense for taxes is the tiny fraction which funds the roads; for abortion, the tiny fraction of cases resulting from medical complications, incest or rape; for *gun control*, the tiny fraction of guns involved in suicide or criminal activity; for welfare programs, the tiny fraction of people who fall on hard times "through no fault of their own"; for militarization, nation-building, and preemptive war, the remotest (and unproven) threat posed without them. These are just a select few examples of the tricks employed by Leftists to manipulate the people and to proceed with their agendas. These are a select few examples of their propensity to abuse and corrupt language, to set the agenda and to narrowly frame the discussion for their own benefit; to equivocate, to conceal, to condition, to obfuscate, to manipulate, to confuse, to distract, to sneakily disarm and enslave the people without their knowledge.

Next to the corruption of the common language, they are occasionally fond of numbers and statistics, but only when they can be manipulated or dishonestly presented to their advantage. The same may rightly be said about their abuse of mathematics, which has been described fundamentally as a concept of numbers. Whether they are altering formulas and methodologies, selectively citing percentages instead of raw figures, comparing figures that are not strictly comparable, or hypnotizing the public with complicated models or calculations, they endeavor to reimagine that broader concept of numbers, and their objective is always the same: to convince the public that the establishment knows what it is doing, that it is justified in its actions, and that the people themselves are hardly capable of understanding. The people are thereby left dealing in arcane terms, units and quantities, measurements and extremes which, like the scale of government itself, the enormity of its expenditures and the public debt, exceed comprehension.

It is in this way that the establishment gets away with using "science" for its own benefit, and yet another way in which it keeps the people bewildered, beguiled, and out of the way. Through this they have the unique advantage of concealing the truth through esoteric models and methodologies, the kinds that read like a foreign language to most of the public. In doing so, they make it progressively more difficult for the people to hold the regime accountable, to expose scandal and deceit, and to defend themselves from the rhetoric and ravages of tyranny; perhaps this is the true meaning of *progressivism* after all.

The tyrants accomplish this end by inventing, eliminating, or modifying words, rambling as if they are paid by the syllable, censoring or condemning inconvenient language, or otherwise reforming their definitions. They intentionally use cryptic, loaded, ambiguous, and euphemistic language in delivering their message, oftentimes of their own construction. They do this in order to avoid committing to any particular claim or proposition; to make their message so abstract and convoluted as to render it virtually incomprehensible; to likewise convince the public that they are on top of things, that they are aware of the public's best interest and that they are keeping it in mind; and that the "experts" know exactly what they are doing, all through the art of what former Federal Reserve Chairman Alan Greenspan described as *syntactical destruction*.

It is in just this way that the Leftists continually seek to discourage the public from even attempting to make sense of things. It is in just this way that they continually seek to make their position more defensible and adaptable; to fashion it beyond reproach; and to make it nearly impossible to dispute or deconstruct, all in order to confuse people into thinking that the Leftists know something that they (the people) don't.

In one *particular* instance, this is actually true: propaganda. They know better than the ordinary citizen how to present their case: for the Leftists, it is a case always opposed to the public liberty, whereas, for the ordinary citizen, his case is rightly in defense of it. Indeed, through its indomitable might and influence, the state enjoys the advantage of making the first move, driving the people into a corner and leaving them to make sense of it.

The people, in turn, grow accustomed to being on the receiving end, to accommodating and adjusting to the state and its every move. Whereas the onus is properly on government to justify its powers, the overreaching establishment places the onus on the people to articulate the reasons why they should be secure in their persons, their property and their personal effects. Indeed, the onus is on the people to not just articulate those reasons but to run a convincing case.

As it turns out, the ordinary citizen is, in many cases, naive or inarticulate, and, in most cases, not nearly as polished or compelling. This comes as no surprise, given that politicians specialize in talk, whereas workers specialize in labor. Of course, the politicians are always busy inventing new terms to give themselves a leg up; to keep the laymen out of the loop; and to make their opposition appear uninformed; concocting reductive titles (i.e. -ist, -phobe, et cetera) to shame the people out of their principles, their traditions, and their standards.

Indeed, the debate between -isms intentionally distracts from the debate between ideas. It is no mere coincidence that the establishment prefers the former, as they reduce people to political agents, whereas the latter distinguishes them as individuals; and individuals and ideas pose the greatest threat to the establishment and its power.

Indeed, by using those titles, they reduce their foes not only to political agents but to caricatures, mere members of a category who are deemed perfectly interchangeable. It is thus determined that those individuals are to be treated as one mass or inventoried under the same names; that there is absolutely nothing to be gained or learned by distinguishing them as individuals; that they are all one and the same, bigots and imbeciles with scarcely any redeeming qualities. This is precisely the purpose of propaganda, the reason that the establishment frames the issues, republishes its tales, parodies the plights of the people, and asserts authority over their language and thereby the index card of allowable opinion.

In the hands of the people, language is their recourse. In the hands of government, it is a weapon or a shield; a kind of shield or barrier which protects the establishment from credible scrutiny, such that any criticisms or challenges that might come their way can be swiftly deflected or rejected as *foolish, insensitive, discriminatory, bigoted,* or *politically-incorrect*. It is a kind of weapon which enables the state to skewer its foes without casting a single spear, to hypnotize the public through mass hypnosis; to program them through reductive terminology, simplistic phrases, and a manufactured vocabulary which is easy to both remember and recite, and which is so convoluted, so irrational and so completely cloaked in rhetoric as to keep the statements as incomprehensible as irrefutable.

In the hands of government, these are tools used to equivocate, to conceal, to condition, to obfuscate, to manipulate, to confuse, to distract, to hide behind, to sneakily disarm and enslave the people without their knowledge. That is why the freedom of speech is indispensable to freedom everywhere, and that is why it is anathema to Leftism: its proponents cannot defend their ideas against it.

This is why the freedom of speech is duly enshrined in the First Amendment to the United States Constitution; why, as the eighteenth-century Philadelphia lawyer Andrew Hamilton put it in 1735, the press has "a liberty both of exposing and opposing tyrannical power by speaking and writing truth." This is not only a matter of justice and ethics, but a matter of good practice.

With the currents beating ceaselessly against the public liberty, the erosion of allowable speech, and thereby allowable thought, is always among the first signs of impending disaster; this being among the many tell tale signs in modern America.

Over the course of recent generations, a great many political, sociological and linguistic transformations, some more literal than others, have coalesced to rally young and impressionable minds around bold ideas scarcely ever met with a willing examination or an adequate understanding by the mainstream, let alone those who loyally wave their banners and line the streets. Before they have even begun to comprehend what they have read, witnessed or encountered, or more appropriately what they have been told to think, they are suddenly involved in an uncompromising movement predicated upon words and statements as bold as their ideas. Unfortunately, while the words may appear bold and compelling, the ideas behind them are just about as flimsy as the paper that bears their message.

Ironically, in the heat of passion — or a fit of boredom — which impels the protest, the participants seem to forget or to overlook the fact that it is that very freedom of speech which enables the protests in the first place. However, for the average opponent to free speech, who is, of course, never opposed to any of his own speech, the only permissible kind takes the form of that which is agreeable, inoffensive, or trivial. Beyond this standard, the only kind of tolerable political speech, that which conveniently qualifies as something other than "hate speech" in their rulebook, is that which opposes the conventions, "antiquated" thinking, or unallowable opinion; or which contests "antiquated" laws and customs, those presumed to have the exclusive support of "bigots" or out-of-touch members of the so-called "privileged" class.

Just as with any set of ideas or series of words that makes us laugh, inspires thought, challenges conventional wisdom, or elucidates an error in judgment, each expression of thought inherently runs the risk of upsetting someone or contradicting popular opinion. In this sense, while the protests against so-called "hate speech" intend to outlaw unpopular or offensive forms of expression, they can serve only to limit the kind of speech which is most meaningful; whether this outcome is secured deliberately or incidentally is wholly immaterial.

Fortunately for those who enjoy free speech and value it as a precondition to a free society, the United States Constitution plainly protects the right against its opponents, regardless of their justifications, their conviction, their sincerity, or their hurt feelings. While people will continue into perpetuity to formulate new reasons to complain about life, other people, and what they say, the value of free speech will endure all the same, regardless of how others wish to define, restrict, or defile it. While these kinds of protests certainly are not new to the human experience, protestors are always inventing new ways to call that freedom back into question.

In the twenty-first century, their trick has been the classification of some expressions as "hate speech", a characterization which appears sensible at first but which crumbles under the slightest of scrutiny or even a hint honest reflection. Clearly, just because someone is offended by another's comment, that does not indicate that the statement is hateful: a fragile ego, a misapprehension, or any number of factors would then, against that standard, theoretically present a case of "hate speech". This is, of course, a dangerous precedent, as wherever the proverbial line is decidedly drawn on the matter, it can serve only as the new basis for further curtailments of speech and liberty into the future, where the laws and their administrators will continue to usurp authority, operating largely free from criticism, given the increasing limitations placed upon the public.

Despite the soundest of intentions, laws endure beyond the final breaths of those who had originally championed the legislation. With their passing, so too degrades the restraints on those powers, where "hate speech" and the like develop into the kinds of insults to liberty that even the original protestors and administrators would have condemned.

By the time that original generation has perished, they will have been replaced by another set of eager, impressionable minds who are prepared to be offended by other forms of expression that have yet to be outlawed. While those original safeguards against "hate speech" may have operated under vastly different intentions, those intentions fail to carry over into the future, where subsequent generations of politicians are able, and even encouraged, to wield this weapon against those who threaten their authority.

Whereas the protestors falsely believe that the people — those who resemble them in countenance and disposition — will reserve the power to determine which speech is allowable, they neglect to acknowledge that it is government and its heavy-handed administrators who assume those powers once they become law. This is precisely why America's Forefathers specified this freedom without condition, qualification, or reservation.

While we all have our own personal concepts of the term "hate speech", or otherwise speech with which we stridently disagree, and we all know of people and comments that we wish we could silence, the freedom of speech is far more important than any convenience attending the silencing of those with whom we disagree.

Take note, "hate speech" did not even exist in the English lexicon until roughly a few minutes ago, in the grand scheme of history, when the politically-minded set out to engineer a divisive term to promote ulterior motives. Indeed, the United States government has never even officially recognized "hate speech", and it has yet no laws defining or outlawing it; that is, not yet.

Just as with most political movements, the laymen and the foot soldiers are scarcely privy to the the greater political strategy, compelled only by whatever faces them in the here and now. In the case of speech, the average opponent to that freedom avails himself of the tools furnished by his sponsors who stand to gain the most through the process and upon the manifestation of the given law.

Second, in the literal sense, "free speech" covers all speech, whether agreeable or disagreeable, whether logical or illogical. The First Amendment reads, "Congress shall make no law... abridging the freedom of speech." The Amendment does not qualify this freedom with any limits or conditions; it is unequivocal.

Indeed, Founders Thomas Jefferson and James Madison — the latter of whom drafted the Bill of Rights in response to political pressure from the Anti-Federalists — even reinforced their intentions through their *Kentucky and Virginia Resolutions*, which rebuked the 1798 Alien and Sedition Acts that served to limit false or critical statements about the federal government.

Through their combined efforts, Jefferson and Madison sought to demonstrate the unconstitutionality of the Alien and Sedition Acts in order to preserve the First Amendment in all of its glory. With history as their guide, the two Founders stressed states' rights and strict constitutionalism to ward off the forces that stood to wear down the very fibers which formed and preserved the fabric of freedom in the New World.

As it turns out, the battle against speech is often a proxy for one's discomfort with truth, unpredictability or the struggle for power. Nowhere is this more relevant than in the realm of politics, where participants and politicians alike commiserate with one another over their disapproval of certain ideas and inconvenient facts. They would like nothing more than to simply eradicate these ideas from their world. Short of this, however, they would settle for the alternative scenario in which they limit their expression through law, whereby they discourage the public from critical thought and honest discussion altogether.

With this arrangement, they believe that they will finally silence their opposition to prove that they are right. Despite their sincerest of efforts, however, they will inevitably squash truth in the process of exterminating everything that ails them. In affording them any such privilege, they will face no incentive to even acknowledge the truth, leaving them blind to it as they snuff out every last threat to their peace of mind.

During colonial times, the English criminal common law of seditious libel made punishable by law all forms of criticism directed at government, notwithstanding any legal defense predicated upon objective truth. In 1704, Lord Chief Justice John Holt explained his rationalization for the prohibition of speech: "If people should not be called to account for possessing the people with an ill opinion of the government, no government can subsist, for it is very necessary for all governments that the people should have a good opinion of it."

In essence, speech which is critical of government poses a threat to the power structure, that apparatus which is presently enjoyed by those in or approving of the establishment. Of course, this is where we find a fundamental distinction between England and the United States: whereas the Magna Carta sought a "better ordering of [a] kingdom" around the English Church, the United States Constitution separated between church and state, pursuing a "more perfect union" to "secure the blessings of liberty to [the people of the United States] and [their] posterity."

The Magna Carta also outlined the rights granted by government to the free men of England, whereas the Constitution expressly enumerated the powers of government to deliberately reserve every other power "to the States respectively, or to the people." In this way, both the United States and the central government made the freedom of speech a core principle within their respective constitutions.

For example, the Constitution of the State of Virginia reads, "Any citizen may freely speak, write, and publish his sentiments on all subjects."

Article I, Section 8, of the Constitution of the State of Missouri reads, "... no law shall be passed impairing the freedom of speech, no matter by what means communicated." The Missouri Constitution continues, "every person shall be free to say, write, or publish, or otherwise communicate whatever he will on any subject."

Article II, Section 4, of the Constitution of the State of Illinois provides: "Every person may freely speak, write and publish on all subjects, being responsible for the abuse of that liberty; and in all trials for libel, both civil and criminal, the truth, when published with good motives and for justifiable ends, shall be a sufficient defense."

Across the United States, a common thread between the states has been the indispensable freedom of speech, and even where that freedom has faced any limits whatever, there it has been met by a thirst for truth, or otherwise the resistance of those unwilling to deal in those terms. The essentiality of the freedom of speech was even powerfully reiterated in a twentieth-century Supreme Court case.

The Supreme Court and the State of California affirmed the freedom of speech in *Pruneyard Shopping Center v. Robins* (1980), where the court held that "[a] state can prohibit the private owner of a shopping center from using state trespass law to exclude peaceful expressive activity in the open areas of the shopping center."

The California Constitution even specifies, "A law may not restrain or abridge liberty of speech or press."

President Kennedy even spoke of the First Amendment in his 1961 address, where he exalted the freedom of speech as that which is protected "not primarily to amuse and entertain, not to emphasize the trivial and the sentimental, not to simply give the public what it wants, but to inform, to arouse, to reflect, to state our dangers and our opportunities, to indicate our crises and our choices, to lead, mold, educate and sometimes even anger public opinion."

This author will here take it upon himself to echo Kennedy's final consideration: the freedom of speech is important even where it may sometimes "anger public opinion."

Were it intended for purposes of agreeable, trivial or humorous applications, the freedom of speech certainly would not require the backing of law to protect it. The First Amendment to the Constitution specifically defines and protects this right because of the predictable response to unpopular speech. A reduction of freedom, any limit against speech serves to prevent meaningful discourse and the kind of speech which is threatening to government and beneficial to liberty.

Remember, the Constitution of the United States was written expressly to limit the central government in order to respect the sovereignty of the several states and the rights of each of its citizens, as the Founders understood that government itself represents the single greatest threat to freedom. With that in mind, we cannot rely upon government to decide on matters pertaining to freedom, as government's record on the subject, wherever it appears or rules on the matter, scarcely accounts for the inherent value of free speech; instead, its decisions represent the pressures of politics and populism. Ultimately, words can no doubt be compelling, but the fear of words can only manage to stoke paranoia and to limit meaningful expression.

The truth of the matter is that people the world over are threatened by speech primarily due to their own personal insecurities, their own emotions and limited apprehensions. In sum, their fear of speech is not as much on account of the speech itself, but rather a reflection of one's insecurities or his inability to deal with the material.

As abolitionist Wendell Philips put it, "He who stifles free discussion, secretly doubts whether what he professes to believe is really true." Whether the repression of speech or the reformation of language, each is essential to the Leftist program such that no individual is permitted, or ultimately even capable of, meaningful expression or critical thought; the kinds, of course, which, in the view of the Left, stand only to interfere with their agenda.

Indeed, language is important not only so that one can articulate his points, but so that he can contemplate complex subjects and defend himself (and posterity) against absurdities and designs of despotism. As Weaver put it, "Thinking requires words of precise meaning. Confuse the vocabulary, and the unsuspecting majority is at a disadvantage when defending themselves against the small but highly disciplined minority which knows exactly what it wants and which deliberately promotes word-confusion as the first step in its efforts to divide and conquer."

Indeed, words and terms are often concocted to infect and control a society: to antagonize and to alienate, to selectively include or exclude groups and ideas. Words and terms are likewise censored to erase the opposition and, more importantly, to prevent the people from even thinking in those terms. This is true for the activist, the politician and the propagandist, and it is true for incompetents, illiterates and the dregs of society who, in their simplistic and reductive conceptions, use rhetoric and ambiguity to appeal to wider audiences; who defame their enemies to restrict the bounds of allowable opinion; who limit the use of words (and tools) to impede further contemplation and understanding; who disguise themselves as compassionate and unthreatening as they have their way.

As the English author Edward Bulwer-Lytton put it in 1839, "The pen is mightier than the sword." However, the pen is merely a tool, impotent against the arbitrary forces deciding what can be written. In the hands of government, or under its direction, the pen is indeed far more lethal than the sword. Whereas the sword can kill, the pen can destroy, and it can do so discreetly. It has the power to destroy life, civilizations, and, most critically, the ability of the people to think. This power tends to wind up in the hands of the people most likely to abuse it, namely pawns, politicians, and propagandists. They use their terms as weapons, and they can be effective in setting the agenda, framing the issues, or otherwise standing in for incomplete narratives and theories that don't really hold any water.

For example, wherever the public poses any resistance, the tyrants term it *insurrection*. In the tyrants' view, *insurrection* is anything that threatens the establishment, and, conveniently for them, when suited for their purposes they claim that the establishment is founded upon *democracy*.

In truth, *democracy* is merely their shield, their illusion, and the pressure relief valve which keeps most of the public at bay as the establishment grows more tyrannical. So long as it claims to be *democratic*, any other means of accountability, wherever the establishment has failed to effect it, are identified by the establishment as *insurrectionist*. When in the presence of such "insurrection", the establishment plays the victim and claims that the whole institution of *democracy* is under attack, when it is actually the failure of their institutions which is so often responsible for impelling the resistance.

It is worth noting that the practical value of democracy or democratic process, insofar as it possesses any value at all, is as a means; it is not the proper end in and of itself. Its value is in its results. From the establishment's point of view, it is a means to power; as for posterity, a means to liberty, a means to oppose tyrants seeking both to strip the people of their God-given rights and to subjugate their heirs in perpetuity.

Democratic process serves the people only when it limits government and keeps it accountable to the terms of its constitution, a process that is quickly corrupted when people and politicians realize that they can use it for more selfish and nefarious ends. Wherever it fails to secure the safety and happiness of the people, wherever it fails to protect life, liberty and property, and wherever it evinces a design to reduce the people under absolute despotism, as the Declaration of Independence states, it is their right, it is their duty, to throw off such government, and to provide new guards for their future security.

Ultimately, the survival of liberty depends upon the people who are willing to stand in its defense. The people must remain vigilant, for, in the case of socialism, despotism comes to assume a wide variety of disguises.

Whether through non-profit organizations or non-governmental agencies, whether sponsored or subsidized by government, or whether a public school indoctrinating the youth or a private company promoting some political agenda or condemning its critics, the tentacles of socialism are upon us, manipulating nearly every aspect of our lives, even the very thoughts that occupy our minds.

The indoctrination runs so deep that even among those who fancy themselves *traditional* or *conservative*, a great number of them have nevertheless been shaped into *instinctual Leftists*. They have been so thoroughly groomed through the public school system, peer pressure and popular media as to completely lack the ability to think for themselves, to conceive of life without the state, or to even imagine their lives with a far more limited form of it.

They are propagandized daily, through both the media and their curricula, by professors, false profits, and self-appointed pundits. They are taught *what* to think, not *how* to think. They are told what to salute and what to condemn. Just as importantly, they are instructed on what *not* to say, what *not* to think, what *not* to explore, examine, or challenge, and what they are forbidden to even suggest. They are conditioned to shrink from controversy; to reduce themselves to the ranks of thoughtless and obedient workers, debtors, and consumers; to reject the very prospect of becoming anything other than a factor of production and one tiny, insignificant part of the collective; to, as Irwin Schiff put it in his work *The Kingdom of Moltz*, "regard obedience as a sign of patriotism".

This has combined with the influence of social media to produce even greater extremes of these results: people habitually looking to others to form their opinions, instead of examining matters for themselves. It is in this way that people have been not only discouraged from thinking for themselves but prepared to forfeit the skills necessary to do so.

Moreover, in the face of so much noise, peer pressure and controversy, the people are far less likely to think for themselves — to run the inherent risks and put in the effort attending independent thought — when others' thoughts and conclusions are so conveniently available for adoption. This has the further benefit of enabling the people to align with more popular and conventional thinking, to, as they see it, avoid the risk of appearing stupid and uninformed.

The pressures around us, sponsored or certified by the beast, evidence its pervasive influence yet leave little trace of it. Instead, the unthinking and unsuspecting pay little mind to the building pressures, the trenches carved around them, and the masses preparing to lay siege. By taking over and controlling their media, the establishment has managed to control their minds, and by controlling their familiar businesses and their neighbors, they have limited all that they are permitted to do or say.

In this way, socialism is not just about determining how to achieve control or justify corporal punishment, but how to limit access exclusively to those who might grow to accept it; in turn, whether for some business interest, self-preservation, or some sense of duty, those who have been granted access will do the bidding of the bureaucracy, whether by encouraging compliance, reporting violations, supporting further impositions, or even enforcing its edicts. While not expressly the work of government, the people and their businesses, succumbing to the pressures around them, do their bidding as agents on their behalf. All the while, of course, the beast keeps its hands clean, rejoicing in the decisions of the public, taking credit while assuming none of the blame.

In this manner, socialism always emerges in clever ways, at first making life easier for those who acquiesce, yet excruciatingly difficult for those who wish only to continue living as freely as they once did. In this way, the scales predictably tilt in favor of socialism once the people figure out how to comply, intensifying the peer pressure upon the diminishing ranks of the few bold enough to stand on principle and defend their liberty. Once the scales have tipped, it becomes nearly impossible to recover.

Once it has become easier to comply than to defend liberty, the people must not shrink in cowardice. They must stand together, shoulder to shoulder, decrying passionately and unequivocally every injustice upon their liberty. This is their final defense against tyranny of any form, and their highest obligation to their heirs and all of posterity: to stay vigilant to every threat, to unveil tyranny in its various forms, and to strip it to the bone in utter humiliation as a reminder of the risk run by any who poses a threat to liberty.

This is an endless battle of vigilance; one against the ambitious aggressors who seek to exploit every weakness in human nature. After all, it is in our nature to survive, not to be free; with survival not only being the priority but seeming to warrant any and every sacrifice in its interest. Of course, the aggressors are always ready to delineate the terms, demanding only that the people submit to them, demanding their compliance if not for the "common good" then at least for their own interests. Indeed, the aggressors succeed not only in intimidating and tempting the people, but in appealing to their sensibilities and their rational interest in self-preservation.

The Leftists tend at first to make compliance straightforward enough that the overwhelming majority will simply acquiesce. As a consequence, this leaves only the few stubborn and courageous defenders of liberty alone to face the unchecked wrath of the establishment; an establishment which enjoys ever more power, influence, and resources under the auspices of the overwhelming majority who acquiesce only under duress, and only in order to avoid the consequences of non-compliance. As such, compliance always appears as the path of least resistance, the surest means to short-term survival, but the people must always keep an eye on the long term, to above all remember that it is liberty which makes life worth surviving; that it is liberty which enables life to be enriching and fulfilling, and to have any real meaning at all. Indeed, it seems true that, unlike any other, the human species is made not merely to survive, but to thrive; to continually refine the meaning of life and what it truly means to be alive.

Indeed, it is certainly true that survival is a necessary condition for living, but, in the estimation of this author, it is not a sufficient case. As it turns out, risk is the key to life. Risks are not only inherent to the human condition, but they are essential in the case of every individual life and in all of his days.

Indeed, with those risks come the possibilities: the possibility of failure, the possibility of learning, and ultimately the possibility of success, whereby there is the honor, the privilege, and the triumph of having accomplished something; having assumed some measure of responsibility; having taken the risk to be sincere, industrious, resourceful, vulnerable, loving and inspiring, and even dangerous where necessary; having committed to some cause beyond convenience; having dared to be passionate, to be a partner and an individual, to think for oneself while thinking of others, and to be a leader as well as a protector; having discovered one's independence and endeavored ever closer to the purest form of freedom; having developed perspective and gathered insight; having enhanced his appreciation for life and liberty, his respect for the lives and the rights of his fellow man; having discovered new frontiers; having explored ever further into oneself as into the wild; having brought greater meaning and purpose into life; and having made a life worth living, a story worth reading, a path worth following, and a legacy worth continuing. These are the reasons to live; survival is merely the opportunity.

As it is with survival, it is with liberty, the precondition for the discovery of meaning and purpose; the precondition for the relationships and the commitments that we keep; and the precondition for the developments, the discoveries, and the revelations which enhance life; preconditions and privileges which are too often taken for granted. For this reason, it is essential to not only ensure mankind's survival along with its liberty, but to immortalize the reasons and the causes which justify the fight to keep them.

In its various disguises, socialism seeks to discredit liberty and erase it altogether from the collective memory. That is why history and heritage are so precious, why it is imperative that each generation guide with wisdom and leave a useful legacy to posterity, and why the people ought never to forget the struggles, the sacrifices, the achievements, and the cautionary tales of their forebears.

Indeed, one of the great tragedies following the passing away of previous generations is that their distant heirs will never know the true price that was paid for all that they now take for granted. It is ultimately up to the people to learn that lesson, to share it, and to preserve it for their heirs.

It is the duty of the people to remember the value of liberty, the costs attending too little of it, the countless hundreds of millions of lives lost in its absence, and the means by which it is threatened today. It is up to the people to remember these, and to continually remind the tyrants of the same; and to do so forcefully from time to time, to reassert the value they place on their liberty, the respect they maintain for the sacrifices of their forbears, and the obligation they have to bequeath upon their heirs a better world.

Indeed, it is up to the people, the freedom fighters, to constantly send those reminders, to fight so ferociously and so remorselessly against tyrants that there will never again be any uncertainty, any doubts about the threats posed by the oppressed; to, as Easy Company's Pvt. David Webster (of the 506th Parachute Infantry Regiment, 101st Airborne Division during World War II) so delicately put it in a 1944 letter, "take the battle to [them]... fight in their villages, blowing up their houses, smashing open their wine cellars, killing some of their livestock for food... litter their streets with horribly rotten... corpses..."; to make plain, and to signal to all, the grave consequences for any and all crimes against the public liberty, and to thereby remind them of the power of the people and the price they are willing to pay in defense of themselves, their heirs, and their liberty.

* * *

As history has shown, socialism is too often praised for its promises despite its repeated results. It is mistaken as charitable until the true costs are made known. It is celebrated as all things good and just; for its stated causes as opposed to its horrid history; for its rhetoric instead of its senselessness; for its provision of social services and its poetic promises of *welfare* and *equality*.

Of course, those endless promises are scarcely anything more or anything other than the means: a means to conquering the public with some applause and approbation. They are promises and initiatives enjoying the benefit of the doubt, the protection of plausible deniability, and the privilege of framing and narrating the story; promises and initiatives typically operating from the middle of the story or otherwise leveraging an outright fiction, a fabricated premise which imagines the plight of individuals or broader demographics unfairly burdened or oppressed, a tale which predictably fails to even remotely account for the attending factors or plausible causes.

Instead, the socialist flatly assumes and boldly asserts that each plight is merely another example of injustice and inequality. Of course, the socialist pays little mind to the fact that inequality is the rule, the organic state of all things in nature, that there are legitimate explanations for unequal outcomes between individuals. Take, for example, the so-called wage gap between men and women, the undisputed fact of male-female income differences. These are differences between averages, and they are explainable. As it is often said, the devil is in the details. As with every false alarm, however, particularly those pertaining to "inequality", the Leftists claim that the differences are attributable to the evil actions of man, to unlawful discrimination and prejudices, instead of the differences in preferences or priorities, instead of differences between the sexes in their preferred roles in their respective households; among such differences the way that women essentially invest in their husbands by voluntarily sacrificing their own employment prospects for the benefit of their husbands' incomes. Indeed, this is not to suggest that there is no discrimination or prejudice against women in hiring or compensation, but that, on average, there are reasonable explanations for the outcomes.

The economist Sylvia Ann Hewlett put it this way upon surveying more than two thousand women and more than six hundred men: "About 37% of women take an off-ramp at some point in their career, meaning they quit their jobs — but just for an average of 2.2 years. Another substantial number take scenic routes for a while — intentionally not ratcheting up their assignments. For instance, 36% of highly qualified women have sought part-time jobs for some period, while others have declined promotions or deliberately chosen jobs with fewer responsibilities." As has been shown, there are legitimate explanations for inequalities in the real world. Despite this, and despite the fact that there are some matters beyond the scope of surveys and data collection, the socialist instead leverages each case of inequality to rally unthinking masses around the political cause, rooted inextricably in covetous greed and envy.

Indeed, the socialist prefers his fantasies and his delusions over the state of nature; in this particular case, the fact that human beings are competitive at birth. Where any should fail on merit, he will either accept that failure and learn from it, remain complacent and undisturbed by it, or compete in still other forms: out of malice or envy, he will threaten and assail, slander and belittle, rob and retaliate, often by allying with others who collectively identify as "victims"; with the list of victims growing by the day, if not by the hour.

Indeed, another subject has entered the social scene in a more meaningful capacity than ever imagined for the most basic of questions about personal identity: gender. The subject has entered casual conversation, the workplace, and even schools, where teachers and professors have been encouraged or even required to gently inquire into the gender identities of their students, so as to avoid mistakenly referring to them by the traditional pronouns that have gotten the job done for so many centuries.

Well, according to the fresh crop of Cal-Berkeley enrollees, there is apparently nothing the average person can say or do that will not offend a member of the protected class; and apparently even gender is not off the table, apparently just another example of the kind of "oppression" running rampant in our community, where some individuals have expressed that these two words, *man* and *woman*, otherwise *male* and *female*, fail to adequately represent them, that they are indeed offensive when used to identify them. Well, here is the cold, hard truth: they were never really designed to represent anyone; they were designed to represent chromosomal composition and reproductive capacity. It is only the assumed and subjective *roles* that have accompanied these basic identifiers, *masculinity* versus *femininity*, which have caused so much controversy among the incorrigible crowd of aimless adults, who are themselves flush with enough college time — otherwise known as the six-year all-inclusive resort for unemployable busybodies — to keep them lying in wait for next weekend's protest against everything that's keeping them down, whatever that ends up being.

In this particular case, the topic of gender subjectivity, gender ambiguity, or "transgenderism", is wholly dismissed by one unanswerable question: how would my infant know to identify as a zeep, or any other gender for that matter, and how would any person know that he is in the presence of one?

Should the respondent succumb to the temptation to actually define the profile of a zeep, or that associated with any other pronoun, that respondent will have effectively established the concept, the rules, the parameters, the conditions and thereby the original stereotypes for that identifier. Ironically, as they attempt to substantiate their claims against traditional gender definitions, their own arguments inevitably undermine the integrity of their very own movement, which ostensibly aims to steer the public *away* from such ruthless and inflexible standards.

In due time, that same respondent will be faced with a stampede of new *progressives* eager to question the completeness of the former camp's definitions; who wish to augment the evolving list with a number of their own unique creations, still uniquely committing only the same error in deviating from the conventional definitions to a more subjective and unscientific set of alternatives. Of course, these alternatives serve not to improve anyone's understanding, but primarily to confuse the conversation around the topic of gender. After all, the original conventions had but modest implications for gender: they formerly sought to represent the person's chromosome profile and, by extension, the individual's reproductive capacity. In the wake of contemporary political rumblings, however, protestors and political activists seek to accomplish much more. Ironically, they fail to acknowledge the fact that gender was never intended to comprehensively define a person, but that is precisely the initiative of the activists who either cannot appreciate the poetic contradiction or otherwise have bigger plans in mind.

As it turns out, the gender test was never really a marker for one's identity, one's personality or the greater nuances which distinguish every individual. In fact, identifiers of all kinds fail miserably to capture these qualities, and any attempt to achieve this end through new words and concepts serves incidentally to prioritize diversity *in form* over diversity *in truth*. After all, there are just as many unique identities as there are people; a figure exceeding 8 billion in number on this planet.

Ultimately, what does it mean to identify as a male or a female, or to be feminine or masculine? Are these traits best encapsulated by John Wayne, a Marlboro ad, Hollywood's hottest couple, or the latest Miss America pageant?

These may indeed prove to inspire some of the conceptions around gender, but they still serve only to distract the individual from the fact that such archetypes are a function of nothing more than the definitions and expectations that we accept, endorse and apply to ourselves.

As such, it need not matter, really, how the chromosomes read, but instead how we manage their real implications and how we view ourselves independently. Everything else is noise, concerns about the opinions of others, matters we cannot always control and which plainly have no bearing on the classic denotative structures whose only purpose has been to lay a *basic* foundation for the most *basic* of human functions.

Unfortunately, the institutions that flex to these political whims, whose professors follow orders by asking their students how they identify, serve regrettably to lend credibility to a condition empirically associated with psychosis, depression and confusion, a condition marked by suicide rates significantly higher than that of the general public in the United States: anywhere from five to twenty times the rate of the general population, depending on age, case study, and years since gender reassignment surgery.

On the surface, there appears to be nothing wrong with requesting that others respect the expressed preferences of those who identify as some other gender beyond male or female, persons otherwise known as *non-binary;* but the oft-ignored side of this discussion centers on the demand that others adjust both their perceptions and their lexicons in order to accommodate a fad, a grammatically-incorrect and plainly unscientific term, while the unseen side of this discussion centers on the perpetuation of an unfounded myth which appears only to bear associations with negative psychological outcomes or, otherwise, a set or persons who will eventually change their minds. As it turns out, this latter group reportedly constitutes greater than 80 percent of the entire transgender community; an inconvenient truth, to be sure.

It is ultimately the duty of leaders and mentors to recognize the impressionability and fragility of the youth, their desperate and often unarticulated quest for direction. It is indeed the duty of leaders and mentors not to enable delusions or destructive behaviors, but to honor their crucial roles in guiding the youth to academic and personal success. This occasionally means taking a hard line, even when faced with political incorrectness, especially when we have the evidence to illustrate the risks of indulging their destructive delusions; delusions around "victimhood" and crises of identity which form the basis for their competitive advantage both socially and politically.

Of course, merely requiring negativity, it is far easier for the failures and the degenerates to compete on this basis, to blame others and to foolishly claim that the advantages enjoyed by some inherently come from a proportional disadvantage incurred by others. Of course, this is a fallacy, but — from their perspective — logic, reason and evidence are unwanted alarm clocks to those dead set on staying in bed; burdens to be shouldered by the "privileged" class; details to be reconciled by those less passionate about "the cause"; standards established to oppress the "victims" and condemn them to their stations in life.

Indeed, the socialist insists that *all* inequalities and disparities in wealth are the result of oppression and exploitation, as if wealth and prosperity were inherently a zero-sum game. They insist that wealthy people can succeed only insofar as they exploit or steal from those among them who are purportedly struggling daily to survive, living paycheck to paycheck, or having a hard time making ends meet. The irony is hardly lost here, however, as, in the course of their misguided protests against free enterprise, the socialists are *actually* lamenting their *own* preferred system; indeed, this is precisely the relationship between the working class and the elites under socialism. Of course, further irony is found in the Leftist diatribe, in this particular case among the politically-appointed "victims", who are typically carrying expensive cellphones and designer handbags; cruising around town in brand new vehicles, and in many cases robbing and looting en masse. Reportedly, this is their way of balancing the scales, taking back what they believe to be rightfully theirs. Interestingly, despite the many clamoring about their struggle, despite their many acts of violence and looting, one scarcely finds any of them burglarizing any grocery stores, or bookstores for that matter; one scarcely sees the establishment equating them with the "insurrectionists".

In still other cases, we find those "victims" joining in "protests" where they are looting and burglarizing designer clothiers and electronics stores; ironically — or perhaps not so ironically, given an adequate understanding of their worldview — it is the socialists who are found mugging people and robbing their stores; it is the socialists who seek equality, not under the law but for their own personal advantage, through theft, violence and intimidation. It is the socialists who take issue with private ownership until or unless that ownership is transferred into *their* hands. As proclaimed in *Psalm 37* of the Old Testament, "The wicked plot against the righteous and gnash their teeth at them... The wicked draw the sword and bend the bow to bring down the poor and needy, to slay those whose ways are upright. But their swords will pierce their own hearts, and their bows will be broken."

CHAPTER X

PROPERTY

Among the necessary conditions for Leftism is the forcible suppression of private property in favor of collective "ownership", or rather that arrangement whereby no individual can officially claim any property for himself; that arrangement whereby his ownership, along with his purpose, is no longer *his*; whereby *true* ownership is, in effect, virtually eliminated from the vocabulary except where the establishment itself claims possession. It is, thus, under the Leftist system that the individual is demoted to the rank of an asset, that he is kept strictly accountable to the demands of the state instead of being the free-willed possessor of his own destiny; that his own personal preferences are made irrelevant; and that "value" is determined and distributed wholly independent of, and with complete disregard for, the individual. Whether it is the "value" of the person, the labor, or the resource, it is a "value" determined not by merit but by protest or politician.

In any free market, however, value is a matter of individual determination, where any given market value is justified only by consent between the relevant parties. Far from the despair and the wickedness brought by Leftism, the free market reaffirms the individual, that the individual owns himself and the product of his *own* labor, that he remains the architect of his *own* destiny and the possessor of his *own* purpose.

Indeed, in any free market, that purpose is owned by the worker, the capitalist and the entrepreneur, respectively, each of whom must necessarily *add* value in any transaction to entice any person to willingly do business with them. As opposed to the sanctimonious and the underhanded, they give generously while "the wicked borrow and do not repay." It is the capitalist and the entrepreneur who invest in plant and equipment to enable their workers to gain in their productivity, and it is this gain in productivity, benefits, stability, and often safety, which entices people to abandon their lives as individuals in order to accept the terms of their employment.

Meanwhile, it is through savings, amassed through economic efficiencies and labor-saving devices, that capital increases and new enterprises are possible. Contrary to the socialist myths, insofar as the capitalist increases his absolute share of the total production, the absolute *and* proportional share of the total production going to the laborer will also increase. As stated previously, the socialist has it entirely backwards. Indeed, the fact of the matter is that it is the capitalist, not the laborer, who stands to benefit least in proportion to the increase in total production. Most ironically, it is, in fact, in the opposite case, where capital is *decreased*, that the laborer stands to suffer most.

It is worth recalling the words of French economist Frédéric Bastiat in his summary of this phenomenon: "In proportion as capital is accumulated, the absolute shares of the total production going to the capitalist increases, and the proportional share going to the capitalist decreases; both the absolute and proportional share of the total production going to the laborer increases. The reverse of this happens when capital is decreased."

It follows, then, that the case for the laborer is made in the case for capitalism, *not* socialism. Through this, we have yet another in a long line of cases for freedom and free markets. As for free markets, the case is based not only on their practical effects but on their moral and ethical constitution.

In any free market, people are free to use or not use their property; they are free to offer their labor or services, just as they are free to withhold them. In a free market, no one sacrifices any of these rights upon launching a business or engaging in trade. Just as every worker is entitled to his wage and the total terms of his employment, so too is the employer entitled to retain the right to his property, which includes the revenue generated by that property and by the contracts negotiated upon the use of that property.

Socialists plainly have no interest in private property, which is to say that they have no interest in freedom. The right to private property is not just a benefit of freedom but a necessary condition for it. Wherever this right is withheld, there is slavery. After all, wherever man is without the right to his own property or the product of his own labor, he is left without the right of self-ownership, and wherever man is said to not own himself, he is either claimed by someone else or, according to the socialist, assumed by his society. The only difference here, as it turns out, is one between a conspicuous form and another which is more abstract, the former being the more honest of the two.

At the very outset of the American republic, the Framers rightly anticipated the dangers inherent to any form of government which pits the rights of people against the rights of property. James Madison communicated his observations on this threat in October of 1788, stressing that "the bulk of the people" ought first to be sufficiently invested in property, or the prospects of the rights of property, with still a sufficient interest in the rights of persons.

Madison sharply described the inevitable power to be suffered at the hands of those "not interested in the rights of property." In his observations, he warned that "one of two things cannot fail to happen" in such a clash of interests: "Either they will unite against the other description and become the dupes and instruments of ambition, or their poverty and independence will render them mercenary instruments of wealth." Madison then concluded that, "In either case liberty will be subverted; in the first by a despotism growing out of anarchy, in the second, by an oligarchy founded on corruption."

As it turns out, Madison has proved rather prescient in his estimation of the risks attending such a conflict, as Americans have indeed come to suffer the power which *slid into the hands not interested in the rights of property*. It is in just this manner that government, not without cunning, has turned homeownership into slavery.

It turns out that Madison was precisely correct in declaring that, in the interest of the rights of property, "Liberty not less than justice pleads for the policy" which seeks to guard each interest against the unwarranted influence of the other. Government, on the other hand, seeks a policy of its own: whether through fiscal or monetary policy, subsidies, debt guarantees, *quantitative easing*, central banking, or tax policy, their policy is a war on liberty. It is, therefore, essential to guard against these pernicious influences, because they are always changing in their forms, rarely in the interest of the rights of property, and rarely obvious.

* * *

One of the great misdeeds in contemporary politics has been the intentional cheapening of money to drive higher real estate prices. This has come not only at the expense of the currency and savings, but with added risk and higher costs in the form of higher purchase prices and higher taxes alike. Herein we find one of the single greatest misdeeds of our time: the conning of the public into accepting as their tax liability some arbitrary percentage of the appraised value of their home — or any other asset for that matter.

From an economics point of view, the cost of government is nowhere a function of the appraised value of real estate; nor does it stand to reason that any person or family, having been saddled already with the higher purchase price, should also stand to pay more in the way of taxes.

Indeed, insofar as government is tenable in any form, no person or family ought to be saddled with any greater liability than that which is assumed by each of their neighbors; that is to say that the liability ought to be rightly apportioned. Contrary to the popular misconception, one's ability to spend more on a property need not imply his ability to pay more in taxes. On the contrary, he is more often than not left with considerably less in the way of expendable income *because* of his inordinately expensive mortgage. Of course, let us not forget that he is condemned to carry this mortgage in the first place because of the artificially low rates of interest which make it altogether impossible for the saver to keep up with the prices of real estate and other costs of living.

Of course, this is no accident at all, as the government is squarely behind this initiative as well, which condemns the people to perpetual work, indebtedness and risk-taking in a vicious cycle which induces their enslavement. They are made to work more in order to pay those higher prices and to make up for the loss of purchasing power, to subsidize the risk-taking and insure against the losses of political and quasi-public entities (through such institutions as the FDIC). The people likewise succumb to debt just to purchase essentials like property; and they accept risk in the form of stocks and bonds, and in the form of their own mortgages, as they seek to enjoy their lives and to manage under the scourge of inflation.

As the government sees it, an indebted populace is far easier to control, and there is no better place to swindle the public into debt than homeownership: after all, homeownership is the most fundamental aspect of life and liberty, heritage and family, dignity and purpose, and it is one for which any people anywhere will suffer virtually any indignity just to keep it. Indeed, this is why the people ought to stand always at the ready to defend the precious principles of homeownership, and *all* property rights for that matter, against the ambitions of politicians who, for their own purposes, seek to redefine the terms and the very concept of "ownership". This is precisely why the people ought to stand ready to defend their rights against the clever schemes of conmen who, through policymaking, salesmanship or otherwise, seek to market lies, to swindle, to extort, to enslave.

The people must remain particularly vigilant to the more discreet forms which tempt the public, which appeal to the public's sensibilities and their own greed, and which exploit emotion and psychology: in the modern context, for example, the clever schemes which keep the people thinking that they are getting wealthier even when they are getting poorer; when, in fact, they are merely in a series of debtors taking on progressively more debt and thus creating the illusion of endless equity through appreciation — nominal gains realized only by taking on more debt against the property or otherwise selling the house, only to, presumably, bid on others at still higher prices; thereby selling the property to still other buyers who have been convinced of the same. Indeed, debt-generated riches and paper wealth are simply an illusion, and they amount to continually more enslavement of the people through (1) the mortgages necessary for the people to compete in such a market, combined with the subsequent refinancing, reverse home mortgages, and home equity lines of credit exploited in order to meet their debts; (2) the ever higher property tax liabilities to be met in order to keep the property; (3) such enormous liabilities as student debt and the perpetual subsidizing of "welfare" and "entitlements", some forms being less conspicuous than others. To be sure, so long as it can be maintained, it is a scheme operating to the perpetual benefit of both lenders and tax collectors, and even corporations who thereby enjoy a distinct advantage at the negotiation table, knowing full well that the employees and the applicants are desperate for funds in order to meet those obligations.

In this way, property becomes progressively more of a liability — as the people take on larger mortgages and their property taxes are assessed at progressively higher levels — while the owners and the bidders are convinced that this scheme makes them wealthier, and that it is sustainable into the future. Of course, this is true on paper, in the abstract. The scheme is indeed sustainable so long as the people can take on more debt and continue the scheme — that is, so long as credit is available and interest rates can be kept artificially low, and so long as the people are willing to tolerate this arrangement whereby even transitory unemployment can jeopardize their living situations; whereby they can be priced out of their homes, even if they "own" them outright, free and clear of any mortgage. For these reasons and others, the property tax is a most cruel and insidious imposition, and one whose risks are often overlooked by so many who are easily confused by percentages and academic justifications, and still others who are otherwise hypnotized by the promises of riches, whether expressed or implied.

Whereas newer homebuyers might appear wealthy for their ability to afford such expensive homes, they have merely committed themselves to stricter terms for homeownership: as opposed to prior generations who paid an average of four times annual household income, our contemporaries pay on average more than six times their annual household income, more than fifty percent higher than their predecessors; and this is a time when both parents are in the workforce, as opposed to the predominately single-income households of prior generations.

Ironically, even despite this, the politicians still claim that women are better off having been "liberated" from their domestic duties: instead of laboring for the benefit of their own families, they now work for CEOs, stakeholders and conglomerates, and according to the politicians and political activists, they are all better off for it. According to them, this is *progress*.

This means that both parents are so busy working to subsist that their children are condemned to daycare centers and public schools so that their parents can afford to clothe, shelter and feed them; or, in other cases, so that their parents can prioritize their own financial affairs, so that they can afford their vacation homes and the other luxuries of life. This means that their children are brought under the care of "professionals" (or the state) instead of keeping them in the care of the ones who are biologically predisposed to love and nurture them, who are (in the main) most capable of doing so. This means that, instead of remaining in the care and custody of their own parents and their own families, they are eventually assumed and treated as the property of the bureaucracy, the state, or the community. Adolf Hitler asserted as much on November 6, 1933:

"When an opponent declares, 'I will not come over to your side,' I calmly say, 'Your child belongs to us already... What are you? You will pass on. Your descendants, however, now stand in the new camp. In a short time they will know nothing else but this new community.'"

This means that, apart from the swindling, enslavement, and the indoctrination of the youth, and apart from the various burdens placed upon posterity, in forms both tangible and intangible, the children bear the brunt of the consequences in the absence and passive obedience of their parents, who are rarely even present to love, nurture and mentor their children. Instead, by forces ill-understood and, as they see it, far beyond their control, the parents outsource or relinquish all of these responsibilities to people whom they don't even know and whom they can't possibly trust, so that their children may stand a chance to do the same. This is a vicious cycle that can only result in decadence, or social ruin.

I posit that this vicious cycle is the direct consequence of taxation: whether upon income or property, or through debt or inflation, it implies taxation all the same. By whatever name and whatever channels, it has proven to destroy families and the very fabric of society; a form of destruction which is highly beneficial to government, which never wastes a crisis or an opportunity to seize more power and levy still more taxes.

This is, of course, part and parcel of the Leftist agenda: to so encumber the economy as to effect its destruction from behind the scenes, to (as the Leftists see it) come to the rescue by seizing more power and control, by achieving stricter social and economic regimentation, or even by taking over enterprise outright. This is precisely how the establishment assumes so much authority over the people: incrementally and surreptitiously, leaving them thoroughly dazed and confused, not knowing *what* has happened, let alone *how* it happened.

Inflation is just one of the invisible tools of despots, in whose hands it quickly becomes one of the deadliest weapons. One of the many advantages of inflation is that the source consistently avoids detection. It is most ingenious in the way that it enables despots to swindle the public and to stack the deck in their own favor without the people noticing; without the people eventually catching on, without them eventually tracing the crimes back to their regular perpetrators. On each occasion, the results are most predictable, among them the inequalities suffered by workers in the form of lost wealth and income; in the form of both a diminished quality of life and progressively lower standards of living.

Inflation is always and everywhere a monetary phenomenon, ultimately tilting the scales in favor of those who have already secured control over much of the wealth and the means of production. It widens the gap between the *haves* and the *have-nots*, and it promotes vast inequalities in wealth and income among the classes. Meanwhile, the perps all too often succeed in placing the blame where it does not belong: in virtually every case, they succeed in placing the blame on *free enterprise* and *capitalism*, so far as they have come to defile those terms to their own advantage. They are always prepared to subject the people to ever more of the state's "solutions", to condemn the people to ever more sacrifice, injustice and humiliation under the banners of *socialism*. This ultimately leaves the people working for ends ill-understood, to serve ends otherwise completely unknown to them.

In this way, the people are left doing progressively more for less: more hours spent working for less in return; wages and salaries always trailing behind the rise in asset prices and the costs of living. This means that the people are ultimately paid less (in real terms), left to work more or to take on additional jobs, while paying progressively more for the resources sold by the ones in control of the assets. It is a most insidious form of slavery, indeed, and one whereby the masters never have to get their hands dirty or even cross paths with their slaves; slaves who, for the most part, don't even notice the chains. Along with debt, inflation is the single greatest source of suffering the world has ever known: from war to economic collapse, countless lives have been lost or ruined under its thumb.

Indeed, debt and inflation are a matter of routine for Leftist administrations: in creating more of it, the establishment succeeds in stealing from the public. It is taxation without legislation, and theft of epic proportions. The scale of the racket, however, is so enormous that scarcely anyone dares to challenge it. After all, there is virtually no limit on the power of this kind of administration, so, in the view of the many, it is a fool's errand to go up against it.

By the time the establishment has seized this much control over the economy (and thereby the social order and all of civilization), there is precious little that can be done diplomatically. Indeed, one of the most dangerous cohorts among us is that which claims to align with the resistance, with the true interests of the commoner and his liberty, yet demands change and resistance only through diplomacy, rejecting all other means, even where diplomacy and democratic process have demonstrably failed.

Indeed, such an environment ushers in a reign of the absurd over the disarmed, whereby all rational thought breaks down, whereby rational discourse becomes all but impossible. That is where absurdity triumphs, whether *diplomatically*, *democratically* or otherwise; where any system tilted explicitly and unconditionally against violence, prohibiting violence of any kind, regarding violence as abjectly uncivilized and unbecoming, that is precisely where the absurdities of sophists and propagandists trample the disciplined and the reasoned, where they do so with impunity; where the disciplined and the reasoned will be thrust into the impossible position of defending themselves diplomatically against those who are impervious to reason and persuasion, and thus against the state and its agents who stand ready to defend the absurdities which threaten to infect and paralyze society.

While disarming the people through social and political means, they do the same through economic controls. Among other means, they accomplish this end by instituting strict "regulations" and compliance requirements; excessive obstacles to entry; "protectionist" tariffs and enforced monopolies; loose monetary policies in the name of "maximum employment", "price stability" and "economic growth"; diminished returns on labor and savings; progressively higher taxes and artificially-higher asset prices; all to condemn the common people to progressively more work, sacrifice and debt for inconspicuous ends, and to continually justify more of the same. The despots make things even worse through their progressively higher budgets and the perpetual raising (or effective neutralization) of the so-called "debt ceiling"; so that, according to the despots, they can cover their *own* rising operating costs without any regard for the operating costs (or the costs of living) for the people. This is one dirty trick.

Accounting for the fact that wages always lag behind inflation, this means that the people are left with not only higher prices but less money to spend; indeed, the people are, by the designs of their government, made to work more and more for the establishment as they struggle to make ends meet.

This is when the despots start licking their chops. By then they know they have got the people right where they want them: struggling and ready to forfeit their liberty for some temporary relief. Indeed, it is not incidental, but by design, that their policies bring about economic hardship, as they know that the people will quickly become so desperate that they will come to accept the despots as their saviors. By the time their policies have crippled the economy, more and more of the people will have rejected the market in favor of the promises of government. This is precisely why the establishment is ultimately so successful: it is always there with new "solutions" to the problems they created, or, in other cases, the problems they will never be able to solve.

Indeed, the establishment is not in the business of solving problems. It is in the business of creating, compounding, and imagining them, and keeping the public eternally aroused in conflict, otherwise hopeful for solutions or results that are never forthcoming. The establishment is always prepared to exploit any emergency, any calamity, and any opportunity for fearmongering; all to, as the investigative reporter Joseph Trento put it in his 2001 work *The Secret History of the CIA*,

"... turn extraordinary power over to a government agency [or set of agencies] run by human beings with weaknesses that we all share." Trento went further, describing an establishment full of extraordinary power coupled with such weaknesses as "careerism, callousness, self-interest, and hubris"; the most dangerous of combinations across all of civilization, the single greatest threat to liberty and the rights of man.

This is precisely why taxation, government debt and regulations are so dangerous: the establishment always insists that, with just a little more, they will finally be able to meet their objectives. Of course, their ambitious ends are always accompanied by still more punitive means. After all, it is not the ends they are after, but the power that is theirs so long as they keep up the charade. Meanwhile, the ends keep the public on their witch-hunt and chasing ghosts, where the tyrants are always ready to point them in another direction. As it turns out, invisibility and witch-hunts are key themes for more than just science fiction novels: they are the modus operandi for the Leftist agenda.

While inflation is the most invisible of taxes, there is no tax that is more fundamentally destructive than the one which seeks to fleece the public for merely owning a home. Under this arrangement, the homeowner is forever liable, as he cannot escape the penalty imposed by government, which threatens to seize his property in the event that he fails or refuses to pay. By definition, no one can truly *own* a home under this arrangement.

This arrangement by government is one part of a web of lies, deception, and coercion which enslaves the public wherever they go, whatever they elect to do, and however they intend to survive. Even where the people seek the humblest of occupations, a meager subsistence, and a tiny plot of their own, they are brought into the fold as servants to the status quo.

The most basic of human ambitions is to build and to own one's own home, and to thereby raise one's own family.

Politicians from time immemorial have been aware of this ambition, and they have sought everywhere to exploit it. At no other time in the history of the world has any government ever been more successful in fleecing the people of so much with so precious few taking notice. Like a magic trick, the government has been busy fleecing the public while convincing some fraction of them that they are getting richer, and still another that they are entitled to some of the loot.

In the case of homeownership, the renters are all too eager to see the homeowners assume the brunt of the taxes. As they see it, the homeowners are wealthy enough to pay them. Of course, the renters pay little mind to the fact that they might be homeowners one day, nor do they busy themselves with the fact that their landlords pay their taxes only upon collecting their rent; nor are they troubled by the fact that property taxes, those based on appraised market value, inherently discourage development and dampen the supply of housing units, thereby increasing rental prices and exacerbating housing crises.

The renters are not concerned with the future nor the finer details, in keeping with the nature of people who have nothing invested in it. Of course, in the face of the consequences, they are just as incredulous to the results of their preferred policies: problems they have (through government) created, compounded, or condoned. Where any policy or set of policies should fail, they are always ready to demand solutions from government, assumed to possess the means, the intelligence, and the incentive to oblige. Meanwhile, government is often just as clueless and almost always uninterested in solutions, especially to problems of its own creation or to those beneficial to its interests.

It is for this reason that government seeks to fill its constituency with desperation, hostility, and the dregs of society. It is for this reason that government seeks to impoverish the people, to stoke division, and to keep them bickering amongst themselves. Indeed, this is how the tyrants guarantee their continued command over the people: wherever the tyrants succeed in splitting them into various camps and factions such that not one of them is powerful enough to wage any meaningful opposition, such that the whole of the people are unlikely to form a capable alliance against the state.

Instead, in such a climate where those various parties are busy with their own internal disputes and conflicts, each of them will be ready to punish its enemies through the state, which stands ready to pummel them all. In this case, the government has laid siege to homeownership, where the soul of humanity and the principles of life, liberty and property are at stake. Meanwhile, the cheerleaders are ignorant to the consequences or otherwise immune to them.

In driving higher real estate prices, the government and the central bank have selected the winners and the losers: they have committed to higher prices to protect the *haves* at the expense of the *have-nots*. This is not to say that they have not distributed some of the loot to the *have-nots*, but that they have distributed only enough to keep them asking for more, or to otherwise keep them quiet. Meanwhile, the ranks of the middle class shrink as the gap between the rich and the poor widens to the satisfaction of the political elite who prefer it that way. After all, this is precisely where the politicians want the middle class: weak and outnumbered. And this is why they keep pounding the table for *democracy*: not because they believe in it on principle, but because they know it will keep the public divided and that they will eventually have the numbers.

The assault upon homeownership is just one of the many ways that government has secured its stranglehold over the people. In their control over property as well as income, combined with their control over the common currency, the politicians can virtually increase taxes at will. With the benefit of so much control, they can increase taxes without the people even noticing. They can, as in the case of homeownership, drive real estate prices progressively higher to induce more debt, more speculation, and more tax revenues to boot.

This essentially subjects homebuyers to prices driven by the government's monetary policy, which thereafter stands to subject them to still another set of prices expressed as a percentage, of the government's choosing of course, of the total purchase price. In this way, the government cheapens the currency, which negates the value of savings; it causes higher prices, namely in stocks, bonds, real estate, and consumer goods; and it stands ready to cash in upon their every sale. This is one of the greatest deceits of the modern era, and one so arcane that scarcely any person will even dare to investigate, let alone question its legitimacy.

For these reasons and more, taxes, wherever they are to be suffered and unopposed, ought only to be tolerated, not accepted; for tolerance may at least keep the people alert to further abuses, whereas their acceptance will invariably form the basis for more of the same until such point is reached that the government asserts itself as the rightful owner of *all* property. By this time, any part left for the enjoyment of the taxpayer is regarded as a form of charity from the government.

The more property claimed (whether in part or in whole) by government, and the greater the taxes and restrictions on property, the weaker the incentive for the people to develop and maintain it. The same is true of any inheritance tax, which serves as still another tax on property, constituting two taxes on the greatest incentive of all: legacy. The threat posed is not just that of wealth redistribution, which alone is destructive enough, but that of routing progressively more of the wealth into the hands of government and its corporate cronies, whereby, as the former Führer of Germany put it in his 1925 manifesto *Mein Kampf*, "A grave economic symptom of decay" is sure to follow through "the slow disappearance of the right of private property, and the gradual transference of the entire economy to the ownership of stock companies." Indeed, whether intentional or incidental, this is precisely the threat posed by the penalty on inheritances and property; the increased costs of ownership making it progressively more difficult to keep property in the family between generations, therefore making it progressively more likely that the two will end up in the hands of the establishment, between the state and their cronies in the form of "stock companies".

Just as the property tax weakens the incentive for the people to develop and maintain their property, an inheritance tax is one which penalizes families for taking an economic interest in their children's future, which fundamentally renegotiates the terms between man and his family, the ends which he most naturally and productively serves. The inheritance tax is just another tax on wealth and property, the most pernicious of taxes for the way in which it redefines the purpose of man, for the way in which it destroys or minimizes not only the incentive for individuals to concern themselves with and invest in the future, but the incentive to produce in excess of their personal needs for the benefit of their heirs and their future security; even heirs who are not yet born. This is a mighty and unquantifiable incentive which is simply irreplaceable by any other.

As the Nobel laureate Milton Friedman once put it, "This is really a family society, not an individual society... The greatest incentive of all, the incentives that have really driven people on, have largely been the incentives of family creation... pursuing the establishing of their family on a decent system."

As Friedman put it, a tax on inheritances encourages people "to dissipate their wealth in high living" with diminished incentives to save, to invest, and to improve technology, to instead waste it in frivolous activities and entertainment. As Friedman put it, a significant share of the world's economic outcomes is attributable to "[t]he extent to which the market system has, in fact, encouraged people and enabled people to work hard and sacrifice... for the benefit of their children." Speaking of the unquantifiable incentive of inheritances, Friedman goes on to say that, "One of the most curious things... is that almost all people value the utility which their children will get from consumption higher than they value their own."

Without the bonds connecting parents to their children, without the bonds connecting elders to the youth as mentors, there is little incentive for the people to pay any mind to the future, to save, to invest, and to labor in excess of their own immediate wants and needs. Indeed, this is why the breakdown of the system of inheritances, the breakdown of that tradition, serves as one of the leading causes of social dysfunction.

More than just the mere inheritance of material wealth, this subject centers around the inheritance of traditions, qualities and skills that are best suited to thrive on this planet, and thereby best suited for the future. It is the responsibility of every child-bearing parent to equip his or her offspring with the physical and psychological tools to survive, lest the parent risk imperiling his or her child through neglect. Unfortunately, many parents broadly misinterpret "neglect" as the active forms of abuse that are visibly apparent, but "neglect" is much more than that.

In the context of parenting, "neglect" takes the form of unmet obligations that are instrumental in enabling children to thrive in life, not limited to the protection, guidance and provisions secured by those parents who have assumed this responsibly. As parents and as families, it is absolutely essential to clothe, to feed, to shelter, and to bathe our offspring, and it is just as necessary to promote learning, confidence, and competence.

In the modern world, where stringent regulations and heavy-handed laws have made life more expensive and less intuitive than before, it appears that the responsibilities of parenthood have grown commensurate with the development of the various complexities and burdens within modern society. These are burdens and complexities not limited to the legal, financial, political, and regulatory difficulties faced in the modern Western world. Whereas our predecessors once freely erected homes on available or otherwise cheaply-acquired lands, modern Americans and most of the Western world now develop properties and build homes at great expense by way of tremendous monetary costs and ongoing tax liabilities, in addition to the myriad costs of compliance with ordinances and regulations; that is, where they are even permitted to build in the first place, in the wake of so many artificial restrictions on the supply of residential and developable land.

This is where modern civilization has witnessed considerable subversion of the customs that once prioritized family ethics and empowered families with stable home lives, that once brought three or more generations to live together to raise children and grandchildren, whereafter those children would inherit the family house to continue the tradition. In upholding this tradition, families achieved stability in the home with the benefit of pooled savings, wide ranges of skills and competencies, and men and women who could work together to raise their children and meet, or exceed, the family's daily needs.

In working together, the family that stays together benefits the children through stability of various kinds, and they also forego the additional, and often unnecessary, burdens of independent living, building or financing another home where they would be without the benefits of those enjoyed synergies and shared costs of living; where the family unit will have been dissolved for the more than doubling of direct costs such as utilities and housing, in addition to those more obscure costs in the form of the time, labor and risks in raising the children alone, maintaining the additional property, paying the additional taxes, and outsourcing the education and care of their children.

Where those marginal costs can be expressed monetarily, we can find one of the many failings that has yielded among us one of the most politicized outcomes in existence: poverty. In bringing a child into this world, one man and one woman have assumed express responsibility for the livelihood of another human being, and ideally there is a supportive family to assume that responsibility.

Where any child inevitably fails or falters, it is the responsibility of the parents and the family to redirect the child and to facilitate his development. In the existence of persistent failure, one can ordinarily trace the outcomes back to the parents and the family unit, their genetics and their parenting methods, the mismatch between one set of expectations and the case of reality, and the divergence between situational demands and parental competency.

Where one fails, it is not the responsibility of anyone other than that individual, and those who birthed and assumed responsibility over him, to rectify his station in life or to otherwise accept the costs of continued neglect. Where parents calculatingly match their projected productivity, competencies and wealth with reality, and where they prove capable of remaining together, raising their children together, and providing those aforementioned essentials for their offspring, their heirs will stand the greatest chance of continuing that trend and empowering their own children to improve the lives of their descendants and so on.

Where we so often find poverty today is where this chain has been broken. It is where parents have failed their children by their absence, by their abuse, by their ineptitude or inadequacy, or by their children misguidedly squandering their resources on needles excesses. In the modern context, one major example of needless excess takes the form of the additional home, which is shown to net a financial loss in excess of ninety percent, as measured by a low-risk opportunity cost of homeownership.

In departing from the tradition of keeping the family together and raising the children with the benefit of the family's combined efforts, the present case amounts to an opportunity cost measuring, by approximation of the average, several millions of dollars over 30 years, which is to say nothing of the unseen costs in the form of the children's personal development. Those millions of dollars represent the direct monetary cost of dissolving the family unit, and the fractured family unit is one of the primary reasons that we see so many individuals now hopelessly mired in debt or otherwise roaming the streets homeless, dejected and directionless.

Rather than working for the benefit of a more plentiful or meaningful future, individuals and couples have come to pursue lives independent from their families and their own parents, where they work more than four months each year to afford housing expenses alone, from rent or mortgage payments to property taxes, maintenance and repairs. Alternatively, in the case of the multigenerational household, those funds can serve to bolster savings, investment and retirement accounts for further wealth creation, higher education, and the improvement of living conditions, advantages bequeathed upon subsequent generations who can continue the tradition.

Wherever the family chain has been broken, wherever familial accountability ceases to endure, one finds the establishment of a new standard whereby offspring are assumed exclusively responsible for themselves, where their failures reflect only on themselves and become the manufactured responsibility of other members of society instead of landing where they originally belonged, with their own families. These breakdowns of the family unit, though costly in the forms of wealth and opportunity cost, evidence themselves in the form of other, even more significant outcomes: one can bear witness to the homeless population, the drug epidemic, the incidence of single-family households, the labor force participation rate, the innumerable cases of academic and professional underperformance, the prison population, the record rates of household debt, the paucity of retirement savings, the death of entrepreneurship, and the tolerated (and even celebrated) expansion of government and the laws that bind, obligate and tyrannize its citizens. However, it is the unseen which is unquantifiable, the underachievement and the underdevelopment of those precious souls who could have otherwise done much better in life.

While the effects of family dissolution vary in form, they are, as shown, costly and extremely destructive to the crucial bonds which have long enabled mankind to flourish on this planet.

The historical record demonstrates that where families remain connected and responsible for each other, whether in tribes or in multigenerational households, there can be plentiful advantages enjoyed across time, reverberating infinitely into the future for subsequent members of that bloodline. If only those families can stay together or else prevent their failures from becoming the burden of others who have managed to sustain their own, then so too can freedom and prosperity survive with them.

For a whole variety of reasons, broken families and the related outcomes among them, the state ultimately succeeds in "justifying" its claim over progressively more property and thereby eroding the foundations of family, liberty and independence. As stated, the more property claimed (whether in part or in whole) by government, and the greater the taxes and restrictions on property, the weaker the incentive for the people to develop and maintain it; the weaker the incentive to labor and invest for the future; the weaker their sense of purpose and their gratification in life; and the weaker their position (and their inclination) to defend themselves and their heirs against the ambitions of tyrants. Whether it is a tax on sales, profits or income, labor or compensation, property or inheritance, dividends or capital gains, however assessed or arbitrarily defined, it is a means to penalizing people for gainful activities and essential possessions which — so far as tangibles are concerned — bring value to life.

In fact, in some jurisdictions, governments are so bold as to levy *value-added taxes*, and that is precisely what all taxes do: all else equal, they penalize people for adding value to life. Big government also has the effect of benefitting big business, specifically those whose interests are served, subsidized, or protected by the establishment. This has the effect of artificially tilting the scales in favor of big business away from small business and labor — as far as negotiations, obstacles to entry, market share, and pricing power are concerned. In this way, the government achieves control through cronies and political allies in private enterprise, where, through a host of advantages secured through the state, they manage to control the people while the government lurks behind the scenes.

It is in this way that bigger government condemns the people to lower standards of living and inferior conditions throughout their communities and their neighborhoods. In the absence or the minimization of the inherent incentive to maintain and to care for one's private property, the government then asserts that the only option left is to enforce standards through the barrel of a gun, neither peacefully nor politely, but through intimidation and force of arms. This is a society rooted not in "progress" or "civility" but in systemic violence and brutishness, in defiance of the very factors and principles responsible for making the people most productive and their living conditions most pleasant.

As this author has already illustrated, the most pernicious form of this kind of abuse is that which is directed at property in the name of so-called *rights* and *entitlements*, the kind which is more aptly termed *extortion*. This kind of liability is lifelong and unavoidable; whether sick or otherwise unable to work, or whether one prefers to subsist on the product of his own land instead of seeking employment or engaging in commerce elsewhere, he cannot elude the government which threatens to dispossess him of his property upon his failure to pay. There is just no way to more accurately describe this atrocity than to simply call it what it is: a form of state enslavement whereby the slaves are afforded a relatively long leash and kept completely unaware of the arrangement, as they are surrounded everywhere by fellow slaves who live in separate homes, who are either too distracted, too ignorant, or too proud to acknowledge the con.

The distinction, then, between property tax and slavery is a matter of form, as they function just the same. The difference, of course, is the proximity of the slave to his master, the chances of his escape, and the opportunity to win his freedom. In either case, each is expected to work for his master, and it is at the master's pleasure only that the subjects enjoy any part of the product of their labor. Ultimately, for those in control, it is not a question of whether man ought to be in chains but whether he ought to know who holds the keys. Ironically, through government the master has convinced the taxpayers that they own their land, whereas the slave is under no such illusions.

A clever ruse, government has swiftly turned homeowner-ship into an instrument for perpetual enslavement; and by its own designs, the people are so busy keeping up, so distracted by cheap entertainment and propaganda, so preoccupied in their petty disagreements, and so fearful of bucking the conventions, that they come to accept their enslavement. All the while, little do they know that they are erecting or otherwise condoning the very institutions that will continue their own subjugation.

Of course, the socialists are always ready to "justify" it all and more, and they are never satisfied until each subject is made to work exclusively for the state. By that time, they are ready to use force to get even more out of their subjects; that is, until they (the socialists) realize that the state will not be sparing them either. By that time, the state will have assumed enough power to do without its cheerleaders, and the very socialists who erected or otherwise supported those institutions will join the ranks of the oppressed. However, this does not keep them from believing in their cherished ideology. On the contrary, they claim that, with just a few tweaks, it can be made to work in the future.

However, those tweaks time and again prove inadequate, unable to overcome the fundamental shortcomings of their ideology: that the inescapable problem with Leftism resides in its scalability, that the model cannot possibly be scaled up without eventually compromising the factors that, in the first place, allowed it to function in any limited form, to any limited extent, and for any limited period of time; and that the factors, in principle, maintaining their friendly intercourse are, at scale, replaced by force.

CHAPTER XI

"NOT REAL SOCIALISM"

Attempting to remedy the deficiencies of socialism is like trying to stop a runaway train or patching the holes of a sunken ship. It is a disaster which the intellectual claims he can resolve, but it is a state of denial, a matter of aesthetics, a fool's errand, or a mental exercise in which he is assessing a problem in slow motion and dismissing the laws of physics, while it is a problem destined for violent impact or already there. It is yet another example of the big abstraction, a model becoming large and complex enough that the individual cannot seem to make sense of it or to appreciate the building blocks of its construction.

Indeed, it is when a system becomes so large, when it exceeds a certain scale, that the factors and values responsible for its success become abstract, if not entirely arcane; that members and beneficiaries of that system begin to betray their former values, to rethink that system and dispense with the vital factors sustaining it.

Whether a politician seeking to reinvent society in defiance of the laws of economics or a corporate manager dispensing with the intangibles of leadership and loyalty, discouraging friendship, or redefining the values of a successful workplace, the scale of the operation, the model or the system, ultimately tricks the untrained eye and confuses the people into thinking that their unproven ideas might work, that they need not account for or worry about the costs or the risks.

In the political context, this tends to be the result of a system yielding so much abundance that it produces the illusion of unlimited (and costless) opportunity, that it keeps an increasing number of agents busy in increasingly menial tasks, insulated from an honest day's work and totally unfamiliar with any real measures of productivity. For this reason, progressively more people are ready to accept the fantastical and the unproven, to propose a reinvention of the wheel without any coherent plans, without any appreciation for the relevant laws and principles, let alone any proof of concept.

This is the predictable result of any system of such scale where power or influence is dealt to those unaware of the big picture: those not in touch with the total mechanics of the system in which they exist and which, in many cases, had previously succeeded without them and may even — for some period of time — continue to succeed despite them and their influences.

Wherever Leftism runs its course, there are those disciples who thus never fully understood the situation or the implications of the proposed actions; those who still do not understand them and thus have no idea why their measures have failed; and thus so many who ultimately refuse to accept defeat, those who cling desperately to their cherished ideology, who, like any alcoholic attempting to justify another drink, claim (and even believe) that they will rectify the wrongs, make the appropriate tweaks, and exercise better judgment and more restraint this time around.

Regardless of ideological preferences, there are eventually throngs of Leftists who abandon ship and defect, seeking shelter from the monster of their own creation. While these Leftists may be welcomed with open arms, and while they may be embraced for (by all appearances) relinquishing their allegiances, they are among their fellow Leftists who are personally responsible for condoning, supporting, or celebrating Leftism until its predictable failures became undeniably clear.

As with their comrades, these Leftists are particularly dangerous because, in their estimation, their conscience is clear. After all, as they see it, they eventually switched teams to join the good guys. So, in their view, they need not repent nor come to terms with their former wrongdoings or their culpability in the events which followed: the violence, the hostility, and the punishment brought upon the people by the tyrants and an establishment empowered by the Leftists who naively worship them.

Few ultimately maintain their allegiances to the failed establishment, and so its advocates and its personnel are seldom held accountable. After all, its advocates and its personnel enjoy plausible deniability: the first hiding behind their "intentions" or their ignorance, the second claiming that they were merely "doing their jobs". This makes for a very dangerous combination, for, as historian and essayist Russell Kirk once put it, "Good natured ignorance is a luxury none of us can afford."

This is precisely why *all* Leftists, both current and former, those who still champion the cause and those who have come to disavow it, are each in their own right part of the problem; and just as the results start coming in, they cannot just abandon ship and expect to be welcomed with open arms aboard the ship of the men and women whom they have so disparaged for so long.

So far as this *is* permitted, so long as the Leftists *are* able to get away with their wrongs, they will never truly learn the errors of their ways; they will never truly repent for the ills they have brought upon their fellow man; and, for the fact that most will have eventually come to abandon ship, nobody will be held accountable. Of course, this is entirely in keeping with the whole theme of Leftism.

Indeed, under socialism it is "society" or the bureaucracy that is responsible, which is to say that, in truth, *nobody* is responsible. On the contrary, the state actually benefits from that distinct lack of accountability, as — in the view of the bureaucrats, at least — the failures seem to justify more of the same: more of the same failed programs, still larger budgets to fund them, and more self-serving rhetoric to keep the charade going. On the other hand, family values and personal responsibility *are* scalable because they are maintained at the most local of levels, whereby, at scale, they are most distinctly capable of preserving the character of a congenial community. This is because, under this model, there is genuine oversight, actual accountability, mutual interest, shared values, and the inherent incentive to continually guard each of these. Indeed, these are qualities essential to any stable society, any state of liberty, and any civilization of free people anywhere. In fact, this is merely another way of viewing *assimilation*: the mutual embrace of that common culture and identity which enables civility, cordiality, comfort, and stability among a people, and a kind of synergy which yields economic strength for the many and maximal mobility for the individual.

As for modern America, unfortunately, it is a case of a people progressively parting with their identity; an identity which had, for so long, uniquely enabled Americans to enjoy and to protect the precious jewel of their liberty; indeed, an identity distinctly opposed to collectivism, and one equally opposed to any such foreign influence. It is an identity, to be sure, but just as importantly it is a most sacred cause, an eternal battle between ideologies, between two radically different views on humanity, between two opposing ways of life: as American chess grandmaster Bobby Fischer is said to have put it in his match against the Soviet Union's Boris Spassky in the 1972 World Chess Championship, it is "the Soviet megalithic system versus rawboned American individualism." For this reason, "The cause of America is in great measure," as Thomas Paine is known to have put it in his 1776 publication of *Common Sense*, "the cause of mankind." It is a cause worth defending at home, first and foremost for the sake of the individual, the family, and all of posterity, but also in order to, by extension, set a shining example of liberty for the rest of the world. Despite what the more politically-minded folks among us might prefer to believe, it is not *the cause of mankind* that is the cause of America, but the cause of America which represents the greatest of mankind's causes.

The political machine, of course, sees things very differently. Always in motion, exploiting semantics, syntactical destruction and social sensibilities, the machine is always exploiting every angle to its advantage, thereby trampling the liberty of the people who are often none the wiser, often even found in celebration of their own sacrifice, whether that be a sacrifice of culture, freedom, heritage, property, or even life itself.

This is true across all of political history, and the story of America is no exception. One striking example of this is found in the pronouncements of President John F. Kennedy, in his September 19, 1960, speech at the United Steelworkers of America Convention in Atlantic City, New Jersey.

In his speech, Kennedy sought to "present to the American people an alternative course of action" for the country. By this, he intended that "the period of the 1960's [be] a period in which we [cannot] conserve, in which we stand still." On the contrary, Kennedy declared this "a time for new go-ahead for this country and the American people." He implored his audience to join him in his campaign, to "[g]ive me your help, your hand, your voice, and we can move this country ahead."

In Kennedy's view, "the great issue in 1960 is for us to take the kind of decisions which will preserve freedom around the world." To corroborate his view, Kennedy called upon the words of the revolutionary Thomas Paine:

"Thomas Paine said in the Revolution of 1776 that the cause of America is the cause of all mankind. I think in 1960 the cause of all mankind is the cause of America. If we fail, I think the case of freedom fails, not only in the United States, but every place. If we succeed, if we meet our responsibilities, if we bear our burdens, then I think freedom succeeds here and also it succeeds around the world."

It is true, as in the words of Thomas Paine during the American Revolution, that "the cause of America is the cause of mankind", that the causes which impelled the Revolution represent the noblest of causes the world over. It is not true, however, as President John F. Kennedy asserted in his coining of the "Revolution of 1960", that "the cause of mankind is the cause of America". While it is true, mathematically speaking, that, by the reflexive property, the two claims are virtually identical, it is simply untrue linguistically, and certainly untrue in the context of Kennedy's speech, given the fact that he himself had determined to distinguish between the two.

Indeed, the first of these, promulgated by Paine, celebrated the cause of America as symbolic of the dearest of causes for all of mankind. In their sacrifice, the American Patriots waged a fight domestically whose consequences would reverberate across the globe as inspiration for the rest of mankind in their new appreciation for concepts not limited to life, liberty and the pursuit of happiness.

Their cause at home, indirectly and without their knowledge, advanced the cause of the world, away from the institution of rights from monarchs and despots or from other mortal men, to the assumption of rights as endowed inherently upon mankind by their Creator. This was, and will forever remain, the cause of mankind, and it was the American Patriot who took up the cause in his own backyard to declare the sovereignty of man and to consequently blaze the trail for the rest of the world.

However, just as President George Washington cautioned "friends and the fellow-citizens" of America in his farewell address, the United States is best served by the avoidance of "foreign alliances" and "the mischiefs of foreign intrigue". Washington appreciated the threats posed by those alliances and others attending the kind of overgrown military which would develop as a consequence of maintaining those alliances. Washington and his contemporaries understood that these were anathema to our constitutional republic and the jewel of the public liberty, a form of liberty that Washington described as "Republican liberty".

Washington also understood that the authority of the general government extended to the affairs between states and to their mutual defense; it did not, in any way, and for good reason, appoint the general government of the United States as the moderator or the policeman of the entire world. These principles were once embraced by the United States, due to the known threats posed to their "Republican liberty" by "the common and continual mischiefs of the spirit of [any political] party"; a spirit threatening to influence government policy at the country's expense for the exclusive benefit of its allies. In the words of Washington, "It opens the door to foreign influence and corruption, which finds a facilitated access to the government itself through the channels of party passions."

Whereas President John F. Kennedy might have described Washington's designs as "a government frozen in the ice of its own indifference", just as he characterized his contemporaries in their misgivings toward the burgeoning welfare state, these were never, and ought never to be, the causes of America,

Washington instead urged that Americans embrace their auspicious isolation from the rest of the world. He thus inquired:

"Why forego the advantages of so peculiar a situation? Why quit our own to stand upon foreign ground? Why, by interweaving our destiny with that of any part of Europe, entangle our peace and prosperity in the toils of European ambition, rivalship, interest, humor or caprice?"

Washington then asserted, "It is our true policy to steer clear of permanent alliances with any portion of the foreign world." After all, the best that any people can seek to accomplish is the defense of their own liberty, and this is precisely where they have the power and the authority to secure it. Wherever they stand to forfeit any measure of that liberty, whether for personal profit, political expediency, or "the cause of mankind", they stand to undermine their own cause.

It is precisely in the view of Washington, as he had laid out in the profoundest of prose, that America undertook the cause of mankind; not by force of arms around the globe, but as an example of a people and a country committed to the defense of their own liberty. This is the cause of America, the identity and the heritage of the American, and they are to be preserved by all means available, to ensure not that the rest of the world follows its lead, but that the people themselves within the country's own borders remain committed to the cause, committed to welcoming newcomers on the expectation that they will do the same; committed to taking pride in their heritage, standing ready to defend it, and demanding assimilation among all who wish to enjoy its plenty.

Regrettably, however, these are an identity and a cause which have, over time, been lost and forgotten. Indeed, rather than encouraging any kind of assimilation to American culture, rather than even daring to suggest that such a culture exists, the modern American has come to believe or to merely accept that, as a "melting pot", the only appropriate identity in America is the one imported from abroad.

Instead of correctly equating the "melting pot" with the assimilation of the peoples, modern Americans have essentially emptied the pot and extinguished the fire, only for the pot to refill and eventually overflow with separate components which then never come to mix but instead threaten to combust. In fact, modern Americans have come to so accommodate the various cultures and customs of the world as to not just shy away from encouraging assimilation or reaffirming their own, but to shy away or even distance themselves personally from their own culture, even going so far as to reject or condemn their forebears and their prior traditions. Indeed, it seems as though the "melting pot" analogy may just have been more destructive to America than a worthwhile point of pride.

Many in the history of America have likened the United States to a melting pot. Already in use as early as the eighteenth century, the term "melting pot" particularly gaining in popularity after the 1908 play of the same name. The term has come to describe America for generations, and it can continue as a fitting analogy so long as the people account for its limitations. After all, an analogy is useful only with consideration to limitations and reason.

The challenge, then, is to determine the extent to which an analogy holds up and where it begins to unravel. In the case of the melting pot, the analogy really serves only to communicate a principle: that America has, on balance, benefitted economically and culturally from a diverse blend of influences. However, in the course of debate and political discourse, people are oftentimes paralyzed by the principle at face value, which numbs them to the kind of critical thinking that would otherwise call into question the veracity and the applicability of the analogy, as well as the degree to which it holds up.

All too often, the principle, taken for granted at face value, precludes any further consideration with respect to degree. In still other cases, the analogy conveniently obscures the risks and the tradeoffs. In the case of the melting pot, America is celebrated for its various influences from abroad, economic as well as cultural, from the wide array of immigrants who have washed upon its shores as they fled the Old World in seeking greener, freer pastures in America. While it is true that America has benefitted from these influences, it is also true that the disagreement between cultures and ethnic groups has led to great strife between the people. However, where the country had flourished, it had flourished for the initiative of its people, who had shared a lot more in common than they had believed.

For one, they had largely appreciated the value of hard work, and they had arrived upon the shores of America prepared to be the architects of their own lives and their own fortunes; and they had prioritized their own families, their faiths, and their communities. In this way, the assimilation to American culture long meant to embrace initiative, hard work, personal responsibility and commitment to faith, family, and community. While the myriad cultural distinctions between Americans at the time were not insignificant, they were at least in mutual agreement over the most important of principles, in the very same way that a healthy diet is in agreement with the necessary components to sustain life.

Insofar as the melting pot analogy holds up, it is as a reference to the mixture produced by blending different ingredients which together produce a healthy, if not delightful, combination. Of course, it is worth noting that this analogy, just as with its social counterpart, has its limits. Indeed, not all combinations and mixtures can be made to work; not all beliefs and world views are compatible or practical. Similarly, not all social influences can peacefully coexist, and certain markers are available to the people, both socially and economically, to alert them to dysfunction, just as their senses inform them of the risks and rancidity of food.

In this way, the objective of any melting pot, whether in the kitchen or in any proper analogy, is to facilitate healthy, stable combinations of ingredients that improve the quality and harmony of the entire mixture. In this way, the limits of the analogy become obvious: it is not a variety or diversity of ingredients which is desired from the melting pot, but rather an optimal combination of ingredients which complement one another. While this might necessitate some variety or "diversity" of ingredients, this is merely incidental to the desired outcome.

Put another way, it is not the variety or diversity of ingredients which is desired, but rather social harmony and economic productivity. While some measure of variety or diversity might produce the desired result, one must not conclude that variety or diversity is a rule or a necessary standard in and of itself, anything more or less than incidental to the desired outcome. In the same way that only certain ingredients can be made to work in any mixture, just as exercise and diet can be made to work only in some kind of moderation, the social melting pot can be described in much the same way: where there is too much diversity or variety, whether in culture, philosophy, morality, resourcefulness or a particular lack thereof, it can be said that a society will suffer dysfunction in the same way that bad food causes illness or indigestion. Wherever the tell-tale signs emerge as evidence of a poor mixture, it is absolutely essential that the mixture be reformulated, that the signs of the dysfunction are heeded, and that they continually inspire us to appreciate those limits and to investigate what went wrong.

The lesson here is that we ought not to conclude that, where any principle or axiom is taken for granted, it must necessarily remain true everywhere and in the extreme. While it can plausibly be stated that America has acted as a giant melting pot for peoples, customs and cultures from around the world, the country is not immune to dysfunction, and it will not benefit from *every* imaginable form of diversity. On the contrary, it is their agreement and the common ground that, despite those cultural differences, enabled them to coexist peacefully and productively in the first place.

In many cases, the kind of diversity which today distinguishes some people, or some groups, is in the abstract or, in a similar vein, the absurd. Whereas those cultural differences once meant minor or relatively innocuous differences in faith, tradition, superstition and fare, the differences which distinguish many today are in forms totally unhinged from reality and completely born from a sense of confusion, inadequacy, or outright contempt.

These are not only highly unproductive forms of "diversity", but dangerously toxic forms to boot. They not only serve to compromise the health, integrity and safety of the individual who entertains these notions, but they pose a very similar risk to all of society at large. After all, society is not a static body of people; it is dynamic, susceptible to changes and influences of various kinds, not least of which those embraced for their "diversity" or uniqueness.

This is just to reinforce the point that "diversity" is neither the worthwhile objective of any process, system or society, nor the justified beneficiary of the melting pot analogy. After all, the melting pot serves primarily to blend and to enhance, not merely to achieve complexity for its own sake, much less to embrace each possible ingredient. Indeed, if the people are not scrupulous about the ingredients, they will be left with a melted mess. It is a mess relished by the many who fancy themselves "progressive", who resent the very prospect of assimilation, but only in their own country; who are, indeed, eager to cast themselves as sophisticates, who are prepared to cast blame anywhere and everywhere except where it belongs; who have together come to epitomize the modern American.

In fancying themselves "progressive", modern Americans indeed pride themselves in "progressing" beyond their prior traditions, in unquestioningly embracing any and all foreign cultures, regardless of attitudes, critical differences, or threats posed.

Indeed, modern Americans have long been in the process of abandoning or even completely forgetting their own traditions, opting instead to stand in solidarity, to stand in the crowd, but to stand for nothing on their own. It is in precisely this way that a people and their traditions are surrendered or squeezed out of existence. Whether through war or indoctrination, the results are just the same: the erasure of one people who are too weak, too gullible, or too feckless, for the benefit of others who stand firm and are ready to do whatever is necessary to defend their own kind.

Ultimately, assimilation is positively essential to a scalable and sustainable society. It is, indeed, necessary for a state of liberty that a people enter into it prepared to assimilate, not only on the basis of culture and values but primarily with respect to ethics and personal responsibility, with respect for the life and property of one's fellow man. Without this kind of assimilation, it is only a matter of time until that civilization begins to break down.

Of course, despite this explanation and the irrefutable evidence to support it, the most incorrigible of socialists never admit defeat. Even in the aftermath of their failed programs and perspectives, and even in the face of social ruin, they claim that "it wasn't *real* socialism". Of course, the truth is that this *is "real* socialism", only its proponents are incredulous to the results. By any other measure or definition, "*real* socialism" is simply unachievable. Whatever the ends, they are always corrupted by the means.

Indeed, upon every failed attempt, and ultimately that is to say *every* attempt, its champions insist that it *is* not, or *was* not, "real" socialism; that, due to human error or forces beyond its control, the administration had failed to see the process through to its ideal conclusion. In still other cases, it is claimed that it is not "real" socialism because, it is said, the system in question merely shares some of the characteristics of socialism; of course the latter being true until the inevitable point of failure, whereafter, on seemingly every occasion, the socialist can then insist that the means had been corrupted along the way, entirely independent of the forces inherent to the proposed system, and that, therefore, the system had failed after having never fully developed into "real" socialism after all. Of course, the most brilliant aspect of this argument is that there will *never* be a program which satisfies the arbitrary standard for "real" socialism, for the fact that the ends are so ill-defined, for the fact that the utopian vision is, as a whole, entirely unachievable, and for the fact that it is predestined for failure on every occasion, so long as human nature remains as it is.

Indeed, socialism of any variety is ultimately doomed for failure, the power necessary to get things started inexorably condemning it to the same fate. It is only upon realizing this fate that it is regarded by its apologists as "not real socialism"; one plea in a long line of such variations of the "no true Scotsman" fallacy.

History decrees, unfortunately, that the socialists never learn from the past. They show up time and again in only slightly different disguises, brimming with confidence and claiming that "this time is different". They make any number of excuses for the historical record, wherever they dare to even acknowledge it: whether it is bad weather, plunging export prices, inadequate compliance, too few programs or too little money, "bigotry" or the plain stupidity of their predecessors, they will blame anything but socialism itself. In each case of unavoidable failure, they are always ready to point to some other factor or -ism. Indeed, what might otherwise be described as *Stalinism* or *Leninism*, et al., is merely another failed attempt at Leftism, the latter always finding cover under the names of new dictators. Whatever the case, the Leftists are always ready to try again, always ready to blame everyone else for every conceivable problem, and always readying for their next assault upon the public and their liberty.

The socialists are everywhere armed with slogans and compassionate-sounding pleas, ranging from scaremongering (in the form of manmade climate change) to the false premise that certain people are doomed to their stations in life, that there is no economic mobility, and that their only salvation can come in the form of government. Ironically — admittedly, the most clever of socialists understand this — the government's response predictably results in only greater adversity, poverty and, in many cases, inequality. Conveniently for the socialists, this only bolsters their ranks as confusion and despondency leave them desperately searching for quick fixes and easy solutions. Indeed, one of the primary objectives of the Leftists is to trap the people in an elaborate maze of lies, to immobilize them by keeping them in a constant state of confusion and desperation.

The psychiatrist Dr. Martin Schotz of Brookline, Massachusetts, put it this way:

"It is so important to understand that one of the primary means of immobilizing the American people politically today is to hold them in a state of confusion, in which anything can be believed but nothing can be known — nothing of significance, that is. And the American people are more than willing to be held in this state because to know the truth, as opposed to only believe the truth, is to face an awful terror and to be no longer able to evade responsibility. It is precisely in moving from belief to knowledge that the citizen moves from irresponsibility to responsibility, from helplessness and hopelessness to action, with the ultimate aim of being empowered and confident in one's rational powers."

This is precisely why Americans must reclaim and embrace their identity, and why they must do so unapologetically; and this is precisely why the state so eagerly seeks to silence and discourage them. At a 1993 candlelight ceremony in Dallas, Texas, author Gaeton Fonzi characterized this identity in his own words, describing it as *the very soul of this country*: in describing his view of that which distinguishes Americans from the rest of the world, he pointed to "the innocent, untarnished belief — naive, perhaps, but gloriously, constantly self-fulfilling — that we are the free-willed possessors of our own destiny."

Mr. Fonzi is surely not alone in his assessment. It is a view shared by many throughout the history of the United States. In fact, in describing the "mysterious factor of difference" which has "wrought such a strangely different result here in our country," as opposed to the "fate of Europe... [which is] to be always a battleground," President Calvin Coolidge concluded in his speech, titled *The Genius of America*, delivered October 16, 1924, to a delegation of foreign-born citizens, that "[i]t was not a single factor but the united workings of at least three forces, that brought about the wide difference." President Coolidge went on to characterize a culture of tolerance unique to the United States, which had demonstrated "peace, harmony and cooperation" in helping "to rid [the countries of the Old World] of the bad traditions, the ancient animosities, the long established hostilities":

"Among these I should place, first, the broadly tolerant attitude that has been characteristic of this country. I use the word in its most inclusive sense, to cover tolerance of religious opinion, tolerance in politics, tolerance in social relationships; in general, the liberal attitude of every citizen toward his fellows. It is this factor which has preserved to all of us that equality of opportunity which enables every American to become the architect of whatever fortune he deserves."

Upon reading President Coolidge's speech, one learns of a number of important American themes, not least of which is the theme of opportunity for those of initiative. However, for the purposes of this particular writing, we shall focus on the importance of the term "tolerance" in the American purview, the particular sort of which, presently taken wildly out of context, inspired so many visitors and immigrants to the shores of the New World.

As President Coolidge described in his speech, it has been a "universal tolerance" which has largely distinguished the United States from the Old World, in particular a "universal tolerance" and "liberal attitude" toward religious opinion, politics, social relationships, and his fellow citizens. By this liberal attitude, of course, President Coolidge meant little more than an attitude of "universal tolerance" whereby one's fellow citizen was unmolested and spared the persecution of the Old World, left generally to "become the architect of [his life and] whatever fortune he deserves."

The reader of the modern age, however, would be quick to translate this "tolerance" into a twisted and expedient form of "acceptance" or "endorsement", but this would amount to a gross misinterpretation of the term and a betrayal of the "natural and correct attitude of mind for each" American. As described by President Coolidge:

"It is the natural and correct attitude of mind for each of us to have regard for our own race and the place of our own origin. There is abundant room here for the preservation and development of the many divergent virtues that are characteristic of the different races which have made America their home. They ought to cling to all these virtues and cultivate them tenaciously. It is my own belief that in this land of freedom new arrivals should especially keep up their devotion to religion."

In his speech, President Coolidge goes to great lengths to characterize the American form of "tolerance" which had distinguished, and arguably continues to distinguish, the United States from the Old World. Far from "endorsing" or broadly "accepting" divergent views or values, President Coolidge celebrates a particular willingness to tolerate those divergences. Indeed, he bolsters this position with his belief that Americans "ought to cling to all these virtues and cultivate them tenaciously." Take notice of the fact that

President Coolidge neither lightly suggests nor even strongly recommends that Americans cling to their virtues; on the contrary, he commands that they "ought" to cling to them and cultivate them "tenaciously".

This command from President Coolidge is one which critically clarifies the meaning of "tolerance" in his speech, one which surely transcends time in the way that it catalogs the sentiments and objectives of its time, and just as importantly the various lessons it affords Americans today: Americans who desperately need to appreciate the value and meaning of "tolerance", who need to be reminded of the value and purpose of their "views" and "virtues", and who need to remember how to develop and protect them along with their continued tolerance for others.

After all, whether in the confusion, some newfound hope or identity, or in their zeal for some new and progressive cause, many have willingly abandoned their values in favor of life without any. President Coolidge spoke prophetically on this very trend: "Disregarding the need of the individual for a religious life, I feel that there is a more urgent necessity, based on the requirements of good citizenship and the maintenance of our institutions, for devotion to religion in America than anywhere else in the world. One of the greatest dangers that beset those coming to this country, especially those of the younger generation, is that they will fall away from the religion of their fathers, and never become attached to any other faith."

In their abandonment of religious conviction, whether in faith or in principle, America degrades the institutions which serve to stave off internal destruction. As Henry Grady Weaver so eloquently articulated in his 1947 work *The Mainspring of Human Progress*, "Our habit of self-criticism, which is so largely responsible for our progress, makes us particularly vulnerable to distorted propaganda which exaggerates our deficiencies and holds out false promises of a short cut to the millennium."

Weaver continues:

"Thus it is that some of our most patriotic, high-minded, and well-meaning citizens succumb to the overtures of those who would make them the innocent tools of subversion. The fact that we are a progressive and open-minded people, always on the alert for new ideas, makes us susceptible to old ideas when they are attractively camouflaged and presented as something new. Being a hospitable, tolerant, and fair-minded people, we are inclined to consider both sides of every question."

Weaver then cautions the reader:

"That's all right up to a point, but when it comes to the eternal verities of moral truth, there are no two sides to the question. Right is right, and wrong is wrong; and any concession to the pagan viewpoint — whether in the name of expediency or open-mindedness — paves the way for the destruction of all moral values."

It is in this way that the agents of destruction bore from within; it is by the grace of the politically indifferent and their widespread "tolerance" of toxic notions among them that their liberty, along with their principles and their heritage, are compromised. Whether an earnest endeavor in faith or toward truth, ideally with one inspiring a strong conviction in the other, it is important to never compromise on the important values, lessons and truths they produce.

While politicians, from time immemorial, have long exploited the decency and respectability of the people, the case is little different for the peoples of the United States who have championed tolerance and who have thereby been swindled into gradually sacrificing their own convictions and values at the altar of allowable opinion and political correctness. The time has long since passed that Americans "ought to cling to [their] virtues and cultivate them tenaciously." They must first reclaim them.

As President Coolidge concluded in his speech, the best method for promoting this action, for maintaining all of our high ideals, for helping other lands and other peoples, is by giving undivided allegiance to America, maintaining its institutions, and, by leaving it internally harmonious, making it eternally powerful, as an example to the rest of the world, in promoting a reign of justice and mercy throughout the Earth.

Leftism, on the other hand, ushers in a reign of darkness, that megalithic system opposed to the individual, his will, his family and his preferred values. Far from the shining example to the rest of the world, the Leftists seek to erase the individual, to dismantle the nuclear family, and to destroy traditional values, indeed preferring to subject the people to the will of the state, and thus the politicians who are to decide what is in their best interest. In truth, the socialist agenda destroys every aspect of human existence, beginning with its economic ramifications. In setting out to achieve nirvana, which proves everywhere elusive, the administration will invariably require prohibitively high taxes, progressively higher inflation, and progressively more control to boot, each of which decelerates economic growth and impairs society's ability to sustainably meet the proposed ends. In truth, as the author George Orwell once quipped, Leftists are motivated not by some love for the poor, but by their hatred for success.

A twisted form of envy and greed, they seek to pillage and plunder, to tear down society and any among them who have enjoyed any measure of success, to foment revolution. Under the banners of socialism and equality, they are more appropriately termed agents of violence and coercion. In seeking "equality" over freedom, the socialist, unwittingly or otherwise, prioritizes a kind of "equality" at the expense of prosperity and liberty.

Where society otherwise enjoys higher standards of living, the socialist, in most cases, insists that we dispense with them in favor of "equality"; in other cases, he even admits that equal suffering is preferable to the kind of prosperity that yields any measure of inequality. For the socialist, in this sense, it is not important that the member of society have the opportunity to improve his lot in life or that he enjoy a higher standard of living; on the contrary, the socialist prefers that every member of society be spared the agony of witnessing others achieve.

Even the egalitarians, who seek *equality* or, more precisely, who seek to condense life into this context, serve either incidentally or intentionally to bring the proles into equal standing under the dominion of the state. Their equal standing, as characterized, breeds subservience to an all-powerful state which has succeeded in bringing about an equality between the peoples; that is, despite their progressive suffering which invariably finds its justification in the state, a state which they have all been made to serve.

Depending on the point of view, this is either accidental and unforeseen or intentional and by design. Indeed, one aspect commonly overlooked by the protestor advocating for "equality" is that she is actually promoting the notion that she herself, among everybody else, is not and shall never be regarded as "special". Needless to say, this is not her intention, not what she truly believes about herself, and, in most cases, not remotely what she intends to convey; rather, she intends to use this ploy (and the appointed "victims") to her advantage, to elevate herself in social standing amongst her peers while tearing down the people whom she envies and regards as members of the "privileged" class. Seldom, however, is there a Leftist who possesses enough integrity to be so honest. Of course, if the Leftist were to truly possess any integrity, she would not be a Leftist for long; and if she were truly intelligent, she would have never become one.

CHAPTER XII

"SOCIAL JUSTICE"

Leftists are masters of deceit, always clever enough to march under the banners of *social justice* and the like, to conceal their motives through the most fashionable and deceptive of language. The scourge of feminism is just one of the various devices employed, and it aids the Leftists in a variety of ways: first, by mobilizing women against men, their protectors, whom they demonize as part of "the patriarchy", the belief that men possess all of the power in society; the irony, of course, being that women wield more power than they think.

Women not only birth and raise the men, but women then decide which men are worthy of sex, which are worthy of their love and their affection; and, therefore, which traits are most desirable, and then, by extension, which are worthy of the future. In this sense, women possess the greatest power in all of the world, and men have historically inherited the responsibility to provide and to protect, and to thereby ensure the survival of both the culture and this very arrangement.

Indeed, men have, historically and necessarily, been the primary defenders of the culture and the family. It is for this reason that the political participation of women is so dangerous: not because they are less valuable but because they are so precious to civilized society that their participation is virtually unimpeachable. It is not only a matter of women's susceptibility to emotion over reason but a matter of their distinct immunity against the ramifications of their politics: at the personal level, women are not drafted into war; they assume a smaller fraction of the costs; and they are assessed not for their ability to reason, but on the basis of their beauty, their grace, their compassion, and their ability to love and nurture.

In their desire for love and intimacy, men will go to the greatest of lengths to please, impress and defend women, even if this means defying logic and abandoning their own principles and beliefs. There is virtually no limit to how far men will go for women and how much men will tolerate and endure in their defense. This is what makes women's participation in politics particularly dangerous to any civilization, and why men — as the primary providers and defenders, and as the more logical of thinkers (on average) — ought exclusively to inherit the sole responsibility and privilege of political participation. This is not to suggest that women are less valuable than men, but that — insofar as government and politics are concerned — civilization, liberty and property are, historically, best served by the steady and calculated judgment of men.

Unfortunately for posterity, those objects are always subject to the incredulousness of the Left, the uncompromising who seek to reorganize society around their edicts under the veil of the ill-defined *common good,* merely an expedient disguise for their great heist. In the name of so-called *social justice,* the Leftists succeed not only by pitting women against men in the realm of politics but by bringing women into competition with men for jobs; by encouraging broken families and single motherhood through alimony and government subsidies; by promoting and even celebrating abortion and promiscuity, thereby compromising the sanctity of life and intimacy, the latter serving as one of the many reasons that so many undervalue the life of the unborn, that so many are so cavalier about the subject of abortion.

Indeed, the topic of abortion is yet another in a long line of insights into the true spirit of Leftism and its complete disregard for the value and the sanctity of life: split into a few particular camps, there are the purists who oppose abortion outright; there are others who are supportive or tolerant of abortion on specific grounds, such as medical complications, rape or incest; then there are those who once described themselves as "pro-choice" but who have come to prefer the title "pro-abortion" as an extension of their wider belief system. Lacking the moral and ethical constitution to appreciate the wickedness of their ideology, they also lack an understanding of the Constitution of the United States, a lethal combination, to be sure.

Upon carefully considering the issue of abortion, this author has become rather curious about whether the "pro-choice" camp would endorse the freedom to terminate the life of an infant; of course, this curiosity is more rhetorical than anything, knowing full well the Left's view on *freedom*. However, we shall uncover here the contradiction in any argument in support of abortion, any argument claiming to be "pro-choice" (albeit only selectively, in most instances only in this particular case).

In considering this issue, it becomes apparent that only a nuanced distinction separates the born from the unborn, chiefly the former's visible existence in our world. The unborn, on the other hand, often reside out of sight and out of mind, leaving the physical bonds between mother and child to produce a sense of power and confuse our sense of *right* and *wrong*.

After all, these bonds are not severed after birth. On the contrary, they merely change their forms. Indeed, during the child's infancy and even throughout his childhood, the offspring remains intimately attached to his parents, albeit not as physically as he once did through his umbilical cord.

Nevertheless, the born and the unborn share mutually in their dependency upon the mother, who could theoretically decide at any time that she is unfit to raise a child. This dependency, then, cannot independently justify or excuse the decision to abort a child, let alone any *right* to do so.

Of course, many impassioned activists and casual comment-ers share in the opinion that every woman should decide for herself whether to continue with the pregnancy, and whether the unborn baby should live or die; the kind of power relished by the members of the Left. Ordinarily, however, for reasons that are fairly obvious, those of this camp avoid framing the subject in this fashion. Instead, they obsess exclusively over the *rights* of the woman, who is, of course, conveniently among the born to do her own bidding. Who, then, will do the bidding of the unborn? Are they without any *rights*? With this in mind, there are the unavoidable questions:

At what stage does the mother lose her *right* to abortion? What is it about that particular stage that qualifies that lifeform for extra protections, whereas just moments earlier that lifeform is deemed expendable? Oftentimes, in the context of this discussion, the members of the "pro-choice" camp claim that the mother ought to reserve the right to decide the appropriate course for her body, to determine whether she wishes to continue with her pregnancy.

This notion seems to stand at odds against the rights of the baby, a baby as alive as the mother, distinguished by dependency on the mother until birth, a notion imploring us to contemplate whether the unborn are people or whether they are to be classified as property instead. For, if the baby is indeed a person, one would be hard-pressed to explain why that baby fails to qualify for the basic human right of life. What's more, wherever *rights* are concerned, they certainly cannot coexist with the compromise of another's; if this were the case, they simply would not be *rights*.

A simple thought exercise demonstrates the point. All reasonable people agree that, once born, a baby enjoys the full suite of rights; that a mother cannot legally abort her child once born. Furthermore, all reasonable people agree that, once born, no other party has the *right* to terminate that child's life. Now, from the perspective of all reasonable people, the same rings true for any unborn baby: no other party possesses the *right* to terminate the unborn baby's life.

Even from the perspective of the *pro-choice* camp, they claim that the *right* of abortion comes from the consent of the mother. At issue here, of course, is whether the mother even possesses that *right* to begin with. However, it is clear that if another party, such as a doctor or any medical professional, were to unilaterally perform an abortion, those persons and all witting participants would be charged with murder. It is just the same for any who murders a pregnant woman: it is rightly considered double-homicide.

Now, in the scope of murder, any and all who carry it out are liable in a court of law; no one enjoys any special privilege for his or her relationship to the victim, and there is certainly not a person among us who possesses the *right* to kill another human being. While a person may formally endow another with the *power* to act in his or her interest (i.e. power of attorney), in some cases including the *power* to terminate the consenting person's life, no person can endow another with the *right* to kill. After all, there is no *right* to kill; there is only the *right* to self-defense, the defense of private property, and the immediate defense of others.

Bearing in mind these facts, the mother who aborts her unborn child is a murderer all the same; she operates only from her intent and her self-regard, without any regard for the unborn baby who is, needless to say, unable to offer consent. In rare cases, the mother may act in accordance with her own self-preservation; indeed, on rare occasions the life of the mother, while suffering from pregnancy complications, may be jeopardized by childbirth.

However, self-preservation does not constitute self-defense. Indeed, such a case does not meet that standard, as it is not the baby who directly and intentionally poses a threat; it is rather the attending medical condition which threatens the mother's life.

Ultimately, wherever any murder is committed, regardless of one's relationship to the victim, it is murder all the same. In the court of law, there is no difference between a mother who murders her child and anyone else who commits the murder: they are guilty all the same. Whoever commits that act upon an unborn baby is just as guilty; whereas a jury would quickly convict any third party in the matter, they ought to hold the mother to that same standard. She does not have the *right* to kill her child, and, regardless of the ongoing debate, she does not possess the *right* to kill her unborn baby.

The intent and the outcome are the two material considerations in the Highest court of law, as they ought to be in ours. Just as no person, neither a doctor nor a parent nor anyone else, possesses the *right* to kill a child, no person possesses the *right* to kill a fetus.

So the abortion debate is not really a question about whether the state — or any government — has authority over decisions affecting the body of any woman, or any person for that matter; rather, it is a question about whether the contrived *right* of abortion trumps the baby's *right* to life. Likewise, this becomes a debate about whether a baby is a person or a form of property, whether a baby has *rights*, and when those *rights* are finally recognized in society: a difficult yet fundamental philosophical consideration, to be sure.

With this in mind, it seems just as difficult to distinguish between the stage in which a baby is believed to be expendable and that in which the baby warrants the same protections of life afforded to the rest of us.

As a mental exercise, let us imagine a pregnant woman who decides that she wishes to continue with childbirth. Unfortunately, this woman later decides that she no longer wants to keep the baby, so she puts her baby up for adoption. In this particular case, one cannot help but wonder why she does not at this time also reserve the right to terminate the baby instead of going through the onerous process of adoption. When and why did she lose that *right*, and why did she even possess that *right* in the first place?

For the purposes of this conversation, let us assume that a *right* is any thing or course of action to which any person is entitled. With this definition, we can safely assume that every person reserves the *right* to reasonably defend himself against a legitimate threat, on the basis of his *right* to life; likewise, that person reserves the *right* to even kill another in self-defense. However, in order to justify a position of self-defense, one must have reasonably feared that her life was endangered by the assailant; this is precisely where a given case is met with a measure of subjectivity. In this particular case, when is a position of self-defense deemed justifiable? At what moment and under what circumstances is a given person's life truly threatened, and how do we determine whether the killing or the form of self-defense was proportionate to the threat?

Well, this is where attorneys and academics complicate the issue, and consequently laws abound attempting to define and then redefine that which is *justified* or *reasonable*, but most *reasonable* people agree — and prevailing law has long supported this — that people reserve the *right* to self-defense, and most of those people, albeit a marginally smaller number, believe that this *right* includes the *right* to kill in self-defense.

In this particular context, the *right* to self-defense, along with the *right* to kill under such circumstances, is valid not merely for ethical reasons but for pragmatic purposes. For instance, it would not be very practical to arrange a society around the notion that people cannot defend themselves against harm, that they are assumed defenseless under the threat of assault or murder. The result of any such social order would inevitably be a society ruled by assailants over a shrinking population of people so paralyzed with fear that they are unable to accomplish much of anything. The people, who might otherwise be productive members of society, would thereby decline in their productivity for fear of losing it to the opportunist or, in still other cases, by joining them to instead exploit their peers who are vulnerable in the absence of their *right* to self-defense.

What, then, can be said about the *rights* of the unborn? Is it practical to promote a social order around the notion that people are expendable, that they can be killed or terminated at one's discretion, or so long as they have not reached a given stage of development?

How do we reconcile this standard with that which applies to any other form of permissible killing? Are people deprived of the *right* to life so long as they are underdeveloped? Are they deprived of this *right* in favor of some other *right* enjoyed by one person, the mother, at the expense of another person, the unborn child? Are *rights* endowed upon birth or upon conception? Are *rights* negotiable — in this case for the interests of the mother? If they are negotiable, are they even *rights*?

Ultimately, in the course of evaluating *rights*, we arrive at the principle of ownership: in the context of the mother, many are eager to recognize that the mother owns herself and her own body, but those same people seem reluctant to extend that principle to the unborn child. In still other cases, they do not even extend that principle beyond the subject of abortion; one such example being their denial of medical freedom, as shown in the case of COVID-19.

With that being said, when and why does a child transition from property to person? What, in particular, constitutes this important metamorphosis from expendable property to full-fledged human being endowed with the same inalienable *rights* as every other person?

While this author is willing to concede that civilization might stand to benefit from the reduction in the number of those born to unfit mothers, the expected benefit is proposed *in theory*, limited in duration, and merely incidental. More importantly, however, in seeking not only to *tolerate* abortion, but to make it *acceptable*, we may then run the risk of continually increasing its incidence, encouraging the practice, and trivializing the significance of life and sexual intercourse; this is a mighty risk for a civilization already so cavalier in its attitudes toward life, sex and personal responsibility.

It is worth noting that these risks extend not only to the unborn baby, but to the psychological wellbeing of the parents, primarily mothers, who are left to regret their irreversible decision in later years. Herein we find an inarguable constant: the importance of mothers and fathers educating their children to make responsible decisions. It is in just this way that we stand to eliminate ninety-nine percent of abortions.

Instead, however, in their haste to support *women's rights*, the *pro-choice* crowd fails to appreciate that they are actually championing irresponsibility. Just as importantly, they fail to appreciate that there are no *women's rights*, only *human rights*; just as there is no justice for society (i.e. "social justice"), only justice for the individual. Of course, they are interested not in the truth but what gets them ahead: that which lets them off the hook or promotes their agenda. They are not interested in responsibility, because, in their estimation, it gets in the way of having fun. According to them, it is just not as fun as taking risks and being unaccountable to the consequences.

From their point of view, responsibility is for old fuddy-duddies who need to get with the times. Fortunately, some of the old fuddy-duddies still remember the value of their traditions. With their help and the benefit of some maturation on the part of the youth, it is still possible (albeit improbable) that responsibility will win out democratically. Ultimately, society will either flourish in its presence or founder in its absence. Either way, responsibility *will* eventually prevail; it will either prevail through its adoption or it will return upon the ruins of civilization.

Regardless of whether we are to institutionalize the concept through the power of law, it will remain one worthy of instilling in our offspring for their own betterment and the collective betterment of society. After all, neither the individual nor society is made any better off for committing these mistakes. For these reasons, the abortion debate ought to center squarely on the question of how we wish to discourage those mistakes, whether generally by law, locally by the same, or informally through peers, friends and family.

In nearly every case, abortion is the consequence of some series of bad decisions; ones inexcusable against any honest measure of responsibility. Whether we are to penalize the misbehavior formally or informally, the desirable outcome remains the same: greater measures of responsibility, fewer unplanned pregnancies, and consequently fewer abortions and fewer impingements on the *rights* of some for the benefit of others who have been casually irresponsible with theirs.

The debate around the means, whether federal, state or local legislation, often serves to distract from the more agreeable ends. In determining which means are justified, we must determine how they are best administered: in this case, just as with most forms of government, the more local the governance and the stricter the accountability, the better.

The matter of abortion, then, as with others under the name of *progressivism* and *social justice*, operates not just from the denial of the construction of the American republic but from the denial of personal responsibility, and the selective denial of rights to some, the unborn and the unrepresented, in granting special privileges to others. Indeed, in the name of so-called *social justice*, the Leftists succeed in completely altering the composition of, and the prevailing attitudes within, society: the moral and ethical constitution of the public, the people's beliefs around *right* and *wrong*, the proper priorities within society, and, as has been shown, life itself.

Indeed, such designs are evidenced by the prioritization of career advancement and social status over family and motherhood; by the discouraging of motherhood altogether through the cause of the "independent" and "liberated" woman; by the inspiring of women to abandon their children (and to leave them in the care of some other party) in pursuit of career development, to serve not their own families but CEOs and shareholders; by the prioritization of financial and material gain, as well as other selfish wants and objectives, over the needs and the development of their children; by the defiling and identifying of men as the enemy, thereby eliminating respect, decency, and honor; by rejecting masculinity in favor of meekness, thereby weakening men in their roles as providers and protectors, both at home and against evil-doers.

In this way, men and women alike are brought under the dominion of the state as fungible soldiers or slaves, not one of whom could possibly conquer their master; after all, they are all equals in dress, appearance, strength and competency, or so they have been conditioned to think. In this supposed state of equality, anyone who might dare to counter the convention is thus made a lunatic or a heretic. In this way, the subjects of the state are fooled into perpetual slavery under the banner of equality, which serves only to bring the people into a nearly equal form of misery. Meanwhile, the state basks in the bounty laid at its table by those who would not dare to suggest that they are anything more or less than equal.

When any people are finally convinced of their equality or otherwise made to submit to this fiction, by definition none is exceptional enough to challenge the authorities and the overlords who determine the status quo, and with it the proposed purpose of life and human capital. In their supposed equality, stripped of their identity and individuality as of their property, they are ultimately stripped of every last authority they retained over their governments, themselves and the property they once considered their own.

In the achievement of equality, they are swindled into a form of political equality whereby the masses are assumed equal in their submission to the new status quo and the regime which fleeces and commands the masses effortlessly and at will. In the achievement of this equality, indeed the only form achievable in the pursuit of equal outcome, they are made to be roughly equal only in misery, destitution and subordination to the regime which commands and rules over them; a destitution which affects a people spiritually, philosophically and economically.

Where they share in that misery, there is not just a growing resignation to their fate but a great many who invite more of it upon their fellow man. In this state, they are constantly scrambling to condescend, belittle, degrade, and disparage their fellow man in order to compensate. They seek selfishly and vainly to cope, to ease their misery at the expense of others; to elevate themselves by putting others down, heaping more troubles upon them, or enlisting henchmen to make their lives worse. They seek likewise to preserve their own perceived status, to humiliate or make a mockery of others so as to make them more miserable, to find joy in others' misery, and to keep themselves from having to truly deal with their own. That is precisely why, under socialism, the decline of society is perpetual; the people, in their misery, starving for more and more company, and through this the consolation that nobody among them is better off or of higher status, a state which serves to enable more and more of the same. The end of this misery shall come only upon the reversal of this practice, the bucking of the conventions, and the determination of the people to sever their bonds with those who wish them ill. As the Greek philosopher Epictetus put it, "The key is to keep company only with people who uplift you, whose presence calls forth your best."

Not only do the degenerates of the Left seek to bring forth the worst amongst themselves, but they aim to bring out the worst in every person and every thing; to promote negativity, scorn and self-pity; to punish success and mock righteous living; to erase the individual and to suspend his pursuit of happiness, to envelop the people in shared misery and to forbid joy to any who has not first obtained approval through the requisite channels. The outcome of this is an interminable misery, and a perpetual one, indeed.

Any endeavor toward equality, then, not in the form of *equality under the law* but in the form of *outcome over opportunity*, serves primarily to bring the people into equal suffering and equal subordination, and to snuff out any leftover resistance guarding or representing the former traditions. Any endeavor toward equality, then, not in the form of *equality under the law* but in the form of *outcome over opportunity*, serves to render the people equally hopeless and powerless, equally insignificant and inconsequential, serving to condemn the people to a rough equality in suffering and subordination, and to extinguish the resistance and their former traditions; traditions in some cases to some degree once enshrined within some form of defined and limited government.

As in the case of Adolf Hitler, three years after he came to power over Germany's Third Reich, in a speech to the old fighters at the Bürgerbräukeller on the anniversary evening on the 9th of November, 1936, he explained one of the objectives he had had in developing the Nazi Party into such a formidable and all-embracing organization: "We recognized," he said in recalling the days when the National Socialist German Workers' Party (NSDAP) was being reformed after the Kapp Putsch, "that it is not enough to overthrow the old state, but that the new state must previously have been built up and be practically ready to one's hand"; that it be "built up" through the existing government and the existing constitution, so far as the first can be abused and the second can be loosely interpreted to serve the party's ends; that the people are thereby kept none the wiser to the trajectory of the state, and in many cases the true extent and character of the revolution which is underway, or which has already taken place. Thereafter, the party is finally able and indeed called to destroy any remnants of the old state, which, in the case of the Nazi Party, took merely a few hours.

In keeping with the Marxist playbook, so as to bring about their extermination, those former traditions are to be so thoroughly attacked as to leave only the most adamant, courageous, competent and fearless of men to defend them, ranks that are always few in number and declining all the time. The politicians and the bureaucrats always have the advantage in this contest. Like queue-jumpers, they impose upon their fellow man, placing him in the awkward and lonely situation of having to defend his position or otherwise lose it. Like the queue-jumpers, the politicians tend to get their way over the people, who are, more often than not, either unaware or unlikely to make a fuss. Of course, the politicians are far less conspicuous in their impositions, so they get away with far more heinous crimes than the queue-jumpers, and they succeed in part by appealing to their victims.

Indeed, they are everywhere promoting positive-sounding policies, winning the approval of the masses with little more than enthusiasm to support their visions, while leaving the sober and honest, and thus far less popular, students to piece it all together and make sense of the mess in order to explain what eventually went wrong. Unfortunately, by the time any thorough study has been concluded and its findings have been published, too few will care to review them, and the politicians will have already moved on to their next foolhardy policy bound to compound the very problems they created and never took the time to truly understand. Indeed, a great measure of our troubles, as both peoples and individuals, would be swiftly averted by thinking more patiently and speaking more carefully, in most cases not speaking at all. Of course, where the few adhere to this wisdom, there are the many who trample over them; this is as true of those in society as in government. Indeed, history shows that there is scarcely any government possessing or promoting these qualities. Instead, the establishment sets out with haste to tilt the scales in its favor.

Make no mistake, every government initiative serves to test the people's tolerance for tyranny, the mettle in their convictions, and their faith in their ancient principles. Whether meddling in domestic affairs or intervening in foreign engagements, whether abusing the public or conquering foreign lands, the state repeatedly tramples man's civil liberties and stretches the limits of its powers until the people eventually come to accept all of it.

Once their faith and their convictions are exceeded by those of the ideologues, and as soon as the ideologues are more willing to lie down their lives for their movement, the cause of liberty is in peril. With the people's support or in their silence, their acquiescence to the usurpations and unlawful commands of government confirms that the despots are completely in control of their rights. Rights that were once deemed natural, derived from our Creator, are gradually redefined as privileges administered or permitted by that government formerly entrusted to defend those rights; governments which, according to Martin Luther, "have bound us with their canon law and robbed us of our rights so that we have to buy them back again with money" or urgent pleas, or otherwise accept the losses.

Over time, in gaining the ill-placed trust of the public, the establishment fortifies its defenses and systematically strips the people of theirs, just before having its way with them and their rights. Indeed, Leftism accustoms the people to getting punched in the mouth, and, through a complicated bureaucracy, having to justify their actions in self-defense (or the defense of their own private property). Eventually, because of the power of the bureaucracy and the difficulty in defending oneself against it, the people stop fighting back or stop defending themselves altogether, opting instead to take the punches and plead for mercy, to bow down to the establishment or to otherwise find clever ways to evade it.

Government pushes against liberty so long as it maintains a hold over some segment of the population, enough to support any campaign, politically or militarily, in order to affirm its institutions. The powers-that-be are always prepared to continue their conquests even so far as to provoke rebellion or assassination; the two representing the best of political outcomes, where, so long as they maintain enough of their constituency, they will be deified and remembered as martyrs for the rest of time.

At such time as rebellion, it is not enough for the rebels to simply stand their ground. Indeed, their mettle will be tested. They will need to see it through to the very end, lest their cause be lost; lest the moment escape them; lest their former government tighten the noose around their necks, or otherwise shatter their spirits (and those of posterity). But rebellion scarcely comes. And government scarcely trembles, for it knows the will and the conviction of the people. It knows that they are at their mercy, and that they require nothing short of a miracle to stand a chance of success. And government is always stacking the odds in its favor, and its subjects are seldom the wiser.

Indeed, the state seeks to be so enveloping, so stifling and ubiquitous that it will make any effort at rebellion seem futile, and even the very thought of it seem dangerous. With the benefit of well-armed security and police, and with a powerful military at their disposal, the tyrants terrorize the public with virtual impunity. The Leftists seek to so thoroughly restrict human action that they render the most significant of action unlawful. They seek to impose so many restrictions, to make them so onerous and paralyzing, indeed, that they themselves necessitate unlawful action and intent in order for the people to exercise their most basic of God-given rights; in order for the people to carry out their business, to defend themselves, and to pursue their various interests.

The restrictions and the impositions become so onerous that they suffocate society, they wear down the individual and make him hopeless; so despondent, in fact, and so depressed that, where people are not dying as a consequence, they are suffering from misery, depression, even thoughts of hostility and suicidal ideation. It is in this way that Leftism kills: not only in the quantity of lives claimed, but in the decline in birth rates, the diminished quality of each life, and the dampened prospects for times ahead.

These restrictions consequently supply the impetus for the people to commit the very "violations" which in turn appear to "justify" still further restrictions and still further condemnation of the people who seek merely to carry on with their lives as normal, who seek to carry on with their lives and their affairs as they are inherently entitled to do so. In due time, the restrictions become so encompassing that they make common criminals out of decent and ordinary people, and they eventually go so far as to necessitate a vocal and physical response by the people, lest they lose any more ground; lest they lose the power or the courage to wage any meaningful resistance at all.

It is, thus, from the comforts and the safety of their offices that despots call for the hollowing out of civilization, the hollowing out of life and the surrendering of dignity among the common man. It is thus that the tyrants whittle the people down in their rights, their honor, and the joys attending their pursuit of happiness. It is, thus, from the safety of their offices that they legislate their way to inducing the last of the resistance into firing their weapons in their last stand for liberty; and it is in the most ironic of twists that the people are always met with agents of the state whom they naively view as their protectors, who wear familiar badges and patches and thereby convince the people that they too are patriotic and that they too are allies of the public.

After all, many Americans today fondly remember *The Andy Griffith Show*, the popular television series that spanned eight seasons from 1960 to 1968. The television show captures the sentiments of a generation and the nostalgia of another, and it represents what law enforcement *could* be.

The show is still especially popular today among conservatives in America, who fondly recall sweeter times and the traditions of a bygone era. The show stars Andy Griffith, the widowed sheriff of the quaint little town of Mayberry, North Carolina. Griffith is the charming and charismatic sheriff who nearly always does right by his community. He is an exemplary citizen and role model who respects his neighbors and leads by example, and he makes people laugh all the while.

Unfortunately, the truth about modern law enforcement in America is far more sinister, yet the politicians are more than happy to exploit the sensibilities of their enemies who remember the good ol' days back in Mayberry.

Have you ever considered how convenient it is for the Left, and for government in general, that "conservatives" and Republicans broadly consider law enforcement their allies? The benefits are manifold: the state can blame their opponents for their own failed policies and abuses of power; they can use their opponents' own allies to force them into compliance, and even to quell or preempt rebellion; they can vilify their opponents for the wrongdoings of their officers; they can further their own political agenda through officers disguised as their opponents' allies, whose disguises even afford the tyrants a friendlier and more familiar disposition. For these reasons and innumerable others, there is nothing more un-American than the people who worship the police (and standing armies for that matter).

Regrettably, even the author's own father has confessed that, as a career law enforcement officer, he was perfectly willing to disobey the Constitution in order to obey a direct order. He has even gone further to claim that, in such cases, it is the responsibility of the judge to figure it out and to effect justice.

Of course, the flaws in this train of thought are many: in such cases, the officers stand to absolve themselves of any responsibility for their actions; they place all of their faith in an unreliable and politically-motivated judicial system; and they stand to suspend the individual's liberty, even on the suspicion that the order is illegitimate or unlawful.

It is always and everywhere the obligation of every officer and every agent of government to uphold and enforce the law of the land, and to accord with the public interest. This means rejecting unlawful orders, even at the risk of losing one's job. After all, those officers are ultimately accountable to the public, the law, and the Almighty who will cast the final judgment on their character, their integrity, and the life they led.

Police officers like to claim that they are public servants, that they go after "bad guys" to "serve and protect" the community, but from their point of view, they cannot help but see "bad guys" everywhere they go. As they see it, their primary tool is the hammer, and the public looks like a bunch of nails.

In modern America, law enforcement officers are trained to view the public as their enemy. They have come to believe that they are accountable not to the Constitution to which they explicitly affirm their allegiance, but to their supervisors, their captains, commissioners and mayors. Truthfully, as far as the officers see it, they are accountable not to the Constitution, which they view with contempt, but to whatever keeps them on the public payroll, whatever keeps them on track for their pensions. As far as they are concerned, they are not in the business of enforcing the law or serving the public; according to them, the public is responsible for respecting *them* and *their* commands, for paying their bills and funding their retirement.

Insofar as they are "enforcing the law", most officers know just enough about the law to be dangerous. In most cases, however, the officer operates at the behest of his supervisors, or otherwise from his own misguided conscience and misconceptions. It is for this reason that so many police officers have grown comfortable with certain phrases and certain courses of action to bail themselves out of disputes with the public.

They will threaten to throw people in jail for disagreeing. They will tell people to "take it up with the judge". They will claim that they are "not going to argue with you", and yet they always insist that they are right; and if you dare to reference the law, some officers will simply dismiss or deliberately misinterpret it, refuse to be troubled by it, or even be so bold as to exclaim, "I *am* the law!" All the while, they claim that they are "just doing their jobs".

As time goes by, the population swells, and the government gains in power, public service becomes less about serving the public and serving the community, and progressively more about "the job": a means to a paycheck, a means for public workers to serve their own selfish interests, to chase their own wants and to spend their way through life, doing so with other people's hard-earned money — other people, or subjects, who effectively have no say in the matter.

Public service has long been in steep decline: once a humble occupation, it has since formed the basis for further subjugation. That same decline is even visible in their appearance. Whereas police officers once dressed professionally and gentlemanly, they have since begun to take on a more intimidating appearance. Indeed, they have gone from the appearance of a steward to that of a soldier, and their attitudes appear to have followed, exercising progressively more force and intimidation instead of respect, reason, and restraint.

There is a rather simple explanation for this development, especially where it coincides with the power and technology to completely dominate the public at will. Quite simply, it is far easier to intimidate than to reason, than to exercise patience, restraint and sound judgment, which is why tyranny is so dangerous, why it is absolutely essential for a people, through courage and eternal vigilance, to defend themselves and the safeguards to their liberty; why, as the American author Edward Abbey put it, "A patriot must always be ready to defend his country against his government." It is essential precisely because, in the possession of so much power, the tendency to take the easy route makes tyranny especially dangerous.

Whereas public servants were previously regarded with suspicion or disdain, whereas they were formerly held accountable to the public, they have since developed a sense of superiority over the people. Indeed, those public servants tend to treat the people as nuisances and lowly criminals, and they would like nothing more than for the people to simply keep their mouths shut, stay out of the way, and pay their taxes; more ideally, of course, they would much rather the people just hurry up and die. Across the board, public servants hide behind their policies and their bureaucracies just as they hide behind their desks and closed doors. They have the privilege of wearing their badges, wielding their weapons, using force against the people, closing their doors on the public, and answering almost exclusively to themselves or, more correctly, nobody at all.

Another set of advantages enjoyed by the establishment is found in its presence, it being ubiquitous; its reach, having its tentacles everywhere; its transcendence, always growing more powerful and enduring across generations. With the advantage of outlasting every generation, the state can tell its own tales. It can push its preferred narratives, write the history and paint the pictures without any fear of opposition from the people who were actually there; the people who might otherwise cast doubt but who have long since passed away. In this way, instead of representing the people and actually *promoting the general welfare*, the agents of the state believe that they themselves are in charge. What's more, they enjoy the benefit of representing a powerful and largely unquestioned institution, one in many cases taken to be so powerful, so fortified and impregnable, so steeped in the collective psyche and tradition, as to stand beyond reproach, such that, instead of representing the people — each of whom see themselves as measly individuals (or subjects) merely passing through — the establishment envelops and commands them. In this way, the establishment is scarcely held accountable to the people, seldom answering to them when and where it counts. On the contrary, it is the people who are expected or (for all intents and purposes) *required* to answer to the establishment, to do so in the manner prescribed and the time permitted, a far cry from the designs of representative government and a country priding itself as *the land of the free.*

Public service ought rightly to be just as the name suggests. Thomas Jefferson famously put it this way: "When a man assumes a public trust, he should consider himself as public property." As such, he is accountable not to his supervisors nor to the political whim, but to the public and to the Constitution to which he has pledged his allegiance.

Regrettably, however, instead of serving the public, police officers generally treat them with contempt, and officers often act with impunity to boot.

On the one hand, they claim to be proud and patriotic Americans, but they are perfectly willing to betray their fellow Americans, and to enforce orders diametrically opposed to American principles and the state's very Constitution. In truth, they are not as ambitious about being good Americans as they are set on looking the part, keeping their jobs and cashing their checks.

Since World War II, the police state has developed into a virtual paramilitary force, and the author's own father has even described his career in just these terms. He sincerely believed that law enforcement qualified as a paramilitary force; perhaps a belief with its roots in not only post-WWII attitudes and technology, but the dreams of little boys who grow up pretending to be soldiers and cowboys, who, in such cases, never grow out of it.

The true American understands that these forces are anathema to the jewel of the public liberty; that our republic and our freedoms can endure only so long as the public remains skeptical and vigilant toward its government; that a decent society is born of respect and family values, from reverence for life, liberty and property, not from heavy-handed government seeking continually to bring the people into conformity.

By all accounts, it appears that Kurt Vonnegut may have been onto something when he stated in a 1987 interview that, "My own feeling is that civilization ended in World War I, and we're still trying to recover from that."

Conveniently for the tyrants, the ignorance and naïveté of the public play right into their hands, as they (the tyrants) hide behind, and wage their assaults through, agents disguised as patriots. Even more insidious is their control over the media, an asset indispensable to their agenda. Indeed, this is precisely how they infect the people with their ideology.

Their monopoly on information is the single most insidious aspect of Leftism. Worse than any virus known to man, it is a contagion that controls what the people think and say; one that, not unlike an uncontrollable pandemic, infects each person ill-equipped to defend against it. With the incessant flow of mistruths, the immunodeficient public, intellectually speaking, succumbs to them without any knowledge of *what* happened or *how* it happened. Once the administration is established as the final arbiter on truth, the people not only fail to form their own opinions, but they eventually lose the ability and even the permission to do so. As a matter of routine, whether out of fear or for having already bought into the propaganda, they instinctually look to the establishment and conventional thinking before adopting an opinion: once established, this is their new religion, one founded upon fear among a congregation of soulless and unwitting servants.

CHAPTER XIII

THE GOVERNMENT FLU

W orse than any virus is the contagion that controls what the people think and say; the virus that spreads through propaganda and half-truths among a frightened public. The public feverishly searching for answers, they latch onto those ideas which appear sensible to them yet go largely unexamined, particularly by those lacking the tools, the acumen, or the initiative to scrutinize the details.

The spread of mistruths, then, much like an uncontrollable pandemic, infects each person ill-equipped to defend himself against it. This is the contagion of Leftism, which feeds off of desperation, ignorance and, above all, hysteria, each serving as the preferred tool for prying into the homes and the lives of the average subject (or voter).

In reflecting upon the list of household names between each administration, one can gain a meaningful insight into the political interests at work. During election years in particular, the many household names of the day succeed in manipulating the people's lives through clever campaigns of grandstanding, virtue-signaling, sounding alarms, poisoning the well, intimidating the public or otherwise talking over their heads.

However sincere or convicted in their beliefs, each of the new household names seeks to improve his party's odds of success in each forthcoming election. On each political subject, a field encompassing more matters by the day, so-called "experts" are always coming out of the woodwork to tell the public both what to think and what to say. Under the pretense of caring about the people, these politicians swindle the public into believing that the politicians are their representatives, when, in fact, the politicians represent themselves and the interests which stand to best serve *them*.

In its exercise of force while erring on the side of caution, Leftism stands to win either way. Either it appears justified in stripping people of their rights to stem the threat or, more commonly, it takes solace in having been "responsible" enough to err on the side of caution. In appearing sensible, Leftism is not only disingenuous but far more destructive than any of its advocates will ever care to admit.

Indeed, operating from the benefit of conscience and false prophecy, the most insidious threat of Leftism is the incredulousness with which its advocates account for its risks. According to the Leftist, every one of the stated risks is a "conspiracy theory" or a remote possibility. In the rare event that the Leftist acknowledges a risk, it is deemed a worthwhile sacrifice; and wherever any legitimate threats are posed to their vile, criminally-wicked institutions, the Leftist decries them as "terrorism" or "insurrection".

There is simply no way to reason with such a cult, as they wiggle and squirm their way out of every debacle and every last debate. Even in the face of fact, whether the laws of physics, those of economics, or those of the United States Constitution, their incredulousness renders them impervious to the dictates of reality. Where they lack the tools to solve any problem, whether physical or abstract, the Leftist will predictably use his words to talk his way out of the problem, to rally public opinion and beat his opponents into submission.

Whether it is a demanding employer, a disagreeable classmate, or an offensive academic concept, the Leftist will publicize his condemnation until that person, that law, or that idea has been virtually eliminated from view; at minimum, the Leftist will not stop until that person, that law or that idea ceases to present itself in public. This means that, while one may privately harbor an unpopular or unapproved view, he is forbidden to share it in public, for fear of the cult making an unfortunate example out of him. As is always the case with the festering of Leftism, whether in the abstract or in execution, it is bound to metastasize; it is bound to alter minds and affect relationships, to command every aspect of society as people yield everywhere for fear of being singled out.

Leftism, treated as some sort of disorder or exotic worldview, festers in a community. Where family and friends hesitate to challenge the Leftist for fear of insulting him, the Leftist is empowered to persist in his ways. All too often, respectable people treat Leftism the same way they would treat any clinical disorder or physical abnormality: for fear of offending the individual, most simply ignore it, look the other way, or at least try to be civil about it. However, Leftism is not a disorder or an abnormality cured by passivity; it is best contested at every margin upon every opportunity.

In the contemporary case, Leftism enjoys the benefit of "protected" status, as each disputed claim, policy or judgment is somehow related to any number of persons or groups regarded as *underprivileged, underserved, disenfranchised, victims* of another's sin or some unfortunate circumstance. So long as these ends are sought, and so long as they are ostensibly justified, the public will yield until they have ceded virtually all power and authority to the establishment. They will have yielded politely and respectfully while the Leftists have pursued their ends relentlessly and unapologetically.

This is not a battle won through "civility" or meekness; it is one wholly dependent upon every free man's will to defend freedom against tyrants who will happily corner their adversaries as they realize their every wish. Predictably, the tyrants seem to get their way by conning the public into playing nicely as they push their legislation, mobilize their troops, and shove their propaganda down the people's throats. And do not think for a moment that any list of laws, however sacred to any land or any peoples, will prevent them from taking aim and laying siege.

Indeed, instead of limiting government per the Framers' intentions, the Constitution of the United States is constantly reinterpreted in an attempt to justify government policies, measures, and rulings; in the majority of cases, it is loosely interpreted or wholly disregarded to undertake others. So long as the state strikes some kind of balance, so long as it appears to be playing remotely within the spirit of the rules, it is unlikely to encounter any meaningful opposition, and it can apparently preempt rebellion so long as its citizens are unaware of the happenings or otherwise willing to afford them some flexibility or leniency on the terms, perhaps on some suspicion that the politicians do not know any better. Unfortunately, that balance is continually tilted away from freedom and the bounds of the Constitution in favor of government and tyranny, a soft despotism that gradually tightens the noose around the necks of a citizenry that is too fearful or uneducated to say anything, much less to mount any meaningful resistance.

With the mutual resentment fostered by class warfare and racial division, and with the total abandonment of logic, the sane American has little cause to fight anyway; severed of his connection with community, his neighbors and his fellow man, not to mention those vague abstractions of country and liberty, he is left merely to fight for himself and his family, ultimately a self-defeating cause in the face of almost certain failure. In this case, he and his family are better off either relocating or simply tolerating each encroachment upon their liberties, so long as they are sharing together in the struggle.

By endorsing the institutions of socialism, communism or whatever style of collectivism — institutions distinguished only by semantics and the means by which they intend to conquer their subjects — the Leftist seeks to con his fellow man, whom he despises with all of his might, into accepting the designs of his own servitude. The Leftist is hardly inclined to socialize, as one might naturally expect from one who fancies himself a socialist. On the contrary, his interests in society extend only as far as he perceives political value in each of his comrades who, in their increasing numbers, form a mob uniquely capable of having their way with the rest of society.

It is no coincidence that collectivistic ideas prevail in times of destitution, when mankind is at its weakest. In this sense, these institutions have always laid claim to comrades and countries prepared to accept a little tyranny for a little relief. Of course, once the state gets a taste of a little tyranny, it goes for as much as it can muster; and after some time, that relief — or at least that perception of relief — is in short order recognized for the burden it poses.

As with modern times, where we find comrades rejoicing in the perception of free money and handouts as they enjoy their time away from work — whether generally unemployed or temporarily so under such cases as lockdowns during COVID-19 — the economic illiterates have been conditioned to view themselves as victims and their employers as villains.

Socialism is popular among the lay and intellectual classes alike because they view their jobs and their bosses as obstacles between them and the goods that they enjoy, as opposed to viewing them as the means by which they are made sufficiently productive to enjoy those goods. It is no mere coincidence that, among the people who believe that workers are exploited by their employers, most were also prepared during the lockdowns to view the jobs themselves as "non-essential". It is also no coincidence that a citizenry better acquainted with debt than wealth is also prepared to endorse socialism as its solution.

Whereas the average citizen has virtually no understanding of investments and sound money, he is well-versed in taking out large sums of debt to indulge beyond his means; oddly enough, this was evidenced during the COVID-19 lockdowns by the average American's spending spree at Walmart and Target upon receipt of each "stimulus" check. Instead of investing the funds, Americans squander them on consumer goods: toys, clothes and electronics. This is precisely the line of thinking which leaves Americans incurably broke and eternally incapable of helping themselves.

Furthermore, this leaves them susceptible to the line of thinking which concludes that their chances of success hinge on their ability — or the ability of some hired help, such as government — to take from some to give to others. They are simply unfamiliar with, or uninterested in, any other way. So long as they have access to Amazon and Netflix, and so long as they can count on their next meal, most Americans are generally unbothered by the gradual encroachments upon their freedoms.

The annals of history are replete with such examples of tyranny and genocide where civilizations succumbed to inaction in the face of "reasonable" or "justified" government overreach. Whether it is a tyrant like Caligula, who indulged in riotous extravagance and tortured hundreds of his subjects for his own personal enjoyment, or it is a more ascetic and industrious one, such as Augustus Caesar, who toiled for the welfare of his empire, its people and Roman world peace, wherever their political means are somehow justified by the ends, tyranny always winds up hurting people and leaving far more casualties in its wake than ever imagined.

Even in the case of an empire as sophisticated as Rome, the designs of their planned economy eventually ushered in restrictive economic regulations and uncompromising directives which left farmers unable to farm and small businessmen starving and suicidal. In the decline of the Roman Empire, just before its collapse into the Dark Ages, the people were eventually left unemployed, so the beneficent government leapt at the opportunity to tax the rich to provide the populace with bread and circus tickets. While this offered some short-term relief to the people, it accomplished nothing in the way of remedying the problems which ailed them, and they were ultimately doomed to ruin, left to suffer centuries of economic despair.

In the recent case of the COVID-19 pandemic, the tyrants needed not to reach very far or to think nearly as creatively in order to swindle their subjects into their own subjection; in this case, the subjects were more than willing to handcuff themselves and their neighbors on the tyrants' behalf while placing themselves under house arrest; what's more, a great many were eager to even celebrate government overreach as they spent each day at home in their pajamas and collected unemployment checks in excess of their normal take-home pay.

Ultimately, as shown, the administration is literally in the business of buying its subjects' acquiescence to tyranny, while the unwitting subjects are, by and large, no less pleased to oblige. After all, it is not terribly difficult to cast a vote, to check a box and cash those checks. Alas, the pitfalls of democracy; the pitfalls of that state which claims to represent the proletariat, which claims to be a *government of the people, by the people, for the people.*

Make no mistake, every government initiative serves to test your tolerance for tyranny. With your support or in your silence, your acquiescence to the unlawful commands of government confirms that the despots are completely in control of your rights; rights that were once deemed natural, with which we were endowed by our Creator, are gradually redefined as privileges administered by that government formerly entrusted to defend those rights. And when that system fails to properly defend those rights and uphold the terms of that sacred agreement, that social contract, it is the right of free people to alter or to abolish it.

Alas, as history has shown, people are generally more willing to follow orders than to challenge them; they are more prepared to obey commands than they are to defend their rights. They are more prepared to align with the status quo and to keep quiet, and they are more likely to fall victim to propaganda, false promises and false narratives, among them the common refrain of "unity", the latter being celebrated as some great achievement and the means to civilized society. In the author's estimation, this simply has more to do with the survival of government than with the general welfare of the people; a government which depends on unity so far as it promotes groupthink, so far as it degrades the individual, so far as enough people are together indifferent, personally invested in the status quo, or willing to obey, and so far as enough power and influence are thereby available to keep them obedient.

Under this sort of tyranny, none dare think for himself, arrive at his own conclusions, or speak the truth; and so, especially where news is so abundant and media so quick to disseminate information and censor the opposition, the views of the public take the form of a hive mind, sharing collectively in both their views and their willingness to obey orders. As a result, this kind of society quickly dispenses with the truth, which comes to be regarded as *hate speech*, *discrimination*, or *politically incorrect*. Indeed, they even come to politicize the sciences themselves, even the very word *science*. However, in doing this, they are sure to straddle the fence so as to interpret "the science" to their advantage or to otherwise emphatically reject "the science" wherever it calls their narratives into question. Fortunately for them, they keep the academics in their pockets, either directly on staff or through sponsored *studies* with predetermined conclusions.

The academics, of course, are more than happy to oblige. After all, they are neither apolitical nor altruists who have forsaken self-interest. Where they are not expressly sponsored by government, they are, as humans, motivated by other powerful factors. Indeed, even the well-intentioned academics crave the attention and the credit that come along with a major theoretical discovery; this is true even among those in any way attached to the field, who, along with their disciples, enjoy the prestige that comes along with being members of the *enlightened class.*

Once they have anointed themselves the enlightened and final arbiters on truth, they decide what "the science" says and doesn't say. Wherever they deem "the science" inconvenient, they term it *heterodoxy, pseudoscience,* or, perhaps worst of all, *conspiracy theory.* Ultimately, whether they are exploiting, manipulating, misinterpreting, or flatly rejecting "the science", it is in service to one particular end: establishing the administration as the final arbiter in all things, and the final word on the bounds of allowable opinion.

On top of all of this, there are the social and psychological factors that keep the power with the establishment: it is challenging enough to take on just one individual, to burst his bubble and shatter all of his illusions. It is a tall task to even broach the subject in most cases, let alone to successfully lead someone to the truth with facts, reason and evidence. Even assuming the cooperation of the other party, it is, in most cases, not enough to just represent the truth; it is just as essential, if not more so, to do so convincingly. Of course, this is even assuming that the other party is interested in the truth, that he is patient and intelligent enough to consider and comprehend facts, reason and evidence.

This is why Leftism succeeds in the first place: too few people satisfy these conditions. Amongst the general population there is too much emphasis on form over function, feelings over facts, promises over results, and confidence over competence; what's more, they are susceptible to the general over the specific. For these reasons, it is prohibitively difficult to have constructive and rational discussions about social or political issues. It is for the same reasons that the establishment tends to win by default, as the people often defer to the government as the final arbiter, and, of course, the establishment happily welcomes any excuse for more power.

While it is indeed a tall task to challenge any given individual, it is nothing short of heroic, á la *David and Goliath*, to question the entire establishment and actually hold it accountable; that is, if they can even find the people in charge, who are typically shielded by the bureaucracy, hiding behind staff members who are "just doing their jobs". For these reasons, precious few ever dare try; for these reasons, it is nothing short of a miracle any time it happens.

It is in this way that the resistance, the so-called *rebels*, are doomed by the establishment. Whereas tyranny in each case provokes the conflict, the resistance is saddled with the blame. Consequently, the ranks of the resistance dwindle over time, as the establishment ups the ante and forces them into submission. In many of these cases, especially in the modern context, some faction of the establishment ups the ante by framing the conflict to their own advantage. Two such examples are the cause of "social justice" and the *war for equality*, more appropriately described as a power struggle between the old guard and the usurpers; in many cases the *old guard* taking the form of the *rebels*, with the *usurpers* taking the form of the *establishment*.

Despite the propaganda, it is not that the old guard necessarily dislikes the usurpers, or that they deny their equal standing as human beings, but that they differ substantially in their fundamental values and preferred systems of government. Indeed, in the modern context this particular struggle is hardly ever based on some insistence that the usurpers are less human, or less important, than the members of the old guard.

On the contrary, for the old guard the struggle is often one directed at the preservation of their traditions: institutions built and defended by them and their forefathers. For the usurpers, the struggle is often directed at dismantling those institutions, ordinarily by discrediting them and the very people who shed blood, sweat and tears in their defense. For this reason, through the usurpers' political causes and their *war for equality*, it is not just a political war, but a war against the old guard's customs, heritage, traditions, and lineage.

In this sense, the usurpers' politics imply the destruction of the old guard's culture. In initiating these wars, whether domestic or abroad, the establishment always wins. While some of the people may stand to win some of the time, the establishment always comes out on top. These wars all have one thing in common: the elimination of the establishment's competition and the few brave souls comprising the resistance.

Wherever the establishment is found sponsoring "social justice" or the *war for equality*, it is almost always a false face for the pursuit of power, in most cases the power to eliminate the very institutions defending the public liberty. Whether due to fear, political correctness, or effective propaganda, the people eventually forfeit their liberty and yield to the state; a state which is as scarcely accountable to truth as it is prepared to sanction it.

Because of this tendency, the cause of liberty is always waiting on a miracle; always waiting for the few brave souls to take up the mantle in its defense. These few brave souls are the men of character and conviction up against the remotest of odds; and yet, by providence, they prevail. In the long run, however, the cause is lost. The people forget and they once again fall prey to the establishment that is always changing hands and disguises, but always somewhere waging its war against liberty; waging its war against the old guard and the men who hold the line as the resistance.

Over time, the establishment wins in the absence of these men, as they and their cause, and the monuments paying tribute to them, are altogether erased from view, the public's collective memory, and eventually their collective conscience. Indeed, in many cases subsequent generations even forget what their ancestors were fighting for, and over time many are even convinced, through sublimation, that *violence is never the answer*; many of whom come to fancy themselves *pacifists*, or otherwise luminaries in the realms of civility and intellectual thought.

Some even attempt to justify their pacifism through Biblical principles, citing in particular a popular misinterpretation of one of the Ten Commandments, *Thou shalt not kill*, instead of the proper translation, *Thou shalt not murder*. Of course, the pacifist prefers the former interpretation as it makes it easier for him to claim the moral high ground, whereas the latter serves to distinguish between *lawful* and *unlawful* forms of killing, thus condoning or even encouraging deadly force when necessary.

Indeed, man is occasionally called to go to such lengths as to kill in the course of self-defense or just war, or as a consequence of particularly heinous crimes and evil intentions; among them, as written in *Matthew 15:19*, "murder, adultery, sexual immorality, theft, false witness, slander." Indeed, as it is written in *Ecclesiastes*, "There is a time to kill and a time to heal. There is a time to destroy and a time to build.... There is a time to tear apart and a time to sew together. There is a time to be silent and a time to speak.... There is a time to love and a time to hate. There is a time for war and a time for peace."

The righteous man seeks not to excuse his inaction, but to be useful in his service to his family and his fellow man; to indeed know when to kill, to destroy, to tear apart, to speak, and to hate, in defense of all which is precious and indispensable to a free and noble people. The pacifist, on the other hand, seeks to build his temple to impress others and to defend himself against obligation and responsibility; to avoid the calls for action or the assumption of risk, and to thereby excuse himself from situations which might challenge his mettle or expose him as a fraud.

Far from the hero whom he imagines himself to be, the pacifist is a rather loathsome specimen who basks in sanctimony, intellectualisms, and spiritual interpretations which he vastly prefers to the harsher realities; realities deemed too uncivilized and thus unfit for the modern world and the future that he can nearly imagine.

As such, the pacifist may tolerate *some* disobedience, but only the kind of "civil" (or "mostly peaceful") disobedience which specifically serves his interests or supports his visions, which likewise aims to overcome those harsher realities, which shall serve only as a means to his preferred *peace* and *obedience;* two separate states of being seldom distinguished in their forms and all too often confused for one another; the latter of the two all too often mistaken as a necessary condition for the former, not necessarily a genuine peace but the kind which demands unquestioning obedience.

Ultimately, the pacifist is either a false face, a shill, or a useful idiot and a mere impediment to the achievement of genuine peace; an intellectual so preoccupied with his own image and self-righteousness that he wholly disregards the sacrifices made and the price paid for the survival of his kind, let alone the kind of peace that he has taken for granted. The pacifist is indeed useless to any initiative which does not already enjoy the support of the status quo, the academics atop the ivory tower, or the body of the people. His only serious initiative or inclination is toward sanctimony, self-preservation, safety and any state which excuses him from taking any meaningful action, risking anything of consequence, or, God forbid, contradicting his precious ideal.

He thereby dishonors his forbears not only by rejecting violence, but by suggesting that they were inferior for their willingness to fight; a willingness which serves as the ultimate means for the survival of any people and their principles, a willingness representing the highest form of man's commitment to any cause. Perhaps worst of all, the spirit of pacifism threatens to hypnotize the people, to reward their obedience, to coddle them into complacency, to render them ever more susceptible to the powerful, and perhaps the less reasonable, who are ready to fight.

Indeed, the people grow so complacent that they come to believe that there is nothing to fear, that they need not remain vigilant to defend themselves, that there are no threats to them or their safety so long as they remain obedient. They grow so accustomed to easy living, to warnings, guardrails, and instructions, to all things abstract and virtual, that they dull the necessary skills, senses and instincts to operate in the real world, to make sound decisions and take full responsibility for themselves.

This kind of meekness is, in turn, beneficial to the establishment, which is inherently violent, which maintains a monopoly over force and coercion, and which has a vested interest in maintaining the status quo. Of course, the establishment seeks to maintain the status quo only up and until the point that it is to be reshaped by the "authorities" who have yet another status quo in mind; an arrangement expected to further the interests, and to improve the security, of the establishment. Once established, it will be yet another endeavor to defend that status quo at all costs; and, under the new arrangement, the "authorities" will possess the purse and the power to better defend themselves and carry out their objectives.

When men have gone too long without war, too long without combat, they forget how to fight; they forget the causes for which it is worth fighting; and they grow accustomed to suppressing those instincts until they lose them altogether, or until they sacrifice the power to effectively act on them. As for the detractors and the nonconformists, the establishment is always prepared to deal with them. In order to maintain their grip around the throats of the people — to put it delicately — the tyrants routinely set out to make examples of them, and to do so swiftly when necessary; cautionary tales for any who dares fall of out line.

Whether it be for "sedition" or "tax evasion" or "insurrection" or "political incorrectness" or anything else deemed offensive to the state, no "crime" goes unpunished, especially any which threatens the state's purse, authority, competency, or its progress, whether politically, economically, or militarily. For these reasons, most simply keep quiet and go along to get along; and most, for understandable reasons, view this as the only rational option. As time goes on, they grow increasingly comfortable and complacent in their relative peace; in their thoughtless obedience, the progressive routine and regimentation of their lives; in the comforts afforded them by keeping quiet and conforming to the status quo.

Indeed, the state uses the term "peace" even where the terms *status quo, submission, conformity*, and *regimentation* are more appropriate; and it permits or demands "peace" when it controls the status quo, or when it is under the threat of losing it. Of course, in the case of the latter, uniformed personnel with weapons are deployed to keep or restore "the peace", and in the former, to protect it and to deter any possible threats to it. When "the peace" or the status quo is challenged, the challengers are termed *the enemy*, whereas the state's own aggression is described officially, and on every occasion, as *war, politics, justice*, or *diplomacy*.

As with their preference for "peace", the state impresses upon the people the importance of remaining "calm" and "civilized"; a mandate not just accepted but in most cases embraced by those eager to accord with the expectations of a "civilized" people, as defined and affirmed by the state through both ordinances and mainstream media. As such, those who dare to honestly express their grief, their anger, or their passion are publicly rejected and ostracized, denounced as *unrefined, disorderly* and *uncivilized*.

The state's preference for such conduct is, as with their penchant for "peace", necessitated by their desire to maintain the status quo; to prevent the kind of unrest and arousal which might elicit scrutiny, pushback or resistance. Therefore, the safest strategy for the state is to impress upon the people the indispensability of "sensible" or "civilized" conduct, the kind which, on virtually every occasion, glorifies, fears, or yields to authority; the kind of authority which keeps the "peace", maintains the status quo, moderates public discourse, silences the critics, tames the people, penalizes, suppresses and humiliates anyone who is agitated or lucid enough to make a compelling case against the establishment.

This is precisely how a society is so thoroughly conditioned, controlled and sublimated as to cease in its ability to defend itself from the sieges upon them, whether from within or from abroad; whether from domestic or foreign influence; whether from forces nearby or afar. Indeed, once the establishment has cemented its standards for "peace" and "civility", and as soon as the people have been effectively neutralized by those standards, the only "proper" and "acceptable" forms of threatening conduct — force, violence, and coercion — are those which accord with the visions and missions of the state.

Indeed, the people are always growing more accustomed to reading the papers, watching the news, and stewing over their grief, with the hope or expectation that the bureaucrats will do something, that diplomacy will prevail; that the men in suits are their leaders, and that, as their "leaders", they have real solutions and the people's best interests in mind. In this way, the people are also made to believe that their only option is to plead for mercy or assistance from government; that the people's causes must be sanctioned explicitly by government in order to qualify as "legitimate"; and that any potential "solution" is possible only in cooperation with that government.

The people eventually come to view the men in suits as the gatekeepers, their chaperones and their superiors, as opposed to their servants or their representatives. They come to view those well-dressed men as icons; men as impressive in their style as in their speech. Still, beware, do not be fooled, as the concept of the "well-dressed man" is as metaphorical as it is literal: indeed, the well-dressed man may opt to dress down for specific purposes, in order to appear more casual and more relatable to his subjects, but he remains the same man nevertheless; a man who, in such cases, dresses down to appear likable, relatable and less threatening, to present his agenda in the same way, but also to secretly express his sarcastic and ironical sense of humor, his contempt for his subjects and the office he holds.

The people come to view those men — those behind the podium, atop the ivory tower, in the newspapers and on the television screens — as parental figures whom the people must beg for answers, permission, approval, and forgiveness, even in the most desperate of circumstances where man's instincts are begging him to defend and represent himself, to take immediate action and to seek his own answers.

Whether a war on principle, a war for self-preservation, a war in defense of liberty, or war for any number of reasons, eventually there are no wars for the people, for *their* causes and the defense of their liberty, but only wars for the purposes and interests of the state; and ultimately, in the long run, wars in service to a new world order, global government, and continued efforts to subdue any opposition which remains or emerges. In their service to the state, these men are often honored as heroes for advancing the cause, but heroes for a distant (and often fleeting) cause both largely impertinent to their lives and well beyond the scope of their understanding.

As a former counter-intelligence officer during World War II, Jesse Glenn Gray wrote of this fear in his classic 1959 work *The Warriors*: "The deepest fear of my war years, one still with me, is that these happenings had no real purpose...".

"How often I wrote in my war journals that unless that day had some positive significance for my future life, it could not possibly be worth the pain it cost."

Ultimately, these men are honored by the state for its own purposes; however, the honorable men themselves, under such conditions as war, have generally struggled alongside the fear, knowledge or suspicion that, as Gray puts it, "these happenings had no real purpose." As such, among the men who have endured such extreme suffering together in such a constant state of tension, among the men who have been casualties in at least some sense of the word, they know that, with or without purpose, they ultimately find their own: they persevere for each other, their heroic actions coming as a consequence of the fact that, in all of it, they become a band of brothers, an honor above all others, unsurpassed by any decoration issued by the state.

Nevertheless, they are decorated as heroes of war, the epitome of man, great symbols of patriotism — for reasons other than those just mentioned, for patriotism beneficial to neither country nor fellow man, to neither liberty nor posterity, but to the interests of the establishment, the undefined visions and objectives of the state; a state as celebrated as its soldiers, and one which fancies itself the noblest of causes and the means to all good things. As state sympathizers are known to have put it, as in their message so brazenly inscribed on their 1927 memorial paying tribute to General Benjamin Lincoln's rout of Shays' Rebellion in 1787, "Obedience to the law is true liberty." Indeed, this is the cause professed by those who so carelessly swear their allegiance and so proudly wear their uniforms; men whose feats and exertions, however impressive, are in service to ends unknown, and in many cases ends specifically contradicting the very oaths which they have sworn to uphold.

These are men who are held as heroes, not only for their courage and their actions in battle, but for the benefit of morale and the people's allegiance to the state; for the boys and men whom they and their stories are to inspire, boys and men to be primed to serve, salute, and sacrifice for the state and its every cause. Indeed, these are men esteemed not only as heroes and valiant soldiers of war, but as exemplars for all men, the highest form of man; a form achievable only in one's sacrifice for the state, a sacrifice deemed the holiest and most "patriotic" of sacrifices that can be made.

The heroes and their worshippers even come to *celebrate* the power of the state, its capacity to manipulate, to dominate and to destroy en masse, as they all begin to mistaken themselves as part of the same team. Indeed, it is in this way that so much destruction is possible with the benefit of a good conscience; that corruption within the state can be found with or without malice; that well-intentioned men conspire to transgress against their fellow man, to manipulate the people and the facts, and to conceal the truth and the ulterior motives. Whether it be troops simply following orders, participating in genocide or other heinous acts, or it be unwitting conspirators "just doing their jobs", as in the more than one hundred and thirty thousand workers on the Manhattan Project who had no idea what ends they were serving, conspiracy is far more common and far more feasible than popularly believed, especially among those merely adhering to the commands of their superiors, assuming no liability in their own limited roles, and thereby keeping a good conscience all the while.

As one "mother in history" (as she often referred to herself) wrote in a letter to several congressmen in 1973 at the height of the Watergate crisis:

"[I]n the name of security, [even] men of integrity and who are the most esteemed, most respected and honored, who have the welfare of the country at heart, would be most likely to do what the White House wanted and thought necessary. The Watergate affair has followed this pattern. Those we believe are above reproach, those who have reached the pinnacle or are near it, those who are guiding our nation's destiny are found to have manipulated events to accomplish certain things they think were for the good of the country. Those who have a deep sense of patriotism and loyalty are most likely to twist events to accomplish their purposes."

Just as misguided patriotism strengthens the convictions of the men who serve those ends, so too have such events proved the theories and strengthened the convictions of those who have maintained their suspicions; the latter are as often vindicated by the truth as they are persecuted by the former who sport the uniforms, salute the flag, and pride themselves in doing their duty or otherwise "just doing their jobs".

Whereas, in the opinion of the state, it is always in the commission of its official duties, always defending the common good, its opponents are always held in disdain, always regarded as existential threats to civilization. From the state's point of view, the citizen is either a team player or one of its opponents; either supporting the cause or threatening to it. In other words, as for policy, *you are either with us, or against us*; as for war, as

President George W. Bush put it in an address to a joint session of Congress on 20 September 2001, "Either you are with us, or you are with the terrorists."

From the state's point of view, there is only one cause. Indeed, those who fight for any other cause are harshly denounced as *criminals*, *rebels*, *terrorists* or *enemies of the state*; and when those enemies kill *anyone*, they are found guilty of massacres and terrorism, whereas, for governments, even where they kill innocent civilians, the deaths are merely considered *collateral damage*. Needless to say, the establishment has the loudest voice and the last word in deciding which outfits are considered legitimate and which actions and wars are considered justified. Thus, precious few ever dare challenge the status quo, for fear of being named *the enemy*, *illegitimate*, and *unjustified*.

Becoming progressively obedient as instruments of the state, held accountable by their comrades who likewise conform, the people exercise the greatest of caution to avoid any association that might render them an enemy or a target; and they ultimately exercise enough caution that they have essentially erased themselves altogether. In this way, they sacrifice meaningful relationships in addition to their individuality. They lose not only their instincts, the courage and the strength to fight, but, over time, the causes for which it is worth fighting.

It is precisely in this way that a society expresses its own value. Indeed, the quality of a society can be measured, in part, by the price which its members are willing to pay in order to defend it from threats posed from either within or without; the costs which they are willing to bear in the defense of their people, their liberty, their property, their culture and their values.

A society whose men deem their own lives more worthy than any possible cause is a society of despicables, the types more interested in their own indulgences and personal safety than any matter concerning the future of their community and their own family. In their indolence and their indifference, they imply the value of both their own communities and their own families, which is to say that they place quite the negligible value on each. This is, indeed, a great tragedy and the hallmark of a society steeped in decadence and selfishness; a society governed by survival without purpose, and one devoid of real principles and values.

In the implied valuation of their community and their people, it is not at all surprising that they are ultimately condemned as *subjects* or *citizens* of an all-powerful establishment prepared to specify the value of the people so far as they are made to serve the political interests of the state. They are then without personal value, but rather reduced to the value of mere tools for the purposes of the establishment. This means that, so far as they value themselves at all, they are either destined for liberty and prosperity or ultimately condemned to some measure of subordination and moral, as well as economic, destitution. It is, thus, up to the people to assert their value, or to otherwise permit others to do so for them.

The English philosopher John Stuart Mill put it this way in his 1848 work *Principles of Political Economy*:

"War is an ugly thing, but not the ugliest of things: the decayed and degraded state of moral and patriotic feeling which thinks that nothing is worth a war, is much worse. When a people are used as mere human instruments for firing cannon or thrusting bayonets, in the service and for the selfish purposes of a master, such war degrades a people. A war to protect other human beings against tyrannical injustice; a war to give victory to their own ideas of right and good, and which is their own war, carried on for an honest purpose by their free choice, — is often the means of their regeneration. A man who has nothing for which he is willing to fight, nothing which is more important than his own personal safety, is a miserable creature and has no chance of being free unless made and kept so by the exertions of better men than himself. As long as justice and injustice have not terminated their ever-renewing fight for ascendancy in the affairs of mankind, human beings must be willing, when need is, to do battle for the one against the other."

Indeed, it may read like a paradox, but it is nonetheless true that a world with some peace is not a world without war. To truly enjoy peace is to know its true price; to enjoy it between the mighty struggles and the hefty costs paid to keep it. Peace cannot be the objective, but the fruit enjoyed through the exertions of those ready and willing to provide it. It must never negate the cause of just war, for that cause is precisely why there will be any peace anymore. A Pvt. David Webster said it best. One of "the boys from Currahee", Webster, a member of the famed Easy Company (506th Parachute Infantry Regiment, 101st Airborne Division) during World War II, put it this way in a personal letter to his mother in 1944: "Those things which are precious are saved only by sacrifice."

A world without war can be only a world full of angels or one governed by select vices and convictions: convictions of those willing to do precisely what is necessary to rule over the rest, the obedient, who are without them; convictions of those determined to define the kind of "peace", if any, that the people will have — whether, as President John F. Kennedy put it in his commencement address at American University on June 10th, 1963, it will be "the peace of the grave or the security of the slave", or instead a "genuine peace, the kind of peace that makes life on earth worth living, and the kind that enables men... to grow, and to hope, and build a better life for their children." You can determine for yourself which of the two is more plausible; which of the two is the world that we inhabit; which of the two is the one called Earth.

This is precisely why, in America's Bill of Rights, the Second Amendment follows the First; the right to keep and bear arms being absolutely essential to the unending pursuit of *true* peace and the continued protection of every other right, especially those which defend the population against tyrannical government and any force imposing upon the public liberty. After all, the greatest threat to liberty is the aspiration to define its terms, in particular by those who have little respect for it; who certainly would not fight for it as much as they are perfectly willing to wage or condone the fight against it; and who conveniently stand to benefit from its loss.

In this environment, faced with no meaningful resistance, the status quo continues and the establishment proceeds with its agenda. Whereas those "civilized" types, as they fancy themselves, insist that change can be effected without force or violence, there inevitably comes a time when this is indisputably incorrect. After all, the establishment always has the upper hand in any debate, as it ultimately reserves the power to defend its position in the interest of the status quo, to defend its position violently under the name of "enforcement", "national security" or "keeping the peace". Indeed, the establishment stands always ready to reassert its authority under the guise of legitimacy — the type of "legitimacy" which goes unquestioned by those who have come to accept it; who have become comfortable with the status quo; who lack the intelligence or the courage to challenge it; or who are otherwise willing to go only so far to defend their principles, their property, their liberty, their loved ones and their heirs.

Indeed, in their defeat, any vestige thereafter remaining of their traditions, their conscience, and their memories is squeezed out of existence. The Leftists conquer their opponents by training (or *rehabilitating*) them to abandon their principles out of fear in the face of peer pressure, political correctness, and persecution.

It is the same with their treatment of truth, whereby the people are made not only incredulous to it but uncomfortable in its presence, whereby the most important of truths are regarded as academic, superfluous, or upsetting to peaceful living. They are conditioned to reject their own instincts, their reasoning and their intelligence, the very qualities which enable a man to discern and to think things out for himself; to contemplate his independence and his self-sufficiency; to entertain the possibilities without accepting them; to appreciate the merits and the demerits of both popular *and* unpopular opinion; and to, likewise, appreciate the merits and demerits of one's own beliefs. These are qualities essential to enlightenment, defense and vigilance, ones indispensable to liberty and anathema to government.

The very pursuit of truth and the practice of critical and independent thought are threats of incalculable proportions to the establishment; an establishment which prefers its lies, which prefers ignorance and uncertainty, desperation and fear, anger and hatred. As it is written in *John 3:19*, "This is the verdict: Light has come into the world, but people loved darkness instead of light because their deeds were evil."

Indeed, the truth threatens to challenge, to expose, to destabilize, to upset, to shake up the status quo and upend the institutions which have perpetuated and presided over the lies. It threatens a call to action among those who so fear upsetting the status quo, who fear that they will be ostracized, exiled or persecuted by the establishment. As it is with truth, it is with facts, honesty, nuance, and logic, which are together nearly always regarded as the *third rail of politics*, impossible to defend or to acknowledge without running the risk of alienating oneself and upsetting the status quo: as Winston Churchill once put it, "Men occasionally stumble over the truth, but most of them pick themselves up and hurry off as if nothing ever happened."

With the benefit of these forces and the relentless barrage of political propaganda, most opt to conform so as to avoid the consequences of speaking the truth or defending their principles, or to relieve themselves of the stress of the lived contradiction: their betrayal of their forebears, their traditions, and the calling which presents too many dangers, too many burdens, too much responsibility, sacrifice and discomfort, to justify the risk of even recalling, let alone defending, those precious principles. Where they themselves are not made to disappear, you can bet that their culture, the truth, and everything else that matters, will be (for all intents and purposes). They will be shunned and humiliated, made to hide and shy away, or they will be accepted, socially and politically speaking, on the condition that they respect the mob and disavow their former loyalties, or otherwise keep quiet and render their salutes.

In the course of the new status quo, there arises even a significant opportunity cost in any attempt to defend the customs and principles of times past. Any attempt becomes costly not merely in the form of social and political disapproval, but in the form of commercial and professional prospects best served by going along with the status quo.

In this way, the subjects, once threatened and intimidated, who first abandoned their cherished customs and principles, give way to subsequent generations willfully rejecting their history, denouncing their ancestors, and defiling their memory; at the same time, they are encouraged by social praise and pecuniary advantages which are more than enough to keep the populace from harboring any second thoughts, let alone any guilt.

It is in this way that a society is reprogrammed and made to suffer the consequences of its own ignorance and selfishness, made to finally appreciate the value of those former values and traditions, for which life and limb were once sacrificed in their own right with hopes that their children and posterity might appreciate the costs attending the defense and survival of their traditions; that they might be spared the agony of ever losing them.

Such is the plight of liberty in the light of spectacular promises. It is only under the darkest of skies, when that light has all but turned to ash, that the value of liberty is once more remembered, but not before it is nearly forgotten and the chances of restoring it all but lost.

All of this is sure to raise the question: why do people still regard socialism as *progressive*? That is the subject of the next point.

CHAPTER XIV

SLAVERY

As Winston Churchill stated, "Socialism is a philosophy of failure, the creed of ignorance and the gospel of envy. Its inherent virtue is the equal sharing of misery."

Recent history demonstrates the ease with which clever politicians have successfully attached the label "socialism" to several causes. These are causes which remain relevant only so far as they serve the interests of the state and the politicians seeking to ensure their electability; seeking their own selfish advantages, among them power and influence, financial and professional gain, or, more likely, some combination thereof.

When considered seriously, those causes have virtually nothing to do with the ideals of socialism; rather, they are false faces for politicians seeking those advantages. For example, the topics of civil rights, welfare, environmentalism, and the end of poverty and racial prejudice, are initiatives often associated with socialism. These causes, as advertised, come to form the pretext by which the people are made to relinquish their freedoms; causes championed only by charlatans and hypocrites, who celebrate those causes not as altruists, but as fools and frauds seeking attention, applause and approval.

It is written thus in *Matthew 6*:

"Be careful not to practice your righteousness in front of others to be seen by them. If you do, you will have no reward from your Father in heaven. So when you give to the needy, do not announce it with trumpets, as the hypocrites do in the synagogues and on the streets, to be honored by others. Truly I tell you, they have received their reward in full. But when you give to the needy, do not let your left hand know what your right hand is doing, so that your giving may be in secret. Then your Father, who sees what is done in secret, will reward you. And when you pray, do not be like the hypocrites, for they love to pray standing in the synagogues and on the street corners to be seen by others. Truly I tell you, they have received their reward in full. But when you pray, go into your room, close the door and pray to your Father, who is unseen. Then your Father, who sees what is done in secret, will reward you. And when you pray, do not keep on babbling like pagans, for they think they will be heard because of their many words. Do not be like them, for your Father knows what you need before you ask him."

The Leftists are the loudest and most lethal of hypocrites the world over. Always sanctimonious and seeking approbation, they have little interest in goodness or righteousness, but in maintaining that pretense. Their initiatives, regardless of their advertised ends, are hardly anything other than self-serving; indeed, they are generally unrelated, or merely incidental, to socialism, a kind of specious humbug designed to conceal its greater desire for economic control. As the French author Albert Camus once wrote, "The welfare of the people in particular has always been the alibi of tyrants, and it provides the further advantage of giving the servants of tyranny a good conscience."

When it comes to tyrants, they are generally, at first, held in the good graces of the people, who confuse congeniality and good-sounding intentions with good character and sound judgment. Likewise, the people commit the mistake of assuming good intentions while ascribing to the tyrants the kinds of charitable qualities that apply in their *own* everyday lives to the company that *they* keep, but which hardly ever apply in the realm of politics.

Ultimately, the kinds of people who thirst for political power have precious little in common with "ordinary" folk. They live entirely different lives with radically different motives and priorities. They are hardly comparable to our friends and family, or any of the company we keep for that matter.

From the politician's point of view, virtue and principle are hurdles to overcome. They are, in the view of tyrants, expendable in their pursuit of power. For them, these values matter only to the extent that they make the tyrants relatable enough to keep the people under their control. For these reasons, as a matter of practice, the people are well-advised to remain skeptical of politicians and governments, not too eager to give them the benefit of the doubt, and certainly not too eager to view them through rose-colored glasses. It is essential to remember their objectives: power, influence and control. With this in mind, the people are less likely to be fooled by their sleight of hand and the various tricks they have up their sleeves. And believe me, they have plenty.

Whether a form of regulation, a series of subsidies, or the construction of forced labor camps, socialism ultimately seeks to broaden its control. Of course, it has achieved this objective diplomatically and with pretense, scarcely admitting of its desired ends in its promise of various benefits and so-called "social safety nets" along the way. Timothy Mellon, businessman and grandson of former Treasury Secretary Andrew Mellon, aptly characterized these "safety nets" as "Slavery Redux", whereby Americans have been made "slaves of a new Master, Uncle Sam." Writing in his 2015 autobiography, Mellon described this arrangement as an exchange of votes for "freebies", all at the expense of freedom and honest, hardworking Americans:

"For delivering their votes in the Federal Elections, they are awarded with yet more and more freebies: food stamps, cell phones, WIC payments, Obamacare, and on, and on, and on. The largess is funded by the hardworking folks, fewer and fewer in number, who are too honest or too proud to allow themselves to sink into this morass."

This is the modern form of slavery in the Western world: a kind of slavery by the ignorant over the meek, the political over the apolitical, the violent over the pensive, the unenlightened over the wise. It is a dysfunction whereby the laymen, the irrational and the uneducated are the ones who are most vocal, the ones who believe that they know enough to shout from the rooftops, to lead armies against their adversaries who might dare to scrutinize the details or disagree; whereas the truly enlightened are wise and intelligent enough to avoid conflict with their irrational and temperamental foes, or to simply avoid them altogether.

This is a kind of slavery which subjects the slave to not just one master but a faceless bureaucracy and a heartless political machine; one devoid of ethics, accountability, and any motivations for truth or righteousness. Whereas socialists often like to condemn particular forms of slavery from the past, or at least they like to bring them up for their own political ends, they seek in the present (and into the future) to bind slaves to their ever-changing concept of the *common good*.

Conveniently for them, the socialists willfully ignore the historical record of the twentieth century, which pinpoints Leftism as the single greatest threat to liberty the world has ever known. Ignoring the horrors of forced labor across socialist states, they also ignore the fact that slavery is still ongoing throughout the world, that they are complicit in afflicting their own communities. Conveniently for them, under their system they are no longer regarded as *slaves* or *serfs*; instead they are regarded as *subjects* or *taxpayers*.

Ironically enough, while lamenting the evils of slavery in the past, they have failed to account for the fact that, as a fraction of productivity, the average serf up through the nineteenth century actually kept considerably more than the average taxpayer today. Moreover, the average slave of the past actually reserved the option to eventually buy his own freedom: indeed, many slaves became freemen in just this fashion.

In the modern context, however, it is virtually impossible for the average taxpayer to ever reclaim his freedom. He is met everywhere with superficial justifications for his continued enslavement, bound indefinitely to the consensus, the *common good* and the tax collectors who enforce their will; tax collectors representing a kind of government which manages to get the people to comply with every directive, "so long as," per Irwin Schiff in his work *The Kingdom of Moltz*, "it comes in an official envelope."

Whether for the layman, the intellectual or the politician, slavery has never been a question of morality but rather a question of how close the slave ought to be to his master, and what ends his work ought to serve. Whether at the behest of a planter or a government, the matter is hardly about whether man ought to be in chains, but whether he should know who holds the keys.

From this particular point of view, virtually every argument ever waged against slavery has amounted to form over substance. Whereas the politicians and the propagandists decry the indignities of the past, they are generally nowhere to be found on its contemporary forms. They have no interest in the responsibilities of the present, unless those responsibilities are placed exclusively upon the public, otherwise known as the accused or the party presumed guilty; nor do the politicians have any interest in the true study of history. After all, the first might expose their guilt, and, as for the second, such a discipline properly prepares the people for the future; the kind of discipline which stands sharply at odds with the visions, the imaginings, the record and the stated intentions of the Leftists. Indeed, this is the kind of discipline which, above all, stands to expose the truth.

Instead they are found in a perpetual state of ignorance, denial or tunnel vision, cherrypicking anecdotes, revising the history, erecting straw men and stereotypes, blaming and harassing businesses and employers for "exploiting" their employees, who are there, mind you, of their own will; conveniently holding the public responsible for select transgressions of the past and present, whether true or contrived, all while excluding themselves (the politicians) and their culpability as members of the establishment, entirely in keeping with their general policy of establishing a rule and exempting themselves.

This is precisely how socialism becomes popular: by appealing to the masses of the *laborers*, who, through the rhetoric, begin to resent their employers, whom they, conveniently enough, vastly outnumber. In this way, socialism gains steam because the lay and intellectual classes alike confuse their jobs and their employers as obstacles standing between them and their paychecks, their wants and their needs; and, in many cases, they foolishly view their paychecks as a reflection of their value as individuals, instead of viewing them as means, rungs on a ladder, or the assessed value of their current occupations.

In the age of plenty, they are dazzled by consumerism and materialistic wants, confused in their perspectives on wealth: a kind of wealth defined by earthly possessions instead of wisdom; the kind centered on things that degrade at the exclusion of great legacies that live on; the kinds of materialism and covetousness which correspond with the sacrifice of principle, virtue and values.

Indeed, so dazzled and confused are the people, so hypnotized and led astray, that they come to even evaluate *each other* against such superficial standards, dispensing altogether with the concepts of wisdom, heritage, and legacy; neglecting the fact that *true* wealth has less to do with the things one owns than with the lives he touches. With such shallow thinking comes a profoundly hollow view of humanity, one's community, his contemporaries, and the purpose of life. Instead of purpose, one begins to view every struggle and every person as a nuisance or an "injustice", a mere impediment to the life he can nearly imagine. It is no mere coincidence that Leftism feeds on such a people; a population as indifferent to the value and the purpose of life as willing to view each other as stock, tools, and weapons when they are not otherwise regarding each other as inconveniences.

Indeed, as employees, they even begin to view their customers through that lens. This is especially true among those in the public sector, who, instead of giving their unceasing allegiance to the Constitution — or the terms of their employment — and the people whom they are expected to serve, grow tired of the very sight of the public, whom they (by default) hold in contempt as their subordinates, as nuisances, criminals and lowlives.

Whether private or public, once under the influence of socialism, the employees seek to hide from the public, to rule over them, to flex their perceived authority, to avoid their bosses and their clients, or to harshly condemn them. They view their work as *abuse* or *exploitation*, as opposed to more appropriately viewing their employers as the investors, the means by which they are made sufficiently productive to afford and to enjoy those goods; the reason that they are able to *specialize* in their respective fields in order to (presently or eventually) meet their wants and needs, instead of having to work more *generally* in hopes of procuring each of them independently. Instead of an honest and sober outlook on their relationships and the world's economic realities, the Leftists busy themselves with outrage, feelings of indignation, and protests around issues where they are lacking as much in research as in understanding.

Nevertheless, as opposed to being honest about the present and the economic reality of scarcity, the politicians and the propagandists find it much easier to focus selectively on the past at the exclusion of the present, unless they can find a way to frame the present in order to fit with their agenda. I suppose it is all too convenient for them to denounce the past; after all, there is nothing they can do to change it, they do not need to burden themselves with any actual work, and yet they get to hold their heads high as champions of the righteous cause.

In this way, they feel like heroes without ever having done anything; while ignoring the indignities of their time, which have merely assumed fresh disguises; and while even condoning the very same institutions which have, in historical context, met with their unqualified disapproval. This implores us to examine the following question: why is it that, in the estimation of self-described socialists, financial slavery is preferable to agrarian slavery? It is certainly not because it is less violent: after all, no fewer than one hundred million lives were sacrificed at the altar of Leftism over the course of the twentieth century alone. As a fellow author once put it, this makes Leftism the greatest catastrophe in human history.

What's more, their own protests against police brutality, still ongoing, suggest that they at least appreciate the kind of force required by government just to make this all work; yet it is clear that, even where the Leftists are aware of the evils attending too much government, in their view the problem is not that the government has too much power, but that the power is in the wrong hands. Alas, this is the perspective of the establishment, the ones seeking to justify the public's interminable enslavement. Desperate for any plausible excuse, they concoct story after story, narrative upon narrative, and yet they are unable to answer the question: why is their variety of slavery preferable to the agrarian kind, and what makes either one justified?

It is certainly not because slavery by way of public debt, central banking and complicated tax codes is any better or more ethical. Is it because agrarian slavery is just a more conspicuous form of slavery, as opposed to the convoluted system which has since replaced it? Perhaps, but it may also be the case that the socialists do not condemn slavery at all; on the contrary, they merely prefer the kind of slavery which best serves them and their personal interests, which best escapes scrutiny by the unsuspecting slaves. After all, if the socialists had any genuine ethical concerns about slavery, they would at minimum offer their slaves the option of buying their freedom back; but dare to ask them what it might cost, and you will invariably be met with the incredulous looks of crooks and thieves in disbelief that you would even pose such a preposterous question, or otherwise in disbelief that you even have something to offer.

As for the Leftists, they are never prepared to answer that question, because it is neither slavery nor any ethical dilemma which concerns them; their motivations extend to any issue only so far as it serves to expand their power and influence over the establishment. Their judgment is the product not of moral righteousness, but of their own personal insecurities. In this particular case, they are too concerned with sparing themselves the agony of having to witness other people succeeding in life and enjoying their freedom, their property and the product of their own labor. They are too concerned with their own lives and how they would get what they want if not for the slaves doing the work.

Ultimately, even if you present the socialists with a blank check in return for your freedom, they will consider it nothing more than a downpayment on further subjugation, yet another excuse to fleece the public. After all, they will claim that their slaves were wealthy enough to make the offer, and therefore wealthy enough to suffer even more at the hands of the tax collector.

Under socialism, there is only the elusive target of nirvana, the empty promises of better tomorrows; yet, in the pursuit of those promises, the people are conned into relinquishing the right to pursue those aspects of life which make it all worthwhile.

The socialists will stop at nothing to deprive the people of every last right, every last freedom, and every last penny. They will continue their onslaught until every last smile is wiped off the faces of their subjects, who by then are measured not by their wealth, but by their audacity to find any pleasure or personal enjoyment in their lives: these will invariably become the "privileged" people who, as the socialists will describe them, are taking life too lightly in the face of so many social indignities.

In their estimation, every living day ought to be hell for those who do not sympathize enough with the agenda, who have not suffered enough already, or who dare to speak out against it. Neither their work nor their lives, nor those of their heirs, will ever suffice (as the Socialists see it) to justify the end of the siege upon the public and its liberty, just as no amount of suffering will ever suffice as "justice" for so much yet-unproven "transgenerational trauma"; the kind lacking merit both scientifically and for the fact that most claiming to suffer from it are those who know virtually nothing about their own family history, who have no experience with the kind of trauma that they describe, but who, in virtually every case, have a vested interest in selling their narratives.

Whether war, central banking, Social Security, Medicare, Medicaid, affirmative action, gun control, environmental or consumer protection, subsidies for business, housing or education, tariffs, price controls, taxes on income, property, wealth, capital gains, inheritance, or any transaction, the means are always justified by their higher ends; and those means, offset in theory by their motivations, invariably transform any civilization into one massive forced labor camp, where freedom goes virtually extinct as its subjects, one after another, lose their freedom to choose the form, frequency and function of their labor, shortly after they have conceded the product thereof.

Indeed, the problem with those programs and regulations is not whether they sound right, just, or sensible, but whether they can achieve the desired results without causing collateral damage and tearing the fabric of a free society; whether government can exercise enough restraint to refrain from abusing those powers, and whether the people can keep the government accountable when it becomes abusive. With enough time and initiative, and without sufficient pushback, the government eventually has its way with the people, seizing control over virtually every aspect of life.

In this way, the people are made to work for the benefit of the administration, the "elite" and the institutions erected around them; institutions maintaining the establishment while favoring specific groups, or "victims", on the basis of political expediency, favoring them only so far as this arrangement continues to serve the true interests and the ulterior motives of the administration and their fellow "elites".

These groups, the select "victims" for whom the public is made to work, namely take the form of the elderly, the "underserved", the "disenfranchised", and the "most vulnerable" among us. Indeed, they are anointed as "victims" only by the choosing of the Leftists, and they remain members of the "protected class" only so long as they remain allies of the establishment in service to its real agenda. Without fail, those interests are secured by the administration's control over the people, where personal freedom stands, as they see it, only to impede their "progress" and their enjoyment of the spoils.

By way of such schemes as Social Security and Medicare, among others, the public is split into groups as beneficiaries and involuntary benefactors, whereby jealousy and indignation inevitably form the basis for the further expansion of the state through still more social programs to pacify the protestors; programs which, of course, only further compound the problems. Indeed, this is the modus operandi for the Leftist establishment, always "justifying" its expansion under the guise of helping the public and solving social crises.

For this reason, they invariably exploit every imaginable excuse, every social weakness and sensibility, to diminish the public liberty. In this way, the Leftists wrest away every last freedom in their unending crusade against every last sorrow, hardship and inequity inherent to life on their planet. Whatever their cause, it is always fleeting, enduring only so long as it serves to accomplish their true objectives, and always changing to keep the public dazed and confused. After all, in the chaos brought upon them, the people are all the more likely to bicker among themselves as the masters of deceit continue to realize their plans. As the journalist H. L. Mencken once quipped, "The whole aim of practical politics is to keep the populace alarmed (and hence clamorous to be led to safety) by menacing it with an endless series of hobgoblins, most of them imaginary."

Likewise, that sole objective, control, is always concealed by claims which purport to advance the "general welfare" or the "common good" of the people. This is, perhaps, the most insidious aspect of socialism: it is all too often appraised for its purported intentions instead of its predictable results. Put another way, it is celebrated, defended and excused on the basis of its theories; theories esteemed sound and noble, even despite the results in execution.

Where the theories should fail, and at scale they are certain to do so, the Leftists invariably claim that "it wasn't true socialism" or that their ideas are "good in theory, just not in practice". Of course, the truth is that any theory which fails in practice is simply a bad theory which neglects to account for the relevant conditions and possible consequences in practice. This is surely the case with Leftism, which is all too often appraised and ennobled for its stated intentions and fantastical theories instead of its oversights, its repeated failings, and its predictable consequences.

Even the popular online encyclopedia Wikipedia defines Leftism on the basis of its intentions, describing it, first and foremost, as "the range of ideologies... that seek to achieve social equality and egalitarianism." While these intentions are part and parcel of Leftist propaganda, if nothing else constituting part of its advertised ambitions, the definition fails to describe the distinct characteristics and practical methods of Leftism, how you will know it when you see it. After all, it is one thing to describe something as it purports to be, as it views itself or otherwise aspires to be, but it is another to describe it precisely as it is. The latter is the only reasonable definition of any system, object, or idea. Regrettably, by equating Leftism with its intentions, the people are led down the primrose path to their own demise. Appraised at first for its intentions, the people are ultimately doomed to the power of the state, the power necessary just to get things going; the new status quo eventually becoming its own justification into the future.

Socialism then, born at once from popular intentions, sets into stone as convention or tradition, taking on a life of its own. Beyond the intentions and the lives of those who once advocated for it, which inevitably perish, a new generation eventually inherits the tools of its forbears. In this way, socialism outlives the banners, the celebrants, the intentions and the designs from which it was born, leaving newfound power in the hands of fallible human beings progressively ignorant to the original intentions and singularly motivated by personal or political gain.

Even in the wake of its most abject failures, the Leftists never admit that the state has become too powerful. Even where the state has committed such heinous atrocities as genocide and assassination, they claim that the wrong people were in charge or that the state was not powerful enough to prevent the atrocities.

As they see it, government can never be powerful enough; indeed, in their view, "progress" is everlasting. Even where the state proves powerful enough to destroy, in their estimation it should be rendered powerful beyond measure; powerful enough to operate completely unfettered, to function beyond reproach; to frighten all of the world into obedience or hiding; to completely eradicate the opposition; to, when necessary, possess the means to mitigate or to repair its own destruction; and, even more importantly, to possess the means to convince the public that it can do just that. All the while, of course, government becomes *progressively* more powerful, more uncontrollable and more destructive upon assuming a *progressively* wider range of control. After all, its "justifications" are just that: "justifications" for *progressively* more power and control over a public led *progressively* further from their faith, their forbears, their convictions, and their freedom.

From their point of view, freedom is never a plausible alternative. It is here that we find the primary objective of every Leftist, which is to pry away every last freedom, every last penny, and every last right from the grasp of the people. All the while, their clever disguises and noblest of intentions keep the public from ever taking notice.

The intentions and the designs of socialism serve merely to advertise on its behalf; upon the acceptance of socialism within any civilization, the people are brought indefinitely under the authority of the new regime, which can be made to work for any period of time only by the powers of force and coercion. The socialists claim that the dictatorship will eventually wither away, but history decrees that it never withers away; that, on the contrary, the force and coercion necessary to get things started become progressively more necessary to support a system that simply cannot be made to work.

The dictatorship indeed never withers away, with most social revolutions merely recreating similar systems based on similarly hollow, yet often more ambitious, promises. Contrary to the empty promises and the preferred narratives of politicians, political and economic prosperity is proportional to as much as political elites are explicitly denied such power, "where," according to Acemoglu and Robinson in their 2012 work *Why Nations Fail*, "political rights [are]... distributed, where the government [is] accountable and responsive to citizens, and where the great mass of people [can] take advantage of economic opportunities."

Indeed, this is precisely the kind of society which in the nineteenth century brought about "a fundamentally different political and economic trajectory, culminating in the Industrial Revolution." As for the politically-motivated, the activists and the opportunists, whether wittingly or otherwise, they ultimately undermine those forces, managing only to replace them with the kinds of force and coercion demanding progressively more of the same — a kind of *naked force*, as author William L. Shirer describes it in his 1960 work *The Rise and Fall of the Third Reich*, demanding always more *naked aggression* — in order to sustain a system socially, politically, and economically destined for failure.

This is precisely why Leftist states are constantly mobilizing for war: as written in the English interpretation of Sun Tzu's fifth-century BC Chinese military treatise *The Art of War*, "War is a matter of vital importance to the state; a matter of life or death, the road either to survival or to ruin."

"Hence," as written in *The Art of War*, "it is imperative that it be studied thoroughly."

Of necessity, Leftist regimes *must*, for their own survival, mobilize for war; this is an endless state of existence, a necessary condition for Leftism and one of its many features. Their policies lacking the abundance and scalability of the free market, they must wage endless wars for resources, keep their citizens from fleeing, and force them to work for the establishment.

This often results in internal conflict between the oppressed and the oppressors, and international wars between despots fighting over resources to fuel their own empires and eliminate their competition. In many cases, warring nations might even share in their ideologies, but they fight nonetheless, not necessarily over ideological differences, but to secure resources and their alliances which guarantee them a share into the future.

In mobilizing for war, the regime additionally succeeds in distracting the public, rallying support around some manufactured cause, and engendering a warped sense of loyalty to the state. In developing their armies for this endeavor, they enjoy still another crucial advantage: more power over the people, and thus the equipment, logistics and manpower to lay siege upon them, to bring them into conformity, and to quell even the faintest hint of resistance.

This is where *progressivism* and *progressivists* reveal their true colors. Indeed, they are "progressive" only in the growing distance between them and reality, their theories and the truth, and the lengths to which they are willing to go in order to redefine and to minimize the significance of the individual life. Indeed, it comes as no surprise that this represents "progress" for them, not only considering just how much loot they expect to take, but given just how abstract and intellectualized all things eventually become; so abstract and intellectualized, indeed, that so many of them are arrogant enough to believe that they can approximate the value and the purpose of life through their simplistic and truly inhumane models.

Ultimately, as with their total worldview, this is yet another way in which the Leftists reduce the value of human life to interchangeable, quantifiable terms, factors of production, and stock for their political farms and their wicked experiments; experiments which have no regard for life, liberty, or property, let alone the pursuit of happiness which makes life worth living. Nevertheless, the Leftists are always the ones who fancy themselves *progressive*; they fancy themselves so perhaps, among the other reasons, for the amount of force that they will ultimately require to take their experiments to the very end, with regard for neither the costs nor the casualties left in their wake.

As for the leaders of this cohort, they are conveniently immune to the results. This is intentional, as they consistently neglect to define their objectives.

Instead of the ends, they are constantly preoccupied with the means: in this case, any method whereby government can punish, ostracize, silence and steal from their opponents. They are not even remotely interested in practical results, but in getting what they want and expanding their influence.

Even where there is good news, or otherwise true progress, facts and evidence which contradict their narrative, they stand always at the ready to move the goalposts and keep their followers in the fight. They are impervious to any news, facts or evidence which threatens to undermine or distract from their agenda.

Despite its packaging, their agenda is neither *progressive* nor beneficial to the *common good*; on the contrary, it is one toward endless destruction. As it turns out, from their point of view, true progress, facts and evidence are not good for business, and so they keep their followers hypnotized and ready to do their bidding.

From the Leftist's point of view, it is essential not only to suppress the truth but to inoculate the public to it, to make them as ignorant to the truth as fearful of it. As for the partisans, the novice is incredulous to reason, facts and evidence, whereas the expert is completely blind to them, defaulting always to a state of outrage or tunnel vision, constantly preparing to slander his foes and reframe every last discussion and debate. This is out of necessity, as their political movement depends upon it. As the economist and social theorist Thomas Sowell once put it, "The leaders of groups that are lagging are often themselves one of the biggest handicaps of those groups, because they have to depict the problems in ways that will allow them to play the role of rescuers."

The problem is only exacerbated by the fact that the people mistakenly identify them as their *leaders*, when in fact they are, at best, public servants and representatives, at worst, tyrants masquerading as the public's heroes. They are constantly grooming the public to relinquish personal responsibility, to suppress their instincts to instead rely on government in times of trouble; to, like children, rely on government to take care of them; and to, thus, view government through that lens, as parents presiding over, and completely in charge of, the public. Indeed, the establishment has to keep the public convinced that they *need* rescuing and that they can be rescued *only* by government. As opposed to rescuing the public, however, they, like Judas, lead the public to slaughter.

Conveniently for the socialists, by the time their experiment has irrevocably failed, they are either already dead or otherwise incredulous to the results and their part in all of it; in the latter case, they have already prepared their excuses ahead of time, readying their defense by blaming other factors that are, as it turns out, inseparable from any system careening toward socialism.

As for its victims, they are all too often more *informed* than *educated*: that is to say, under socialism they are trained to know *what* to think instead of *how* to think. As it is, by the time all of this finally reaches a head, most of the people are simply too far removed from its origins to truly appreciate the sinister sequence of events which put all of this in motion. As such, in their failure to sound the alarm for all of posterity, they confess their ignorance in condemning their heirs to the same, and the cycle of statism continues unabated.

Not only are their heirs unprepared to articulate the case for freedom, due to fear or incompetence, but they are wildly ill-equipped to physically defend themselves against the monster empowered by their parents to regiment every conceivable aspect of their lives. Whether in their silence, their acquiescence or their activism, the monster lays waste to their freedom and that of their heirs, with the benefit of their approval, implied or otherwise. This is precisely why free people everywhere ought always to stand ready to stand up to despotism where speech and protest have failed; and this is precisely why the Second Amendment to the United States Constitution enshrines that most essential right of the people to defend themselves, their right to keep and bear arms. And this is precisely why that right ought never to be infringed.

For their own reasons, the politicians are always ready to threaten this right. Whether out of ignorance or naïveté, or some measure of both, by the time this right has been sufficiently undermined, by the time the people (as a whole) have surrendered the ability to defend themselves, they are eventually swindled out of their rights, whatever remains of them. This is why it is indispensable to any free people to appreciate and defend their right to keep and bear arms. They owe it not only to themselves but to their heirs, who otherwise stand little chance at enjoying the freedoms once so foolishly taken for granted.

CHAPTER XV

ARMS

For generations, Americans have intensely debated the meaning of the Second Amendment to the United States Constitution. Many of them simply read into it what they prefer to believe, interpreting it to fit with their own particular views on the subject. Fortunately for those in pursuit of the truth, the tools of grammar and the annals of history are at our disposal to wade through all of the noise.

First, it is essential for readers to understand that every power reserved to Congress is expressly enumerated within Article I, Section 8, of the Constitution. Not one of those powers pertains to regulations, limitations or prohibitions on firearms; indeed, not one part of the section pertains in any way to firearms, whether specifically or generally. Remember, Congress reserves the power *to make all Laws which shall be necessary and proper for carrying into Execution the foregoing Powers*, which in this case, regardless of subsequent acts or measures, do not extend to the matter of firearms.

Congress has the power only (1) To lay and collect Taxes, Duties, Imposts and Excises, to pay the Debts and provide for the common Defence and general Welfare of the United States; but all Duties, Imposts and Excises shall be uniform throughout the United States; (2) To borrow Money on the credit of the United States; (3) To regulate Commerce with foreign Nations, and among the several States, and with the Indian Tribes; (4) To establish a uniform Rule of Naturalization, and uniform Laws on the subject of Bankruptcies throughout the United States; (5) To coin Money, regulate the Value thereof, and of foreign Coin, and fix the Standard of Weights and Measures; (6) To provide for the Punishment of counterfeiting the Securities and current Coin of the United States; (7) To establish Post Offices and post Roads; (8) To promote the Progress of Science and useful Arts, by securing for limited Times to Authors and Inventors the exclusive Right to their respective Writings and Discoveries; (9) To constitute Tribunals inferior to the supreme Court; (10) To define and punish Piracies and Felonies committed on the high Seas, and Offenses against the Law of Nations; (11) To declare War, grant Letters of Marque and Reprisal, and make Rules concerning Captures on Land and Water; (12) To raise and support Armies, but no Appropriation of Money to that Use shall be for a longer Term than two Years; (13) To provide and maintain a Navy; (14) To make Rules for the Government and Regulation of the land and naval Forces; (15) To provide for calling forth the Militia to execute the Laws of the Union, suppress Insurrections and repel Invasions; (16) To provide for organizing, arming, and disciplining, the Militia, and for governing such Part of them as may be employed in the Service of the United States, reserving to the States respectively, the Appointment of the Officers, and the Authority of training the Militia according to the discipline prescribed by Congress; (17) To exercise exclusive Legislation in all Cases whatsoever, over such District (not exceeding ten Miles square) as may, by Cession of particular States, and the Acceptance of Congress, become the Seat of the Government of the United States, and to exercise like Authority over all Places purchased by the Consent of the Legislature of the State in which the Same shall be, for the Erection of Forts, Magazines, Arsenals, dock-Yards and other needful Buildings.

Among the enumeration of powers in Article I, Section 8, there is not a single mention, whether expressed or implied, of any power of Congress to regulate, limit or prohibit the sale, distribution, manufacture, use, possession or bearing of firearms.

Indeed, the right to keep and bear arms, as enshrined in the Second Amendment, is ironclad, as immutable as the law of gravity. Any law-abiding American keeping or bearing arms is, in fact, by this enumeration and his divine right, forever free to exercise this right, as with any other, and to do so free from harassment (i.e. *unreasonable searches and seizures*, per the Fourth Amendment), the "Laws of any State to the Contrary notwithstanding" (Article VI, Clause 2).

Those who are desperate to find a Constitutional basis for federal regulations, limitations, or prohibitions on firearms predicate their assertions on the Commerce Clause, which is described above as the power to *regulate commerce with foreign Nations, and among the several States, and with the Indian Tribes*. It is important to note that this clause was never intended to authorize the federal government to regulate business or industry or to determine the bounds of allowable production, pricing or trade. Clearly, the federal government has no jurisdiction in foreign Nations or within the Indian Tribes; likewise, the federal government is equally powerless within the several States.

As written and as intended, the Commerce Clause applies exclusively to the regulation of commerce; in the language of the period, *regulation* being synonymous with *regularization*. As such, the Commerce Clause served only to ensure that interstate commerce (commerce among the several States) would be subject to uniform laws, rules and customs; that no artificial barriers (i.e. taxes, duties or tariffs) nor special privileges in trade or contract enforcement would be implemented between the several States.

This means that any related dispute between the several States would not be left to the States independently, but that they would instead be adjudicated by the federal government in accordance with the law. Remember, the adjudication or *regulation* extends not to the industry nor to the enterprise but explicitly to the *commerce* among the several States. The lone objective of this clause was the interest of free trade between the several States; and that, consistent with the character of free trade, commerce between the several States would enjoy the protection of rights under a uniform rule of law.

It is important to note that the term *regulate* has evolved in its contemporary uses; however, where it appears in the Constitution, it refers explicitly to the maintenance of the cited associations. In the case of commerce, *regulation* thereof was meant only to facilitate free trade among the several states by preventing the institution of artificial barriers between them; and to adjudicate interstate disputes through an impartial judicial system.

The same rings true for the militias, which were meant, when *employed in the Service of the United States*, to serve in cooperation with the several states in order to *execute the Laws of the Union, suppress Insurrections and repel Invasions.*

This is the only condition on which the federal government enjoys any authority at all to govern the militia, whereby their power to *govern* is subject to the authority of Congress and limited to *organizing, arming, and disciplining.*

Indeed, those three powers are precisely the meaning of a *well regulated militia.* There is unmistakable evidence of this in President Thomas Jefferson's first inaugural address on March 4, 1801, where, in the course of outlining *the essential principles of our Government*, he referred specifically to *a well-disciplined militia, our best reliance in peace and for the first moments of war till regulars may relieve them.* As it is written, the Second Amendment attaches the term *regulated* to the *Militia*, not to *the right to keep and bear Arms.* After all, it is that *right* which *shall not be infringed*; and it is *the right of the people*, not of the militia.

As it turns out, the term *regulate* has no bearing at all on the immutable *right to keep and bear Arms.* A *well regulated Militia* is neither a condition nor a qualifier for that right, nor its exclusive purpose. It is, on the contrary, indispensable to the defense of liberty and *the security of a free State*.

Note that this is not its exclusive purpose, because it is otherwise a right more commonly exercised in securing, defending and providing for oneself and his family. It is also worth noting that, in the words of the Constitution, *the right to keep and bear Arms* is essential not for the preservation of the Union, but for *the security of a free State*.

The purpose of the Second Amendment, just as with the enumeration of certain rights in the Constitution, was "not [to] be construed to deny or disparage others retained by the people." This accords with the very conception of the Constitution, drafted at the behest of the several states in seeking to enumerate the "few and defined" powers of the federal government.

Ultimately, the Constitution grants the federal government no power to define or qualify the rights of the people among the several states. After all, governments do not define the rights of mankind; they merely determine just how many of those rights they will honor or otherwise trample. As we are reminded by the Declaration of Independence, the people are endowed with their unalienable rights *not* by government, *nor* by any constitution, but by their Creator; governments are instituted among men to secure those rights.

Now, another argument posits that *the right to keep and bear Arms* extends only to the Militia, on the basis that Congress, per Article I, Section 8, of the Constitution, reserves the power to *provide for organizing, arming, and disciplining, the Militia*. The popular claim is that, through its power over the Militia, the federal government also reserves the authority to regulate, limit or prohibit the manufacture, sale, distribution, and possession of firearms. Of course, members of this camp conveniently omit the next part of the clause in question, which applies to the limits of their power in governing only *such Part of them as may be employed in the Service of the United States*. This particular clause within Article I, Section 8, authorizes the government to *provide for organizing, arming, and disciplining, the Militia* for the express purpose of suppressing insurrections and repelling invasions. It does not confer any authority upon the federal government in the matter of regulating, limiting or prohibiting firearms within the States or among the people.

In total, the term *Militia* appears six times within the Constitution of the United States. The term appears three times in the clauses just described: once in the authorization of the President as the Commander in Chief over the Militia of the several States *when called into the actual service of the United States*; once in characterizing its necessity in the *security of a free State*; and finally once in an exception to the Fifth Amendment *when in actual service in time of War or public danger*.

While some opponents to the Second Amendment have claimed that the amendment applies only to the Militia, their criticisms are not only syntactically untrue in accordance with the rules of grammar, but they also ignore the framework of the Constitution, which enumerates the limited powers of each branch of government in its first three articles, whereas the Bill of Rights seeks to secure those "additional guards in favor of liberty" for the people and the States, respectively.

It is worth remembering that the famed Father of the Constitution, James Madison, wrote strongly in favor of an armed citizenry in *Federalist No. 46*, where he celebrated the ability of the "State governments, with the people on their side... to repel the danger [of a regular army]."

Acknowledging that "governments are afraid to trust the people with arms," Madison wrote:

"Besides the advantage of being armed, which the Americans possess over the people of almost every other nation, the existence of subordinate governments, to which the people are attached, and by which the militia officers are appointed, forms a barrier against the enterprises of ambition, more insurmountable than any which a simple government of any form can admit of."

It is for this reason that the Second Amendment follows the First, and that it seeks to preserve *the right of the people to keep and bear Arms*; this right is most indispensable in the defense of the others that make life worth living, as it stands as the last resort against the "enterprises of ambition" which threaten the public liberty. Thus, in order to defend against the "enterprises of ambition" which threaten the public liberty, it is incumbent upon the people not only to keep and bear Arms, but to properly equip and organize themselves to offset the threat posed by the regular army; it is precisely for this reason that *the right to keep and bear Arms* is unqualified and unconditional, and that the Constitution decrees that it *shall not be infringed*.

It is in just this spirit that the Militia is formed; not as part of the regular army, but as consisting of the people of the several States in defense of their liberty. The Militia, wherever formed, organized or called upon in the defense of liberty, sovereignty, or the United States, depends squarely upon the preparedness of the people in their exercise of this most vital right; for these purposes they may be called upon at a moment's notice, and therefore their right to keep and bear Arms serves not only their personal interests but the general welfare of the people. After all, had the Second Amendment applied exclusively to the Militia, the amendment would have characterized *the right to keep and bear Arms* as one *of the Militia* instead of that *of the people*; moreover, it would have been redundant after Clause

16, which had already enumerated the power of "Congress... to provide for organizing, arming, and disciplining, the Militia."

What's more, it is important to note that governments do not have rights; only persons have rights. Governments are constituted only by the powers that the people cede to them, or alternatively by the impositions generally tolerated among them. It is, indeed, up to the people to decide whether they will accept or tolerate, or otherwise reject or denounce. As etched into the Declaration of Independence, and thereby into the very foundation of these United States, "Governments are instituted among Men, deriving their just powers from the consent of the governed."

Wherever one cites the Second Amendment as a right enjoyed exclusively by the Militia, the individual States or the federal government, it is critically important to remember that the Constitution of the United States does not exhaustively enumerate the rights of the people, but rather the limited powers of the federal government; and that the Bill of Rights does not grant rights but instead seeks to protect some of the rights deemed most vital for the preservation of liberty, state sovereignty and limited government. Indeed, as demanded by the Ninth Amendment, "The enumeration in the Constitution, of certain rights, shall not be construed to deny or disparage others retained by the people." This disposition is subsequently bolstered by the Tenth Amendment: "The powers not delegated to the United States by the Constitution, nor prohibited by it to the States, are reserved to the States respectively, or to the people."

Ultimately, the Second Amendment, as with each of the Bill of Rights, serves to protect the rights of the people and the States, respectively; it is unqualified and unconditional. Indeed, the Second Amendment, as unconditional and as indispensable to liberty as the First Amendment, was conceived as a natural check against the risks attending a central government and a standing army, institutions antithetical to liberty and anathema to the very Spirit of '76.

In the Spirit of '76, it is critically important to remember that it was the several States which achieved independence at the conclusion of the War of Independence and upon signing the Treaty of Paris; that Great Britain recognized not one nation but the States severally in possessing the full measure of their sovereignty and independence. It is important to note this in order to appreciate the character of the Articles of Confederation and the later Constitution of the United States.

The powers of the federal government are derived from the continued consent of the States, respectively, and the States (and the people of those States) respectively assume every power not conferred by them upon the federal government; once that consent is withdrawn, the States individually possess the authority to resume the powers previously conferred.

As such, the Constitution of the United States was written to specify the "few and defined" powers of the federal government; to make plain that the States and the people respectively possess every power not expressly conferred upon the federal government, and that those powers reserved to the States and the people are "numerous and indefinite". Therefore, should any power fail to appear specifically and unequivocally within the Constitution, it is not authorized by the Constitution, and thus it cannot be made law. The case, then, is unequivocal on the matter of the Second Amendment and *the right to keep and bear Arms*: it shall not be infringed.

* * *

"A well regulated Militia, being necessary to the security of a free State, the right of the people to keep and bear Arms, shall not be infringed."

No solitary sentence has been the subject of greater debate than the Second Amendment to the United States Constitution, and no sentence has been more wildly misconstrued or misrepresented. Whenever mankind suffers any devastating loss of life, it appears so common that so many among us leap at the opportunity to cast blame well beyond the individuals responsible for the violent acts.

Many among us automatically conclude that the acts represent some greater trend, a systemic problem, or an eradicable evil. On the one hand, the morbid events that surround us expose the primal instincts of the human race, while the campaigns that leverage them to advance their agendas expose much of the same: the human being is thrust into the position of fighting for survival, and this remains just as relevant for the wilderness as for the political arena, just as relevant for species of animals as for species of thought.

Nowhere can one find a more dogmatic yet violent fight for survival than in the shallow expanses of debate on the subject of America's Second Amendment. Only a limited few subjects can possibly rival this one, and yet while so many people have shared their thoughts on the subject, so little seems to actually be commonly understood about its origins and its purposes.

First, despite popular (and even possibly forgivable) claims that the amendment is modifiable, the Second Amendment is an absolute pinned to the Constitution as an unequivocal imperative with only added context. In the given context of the Second Amendment, that "well regulated militia" describes not a condition but the purpose of including in the Bill of Rights "the [presupposed] right of the people to keep and bear Arms."

In fact, James Madison's first proposed passage for the Bill of Rights, pertaining to arms, was worded even more unequivocally: "The right of the people to keep and bear arms shall not be infringed; a well armed and well regulated militia being the best security of a free country: but no person religiously scrupulous of bearing arms shall be compelled to render military service in person."

In reviewing the Second Amendment and its first draft, it is important to remember that the "right of the people to bear arms" is presupposed, not granted by the Framers of the United States Constitution. What's more, when the Second Amendment refers to "the security of a free State," the text refers not to the Union, but to the several states individually.

As such, during the adoption of the Bill of Rights, the Second Amendment served the mutual interests of both contemporary movements as a means to strengthen the greater resiliency of the Union, while protecting the right of the individual and each sovereign state to use the most effective instrument for defense against their foreseeable enemy: namely the increasingly-powerful and -influential central government.

Remember, the Bill of Rights was attached to the Constitution as a means to placate the so-called Anti-Federalists, who intensely opposed the new Constitution, who preferred the form of federalism established by the foregoing Articles of Confederation. By the way, the "Federalists" merely appropriated the name after the American Revolution, whereupon they denounced their opposition as "Anti-Federalists" in a political campaign aiming to discredit their positions as expressions of disloyalty to the cause of the Revolution.

In the midst of this political jockeying, James Madison moderated his own position just before his election to the U.S. House of Representatives, when he faced a formidable challenger in the form of James Monroe. Formerly opposed to amending the Constitution, Madison campaigned on the promise to seek amendments to secure "additional guards in favor of liberty."

Madison wrote strongly in favor of an armed citizenry in *Federalist No. 46*, where he embraced the capacity of the "State governments, with the people on their side... to repel the danger [of a regular army]."

Acknowledging that "governments are afraid to trust the people with arms," Madison wrote:

"Besides the advantage of being armed, which the Americans possess over the people of almost every other nation, the existence of subordinate governments, to which the people are attached, and by which the militia officers are appointed, forms a barrier against the enterprises of ambition, more insurmountable than any which a simple government of any form can admit of."

In *Federalist No. 45*, Madison described the enumerated powers under the proposed Constitution:

"The powers delegated by the proposed Constitution to the federal government, are few and defined. Those which are to remain in the State governments are numerous and indefinite. The former will be exercised principally on external objects, as war, peace, negotiation, and foreign commerce; with which last the power of taxation will, for the most part, be connected. The powers reserved to the several States will extend to all the objects which, in the ordinary course of affairs, concern the lives, liberties, and properties of the people, and the internal order, improvement, and prosperity of the State."

Regarding the militia, the Constitution offers two concise clauses in Article I, Section 8:

According to Clause 15, "Congress shall have Power to provide for calling forth the Militia to execute the Laws of the Union, suppress Insurrections and repel Invasions."

According to Clause 16, "Congress shall have Power to provide for organizing, arming, and disciplining, the Militia, and for governing such Part of them as may be employed in the

Service of the United States, reserving to the States respectively, the Appointment of the Officers, and the Authority of training the Militia according to the discipline prescribed by Congress."

While some opponents to the Second Amendment have, indeed, claimed that the amendment pertains only to the militia, their criticisms are, as previously noted, not only syntactically untrue, in accordance with the rules of grammar, but they also ignore the very framework of the Constitution, which enumerates in its first three articles the limited powers of each branch of government, whereas the Bill of Rights seeks to secure those "additional guards in favor of liberty" for the people and the states, respectively.

As previously noted, had the Second Amendment applied exclusively to the militia, the amendment would have characterized "the right to keep and bear Arms" as one "of the Militia" instead of that "of the people"; moreover, it would have been redundant after Clause 16, which had already enumerated the power of "Congress... to provide for organizing, arming, and disciplining, the Militia." Remember, governments do not have rights; only people have rights. Governments are constituted only by the powers that the people cede to them, or alternatively by the encroachments broadly tolerated among them.

As etched into the Declaration of Independence, and thereby into the very foundation of these United States, "Governments are instituted among Men, deriving their just powers from the consent of the governed." It is only by some compromise by the people that governments are instituted at all; compromise which is tolerated so far as it serves to preserve man's liberty, to promote man's mutual respect for each other's rights and property, and to ensure, through its limited powers, that, as the French philosopher Montesquieu famously put it, "no man need be afraid of another." Likewise, according to the founding principles of these United States, any and all just power exploited by their central government is derived purely from "the consent of the governed" who are "the creators, not the creatures, of the general government." This means that the people are the possessors of their own unalienable rights and their consent to be governed: their rights are not forged out of thin air by the conceptions between pen and parchment, but rather preexist the instruments which serve to acknowledge or protect them.

Furthermore, wherever one cites the Second Amendment as a right enjoyed exclusively by the militia, the individual states or the central government, it is critically important to remember that the Constitution of the United States enumerates not the rights of the people but the limited powers of the central government, and that the Bill of Rights does not *grant* rights but instead seeks to *protect* some of the rights deemed most vital for the preservation of liberty, state sovereignty and federalism. Indeed, as declared by the Ninth Amendment, "The enumeration in the Constitution, of certain rights, shall not be construed to deny or disparage others retained by the people."

This disposition is subsequently bolstered by the Tenth Amendment: "The powers not delegated to the United States by the Constitution, nor prohibited by it to the States, are reserved to the States respectively, or to the people." Ultimately, the Second Amendment, as with each of the Bill of Rights, serves to protect the rights of the people and the states, respectively. Indeed, the Second Amendment, as unconditional and as indispensable to liberty as the First Amendment, was conceived as a natural check against the risks attending a central government and a standing army, institutions antithetical to both liberty and the cause of the Patriots, the Sons of Liberty.

The Framers of the Constitution, America's famed Forefathers, lamented the notion of a standing army, not merely for the fear that such a force would inevitably become oppressive, but that it would, through its mere existence, suppress the kind of confidence among the people which stands to resist that threat. They rightly feared that such an oppressive force would serve not only to quell resistance but to prevent the very thought of it; a thought which, under such conditions, comes to be regarded as laughable due to the growing disparity in weapons, resources, and power. The very existence of such a powerful and trained force, standing always at the ready to follow the orders of politicians and propagandists, dampens the spirit of liberty, which is choked of life in the presence of unquestionable authority and precious little hope to prevail.

It is, after all, the people and the states, respectively, who possess, in their sheer numbers and the potential for resistance, that most vital check on ambitious government; in the absence of this check, government stands just as ready to press where resistance has relented or altogether capitulated, and nothing is more certain to achieve this end than such a force unfailingly capable of silencing every hint of it. Wherever that spirit of liberty is born, the sobering odds of failure will invariably repress it, suffocating it ahead of its first breath, even before the first volley of fire.

Just as the rights indelibly etched into the Constitution are indispensable to liberty, so too is the standing threat against anyone who aims to curtail them. For this very reason, Thomas Jefferson remarked in his 1787 letter to William Stephens Smith, the future congressman from New York and son-in-law of John Adams, "The tree of liberty must be refreshed from time to time with the blood of patriots and tyrants."

That following year, fellow Founding Father and Virginia Governor Patrick Henry, popularly known for his "Give me liberty, or give me death!" speech to the Second Virginia Convention, argued his point unequivocally at the Virginia ratification convention in 1788, where he advocated in support of the right of man to arm himself and to defend himself against oppression:

"Guard with jealous attention the public liberty. Suspect everyone who approaches that jewel. Unfortunately, nothing will preserve it but downright force. Whenever you give up that force, you are inevitably ruined."

Politicians, everywhere clever and calculated in their attempts to make subjects of their constituents, to disabuse them of the necessity of liberty, to deprive them of that power and that most precious jewel, are constantly vigilant of political opportunities. It is said that a politician never allows a crisis to go to waste, and this adage applies nowhere more so than it applies to this subject. It is for this very reason that free peoples everywhere ought to "guard with jealous attention the public liberty" and the rights which enable them to protect it.

Oftentimes, the threats to their rights and to the public liberty are discreet, cloaked like a wolf in sheep's clothing. Indeed, through the state's myriad disguises, it has never been more successful as the predator. It has been so successful, in fact, that it has convinced many among the prey that there is virtue in their sacrifice and their subordination.

In the modern context, the people have even been fooled into believing that, in becoming *citizens*, they have transcended the rank of *subjects*. Quite the contrary. Where a people are sublimated into citizens, they are, in virtually every case, made into even finer subjects; and, in time, they are made into most willing and obedient ones, citizens who fancy themselves members of civilized society. As the American author and journalist William L. Shirer wrote in his 1960 work *The Rise and Fall of the Third Reich*, the authoritarians eventually succeed in "[making] blind obedience to temporal rulers the highest virtue," whereby, as Shirer puts it, customs evolve to "put a premium on servility."

As such, the greatest threat to *the right to keep and bear arms* is not an outright gun ban, but rather any measure or set of measures which encourages the people to so worship or fear the state that it is popularly viewed as the unquestionable authority on all things proper; that, because of this, there is no reasonable justification for the citizen to even own a firearm; that even the mere thought of obtaining one becomes either superfluous or threatening to the social order. It is precisely in this way, and through all of the "regulatory" hoops, "permitting" processes, and additional financial burdens, that the state makes it ever more unlikely that the average law-abiding person will ever go through the toil of obtaining a firearm.

Through this, and by any measure which makes it unlikely that the average person would ever publicly bear arms or even disclose any information about his firearms to his own allies, war is either ongoing or imminent between the state and the people; a people woefully incapable of defending themselves against any threat. Whether from a lack of firepower or for fear of being exposed as a firearm owner, that society will be rendered defenseless while *the right to keep and bear arms,* among the various other rights essential to liberty, remains intact, albeit only nominally, by technicality or clever legalese.

Prussian general and military theorist Carl von Clausewitz put it likewise in his treatise *Vom Kriege (On War)*, published unfinished in 1832, a year after his death: "War can be of two kinds, in the sense that either objective is to overthrow the enemy — to render him politically helpless or militarily impotent, thus forcing him to sign whatever peace we please."

Of course, this kind of "peace" is more appropriately italicized. This is a kind of *peace* enforced by weapons of war, and, in the case of Leftism, one in which the weapons are used against the people of their own country; one whereby the people are forced to silently submit to the demands of the state, to accept that, as Eric Arthur Blair put it in his work *Nineteen Eighty-Four, war is peace, freedom is slavery,* and *ignorance is strength.*

In this way, any measure or set of measures which induces secrecy among firearms owners, and which makes it unlikely that the average law-abiding person would ever go through the toil to obtain a firearm, is virtually tantamount to a gun ban, different in language but identical in effect. It is for this very reason that the price of liberty is eternal vigilance, and that eternal vigilance is nowhere more necessary than in the matter of man's right to keep and bear arms.

Interestingly enough, we find that the data around gun violence, and around violent crime in general, is actually quite relevant to a wide array of other matters which are intentionally confounded or otherwise met with confusion in the ranks of the Left.

One such example is found where the Leftists cast blame for gun-related crime, of course focusing particularly on the aspect of guns due to their preference for a most obedient citizenry; an objective served, no doubt, by the progressive disarmament of the people.

Indeed, some people attribute the incidence of gun-related crime in America to backward or insensible gun laws, but the data simply do not bear this out. Indeed, up until 2020, the long-term trend had indicated that progressively fewer Americans were dying as a result of gun violence. Indeed, this was the continuation of a trend that began about three decades earlier. Contrary to the popular misconception that America has become more and more violent over time, the data suggest that, up until 2020, it had actually become considerably safer. However, this is not the only story in the data. Indeed, there is a far more interesting tale to tell. Before we get there, let us start with the facts.

First, let us settle the debate on whether America, *prior* to the unsettling events around the lockdowns and the "Black Lives Matter" and "Antifa" riots, had actually become a more violent place over recent decades. Fortunately, the facts are indisputable. As it turns out, the number of privately-held firearms and the incidence of gun-related homicides (each expressed by percentage change over that period) had managed a near-symmetrical divergence over the past three decades; the same being true of the relationship between the average number of guns per person and the number of gun-related homicides per capita.

This decline in gun violence was part of an overall decline in violent crime in America. In fact, according to the FBI's data, the rate of violent crime in America had declined by nearly fifty percent since its peak in 1991. On balance, up until 2020, America had become a much less violent place, at least as measured.

Second, despite the long-term trajectory of gun-related crime, the United States has never before been in such steep moral decline. At no time in American history has there ever been a higher incidence of single-parent households: seventy-five percent among black families, sixty-one percent among Hispanic/Latino families, thirty-nine percent among white families, and twenty-three percent among Asian families.

These figures are vastly different from the data compiled half a century ago. Indeed, since 1970, out-of-wedlock birth rates have soared. In 1965, twenty-four percent of black infants and three percent of white infants were born to single mothers. By 1990, the rates had suddenly risen to sixty-four percent for black infants, eighteen percent for whites; and, it is worth noting, there are a number of alarming outcomes particularly associated with single-parent households, not least of which is the prevalence of economic instability, welfare dependency, academic and professional underperformance, criminal activity and psychological disorders — not to mention this demographic's tendency to favor Leftist administrations.

Indeed, upon assessing the profile of the majority of the gunmen involved in mass shootings, it is apparent that the majority of them come from broken and dysfunctional households, characterized by single parents, fatherlessness, and drug addictions, each of which has been on the rise since the New Frontier and the Great Society campaigns of the 1960s.

It is also worth noting that the United States is not even remotely one of the most violent countries in the world. Latin America, Africa, and the Middle East are far more violent; and for those who are prepared to refer to Canada or European examples, take note of their scale and their demographics, as they are not nearly as large or as multicultural. Note that this author did not say "diverse". This author has intentionally used the term "multicultural". There is a significant difference between "diversity" and "multiculturalism", and these considerations, in addition to all of the others described here, distinguish America from every country of the world. Of course, these considerations are positively indispensable to any like comparison between data sets and for any scientific assessment of any kind.

As part of any such assessment, it is also important to note that the United States has far more major cities than any other country, and that the incidence (per capita) of gun-related crime is concentrated in those major cities and metropolises. It is also worth noting that, relative to the likes of China's major cities and others across the globe, American cities are not demographically representative of the country's total population.

This means that demographic influences are particularly relevant in the American case study. And no, contrary to the common misconception, population density need not necessarily drive a higher incidence of gun-related crime, relative to rural counterparts. Although generally true in America, certain comparisons reveal just the opposite; but once again, these outcomes directly relate to demographic compositions of the respective case studies. In the first, they are dissimilar, whereas in the second they are more alike.

To demonstrate this point, we need not look any further than the city of El Paso, Texas. More than eighty percent of El Paso's residents are Hispanic, and the vast majority of these individuals are of Mexican origin; and, as it turns out, El Paso is one of the safest cities in the United States, with a homicide rate of 2.4 per one hundred thousand residents.

While there are plenty of crime-ridden cities in America with significant Hispanic populations, El Paso is just one example of monocultural harmony. This is one consideration that is, for obvious political reasons, routinely overlooked or ignored, but one that is absolutely essential for any honest assessment of this kind. In such cases where monocultural cities, towns, or neighborhoods have otherwise lacked in harmony, it is, among other factors, due to the character of the culture itself; in most cases a lack of harmony within the household to begin with.

Now, because of their respective population densities and various ethnicities, China and India are often referenced for purposes of further comparison. However, despite their apparent ethnic diversity, they are not nearly as *multicultural* as the United States; their cities are, unlike the United States, fairly representative of the total population; and their incidence of single-parent households is not even remotely comparable to that of the United States.

The same goes for Canada, any European nation, and every other country across the globe. Upon a close and honest assessment of the data, one invariably finds that these outcomes have corresponded most reliably with the incidence of single-parent households in the United States, and that countries elsewhere across the globe still retaining their traditions and family values have not suffered the same fate. In a 2022 interview with ABC News, John Hinckley, the man who attempted to assassinate President Ronald Reagan in March of 1981, likewise described his condition in these terms: "I was just totally depressed, totally despairing of my life. I thought I had nowhere to turn. I had become totally estranged from my family. That was the worst part of it."

It is only through dishonesty or incredulity, generally one and the same, that so many are led astray from the truth. In this case, if we were to indulge the arguments made in favor of other nations and their favored policies, those of Chinese or Indian ethnicity would be expected to be far more violent in the United States, and yet they are no more violent in America than they were in their native lands. The same rings true for those of German, Canadian, and Scandinavian ethnicity. Indeed, this principle rings true for virtually every ethnic group across the globe; that, upon legally becoming an American, scarcely one of them spontaneously becomes more violent. Of course, this is not to say that immigrants are not violent, but only that they scarcely become *more* violent upon legally becoming Americans.

On the demographics front, the two groups disproportionately responsible for gun-related crime in America are blacks and Hispanics/Latinos; they also happen to have the highest incidence of single-parent households. It is also worth noting that the incidence of gun-related homicides is highest (by total) in predominately-black cities and (per capita) throughout the regions of the United States dominated by blacks and Hispanics/Latinos.

Ultimately, an honest and objective assessment of the data reveals a variety of factors generally responsible for the outcomes described in this writing. While no writing could, in the interest of brevity, possibly seek to account for every conceivable factor, we are ultimately left with two particular factors strongly correlated with criminal activity: demographics and single-parent households. Where anyone seeks to resolve the problem of crime in America, especially gun-related crime, without first accounting for these factors, you can rest assured that his work is in service to some unrelated political agenda; thus warranting every bit of the suspicion attending the subject of *gun control*, and indeed necessitating the highest form of vigilance in order to maintain the public liberty.

In keeping with that concept of public liberty and that suspicion toward government, it is worth remembering that the official purpose of the Bill of Rights was "to prevent misconstruction or abuse of [the Constitution's] powers" and to "extend the ground of public confidence" through the complement of "further declaratory and restrictive clauses" that "will best ensure the beneficent ends of its institution."

So when the savvy politician capitalizes on public despair and grief, or when the political contagion takes hold over family and friends who are susceptible to the message, unveil the fraud and remind them of the origins of the right to bear arms. Remind them of the perils of sacrificing on the margin any measure of this right. Remind them that it is government that beats ceaselessly against liberty, carving out its place insofar as the once-free people have relinquished control over their own defense, and effectively freedom in their lives. Once this obstacle is finally overcome by government, there is absolutely nothing to restrain the orders that follow.

Once a free people are no longer free and prepared to defend themselves against oppression, their freedoms, their votes and their rights are rendered moot; they will survive no longer than their founding documents to the fiery inferno, whose intensity will be predictably outmatched by the fervor of impassioned politicians and opportunists who will, reminiscent of Sherman's March to the Sea, exterminate every last "enemy" or "traitor" as they realize the "National Will" by "[making their opponents] to feel... the existence of a strong government, capable of protecting as well as destroying" and, as Sherman's wife described it, driving them "like Swine into the sea."

In the course of their extermination, they will make haste to exterminate any form of truth, resistance or dissension which stands in their way; and, just as with Sherman's deadly March to the Sea, which witnessed the razing of towns, the pillaging of homes, and the ruining of lives, they will scarcely spare the precious artifacts of history and heritage which serve to enshrine their memory. Just as poetic in its symbolism as devastating in its consequence, this is precisely what happened during Sherman's wretched campaign across the South, which led to the destruction of one of the largest collections of books and Revolutionary War manuscripts in the country, at the home of William Gilmore Simms, whom Edgar Allan Poe regarded as the best novelist America had ever produced.

In this way, "the right of the people to keep and bear Arms" serves not only to faithfully secure the freedom and sovereignty of any people but to reliably defend heritage, history and, above all, truth.

The right to keep and bear arms is as essential to liberty as it is to life and the pursuit of happiness. It is the final check against the abuses of government, and the final safeguard for liberty and the sovereignty of man. It is for this very reason that America's Founding Fathers hotly debated the terms of their Union, and that they sought to preserve this right along with the sovereignty of the several states. Indeed, these issues were at the forefront of the American Revolution, and nearly a century later they would culminate in a not-so-civil war at the cost of nearly one million lives and the cause for which our forefathers so fervently labored to defend.

CHAPTER XVI

"MIGHT MAKES RIGHT"

In the aftermath of the War between the States, the federal government asserted the notion that "might makes right". As the Federals mobilized troops throughout the Southern states, during and for many years following the war, they busied themselves with political *reconstruction* of the Union, flatly disregarding the question of constitutionality.

Upon the surrender of the Confederate States, the federal government firmly established its claim, and it has since gone without question. However, one particular judge has issued a dissenting opinion: that is the judge of reason, which implores us to reexamine this claim and to reassert the truth in the matter of states' rights, a matter indispensable to the case for liberty and limited, representative government.

Upon claiming victory in their siege upon the South, and after shredding the very fabric of the Constitution, the Federals celebrated the "preservation of the Union" as they brought the Southern states under their control as "conquered provinces". From their point of view, the truth was simply irrelevant, or otherwise whatever they determined it *should* be. Strangely, their assertion that "might makes right" seems to stand alone today, as it did then, as a sufficient case for its acceptance. After all, upon having proven sufficient might, what use is there in any argument?

Should the argument prevail in reason, and should it accord with the facts, it is still impotent against the conquerors who assert that *might makes right*. After all, wherever the conquerors succeed, they are unaccountable to the truth; after all, they write the history and, at their will, determine the bounds of allowable opinion, penalizing those who dare to do anything more with the truth than to contemplate it. Even still, one's sympathy, whether expressed or suspected, is often sufficient cause for public harassment or arrest.

Apart from their steel swords and metal shields, the tyrants are always ready to use their weapons of choice: their fountain pens and their silver tongues. In fact, those are the only weapons the politicians personally know how to use, and they are always prepared to use them to con the people out of their resources and their liberties, and to confuse them into thinking that they are getting a good deal. What's more, they always have the advantage of plausible deniability, prepared on every occasion to blame their failures on inadequate resources, insufficient compliance, or too little power; in this way, they weaponize their failures in their attempt to justify seizing still more resources from, and more power over, the people, relentlessly shaming the public into compliance and conformity.

The tyrants are always crafty in their excuses. In some cases, they will place the blame on "a few bad apples" in their ranks when it is actually a whole orchard full of them. They will point to a few rogue agents when in fact the entire agency has gone rogue. They will point to a fixable fault when it is essentially the entire system that is corrupt. The tyrants have the further benefit of coupling their persistence with their power and the (virtually unlimited) resources stolen from their victims; and so long as they insist that they are right and just, so long as they never admit that they were wrong, few will be brazen or knowledgeable enough to challenge them, and even fewer will have the power to effect any meaningful change. After all, once the tyrants have asserted and affirmed *that might makes right*, the truth is little more than academic: something whispered, readily abandoned, and forgotten as soon as it becomes too dangerous to contemplate.

So, what use is there in seeking the truth about the matter when the findings stand to change nothing of any material consequence? Like any other inheritance left to our heirs, we may not enjoy it materially in our time, but we shall enjoy the prospect of its impact in theirs. While it may be of little consequence today, its survival is key: the abandonment of truth is even more dangerous than the regime which suppresses it. The value of truth is within itself; it is, like virtue, its own reward, independent of appraisal and approbation. He who pursues the truth makes an honest living, and thus makes a sufficient case for its practice.

In the case of truth, as in life, the journey is often more important than the destination. In the case of truth, the journey brings unrivaled riches in the form of knowledge, wisdom and discipline; it serves likewise as a beacon for others in pursuit of the same, and it blazes the trail for continued discovery and preserves its findings for future generations. While the discoveries may not revolutionize public opinion, and while they may even face rejection or outright condemnation, they are more important than one can possibly fathom.

In short, a commitment to truth affords our heirs a chance of knowing it, and with it a chance of an honest and fulfilling life. The forces which seek to suppress the truth are more pernicious than one can possibly imagine; not even those undertaking its suppression can appreciate its implications.

Once a people abandon the truth, in time they can be made to believe almost anything. As a matter of practice, the truth keeps a people honest, principled and prepared to defend themselves against mischief and deceit. At the interpersonal level, the abandonment of truth will corrupt; at the social and political levels, it stands to destroy.

In the case of the War between the States, the author's cause is to determine the truth in the matter of states' rights. With the help of the architects of the United States, we will seek to ascertain the truth about the designs and the intentions of their Union. We will ascertain whether "might makes right", and whether the federal government even possessed the authority to exercise its might. For these purposes, we will rely exclusively on personal testimonies and the written word; piece by piece, we will exhume the truth. As Jefferson Davis proclaimed, "Truth crushed to the earth is truth still and like a seed will rise again."

For the purposes of seeking the truth about the designs and the intentions of the Union, we shall examine its foundations through the eyes of its architects, the proceedings of their conventions, and the contents of their final product: the Constitution. Let us begin with the Declaration of Independence:

"We hold these truths to be self-evident, that all men are created equal, that they are endowed by their Creator with certain unalienable Rights, that among these are Life, Liberty and the pursuit of Happiness.–That to secure these rights, Governments are instituted among Men, deriving their just powers from the consent of the governed, – That whenever any Form of Government becomes destructive of these ends, it is the Right of the People to alter or to abolish it, and to institute new Government, laying its foundation on such principles and organizing its powers in such form, as to them shall seem most likely to effect their Safety and Happiness."

These sacred words are underscored here to stress their necessity in the preservation of liberty, the conditions for the just powers of government and, ultimately, the authority which inherently enables "the consent of the governed" to confer those powers: authority in the form of man's own self-ownership. It is the sovereignty of man, as expressed by his consent through his representatives, which, to any extent, legitimizes the state; thus, it is through the sovereignty of man that any state enjoys any measure of sovereignty at all. It is through sovereignty that one possesses the authority to consent to any association, and it is only by one's continued consent that the association is maintained. It follows logically, then, that where any state, having once consented to any union, withdraws from that union, it is always free to separate and to thereby reaffirm her sovereignty. Indeed, this is the very case pronounced by the Declaration of Independence, and it was a case reaffirmed in the United States up to the dreaded War of Northern Aggression; and, as Jefferson Davis put it, "There was a time when none denied it."

In his 1881 treatise *The Rise and Fall of the Confederate States*, Davis elaborates on the right of secession, a remedy indispensable to American tradition and the defense of that principle which asserts that "there [is] no divine right to rule; that no man inherit[s] the right to govern." Davis explains that "[Secession] is to be justified upon the basis that the States are sovereign", whereafter he expresses his "hope [that] the time may come again when a better comprehension of the theory of our Government, and the inalienable rights of the people of the States, will prevent any one from denying that each State is a sovereign, and thus [that each] may reclaim the grants which it has made to any agent whomsoever."

That time, should it ever arrive, will come no sooner than a better comprehension of our forbears, the stake consistently defended throughout our history, and the clues left behind to lead us to the truth. This truth and "[t]he impartial and enlightened verdict of mankind" will vindicate the Confederacy in their separation; it will vindicate "the rectitude of [their] conduct" and the men who labored so sincerely "to preserve the Government of our fathers in its spirit." We shall remember that spirit through the words themselves, as written by the men who delivered them, who constructed a truly new form of government on the "consent of the governed", and whose cause inspired them to "pledge to each other [their] lives, [their] fortunes, and [their] sacred honor."

In this endeavor, it behooves us to remember the words of Thomas Jefferson. With reverence for sound practice and the principles duly enshrined within the Constitution, Jefferson believed that allowing a state (or any number of states) to secede would demonstrate the general government's commitment to the First Amendment's guarantee of free speech, in addition to their express protections enumerated in the Tenth Amendment. It behooves us to remember that President Jefferson, in his First Inaugural Address in 1801, declared, "If there be any among us who would wish to dissolve this Union or to change its Republican form, let them stand undisturbed as monuments of the safety with which error of opinion may be tolerated where reason is left free to combat it."

Notice that, on the matter of any state seeking secession or, specifically, "wishing to dissolve this Union", Jefferson declared that the Union shall "[l]et them stand undisturbed". In his First Inaugural Address, Jefferson made plain his interest in defending that sacred right of secession even where he estimates an "error of opinion". Jefferson even wrote to Madison in 1787, stating that "a little rebellion now and then is a good thing, and as necessary in the political world as storms in the physical... a medicine necessary for the sound health of government."

Jefferson maintained this position fifteen years later, after the New England Federalists attempted to secede from the Union, stating: "If any state in the Union will declare that it prefers separation... to a continuance in Union... I have no hesitation in saying, 'let us separate'."

Even John Quincy Adams, a staunch Unionist, in his 1839 speech celebrating the Jubilee of the Constitution, defended the essential right to secession: "The indissoluble link of Union between the people of the several states of this confederated nation is, after all, not in the right but in the heart. If the day should ever come (may Heaven avert it!) when the affections of the people of these States shall be alienated from each other; when the fraternal spirit shall give way to cold indifference, or collusion of interests shall fester into hatred, the bands of political association will not long hold together parties no longer attracted by the magnetism of conciliated interests and kindly sympathies; to part in friendship from each other, than to be held together by constraint. Then will be the time for reverting to the precedents which occurred at the formation and adoption of the Constitution, to form again a more prefect Union by dissolving that which could no loner bind, and to leave the separated parts to be reunited by the law of political gravitation to the center."

Alexis de Tocqueville supported the same in his own interpretations:

"The Union was formed by the voluntary agreement of the States; and in uniting together have not forfeited their nationality, nor have they been reduced to the condition of one and the same people. If one of the states chooses to withdraw from the compact, it would be difficult to disprove its right of doing so, and the Federal Government would have no means of maintaining its claims directly either by force or right."

Alexander Hamilton even asserted the same principles in *Federalist No. 81*: "It is inherent in the nature of sovereignty not to be amendable to the suit of any individual without its consent. This is the general sense and the general practice of mankind; and the exemption, as one of the attributes of sovereignty, is now enjoyed by the government of every State in the Union... The contracts between a nation and individuals are only binding on the conscience of the sovereign, and have no pretensions to a compulsive force. They confer no right of action, independent of the sovereign will. To... authorize suits against States for the debts they owe... could not be done without waging war against a contracting State... , a power which would involve such a consequence, would be altogether forced and unwarranted."

America's early history reasserted these principles, securing their enjoyment, as Hamilton put it, *by the government of every*

State in the Union. Indeed, during the New England secession crisis, the New England Federalists publicly threatened secession while Federalist newspapers and clergy demanded it, and the Hartford Convention proceeded without any interference from the general government. New England even went so far as to refuse to send militia upon Madison's request, effectively signaling secession while agitating for it officially during the War of 1812.

These principles were so essential to the formation of the United States that the Founders and the Framers hardly expected an eternal Union, but rather anticipated a splintering into confederacies with congenial characters whose mutual wants would render a friendly and commercial intercourse inevitable. As Colonel Timothy Pickering wrote on December 23, 1803, "The Southern States would require the naval protection of the Northern Union, and the products of the former would be important to the navigation and commerce of the latter." In the formation of the original confederation, just as in the establishment of the *more perfect Union*, there was never any misconception or legal principle which led the states or the people to conclude that they were bound to the Union by force. Such a concept would have hardly satisfied the Patriots who had just defended their liberty and independence against that very foe.

The powers, privileges and rights which exist beyond those few and defined powers, which are to remain with the states and the people, are numerous and indefinite. It is, thus, the prerogative of the sovereign states, and the people who comprise them, to defend those rights with the tools at their disposal, among them the right of secession.

In summary, the War Between the States was a veritable war of aggression in response to an expression of independence by eleven states that reserved every constitutional and natural right to secede: the Tenth Amendment to the Constitution reads, "The powers not delegated to the United States by the Constitution, nor prohibited by it to the States, are reserved to the States respectively, or to the people." Since the Constitution omits any mention of the power of the federal government to prevent separation or secession, this power is rightly reserved to the "States respectively, or to the people."

Article II of America's original Articles of Confederation expressed this right in even clearer terms:

"Each state retains its sovereignty, freedom, and independence, and every power, jurisdiction, and right, which is not by this Confederation expressly delegated to the United States, in Congress assembled."

Upon the release of the official Declaration of Independence on July 2, 1776, after securing support from twelve of the thirteen colonies, two days before it was formally approved by Congress, the Pennsylvania Evening Post reported, "This day the CONTINENTAL CONGRESS declared the UNITED COLONIES FREE and INDEPENDENT STATES."

The following day, the Pennsylvania Gazette reported, "Yesterday, the CONTINENTAL CONGRESS declared the UNITED COLONIES FREE and INDEPENDENT STATES."

Likewise, the Declaration of Independence itself stated, "Resolved, That these United Colonies are, and of right ought to be, free and independent States... That a plan of confederation be prepared and transmitted to the respective Colonies for their consideration and approbation."

By all accounts, both formal and informal, *de jure* and *de facto*, enumerated and intended, the Union was formed as a confederation of free and independent states. As such, the several states are not as much bound by the federal government as the federal government is bound by the will and the consent of the sovereign states. Indeed, the merits of these words are found not in the canonization of text but rather in the sound reason which guided the quill.

It is the natural course of representative government to separate into smaller bodies, where the proportion of inhabitants to representatives remains conducive to representative government. James Madison wrote in *The Federalist Papers*, Numbers 55 and 56, that the Federal government would consist of "one [representative] for every thirty thousand inhabitants."

Secession, not only an essential course for representative government and developing populations, produced several of America's states: Franklin (later Tennessee) from North Carolina in 1784, Kentucky from Virginia in 1791, and Maine from Massachusetts in 1820.

The founding of the United States was itself born out of this very principle once the states declared their independence from Great Britain in 1776; seven years later in the Treaty of Paris in 1783, Great Britain would even formally recognize not one Union but the existence of thirteen sovereign states, three of which — New York, Rhode Island, and Virginia, respectively — would expressly enumerate the right of secession, in their own specific language, in their ratification of the United States Constitution.

New York expressed herself as follows:

"That the powers of government may be reassumed by the people whenever it shall become necessary to their happiness; that every power, jurisdiction, and right, which is not by the said Constitution clearly delegated to the Congress of the United States, or the departments of the Government thereof, remains to the people of the several States, or to their respective State governments, to whom they may have granted the same; and that those clauses in the said Constitution, which declare that Congress shall not have or exercise certain powers, do not imply that Congress is entitled to any powers not given by the said Constitution; but such clauses are to be construed either as exceptions to certain specified powers or as inserted merely for greater caution."

Virginia expressed herself similarly:

"That the powers granted under the Constitution being derived from the People of the United States may be resumed by them whensoever the same shall be perverted to their injury or oppression and that every power not granted thereby remains with them and at their will."

Rhode Island reinforced the same in her own ratification documents:

"That Congress shall guarantee to each State its sovereignty, freedom, and independence, and every power, jurisdiction, and right, which is not by this Constitution expressly delegated to the United States."

Even South Carolina and North Carolina went out of their way to unequivocally condition their assent to the new Constitution on their retention of powers "not expressly relinquished by them and vested in the General Government of the Union."

South Carolina expressed herself thus:

"This Convention doth also declare that no section or paragraph of the said Constitution warrants a construction that the States do not retain every power not expressly relinquished by them and vested in the General Government of the Union."

North Carolina likewise affirmed the same:

"Each State in the Union shall respectively retain every power, jurisdiction, and right, which is not by this Constitution delegated to the Congress of the United States or to the departments of the General Government."

Whether America's War of Independence, the Hartford Convention, the Tariff of Abominations, the Louisiana Purchase, the annexation of Texas, or even the very Constitution ratification documents of several states, the American tradition is expressly one of state sovereignty, secession and cautious apprehension toward government.

In this sense, secession is truly an American tradition and an essential course for representative government.

Indeed, even far in advance of the War Between the States, in the very infancy of the newfound republic, Colonel Timothy Pickering, formerly an officer in the cabinet of General Washington of the Continental Army during the Revolution who had afterward successively served as Postmaster General, Secretary of War, and Secretary of State, was one of the leading secessionists of his day.

Writing from Washington to a friend on December 24, 1803, then-Senator Pickering of Massachusetts proclaimed prophetically:

"I will not despair. I will rather anticipate a new confederacy, exempt from the corrupt and corrupting influence and oppression of the aristocratic democrats of the south. There will be (and our children, at farthest, will see it) a separation. The white and black population will mark the boundary."

Pickering wrote subsequently on January 29, 1804, denouncing the wrongs and abuses perpetrated by the existing administration upon expressing his views of the remedy to be applied:

"The principles of our Revolution point to the remedy — a separation. That this can be accomplished, and without spilling one drop of blood, I have little doubt."

Pickering then affirmed the Jeffersonian view of a continent settled separately by a greater number of republics sharing mutually in their economic and political interests without compromising the designs and the fruits of representative government by the consent of the governed:

"I do not believe in the practicability of a long-continued Union. A Northern Confederacy would unite congenial characters and present a fairer prospect of public happiness; while the Southern States, having a similarity of habits, might be left to 'manage their own affairs in their own way.' If a separation were to take place, our mutual wants would render a friendly and commercial intercourse inevitable. The Southern States would require the naval protection of the Northern Union, and the products of the former would be important to the navigation and commerce of the latter."

Pickering then specified the strategy for such a separation:

"It must begin in Massachusetts. The proposition would be welcomed in Connecticut; and could we doubt of New Hampshire? But New York must be associated; and how is her concurrence to be obtained? She must be made the center of the Confederacy. Vermont and New Jersey would follow of course, and Rhode Island of necessity."

Decades later, it would appear that, as President Jefferson Davis penned in his own memoirs, "we find the suggestions of 1860-'61 only a reproduction of those thus outlined nearly sixty years earlier." Indeed, the reproduction becomes clear upon substituting South Carolina for Massachusetts; Virginia for New York; Georgia, Mississippi, and Alabama for New Hampshire, Vermont, and Rhode Island; Kentucky for New Jersey, et cetera.

In *The Rise and Fall of the Confederate Government*, Jefferson Davis wrote of another such instance of the asserted right of secession:

"In the prior history of the country, repeated instances are found of the assertion of this right, and of a purpose entertained at various times to put it in execution. Notably is this true of Massachusetts and other New England states. The acquisition of Louisiana in 1803 had created much dissatisfaction in those states for the reason, expressed by an eminent citizen [George Cabot] of Massachusetts, that 'the influence of our {the Northeastern} part of the Union must be diminished by the acquisition of more weight at the other extremity.' The project of a separation was freely discussed, with no intention, in the records of the period, of any idea among its advocates that it could be regarded as treasonable or revolutionary."

Thus, secession was not merely the spirit of the Revolution; indeed, it was the natural and expected course of the American Republic, a right expressed at various times for different reasons, and by separate states. Needless to say, the right of secession was not just reserved to the states but universally respected among them. Above all, it is an established and indispensable right, and one historically exercised by those in the North as with those in the South.

In his 1804 letter to Theodore Lyman, Pickering elaborated further against hostile feelings or ill will toward the South:

"While thus contemplating the only means of maintaining our ancient institutions in morals and religion, and our equal rights, we wish no ill to the Southern States and those naturally connected with them. The public debts might be equitably apportioned between the new confederacies, and a separation somewhere about the line above suggested would divide the different characters of the existing Union. The manners of the Eastern portion of the States would be sufficiently congenial to form a Union, and their interests are alike intimately connected with agriculture and commerce. A friendly and commercial intercourse would be maintained with the States in the Southern Confederacy as at present. Thus all the advantages which have been for a few years depending on the general Union would be continued to its respective portions, without the jealousies and enmities which now afflict both, and which peculiarly embitter the condition of that of the North."

Pickering concluded, "It is not unusual for two friends, when disagreeing about the mode of conducting a common concern, to separate and manage, each in his own way, his separate interest, and thereby preserve a useful friendship, which without such separation would infallibly be destroyed."

During his tenure in the House of Representatives, Abraham Lincoln even acknowledged the vital right of secession in his polemic against US aggression during the Mexican-American War:

"Any people anywhere, being inclined and having the power, have the right to rise up, and shake off the existing government, and form a new one that suits them better. This is a most valuable – a most sacred right – a right, which we hope and believe, is to liberate the world."

If only these were more than words to Lincoln, and if only he actually upheld the Constitution which he swore an oath to preserve, protect and defend, the War Between the States could have been swiftly averted.

Ultimately, the right of secession was so solemnly defended that Confederate President Jefferson Davis defended it even "when the doctrine of coercion was rife" for "the rescue of a fugitive slave in Boston." As Davis wrote in 1881, "My opinion then was the same that it is now... that if Massachusetts — following her purpose through a stated line of conduct — chose to take the last step, which separates her from the Union, it is her right to go, and I will neither vote one dollar nor one man to coerce her back; but I will say to her, Godspeed, in memory of the kind associations which once existed between her and the other States."

Indeed, among the founding generation, free speech, freedom of association, and the right of secession were rights to be jealously defended. The proceedings from the Constitutional Convention offer only further support for these American institutions.

During the Constitutional Convention, an early proposal sought to confer upon the Congress the power "to call forth the force of the Union against any member of the Union failing to fulfill its duty under the articles thereof." Upon consideration of this proposition, a certain observer noted that "a union of States containing such an ingredient seemed to provide for its own destruction." The observer continued: "The use of force against a State would look more like a declaration of war than an infliction of punishment, and would probably be considered by the party attacked as a dissolution of all previous compacts by which it might be bound."

The observer hoped that such a system would be framed as might render this recourse unnecessary, and moved that the clause be postponed. This motion was adopted, and the proposition was never again revived. The same observer subsequently commented on an appeal to force: "Was such a remedy eligible? Was it practicable? Any government for the United States, formed on the supposed practicability of using force against the unconstitutional proceedings of the States, would prove as visionary and fallacious as the government of Congress."

Every such proposition seeking the same or any similar object was promptly rejected by the convention. Who was that observer? Of course, it was James Madison, otherwise known as the "Father of the Constitution".

On the subject at hand, we have still further context from a fellow observer, George Mason of Virginia, who said of such a proposition: "Will not the citizens of the invaded State assist one another, until they rise as one man and shake off the Union altogether?" As urged by their own Declaration of Independence, "when a long train of abuses and usurpations, pursuing invariably the same Object evinces a design to reduce them under absolute Despotism, it is their right, it is their duty, to throw off such Government, and to provide new Guards for their future security."

In the case of invasion or war upon any fellow state, the Constitution is most unequivocal on the subject: per Article III, Section 3, "Treason against the United States, shall consist only in levying War against them, or in adhering to their Enemies, giving them Aid and Comfort." Consistent with the rest of the Constitution, the term "them" refers to the "states respectively", each constituting "one of the United States"; they were not, in acceding to the Constitution, to be taken as part of one monolithic body.

Thus, the Northern onslaught upon the Southern states, as one Charles Dickens described it in 1862, qualified as treason; it forever mutilated their compact in both form and spirit, and it irrevocably shattered the designs of American federalism. Their onslaught upon the Southern states not only justified the separation, but made it mankind's "duty" to "throw off such Government, and to provide new Guards for their future security."

Likewise, the general government's onslaught not only disgraced the Declaration of Independence, but plainly violated the very Constitution that brought that government to life. It stands to reason, thus, that the sovereigns which brought it to life ought rightly to reserve the power to secede, to resume the powers formerly conferred to that government, and, if necessary, to destroy the monster to prevent any further damage. As written in the Declaration of Independence, "[they] are, and of Right ought to be, Free and Independent States," free to associate, just as they are free from coercion and thus free to dissolve their associations.

On the subject of dissolution, otherwise termed *secession*, there is the question of whether this power remains with the states, respectively. There is, at first, the question of whether the states are even sovereign and independent. Fortunately, the Father of the Constitution was unambiguous on this particular subject. The reader finds a clear answer to this question in *Federalist No. XL*:

"We have seen that, in the new Government as in the old, the general powers are limited; and that the States, in all unenumerated cases, are left in the enjoyment of their sovereign and independent jurisdiction."

In a letter to George Washington on October 23, 1786, U.S. Secretary at War Henry Knox affirmed the same, regarding "[o]ur political machine" as "constituted of thirteen independent sovereignties."

This principle was ultimately enshrined in the Constitution's Tenth Amendment, which Thomas Jefferson regarded as the cornerstone of the Constitution:

The Tenth Amendment to the Constitution reads, "The powers not delegated to the United States by the Constitution, nor prohibited by it to the States, are reserved to the States respectively, or to the people."

Since the Constitution omits any mention of the power of the federal government to prevent separation or secession, this power is rightly reserved to the "States respectively, or to the people."

As noted, Article II of America's original Articles of Confederation asserted this right in even clearer terms:

"Each state retains its sovereignty, freedom, and independence, and every power, jurisdiction, and right, which is not by this Confederation expressly delegated to the United States, in Congress assembled."

For those who might dare to question the appropriateness of any reference to the Articles of Confederation, it is worth noting that James Madison, in *Federalist No. XL*, described the principles of the Constitution as being substantially the same as those of the Articles of Confederation. According to Madison, "The truth is that the great principles of the Constitution proposed by the Convention may be considered less as absolutely new, than as the expansion of principles which are found in the Articles of Confederation."

On the subject of association, the "American Confederacy" has been described as a "perpetual union". How does this alter the power of secession? In short, it affirms it.

According to Theophilus Parsons, the eminent jurist of Massachusetts, in his work *Rights of a Citizen*, "If the articles between the partners do not contain an agreement that the partnership shall continue for a specified time, it may be dissolved at the pleasure of either partner."

It is clear, then, that the states independently possess the power to dissolve their associations with the "perpetual union" at their own discretion. While this singlehandedly invalidates any argument for coerced association, we shall deal with it nevertheless.

First, it is worth noting that the opponents of the right of secession claim that the Union could not long endure so long as its members reserve the power to withdraw. These opponents claim that even the most trifling of differences would then threaten its survival. As it turns out, the Founders addressed this very subject in the Declaration of Independence: "Prudence, indeed, will dictate that Governments long established should not be changed for light and transient causes; and accordingly all experience hath shewn, that mankind are more disposed to suffer, while evils are sufferable, than to right themselves by abolishing the forms to which they are accustomed."

It is, thus, all the less likely that mankind will reliably dare to perform such a miracle as secession, even on its most warranted occasions. On the contrary, it is all the more likely that the people will suffer the status quo from their own indolence until they are clamoring desperately for their survival under the thumb of the most lamentable despotism.

Indeed, in the case of government, the inertia of the status quo is likely to secure the same ends as the power of coercion. However, wherever that power of coercion is left to maintain the association, it is sure to emerge upon the most desperate of occasions; and wherever that power has been established *de jure* or *de facto*, it is sure to stifle accountability, to suppress opposition, and to beget ever further abuses of power.

You can rest assured that, wherever any government has established the power of coercion, the power is a prelude to future ills. After all, the power to secede, to dissolve one's associations, serves as the final check against tyranny; it is, above all, the last resort for liberty.

Per the Declaration of Independence, "Governments... derive their just powers from the consent of the governed." Wherever that consent is withdrawn, the association is null. This vision of government was intentional, as it empowers the people and the states, respectively, as the final arbiters in their associations; as the Declaration of Independence states, it empowers them on occasion to "institute new Government, laying its foundation on such principles and organizing its powers in such form, as to them shall seem most likely to effect their Safety and Happiness." After all, it is "Safety and Happiness" that we seek, not the preservation of those associations which have become destructive of those ends. The latter is the object of coercion.

On this subject, there has been quite a ruckus around Article VI, Clause 2, commonly regarded as the Supremacy Clause of the Constitution. Some loose interpretations and judicial activists have taken the clause to afford the general government carte blanche in carrying out the affairs of government, and, by extension, to thereby justify the continued Union at any cost, by the most coercive of means. They claim that, in reigning supreme over all matters pertaining to law, the general government is the final and only arbiter thereof, and that the states are bound eternally to their association.

Article VI, Clause 2, reads as follows:

"This Constitution, and the Laws of the United States which shall be made in Pursuance thereof; and all Treaties made, or which shall be made, under the Authority of the United States, shall be the supreme Law of the Land; and the Judges in every State shall be bound thereby, any thing in the Constitution or Laws of any State to the Contrary notwithstanding."

It is worth noting that, by law, convention and the knowledge of the Framers, the designs of the Republic were assumed neither permanent nor *absolutely* supreme but strictly limited to the enumerated powers conferred thereupon by individual states which, in their own sovereignty and independence, first (and conditionally) authorized those powers. Indeed, it is not the general government nor the Republic itself which is supreme, but rather "The Constitution, and the Laws of the United States which shall be made in Pursuance thereof."

It was not the Republic itself which was to be regarded as supreme, but rather the few and defined powers of the Constitution and the laws made in pursuance of it. However, those powers were not intended, by any liberal interpretation, to nullify the powers reserved to the states, respectively; nor to deny or disparage the rights of the people of the several states. Indeed, the Constitution was proposed, scrutinized, and ratified as a construction between the states, respectively. In fact, the original draft of the preamble actually consisted of the names of the several states, but it was later reduced to "the United States" in the plural after concerns that some of the states would ultimately refuse to ratify the new Constitution.

One vital aspect of sovereignty is that the sovereign can willingly agree to delegate authority without necessarily precluding the resumption of that authority. In the case of the Supremacy Clause, it does not preclude the resumption of any powers by the states, respectively. It merely declares supreme the Laws of the United States, in pursuance of the Constitution, and thereby binds the Judges of every state (critically) on the assumption of each state's continued membership in the Union. This is precisely where the "Authority of the United States" is vested: in the authority of the states (independent of each other, and each as part of the whole), as expressed by the sovereignty permitted them by the people.

The truth is that sovereignty, from the people through their representatives, is the underpinning for just government. Put differently, just government is derived from the continued consent of the governed; a form of consent which can be revoked at their pleasure, so long as it compensates for any injury to the other party. Ultimately, the general government was devised to secure the mutual interests of the several states, and their inhabitants, not to bind them unconditionally. Their compacts, first the Articles of Confederation then the Constitution, were held as the expression of the several states in their effort to form a more perfect Union; neither their compacts nor the general government were ever to be regarded as their captors.

Indeed, the Constitutional Republic of the United States was designed not as an omnipotent central authority but rather as the expression of individual states through their representatives for the mutual advantages of defense and free trade. At no time did any of the states relinquish their independence or their sovereignty. Indeed, several of the states even made certain to unequivocally declare their independence and sovereignty in their ratification documents, and therein even reasserted their authority to resume, at their own discretion, the powers formerly conferred.

Whether nullification or secession, the states reserved every power to check the central government and, by their own conviction and discretion, and in accordance with the law, to nullify abuses of power and dissolve their union. Ultimately, it is the "few and defined" powers of the Constitution, not the Republic itself, which were to be regarded as supreme.

Of course, as already stated, the Constitution's supremacy is limited to the pursuance of the law as explicitly written, not as implied nor as exigent circumstances may seem to permit. What's more, its supremacy binds none of the states, but specifically the "Judges in every State".

However, just as with any consensual association, the Constitution was and, by law, remains binding only through the continued assent of the states, respectively. Just as any member of any indefinite association is free to dissolve that association at any time, not a single state is bound to the Union; each is free to resume the full measure of its power without penalty but, in Parson's words, only so long as it does not "exercise this power wantonly and injuriously to the other partners, without making himself responsible for the damage he thus causes."

On the subject of coercion, we have still further testimony from Oliver Ellsworth of Connecticut, the future senator and Chief Justice of the United States, who noted likewise in the ratifying convention of Connecticut: "This Constitution does not attempt to coerce sovereign bodies, States, in their political capacity." Ellsworth continued: "No coercion is applicable to such bodies but that of an armed force. If we should attempt to execute the laws of the Union by sending an armed force against a delinquent State, it would involve the good and bad, the innocent and guilty, in the same calamity."

Alexander Hamilton said likewise in the convention of New York: "To coerce the States is one of the maddest projects that was ever devised."

Hamilton continued:

"What picture does this idea present to our view? A complying State at war with a non-complying State: Congress marching the troops of one State into the bosom of another: Here is a nation at war with itself. Can any reasonable man be well disposed toward a government which makes war and carnage the only means of supporting itself — a government that can exist only by the sword? But can we believe that one State will ever suffer itself to be used as an instrument of coercion? The thing is a dream — it is impossible."

Formerly a mover of the original proposition to authorize the forces of the Union against a delinquent member, Edmund Randolph, governor of Virginia, afterward, in the Virginia convention, protested against the idea of coercion against any state:

"What species of military coercion could the General Government adopt for the enforcement of obedience to its demands? Either an army sent into the heart of a delinquent State, or blocking up its ports. Have we lived to this, then, that, in order to suppress and exclude tyranny, it is necessary to render the most affectionate friends the most bitter enemies, set the father against the son, and make the brother slay the brother? If an army be once introduced to force us, if once marched into Virginia, figure to yourselves what the dreadful consequence will be: the most lamentable civil war must ensue."

On this particular subject, it is worth noting the words of another distinguished statesman who spoke of the states as enjoying "the exclusive possession of sovereignty" over their own territory, who termed the United States "the American Confederacy", and who declared, "The only parties to the Constitution, contemplated by it originally, were the thirteen confederated states." The statesman continued:

"As between the original States, the representation rests on compact and plighted faith; and your memorialists have no wish that that compact should be disturbed, or that plighted faith in the slightest degree violated."

The statesman and his committee publicly voiced these views, among others, in a memorial to Congress among citizens of Boston on December 15, 1819. He served as chairman of the committee which, on the admission of the state of Missouri, affirmed that new states "are universally considered as admitted into the Union upon the same footing as the original States, and as possessing, in respect to the Union, the same rights of sovereignty, freedom, and independence, as the other States."

Near the end of his life, the statesman delivered a speech at Capon Springs, Virginia, in 1851: "If the South were to violate any part of the Constitution intentionally and systematically, and persist in so doing year after year, and no remedy could be had, would the North be any longer bound by the rest of it? And if the North were, deliberately, habitually, and of fixed purpose, to disregard one part of it, would the South be bound any longer to observe its other obligations?"

The statesman continued: "I have not hesitated to say, and I repeat, that, if the Northern States refuse, willfully and deliberately, to carry into effect that part of the Constitution which respects the restoration of fugitive slaves, and Congress provide no remedy, the South would no longer be bound to observe the compact."

The statesman concluded: "A bargain can not be broken on one side, and still bind the other side."

This statesman, of course, is the venerable Daniel Webster, the former Federalist who represented New Hampshire and Massachusetts in Congress before serving as Secretary of State under Presidents William Henry Harrison, John Tyler, and Millard Fillmore. In addition to his illustrious political résumé, Webster was considered one of the eminent lawyers of the nineteenth century, arguing more than two hundred cases before the Supreme Court between 1814 and his death in 1852.

Now, it is worth noting that Webster, in citing "the restoration of fugitive slaves" in his 1851 speech, specified merely one justification for any state to dissolve its association with the Union.

According to the quote itself, "... if the Northern States refuse, willfully and deliberately, to carry into effect that part of the Constitution which respects the restoration of fugitive slaves, and Congress provide no remedy, the South would no longer be bound to observe the compact."

That quote provides an example of a *sufficient* condition, but not a *necessary* condition, for the dissolution of their compact. There are nearly infinite conditions which would suffice to nullify their compact, and there were indeed several causes which impelled the Southern states to the separation: among them were the issues of states' rights, profligacy, special interests, nullification, economic oppression, and the inviolable tenets of their Constitution.

As declared in a familiar resolution, "When a long train of abuses and usurpations, pursuing invariably the same Object evinces a design to reduce them under absolute Despotism, it is their right, it is their duty, to throw off such Government, and to provide new Guards for their future security." That example by Daniel Webster is merely one of a "long train of abuses and usurpations" which have ultimately, in the wake of federalism's defeat, established precedent for more of the same.

In response to this "long train of abuses and usurpations", the Confederate States remedied the deficiencies of the United States Constitution in the construction of their own. In his inaugural address on February 18, 1861, President Jefferson Davis humbly declared the same at the Alabama Capitol in Montgomery: "The Constitution formed by our fathers is that of these Confederate States, in their exposition of it, and in the judicial construction it has received, we have a light which reveals its true meaning."

Their new construction, inspired in part by an inequitable series of abominable tariffs, specifically prohibited "duties or taxes on importations from foreign nations [to] be laid to promote or foster any branch of industry." Intending to further prohibit the misappropriation of the public purse, their Constitution asserted that none of its clauses "shall ever be construed to delegate the power to Congress to appropriate money for any internal improvement intended to facilitate commerce."

The Confederate States made only one exception "for the purpose of furnishing lights, beacons, and buoys, and other aids to navigation upon the coasts, and the improvement of harbors and the removing of obstructions in river navigation." In all such cases, however, their Constitution required that "such duties shall be laid on the navigation facilitated thereby as may be necessary to pay the costs and expenses thereof."

Their Constitution further demanded, for "all bills appropriating money," that Congress "shall specify in Federal currency the exact amount of each appropriation and the purposes for which it is made." The Confederate States' apprehensions about "internal improvements" emerge here as well, along with their disdain for the pilfering of the public purse. There is perhaps no clearer indication of this disdain than in Article I, Section 9, Clause 10: "Congress shall grant no extra compensation to any public contractor, officer, agent, or servant, after such contract shall have been made or such service rendered."

Clause 20 of the same section enumerated yet another demand upon Congress, so as to further prevent obfuscation and encourage transparency within government: "Every law, or resolution having the force of law, shall relate to but one subject, and that shall be expressed in the title."

What's more, in Article II, Section 1, Clause 1, the Confederate States limited each of its presidents to a single term of six years, after which "the President shall not be reeligible."

In Article IV, Section 3, Clause 4, the Confederate States issued their most urgent guarantee. In this clause, they committed themselves precisely where their former Union had failed them: "The Confederate States shall guarantee to every State that now is, or hereafter may become, a member of this Confederacy, a republican form of government; and shall protect each of them against invasion; and on application of the Legislature or of the Executive (when the Legislature is not in session) against domestic violence."

Through these provisions, it is clear that the Confederate States were indeed troubled by a "long train of abuses and usurpations" and that they sought to remedy each of them in their new construction. Among their remedies were designs for the several causes which impelled their separation, more aptly termed "new Guards for their future security".

For all intents and purposes, the Constitution of the Confederate States reasserted the principles of the United States Constitution, revealing its true meaning in so few modifications. Their construction reaffirmed, as Webster put it, their respect for "the restoration of fugitive slaves"; their guarantee of mutual defense, a republican form of government, and the privilege of the writ of habeas corpus; and their rejection of political corruption and protectionist tariffs which have, for so long, plagued the Southern states. Their construction was truly, in both its spirit and its expression, the Constitution formed by their fathers.

Whereas the sources cited throughout this work are of various political perspectives, they agree mutually on the objects of sovereignty, secession, and the inherent incompatibility of their Union with any instrument seeking to maintain it by force or coercion. These were then, as they ought rightly to have always been, principles virtually uncontested in the halls of the various conventions. These were, as it turns out, non-partisan views of their time, perverted merely for the benefit of politicians, their benefactors and their beneficiaries as they laid waste to their fellow man and the principles on which they based their Union.

These are but a few of the precious artifacts of truth unearthed beneath the growing mountain of lies, the implications of which are enormous. Not only do these truths stand to shift the manner in which students view the War between the States, but they also have the power to debunk the misconceptions about the men who fought admirably for the stake of the Constitution and the cause of states' rights. They have the power to remind the students that these were flesh-and-blood human beings after all, not the caricatures they have been led to imagine.

Above all, these truths stand to demonstrate that the cause of the Confederacy was the cause of America, the cause of federalism and limited, constitutional government, and the cause of truth; that the Confederacy was merely the continuation of the bygone "American Confederacy"; that their cause was to defend their homes, their communities and their states from the unwarranted influence of the federal government.

The cause of the federal government, on the other hand, was, as it is on nearly every occasion, the achievement of further control through the concealment of its motives. This was just as true before and during the war as it was upon its conclusion; in fact, it may rightly be said that the war never ended, that it merely changed forms through Reconstruction onward. After all, the war on truth is still ongoing. Its course depends upon the courage of those in possession, or otherwise in pursuit, of the truth.

As President Jefferson Davis proclaimed in his inaugural address, "The impartial and enlightened verdict of mankind will vindicate the rectitude of our conduct, and He who knows the hearts of men will judge of the sincerity with which we labored to preserve the Government of our fathers in its spirit."

In the preservation of that form of government, there is the determination to affirm the rights we have inherited from our Creator; there is the preservation of life, liberty, and the pursuit of happiness; there is the kind of sovereignty which is best kept in the hands of free and disciplined men eager and ready to secure the blessings of liberty to themselves and their posterity. In the defense of sovereignty, there is ultimately the defense of the individual, the most basic and essential atom of civilization. In the possession of his sovereignty, he is not the product of society, nor *the sum of interrelations*, but rather the free-willed possessor of his own destiny. As the despots see it, their case is all the better for it: where the people are stripped of their individuality, they are just as soon stripped of their ability to think for themselves, or otherwise stripped of their courage to challenge the new status quo. In most cases, this leaves most of them unwilling to even harbor such doubts, questions, or curiosities.

Under socialism, the individual is not only the single greatest threat to the establishment, but he is a danger to himself if he lets his comrades in on his secrets. Under socialism, the individual is best served by keeping his mouth shut or otherwise suppressing his own thoughts, lest he risk life or limb by suggesting that he might dare to think for himself.

There is simply no place for an individual under socialism; as the socialist sees it, the individual stands only to threaten the new status quo. Under socialism he is met swiftly with force which reminds him of his place in society, and which keeps him from disturbing the gears of the great social machine.

Socialism is either a fantastic dream, a palatable lie, or a great deceit, but it is not and never will be *progressive*. Despite the compassionate packaging of socialism, it is effected and maintained only through force, democratic or otherwise. After all, the "democratic" means are just that: the means to sweeping social control.

Put another way, socialism is merely an elaborate power grab by intellectuals at first lacking enough might to assert their control, who therefore initially pursue their ends through cunning. After all, the intellectual is the one who endeavors toward truth *or* cunning, who otherwise lacks the power in force.

The intellectual is the one who seeks to convince the public of his vision, to convince the people that he knows what he is talking about, to convince them that he has both the knowledge and the practical expertise to execute his plans. In reality, all of the talk is just that: talk for the purpose of deception, for the purpose of getting out of real work, for the purpose of obscuring the truth, and, finally, for the purpose of conning others into accepting mistruths and doing all of the work for him.

Of course, the ends of the socialist are self-evident: truth is scarcely of any interest to the socialist, but rather an obstacle to be overcome or otherwise a case to be made subjective, relative, or politically incorrect. Once the means are secured, the administration remains *democratic* in name only, beyond reproach because of its stated intentions and the people who have come to depend on it; unconquerable due to its insurmountable power; unaccountable to the public whom it purports to represent; unassailable for the assumed consensus which theoretically corroborates its very existence; and progressively more incomprehensible for the arcane methods and elaborate schemes employed by the dishonest intellectuals on the payroll. It is for this reason that William F. Buckley Jr. was often quoted as saying, "I would rather be governed by the first 2,000 people in the Boston telephone directory than by the 2,000 people on the faculty of Harvard University."

Wherever "democracy" either dominates or condones oppression, it invariably prevails over a people devoid of principle, aptitude and ambition, or otherwise lacking the profound desire to truly live. Indeed, even in the presence of some semblance of the latter, it is ultimately in service to some ulterior motive.

Oppression by consensus, implied or otherwise, is oppression all the same. Oppression by the designs of democracy is merely more insidious, serving to pit the public against each other instead of their rulers; serving to distribute the guilt such that no one person is accountable; serving to operate from the presumed approval of the masses, and to likewise enjoy the benefit of their conscience in continuing the oppression. Indeed, with the help and the approval of the people no less, the establishment eventually grows to such a size that it exists and operates despite and independent of the people, their wishes, their opinions, and their misgivings; and, thus, the ability of the people to restrain it.

The establishment thereby develops a character and a presence of its own, independent of both its constituents and its agents. In such cases, the establishment's actions are largely predetermined by existing commitments, alliances and obligations, so-called political correctness and party allegiances; it is, likewise, beholden to perceptions, the status quo, the party platform, and the terms of each agent's employment. Upon assuming its own presence, character and identity, the establishment carries its own momentum and thereby deters independent thought; it steamrolls the opposition and the detractors, whether among the public or among the agents responsible for its operations. In this way, the establishment operates not just beyond the consent of the governed but beyond the control of any individual's better judgment and discretion. The establishment itself seems to dictate outcomes and narratives in this way, through agents too career-driven, too afraid, too cowardly, and, from their perspective, too diminutive compared to the everlasting and all-powerful machine.

Ultimately, the risk of democracy is in the illusion of consensus, and in the legalization of plunder and suppression under its auspices; under the auspices of an illusion convincing the people that they are in control through their votes and their representatives, and that their representatives are in control through their uncompromised judgment and discretion.

Indeed, this is one of the many advantages enjoyed by any system stylized as a *democracy*: it keeps the public at bay and in its pockets, as the machine employs them to do its bidding and to fund every conceivable political agenda; even if that means suppressing the very people who seek to preserve the public liberty, the very people whom the establishment purports to serve and represent.

CHAPTER XVII

DEMOCRACY DESTROYS

Democracy destroys. It keeps the people busy fighting amongst each other, and it keeps them hopeful and believing that they are just one election away from redemption. As more and more people are seduced by the promises of democracy, the state wages every one of its efforts, however deplorable, with the help of its loyal benefactors who dutifully pay their tribute to escape the wrath of their rulers.

As their rulers impose more obligations upon the public, and as they raise taxes and plunder the public treasury, they fortify their defenses against a public that might finally awaken to the con. Unfortunately, by this time the public's efforts to reclaim their liberty are met with an insurmountable force: not only a standing army more than prepared to quell any resistance, but their fellow man who is reluctant to join in the fight.

By this time, that standing army will consist of familiar friends and family who have since developed a sense of duty to their rulers and who are more interested in their jobs and their own personal welfare than that of the public, let alone posterity. Unlike the resistance, that standing army will enjoy an endless supply of resources from taxpayers who will continue to fund their efforts, whether out of fear, loyalty, indifference, or acquiescence. Indeed, the government always enjoys the advantage when it comes to blows. This is true not only in force and technology, but in the perspective of the many who view the government as the enforcers of law and order, as the *keepers of the peace*, as workers "doing their jobs" against the resistance of an "uncivilized" few; the few regarded variously, and in these particular cases inaccurately, as any of the following: *rebels*; *insurgents*; *insurrectionists*; *brutes*; *savages*; *barbarians*; *partisans*; *revolutionaries*; *extremists*; *fanatics*; *nuts*; *bigots*; *criminals*; *terrorists*; *enemies of the state* or *Public Enemy No. 1.*

Meanwhile, the true savages (et al.) are often allies of the establishment, often encouraged, enabled and welcomed by it. Whether the savages are ennobled as "victims" or "the oppressed" for their crimes, whether their crimes are redefined as "reprisals" or "reparations", or whether the savages are treated as ordinary criminals, they serve the same ends: to "justify" more power to the state. Of course, this is not to completely invalidate the threat of true savages, but to encourage the people to draw the necessary distinctions; to recognize that the establishment makes a habit of imagining and importing problems while vilifying a particular group: their own enemies.

This is the uphill battle faced by the resistance, the veritable Sons of Liberty who are left, on every occasion, to wage the desperate and often futile fight against tyranny. In the case of *democracy*, or any system so stylized, it is not only a fight against tyranny, but one against theory. This is precisely why Leftism is so insidious.

While it could plausibly be theorized that a democratic socialism might arise from the consensus of a well-intentioned constituency, their ranks predictably wane over time in favor of a constituency which prefers socialism not for its stated intentions but for its expedience in fleecing their contemporaries and silencing their opponents. For these reasons and others, once this apparatus is sent in motion, it becomes virtually impossible to stop. As the economist Milton Friedman warned in his 1984 work *Tyranny of the Status Quo*, "Nothing is so permanent as a temporary government program." For shining examples of just this kind of program, one need not look any further than the Social Security Act of 1935, the Revenue Act of 1942, or the end of Bretton Woods in 1971; each considered "temporary" at the time of becoming law.

Ultimately, whatever the seemingly-virtuous or -noble ends, under socialism they are corrupted by the means. After all, the virtue of charity is found not in the regimentation of society, but in the voluntary will and compassion of individuals; the efficacy of charity is found there as well, as individuals are always better stewards of charity than any thoughtless system which seeks to replace them. As it turns out, through socialism, charity and compassion are together gutted from society and replaced with the thoughtless and uncaring mechanics of tyranny, commonly corroborated on the surface by some agreeable "common good".

As told in the fabled story of Horatio Bunce in his speech to Congressman David Crockett during the congressman's reelection campaign:

"It is not the amount that I complain of; it is the principle. The power of collecting and disbursing money at pleasure is the most dangerous power that can be entrusted to man. Congress has no right to give charity. Individual members may give as much of their own money as they please, but they have no right to touch a dollar of the public money for that purpose."

As the story goes, Bunce then stressed the living contradiction of so many in Congress:

"Money with [Congressmen] is nothing but trash when it is to come out of the people. But it is the one great thing for which most of them are striving, and many of them sacrifice honor, integrity, and justice to obtain it."

It is in just this manner that a soft despotism envelops a people, and even elicits their acquiescence or approbation in the process. Once the state has convinced enough people to tolerate, accept or even champion its initiatives, it comes to support itself and to assume ever further control with the implied approval of the people, who, by casting their votes, imply continued confidence in that failed system. It is then, by both cunning and force of arms, that the state comes to fill its treasury for its own benefit and, to a lesser extent, the benefit of its constituents.

As Professor Alexander Tytler of the University of Edinburgh commented, in 1787, about the fall of the Athenian Republic some two thousand years earlier:

"A democracy is always temporary in nature; it simply cannot exist as a permanent form of government. A democracy will continue to exist up until the time that voters discover that they can vote themselves generous gifts from the public treasury. From that moment on, the majority always votes for the candidates who promise the most benefits from the public treasury, with the result that every democracy will finally collapse due to loose fiscal policy, which is always followed by a dictatorship."

In his 1947 work *The Mainspring of Human Progress*, Henry Grady Weaver described socialism in just this way, warning of the pernicious threat of dictatorship in the very designs of socialism:

"In line with the teachings of Marx, the proponents admit the necessity but argue that it is merely a temporary measure — that the dictatorship will automatically 'wither away' just as soon as things get going. They contend that history decrees this withering away, but the facts do not bear out this theory. In all history, there is no evidence of any dictatorship ever withering away. Dictatorship always feeds on itself. The ruthless tactics necessary to get it started becoming increasingly ruthless in the efforts to conceal the errors and defects of a scheme that can't be made to work."

Socialism cannot be made to work precisely because of its inherent defects, three of them in particular. First is the *incentive problem*, the failure of socialism to respect creativity, to incentivize production, saving and investment, to impose discipline, whether personally or politically. This, in turn, stifles innovation and atrophies industry. This deficiency ultimately corresponds with the abandonment of private property, the repurposing of life and labor, and thus the redefining of life itself. In the face of these troubling themes, the French economist Frédéric Bastiat published his own criticisms in his 1850 treatise *The Law*:

"And what part do persons play in all this? They are merely the machine that is set in motion. In fact, are they not merely considered to be the raw material of which the machine is made?"

Indeed, this begs of socialism an answer to these and other questions: What is the purpose of the individual? What is the meaning of life? Of course, these are questions that socialism universally fails to address. On the contrary, socialism hastens to assume that the individual and the family are unimportant, dispensable for the welfare of society or the utopia they can nearly imagine. In their lust for utopia, however, they fall short of approximating the very real risks and the predictable consequences of any such design which rejects the sovereignty of man.

Indeed, Leftists prefer to treat societies as systems without an adequate appreciation for the relevant variables and controllables, the unintended consequences, and the fact that they are dealing not with a fixed or controlled system, not with mere factors or figures, but with human beings capable of feeling and thinking, adapting and suffering. Those human beings are not lab rats, not *only* worthy of dignity and respect; they are individuals and far more complex than buttons, keys, levers, and material that can be manipulated, programmed or designed for any given purpose or outcome. They are not born to participate in some experiment, to be held in the hands of a select few, to be subjected to the whims, the mercy and the curiosities of experimenters; and they are simply incapable of appreciating the real and lasting consequences of such experiments, projects whose effects are both irrevocable and beyond measure. The dangers posed simply exceed the bounds of understanding. They are confused with the risks attending any other experiment, or they escape or otherwise do not concern the experimenters, who come to prioritize their own interests and aspirations and refuse to accept that they cannot perfectly (or "scientifically") control society.

As Russian philosopher Fyodor Dostoevsky wrote in his 1864 novel *Notes from Underground*, "Shower upon him every earthly blessing, drown him in bliss so that nothing but bubbles would dance on the surface of his bliss, as on a sea... and even then every man, out of sheer ingratitude, sheer libel, would play you some loathsome trick. He would even risk his cakes and would deliberately desire the most fatal rubbish, the most uneconomical absurdity, simply to introduce into all this positive rationality his fatal fantastic element... simply in order to prove to himself that men still are men and not piano keys."

After all, despite waxing poetic about designs for nirvana, all that man naturally desires is in his struggle for the benefit of himself and for that of his family; and the love, the affection, and the satisfaction that come along with it. The socialist, or any collectivist by any other name, seeks to rewrite the human condition. In this, he seeks first to convince his unwitting subjects of another world order, something distinct from the natural course just described. Upon convincing his followers, he rearranges the ends they serve in their daily toil. Eventually, they turn on their newfound system, either for sport or upon finally recognizing the value of their former traditions. After all, once a civilization has compromised its values, there is precious little that can be done in the way of politics to reverse its decline without somehow compounding its problems.

As the German philosopher Frederic Nietzsche wrote in his 1901 work *The Will to Power*, "nihilism represents the ultimate logical conclusion of our great values and ideals —

because we must experience nihilism before we can find out what value these 'values' really had."

Indeed, a disillusioned Marxist once wrote of his stint in Soviet Russia upon defecting from the United States in the fall of 1959. After nearly a year in the Soviet Union, he came to regard Russian Communism as yet another brand of slavery. He wrote the following in his diary near the end of summer in 1960:

"As my Russian improves I become increasingly conscious of just what sort of a society I live in. Mass gymnastics, compulsory afterwork meeting, usually political information meeting. Compulsory attendance at lectures and the sending of the entire shop collective (except me) to pick potatoes on a Sunday, at a state collective farm: A 'patriotic duty' to bring in the harvest. The opinions of the workers (unvoiced) are that it's a great pain in the neck: they don't seem to be especially enthusiastic about any of the 'collective' duties a natural feeling."

The same Marxist wrote in a letter dated January 4, 1961:

"I am starting to reconsider my desire about staying. The work is drab, the money I get has nowhere to be spent. No nightclubs or bowling alleys. No places of recreation, except trade union dances. I have had enough."

Upon his return to the United States, he later delivered a speech on July 27, 1963, at Spring Hill College in Mobile, Alabama. In a speech before an audience of Jesuit priests and scholastics, he lamented the unspeakable crimes committed by the Soviets, "the imprisonment of their own peoples, the mass extermination so typical of Stalin, and the individual suppression and regimentation under Khrushchev." He continued further in lamenting "the deportations, the purposeful curtailment of diet in the consumer slighted population of Russia, the murder of history, the prostitution of art and culture."

This is a familiar theme amongst those who have witnessed the depravity of Leftism. Indeed, a German soldier once wrote in his diary of his own experience on the Eastern Front during World War II: "The Soviet Russians live damned, miserable lives. Today I went inside the house of one of these collective farmers. There is no way to get rid of the stink one finds in these one-room shacks, not even with hours of ventilation."

Regrettably, Leftists are all too often consumed by designs of nirvana; their pursuit of fame, fortune and power, paired with some fantastical imaginings, blind them to the very real costs of it all, as they pertain not only to the economy and the social order, but to the rights of man and his very purpose on planet Earth. These are rightly described as costs which are impossible to bear; taxes which, after gnawing on the flesh, suck the marrow straight from the bones of mankind.

The Leftist, of course, can scarcely even conceive of the harsher realities. Incredulous to the misgivings of his opponents, he must first suffer the scourge of his own imaginings, but not before effecting the destruction of his country and their former traditions. After all, this destruction is an essential condition for the implementation of his wretched system. Whether through war or genocide, historically regarded in Leftist circles as *cleansing* or *disinfection*, the socialist state must first endeavor through one or the other, or more likely both.

As Prussian general and military theorist Carl von Clausewitz wrote in *Vom Kriege* (*On War*), "War is thus an act of force to compel our enemy to do our will." It is, as Clausewitz put it, "... the continuation of policy with other means." It is, in the case of Leftism, an act of force internally as well as externally, each being essential to the endurance of such a scheme destined for failure.

Despite the impassioned talks of *equality*, the working class and the political elite never share equally in the suffering. As the aforementioned German soldier wrote in his diary, "the working population suffers most." The soldier continued with a question: "Am I too much of a materialist if I claim that the upper levels of the population can bear the loss of their ideational values much better than the working class can bear their material loss?"

It is in just this way that the ideological struggle plays out, whereby the political elite manipulate the public like pawns in the most dangerous game; whereby the political elite, scarcely lacking any material need, enjoy the protection of the state, the spoils of war and the product of forced labor.

The political elite have the distinct privilege of basking in the abstract, specifically because of the working class, who are left operating in reality. Their ideological assertions, just as with the ideologies themselves, offer the ideologues a wide variety of benefits; not least among these benefits are camouflage, in the form of their stated intentions, and social capital by ingratiating themselves with the miserables, the dregs, or collectively the "victims" of society, the latter of whom are more than delighted to play along; indeed, out of a personal sense of inadequacy, they are more than willing to cast blame, chase ghosts, and identify as "victims".

Indeed, so effective is the "victimhood" propaganda that, in time, the state succeeds not only in placing the blame on the common man but in convincing him that he is somehow responsible; that the "victims" are entitled to his sympathy, his apologies, and reparations. Indeed, so successful is this scheme that it even serves to excuse the behavior and the most heinous acts of criminals who happen to qualify for "victim" status. After all, "victimhood" is, politically speaking, the perfect excuse for failure, the easy way to "win" the debate, to silence and blame their enemies; enemies of their own construction, mind you. It is an effort at justifying malice and violence in the stead of honest work. It is the glorification of misery and the arming of the "victims" against the "evil-doers". In other words, victimhood is power.

The glorification of victimhood comes with the glorification of poverty and destitution, engendering a sense of resentment and indignation toward the *haves* among the *have-nots*. This pits not only the *have-nots* against the *haves* but the *haves* against each other on the basis of their political identities, making business progressively more political while driving progressively more loyalty and obedience toward the establishment; the kind of loyalty and obedience which keeps a business in the good graces of the state. The glorification of misery or failure also engenders a sense of pride, an eagerness to share in the misery as a challenge to be overcome, as a kind of lifestyle or fashion statement, or as a means to supporting the *common good*; to be esteemed as heroes or altruists as the political elite continue their con in the lap of luxury.

As a result, the ideologues and the "victims" are validated through instant gratification in the form of praise, power and perceived righteousness; meanwhile, their followers enjoy the same in the form of splendid illusions. However, that instant gratification comes at a cost over the long run. In the short run, however, a confluence of factors sustains the illusions, not least of which economically through — in view of the bigger picture — cheap money and debt.

CHAPTER XVIII

ILLUSIONS

As it turns out, cheap money and debt have the effect of making things appear more achievable. Whether affordable goods or gainful employment or capital gains, it is an illusion whereby people are made to believe that they are easy to come by; in the splendor, they are inclined (by guilt or self-righteousness) to celebrate initiatives seeking to share the plenty.

Little do they realize, or otherwise mind, just how fleeting the splendor and short-lived the arrangement will prove to be, that such redistribution schemes encourage still more dependency while discouraging the very production that makes any of it at all viable (for any period of time); that the systematic sharing of wealth at scale amounts to the guaranteed sharing in misery. When the party is finally over and the bill comes due, they are quickly reminded of the cold, hard truth: as the author Robert Heinlein so famously put it in his novel *The Moon is a Harsh Mistress,* "There ain't no such thing as a free lunch." As is always the case with public service, the cost is consistently higher than the price advertised on the menu (if listed at all), and, in the case of deficit spending, it is a tab eventually paid with interest.

Indeed, the costs are ultimately borne out over years and generations, paid by those who knew little of the consequences; or, in the case of the youth and the unborn, those who never had any say in the matter. In any case, the costs are paid in various forms, economic and social, by those who can least afford them; who act as pawns for the man behind the curtain, and who, in many cases, hide behind their *own* camouflage in war, either domestically or internationally, in order to keep the system going. In turn, their work serves to sustain their overlords, who, instead of *social* capital, turn to *physical* capital by any and all means, however vile or underhanded, never shying away from threats of imprisonment or forced labor. Rest assured, they are never short on excuses or empty promises.

In the end, when their socialist experiment eventually implodes, it is not the elite who suffer the most, but the people who did the fighting and labored tirelessly to keep the experiment going. Meanwhile, the wiser among us know to expect the disaster; to them, it is not an experiment at all but a performance with a predictable ending. Whether it be the historian or the social theorist who sounds the alarm, whether it be the propagandist or the aspiring despot in pursuit of absolute power, social destruction is a known and defining quality of Leftism; it is not only the ultimate end, but the means by which Leftism takes hold of a people.

Socialism, or any form of collectivism for that matter, must first endeavor to denigrate and then destroy the existing power structure and every authority ruling over it. Whether a god or a set of traditions, the new order must abolish the old. For the purposes of socialism, this means the disintegration of the family and erasure of the individual. Karl Marx writes plainly of this in *Fundamentals of a Critique of Political Economy*: "Society does not consist of individuals, but expresses the sum of interrelations, the relations within which these individuals stand."

According to Marx, the individual is nothing more than a member of an economic class, basically irrelevant without his society or the relations within which he stands. According to Marx, society is not a macrocosm of individuals nor the sum of individual decisions, but rather the expressed purpose of the individual, insofar as he is regarded as having any independent purpose or value at all.

According to Marx, or broadly any collectivist, it is the interest of society, however defined, which ought to limit the purpose and thence the labors of the individual. After all, it is the individual who poses the greatest threat to this kind of system. Indeed, there is no greater threat to the establishment, or any enemy for that matter, than a young man willing to die for his country. As H. L. Mencken once wrote, "The most dangerous man to any government is the man who is able to think things out for himself, without regard to the prevailing superstitions and taboos."

It is not by accident nor incident but by deliberate design that the individual and the family are marginalized under socialism. Contrary to the interests of the individual or the family, under socialism it is *society* — the *collective*, the persons and the institutions masquerading as representatives of the people and purveyors of the "common good" — that defines the meaning and the purpose of life; that gives life its value, assuming that it is then regarded as possessing any value at all; that decides what is good and just, what is expected of each person, and what the consequences ought to be for any failure to meet those expectations, for failing to fulfill one's "duty" in society.

Socialism, then, is tantamount to the destruction not only of the person but of humanity. It is the attempted reformation of community and identity, the cause and the function of man. It is the intertwining of peoples irrespective of cultural differences, the forced association between peoples regardless of will and compatibility, a manufactured identity for peoples despite what little they may have in common.

This is precisely why the state seeks to preoccupy the people with endless work and designs for *the common good*. This is why the state seeks to undermine faith and family; to dumb the people down, and to bring them into conformity through public schooling and political propaganda; to encourage them, through television sitcoms and sardonic rhetoric, to take their lives and their heirs less seriously.

This is why the state seeks to maximize employment, celebrate *equality* and denounce greed; to busy parents with work as they condemn their children to "professionals" at daycare centers; to develop social *welfare* programs and *entitlements* to encourage individuals to live independent of their own families and their former traditions; and to, in turn, strip families of their inherent responsibilities and, thus, their influence over their own children.

In many such cases, the people are pleased to finally be free of their obligations and the demands of their faith and their former traditions; they come to regard those rigid rules and principles as the very source of their misery and the apparent "inequities" within society. In still other cases, they pretend to take pleasure in their defection, in service to some political, business, or social interest. In whatever case, however, they are often blissfully unaware of the tradeoffs; they know neither the true extent of their concessions nor the long-term ramifications attending their indiscretions.

Indeed, in order to satisfy the ever-changing conditions for *political correctness*, they hasten to reject the rules of reality, to scoff at their fathers, and to make enemies, whether seen or unseen, in the flesh or in the mind, provable or otherwise. As misfits, miscreants, and malcontents, they scarcely hesitate to make a mockery out of life, to stand between the people, the truth and the light. They condemn *capitalism*, at least as they know it, and yet *they* are the ones guilty of subjecting the people to cheap transactional and involuntary associations. They are the ones who denounce money, but only so far as this enables them to acquire more for themselves, only such that they can successfully rearrange resources for their own personal benefit.

They are the ones who measure and compare men on the basis of their wealth (otherwise race or some other arbitrary metric or identifier), who seek to limit their lives by the "common good" and to thereby perfect the people as resources for the establishment; resources hardly any different from raw material at a mill. They are the ones who reduce the individual in rank to a pestilence, a nuisance, the butt of a joke, a menace to society, one part within a machine or an arsenal; one pathetic and powerless creature who can, from all such accounts, do, say, and know precious little of consequence beyond the wishes and commands, the determinations and delusions, the ever-changing rituals and superstitions of the establishment.

Indeed, Leftist ideologues, Keynesian economists, and central planners prefer to view all of human action as part of some mechanism whereby the people and their exchanges are but the necessary gears to get it moving. Insofar as the people and their exchanges affect the performance of the machine, the ideologues and the central planners seek to bring the gears into hyperdrive, eliminating every delay and discretion that might otherwise prevent a transaction from moving the gears.

In this way, the economists and the central planners view the people as being merely incidental to economic growth. The former lament the fact that their field of study has them dealing with mere human beings instead of raw, inanimate material; but this hardly keeps them from treating their human subjects any differently than the material they might otherwise manipulate at will.

In this way, the Keynesians and the central planners view the people and their actions as constantly grinding the gears or needlessly slowing them down. It is for this reason that the Keynesians and the central planners glorify debt and spending, as they view savings as deferred consumption merely delaying the fruition of economic activity. Indeed, they take no interest in the prospects of savings where they stand in anticipation of a rainy day or in preparation for future investment or retirement; they would much rather have somebody, anybody, spending that money on something somewhere.

Just as all Leftists' ideas are either incomplete or shortsighted, inhumane or impractical, their economic priorities are in political expedience and the velocity of money, not in sustainability or the preservation of purchasing power, nor in accordance with the preferences of those who actually earn that money. Indeed, they seek to drive the velocity of money for a number of reasons. A higher velocity causes the proverbial gears to turn more rapidly, and with that higher velocity government stands to benefit in a number of ways: it gets in on more of the action through taxation; it keeps the people perpetually busy and assuming progressively more risk in their hopes of retiring or enjoying more leisure time. It thus keeps the people assuming more risk through preferred asset classes and shares of business as their dollar-denominated savings and bonds, once regarded as safe stores of value, continue losing value by design; thereby keeping the people progressively more dependent upon and amenable to the establishment, albeit economically, for their livelihood, their future prospects, and their ability to manage their debts and meet their tax obligations. Indeed, it is such failed stores of value as these which are behind the sharp rise in equities as a share of state and local pension fund allocations, at a time when pension funds have come to constitute an ever greater share of personal and household wealth; at a time when speculative ventures have come to replace business assets. And it is this very kind of instability and speculative fervor which is behind the absurdity of the proposed alternatives of the modern era; which has made cryptocurrency, such as bitcoin, all the more appealing, the latter being merely another form of risk-taking, in this case within an unproven and highly speculative "asset" class; and, not unlike Leftism itself, one always in the midst of a serious identity crisis and having everywhere the makings of a racket.

Indeed, since its conception, bitcoin enthusiasts have characterized the cryptocurrency as an alternative monetary asset, namely "Gold 2.0". They have likened certain qualities of bitcoin to those of gold, and they have claimed that Bitcoin improves upon gold just as every other digital asset has improved upon its predecessor: whether e-mail, audio files or online shopping, the bitcoin enthusiasts claim that the digital space is the preferred domain for all things.

Unfortunately, the bitcoin enthusiasts have forgotten that e-mails can be substituted for physical letters because you can still read them; audio files can be substituted for tapes, records and CDs because you can still listen to them; and online shopping can be substituted for in-store shopping because you can browse inventory then actually take physical delivery of the goods. With bitcoin, however, you can neither see nor hold the "asset"; on the contrary, the bitcoin speculator must simply accept that, because it carries a price today, it will always be there and it will always remain valuable.

As opposed to gold, which is tangible, recognizable and indisputably valuable for its unique elemental properties, a bid on Bitcoin is predicated on sheer faith, the belief that some greater fool will pay more for it tomorrow, the next day, or next year: this is virtually the only "use case" for bitcoin, which is to say there is no use case at all for bitcoin; it is nothing more than a speculative risk asset.

It is worth noting that, just because people prefer digital alternatives for some things, that need not necessarily imply that digital alternatives are preferable for *all* things. Sure, the tradeoff between the physical CD, tape or record for the weightless, portable and easily-transferrable digital audio file often justifies the latter, but not in *all* cases. Sure, e-mail is faster and cheaper than sending a letter by mail, but the former has not *completely* replaced the latter. Meanwhile, online shopping is often cheaper and easier than in-store shopping, but once again the former has not yet altogether replaced the latter.

Indeed, there are still qualities about the more antiquated methods that appeal to people: some people prefer the sound quality of a vinyl record, the connection fostered between the record and the listener, or the fact that you do not need to rely on a computer to store music; some people prefer to hold a physical letter with one's handwriting and a personal touch; and some prefer in-store shopping in order to try on clothing or to enjoy the experience. While the digital world can help to facilitate many wants and needs, it cannot entirely replace the physical world.

Indeed, whereas the digital domain functions fairly well in logistical operations and transmitting information, it cannot form the basis for all human affairs. This is especially true in the performance of affairs which require absolute and unquestioned fidelity. Just as a parent would never hire a virtual babysitter to look after her children when she is away, there are many tasks in the human experience which require tangible assurances. The reason for this is clear: fidelity.

A babysitter is effective only insofar as she is present to observe and manage the children, to keep them safe and to prevent them from destroying the house. A residence is effective only insofar as it physically provides shelter. Transportation is effective only insofar as it physically transports goods and people. And money is effective only insofar as it reliably insures the fruits of our labor, and the reliable exchange thereof: whether it takes the form of one commodity or another, the fruits of our labor are best kept in a stable and reliable store of value, one that can withstand the test of time and still retain its useful properties.

In the case of money, its best form is that which preserves its purchasing power over time, which reliably returns value upon receipt, which exacts not too hefty a cost in storage or exchange, which is divisible, transportable and easily recognizable. Above all, sound money must insure the fruits of man's labor, meaning that sound money minimizes the role of faith through its timeless demonstration of value, and that it stands to remain useful even in the absence of an outside appraisal.

This is where bitcoin misses the mark: in their irrational exuberance to get rich, the bitcoin enthusiasts are complicit, albeit most unwittingly so, in an elaborate wealth transfer scheme with enigmatic language and elaborate protocol which seeks to superficially simulate some of the features of money. However, bitcoin fails miserably where it counts most of all. In the end, bitcoin will not be remembered as "Gold 2.0"; it is more than likely to be remembered as a contemporary iteration of fool's gold.

Real gold does not require an appraisal to justify its use: gold inherently possesses physical properties which uniquely satisfy consumer and industrial demands. It is useful in and of itself; it is relatively scarce; and, historically, it is mined at a fairly consistent and predictable rate. Furthermore, gold can never be used up; regardless of its applications, gold that is recovered, recycled or repurposed presents the same properties as when it was originally refined. Whether it is panned from a stream, unearthed within a mine, recovered from a shipwreck or elsewhere, it is gold all the same. This is to say that gold is durable and fungible; that, in possessing these unique elemental properties, it will function indefinitely; and that, in this way, it functions as a true store of value. Remember, price and value are two separate measures: whereas they tend to correspond over the long run, they can diverge over the short term, especially during speculative booms and manias.

Bitcoin, on the other hand, requires an appraisal in order to justify a bid; absent any appraisal, bitcoin possesses no inherent properties to offset market risk, and it is precisely because of its price action that it presents any use case at all. Put another way, bitcoin has no value where it does not have a price. Of course, because of this, bitcoin's "use case" is limited to use as a speculative risk asset; for this reason, bitcoin suffers from a distinct lack of downside insurance. Ultimately, no asset can possibly function as a store of value that does not first present a use case independent of its price.

Whereas gold offers insurance through its physical properties, its increased scope of application, as well as its historical performance and relationships, bitcoin offers merely the illusion of endless upside potential: wherever bitcoin assumes a secular price decline, there is absolutely no case for holding it. This is not the case with gold, which, independent of its price, presents more use cases virtually every year.

As opposed to bitcoin, a "position" held by speculators praying for higher prices, gold's use cases operate entirely independent of its price action. Even if gold were hypothetically assigned a market price of zero, it would still present the same use cases through its physical properties. Whereas bitcoin operates exclusively as a speculative vehicle, gold's tradability is merely one of its many features. Indeed, as opposed to bitcoin, which depends exclusively upon this feature in order to survive in any form, gold's tradability is the result of its inherent, unparalleled and timeless properties.

Whereas some people value Bitcoin for its promise of future riches in still other forms (i.e. US dollars), investors and end users utilize gold for a wide variety of purposes. Whereas bitcoin speculators aim to get rich in other terms, namely dollars and other fiat currencies, gold buyers and investors seek to actually use gold or to hold it as a store of value. Gold is physically scarce and it possesses unique qualities not possessed by other assets: this lends to its timelessness, its recognizability, and its unrivaled application in industry across the globe.

Indeed, the world is truly richer and better off with the marginal ounce of gold, whereas the marginal unit of bitcoin makes the world hardly any better off at all, and in fact that marginal unit stands only to dilute the purchasing power of its pre-existing supply. This is not a problem for gold, as its mine production is essentially inelastic and predictable over time: in fact, between 1917 and 2013, the supply of gold increased by only 1.52 percent per year. If one looks at the rate of change since the beginning of the new monetary era, since the end of the Bretton Woods agreement, the growth rate of base money (USD) is actually significantly higher at 9.95 percent. The gold supply, by comparison, grew by only 1.5 percent per year during the same time period. This relative scarcity is one of the main advantages of gold compared to fiat currencies, and one of the only qualities that bitcoin can, in its current form, seek to simulate.

Moreover, gold also presents an extraordinarily high stock-to-flow ratio. The total amount of gold amounts to approximately 177,000 tons: this is the stock. Annual mine production amounted to roughly 3,000 tons in 2013: this is the flow. If one divides the total gold mined by annual production, one arrives at a stock-to-flow ratio of approximately fifty-nine years. The ratio expresses the number of years it would take to double the total stock of gold at the current rate of production.

Since the year 1900, the stock-to-flow ratio has managed a mean of 66. This means that gold is relatively scarce, that mining and future supply are fairly predictable, and that supply changes tend to weigh minimally on the long-term market value of gold. As stated previously, however, while these market dynamics can influence the price of gold, and while Bitcoin can artificially simulate some of these properties, gold's use case is still wholly independent from its price performance.

On the other hand, bitcoin relies *exclusively* upon its price performance, and from its very conception it has sought to artificially simulate the properties of gold; however, in aiming to simulate those properties, Bitcoin has failed to replicate the finer qualities which actually make gold reliable and progressively more valuable by the day.

Whereas the supply of bitcoin is artificially limited — its maximum supply is limited to 21 million Bitcoins — the supply of bitcoin might as well be measured by the Satoshi, its smallest unit, equivalent to 100 million Bitcoins. You see, the difference here between gold and bitcoin is rather simple: whereas gold can likewise be reduced to progressively smaller quantities, the marginal unit of gold (of whatever quantity) physically improves upon the wealth of the world; it is constant and measurable, independent of valuation. However, the difference between a Satoshi and a Bitcoin is a contrived ratio conceived out of thin air, whereby an artificial supply of one arbitrarily implies the quantity of the other.

In yet another effort to simulate the increasing difficulty in mining new gold supply, bitcoin undergoes "bitcoin halvings" whereby the number of bitcoins entering the system with every new data block, every 10 minutes or so on average, is cut in half. These "halvings" take place roughly every four years, suggesting that bitcoin will theoretically become progressively driven by demand over supply. By this particular protocol, the bitcoin enthusiasts claim that they can simulate the performance of gold. Of course, they cannot, as their entire model relies squarely on the assumption that the scarcity of Bitcoin alone should drive value, but this may not be the case into the future.

Beyond the fact that bitcoin is far more numerous depending upon the preferred unit of measure, whether Bitcoin or Satoshi, it is not entirely immune to competition. There is virtually nothing which prevents future innovations and technologies from rendering Bitcoin completely obsolete, which implies that the supply is effectively unlimited. Eventually, this will happen, and Bitcoin will be left as nothing more than a marginal trading vehicle, or an abstract relic of a time gone by.

Gold, on the other hand, is an element with unmatched properties that will survive at any price and against any and all competition. Even if a new element were theoretically discovered which improves upon each of gold's properties, gold would still be useful. However, the trend has decisively indicated that the applications for gold will only continue to grow into the future.

Whereas the progress in industry, and that within the market for cryptocurrencies, would subject bitcoin to still stiffer competition, developments in industry will uncover only further applications for the yellow metal. Whatever the case, whatever the circumstances, whether beloved or ignored, gold will continue to shine and perform. Bitcoin, on the other hand, is forever beholden to the whims of speculators and popular opinion.

Like a plastic bag in a storm, bitcoin is nothing more than the direction of the wind; and like any populist movement, it is full of air and endless empty promises. It simulates the properties of gold the way a cartoon simulates life: both simulate the conspicuous features yet ignore the inherent qualities which make them viable in truth, not only in principle. While the cartoonist can make his characters lifelike, they will never have life; in just the same way, while Bitcoin can seek to simulate the qualities of gold, it will never be gold. And where it fails in this particular regard, it fails in every regard which would otherwise make it viable.

Bitcoin is ultimately a fool's errand, and the only winners are the people who ultimately sell out of their positions. There are only two kinds of Bitcoin fans: those who truly believe in it and those who seek to exploit the ignorance and the gullibility of the first. In the end, the only winners will be those who are lucky enough to leave their bags with the other guys who are so eager to hold them that they do not even bother taking a look to see what is inside. Unfortunately for the latter, it will eventually be all too late by the time they realize that they don't even get to keep a bag as a souvenir or a consolation prize. It will be all too late by the time they realize the true extent of the risks that they had taken, and, contrary to having believed that they were challenging the conventions, they will take part in the continued case for more government and more "regulation".

Indeed, as a consequence of the increasing measures of risk, the state appears "justified" in yet another role, in this case expanding government oversight, "regulation", and "insurance" programs as part of every "new deal", despite its primary role in producing or otherwise encouraging the trends. Additionally, due to the higher levels of consumption and government spending, as noted previously, the state can boast a higher gross domestic product and booming economic growth, which in turn makes the politicians look good and enables the state to take on progressively more debt, to celebrate its existing programs and to "justify" the creation of still others in the future. Finally, higher tax revenues and more debt mean that the government can continue to maintain the illusion of the new economy; that it can expand in its reach and its power to bid for more of the public's acquiescence, and to further intimidate and exploit the honest and hardworking people who, as the Keynesians and the central planners see it, exist merely to keep the gears turning, to keep the currency moving.

One way or another, the Keynesians and the central planners induce that higher velocity by cheapening the money. Whether intentionally or incidentally, cheap money has the effect of distorting the economy and distorting prices, but it also has the effect of distorting incentives; and in a society governed progressively by monetary incentives, it has the effect of cheapening the values of the people.

That is because cheap money isn't honest; it's speculative. It does not impose discipline or encourage investment. It invites frivolity and decadence. It not only corrupts an economy; it destroys a society.

Whereas the people are inherently motivated to do well for themselves, their own families and their own communities, the monetary system has served to improve each individual's contribution and his own reward. This has offered plentiful advantages in economies of scale and division of labor, while generally promoting the values of the people.

However, wherever that system has been corrupted by political expedience, that system stands to exploit the people in support of politicians, their cronies, and *their* preferred objectives. This is perhaps the most pernicious effect of cheap money, and one which commonly eludes the untrained eye of the public. Of course, by the time this effect has reached a fever pitch, the public has long abandoned its traditions and its scruples in favor of the more tangible monetary advantages. All the while, the unsuspecting public has been swindled out of its values by cheap money, printed or digitally imagined out of thin air.

In this way, the people have been conned into worshipping a false idol under the control of central planners. Of course, the Keynesians and the central planners are generally clever enough to cover their tracks or to otherwise leave their victims feeling richer and better about themselves in the process. After all, so long as inflation is driving wages and assets nominally higher, the people start to actually believe in their big lie.

Ultimately, in discreetly stripping the people of their savings through the inflation tax, conceived explicitly for the purpose of boosting spending and thereby supporting government, those honest and hardworking people are stripped of their livelihoods, their freedom, their peace of mind, the product of their own labor, their rightful property, and the most gratifying aspects of life. They are condemned to spend more time at work, and they are left ever more defenseless against the onslaught of government, its cronies and its supporters, ranks always expanding as the government spends more of the people's money. After all, a broke and indebted populace is far easier to intimidate and to control than the alternative; by definition, they have fewer resources to practically defend themselves, and for precisely this reason they are made progressively more amenable to the commands of the regime which promises safety and security at the expense of their freedom.

In the course of having precious little in the way of wealth and yet so much in the way of debt, they become more willing to depart with their freedom for some measure of temporary relief; whether it be in the form of food or in their ability to repay their debts, they come to participate directly or indirectly in their own subjugation. In this manner, the people are beset by a veritable mob, in forms both systemic and physical; a mob that is just as enthusiastic about theft as they are ready to accept any justification for their actions, however convoluted or irrational.

Fortunately for the mob, the business of government is booming, and its payroll has afforded the state, its cronies and its advocates ample support in order to continue their siege. Unfortunately, the mob consists of many who passively condone the misdeeds and, in still other cases, active members who appreciate neither the true implications of their actions nor the various losses that they personally stand to incur wherever the mob stands to succeed.

Whether through force of arms, pseudoscience, entitlements, economic policy, or outright propaganda, the siege becomes progressively more destructive as the mob operates not only with malice but with the benefit of its conscience and the advantage of the status quo. There is perhaps nothing more dangerous than a mob of this kind; unless you ask government, of course, which would have you believe that the most dangerous entity in the world is the person who thinks for himself.

Of course, that is precisely why the state keeps itself busy in its assault on the individual. That is precisely why the state prefers its own caricature of the individual: one pathetic and powerless creature who can do, say, and know precious little of consequence beyond the wishes and commands, the determinations and delusions, the ever-changing rituals and superstitions of the establishment.

Upon acceptance of this caricature, it is expected by all that no individual will take himself too seriously, that no person will take too much pride or pleasure except where obligated in his labor, and except for those persons representing or working directly on behalf of the establishment; that is, those with the power and the sense of authority to impose their will upon the former, the individual, who is conditioned to champion the establishment, to view himself and his own life as components within a circuit, as props for the set of some sitcom or tragic comedy, as drawn-out infomercials for anything and everything that the establishment is prepared to sell.

The individual scarcely survives in this environment, either erasing or concealing himself from the public or otherwise being erased by those with the power of permanence; the power of the eraser often proving as mighty as the sword and the pen in this capacity. Thereafter, wherever the individual survives, it is in physical form. There, he inevitably responds to the establishment as his master and his leader, his provider and his savior. The new conventions are his "safe space" from realities too rigid and truths too "triggering"; his commendations his badges of honor in place of his heritage and the legacy once inherited; the establishment the new institutions, the new religion, and he a measly member of the communist constitution.

A constitution of unworkable institutions, it is the constitution of wretches and profiteers, and according to them the proudest of all queers; it is the constitution of killers and quitters, deniers and dwellers, it is the keeper, the reaper, and the sum of all fears. It is a constitution not for "common good" but for common corruption. It is born not from inspiration but from agitation. Its promises are plenty but empty: selling caves as castles, defaming their slaves as rascals, securing support with pay, praise and tassels. Dispatching the man with discipline, the man who saves; the collector, the protestor, they rant and they rave. Once more into battle, they conquer the day. 'Tis the despots, the deceivers, who have the final say.

Among their ranks, there are the demagogues and the grandstanders, the self-appointed pundits and the paper tigers, the purveyors, the agitators, the illusionists, and the propagandists. When they come upon an inconvenient truth or an unfortunate reality, they set out not to understand it or to reconcile with it, but to conceal, to disguise, or to avoid it. Indeed, where reality presents a real problem or a real challenge, the Leftists are always prepared, not to resolve it but to find clever ways to "justify" more power and to blame their enemies; enemies apparently not only connected to the former traditions but, as messengers for the rigid rules and the uncompromising realities of life, presumed responsible for them, or otherwise guilty of acknowledging them, wherever any of them are decried by the Leftists as a source of their misery or any apparent "inequity".

After all, reality can be very unpopular, especially so where the state purports to offer a more convenient alternative. And where the state has succeeded in convincing some segment of the population of its merits, or otherwise the soundness of its intentions, the people are made to believe that each person is to serve a particular role within society; that one's obligation is to neither faith nor family, but to nothing other than his society; and that there are "professionals" for every task, who are considered both interchangeable with the family and officially "more qualified" to raise and educate the children.

In the planned disintegration of the family unit, women have even been conned into believing that they have been *liberated* from their domestic duties; yet, instead of laboring for the benefit of their own families, they now work for CEOs, stakeholders and conglomerates, and according to the politicians and political activists, they are all better off for it. According to them, this is *progress*.

CHAPTER XIX

"PROGRESS"

"Progress" for the state is not "progress" as it is commonly known by the people. "Progress" for the state means progressively less for the individual and progressively more for the establishment. It means progressively more in the way of regimentation and the work required to keep it moving.

It means that both parents are so busy working to subsist that their children are taken to daycare centers so that their parents can afford to shelter, clothe and feed them. This means that their children are brought under the care of "professionals" instead of keeping them in the care of the ones who are biologically equipped to love and nurture them.

It is a shame indeed that so many parents have bought into this con, and that so many have been led to believe that they can both ignore nature and suppress their instincts without consequence; that fulfillment, for women, can come without service to one's own family and children.

It is in this way that modern women, feminists, have been conned into believing that they are oppressed by their husbands and their household duties, that they are imprisoned domestically by children and chores, rather than privileged to care for their families. In due time, these are myths contested by anxiety and depression, so prevalent in modern society, which emerge from unfulfilling work and meaningless preoccupations outside of the home. These are women, with male enablers among them, who are in denial of the merits of tradition, nature, and even biology; who are prepared, if not eager, to dismiss gender roles, to subjectify gender identity, to diminish the sanctity of life and marriage, and to equivocate the point of conception and the rights of the unborn; who are otherwise, especially among the men, seeking status, respect and admiration, not for being honest or accurate, but for merely supporting those fashionable and "politically-correct" beliefs.

Little do many of them realize that, in so rejecting reality, they are stripping themselves of the most glorious of all purposes in life; that they are condemning themselves to lives in service to people whom they neither know nor care about, who in turn offer no long-term commitment and are prepared to replace them as soon as it is convenient or necessary. Little do they realize that this brings them into competition with fellow women to spawn still further jealousies and insecurities. Little do they realize that these jealousies and insecurities make joy and fulfillment even more elusive; that, apart from their mighty influence as gatekeepers for sex and romance, the new order, in many cases, pits women against each other, and against men, by appointing a select few as the gatekeepers for (that new form of) "success": professional success and career advancement.

Indeed, numerous studies have corroborated this story, finding that "women are [not only] overwhelmingly responsible for deciding which candidates to invite for an interview," but that "female jealousy of attractive competitors in the workplace is a likely explanation for the penalization of attractive women" and women in general. Little do they realize that this competition is, among other factors, responsible for not only that anxiety, depression and general dissatisfaction, but also a great number of the disparities perceived or existing in modern society. Little do they realize or appreciate that the antidote is found in traditions once honored by women in the family; by accepting that they, as women, are so precious to our species as to warrant the unceasing protection and service by men; to have, in turn, the honor of serving their own children, husbands, and families.

This is all by the designs of Leftism, which requires the dissolution of the family unit so that the people can be made to work for the *common good*, a clever euphemism for the political elites who define it.

This is not for the good of the people or the family but for the benefit of the state as the people are made to serve and even worship its interests; and they are often left so busy and utterly desperate for assistance that they hardly think twice about their sacrifice. From the state's point of view, this has the further benefit of presenting government in a positive light as a savior for some and a benevolent influence for others. This, in turn, has the effect of gradually anointing the state as the unquestioned authority over nearly every aspect of life.

Of course, by the time the government has succeeded in dismantling the family and convincing the public of their equality under the state, they will have already lost touch with the kind of love which might otherwise serve to defend their better interests; and they will have been left equally powerless against the state which they have all come to support, condone, or to which they have even pledged their unconditional allegiance.

In this way, where the state succeeds in dismantling the family, their faith and their traditions, it ultimately succeeds in replacing those institutions with its own; and in replacing those institutions, the state expects the full faith and unquestioning devotion of the people. Once the state has achieved this end as the ultimate authority and the final arbiter on all things, tyranny is a foregone conclusion, and one that will be suffered to the bitter end, albeit in the name of "progress". After all, where society has been stripped of love and family, there is nothing left to stand in the way of tyranny; and so the end will come only upon its disastrous collapse and some unspeakable suffering, not from the triumph of love, reason or sound judgment.

Indeed, where the state succeeds there is hardly even a whisper of dissension in their midst, where every individual fears social rejection or upsetting the establishment which claims to prioritize *the common good*. In this way, as Mencken put it, such a critic becomes "the most dangerous man to any government", the enemy of the state, and a convenient example for any other who might dare to raise any questions. After all, what kind of monster could even consider prioritizing anything above "the common good"?

From this and upon the dissolution of the family, the individual and the doctrine of their faith, Marx promulgates his new world order: "From each according to his ability, to each according to his need." Here, Marx makes no mention of free associations, ambitions, wants or desires; he makes no mention of any plausible method for determining *ability* or *need*; and he entirely omits the fact that one's *abilities* and *needs* are always subject to change as a consequence of circumstances and incentives.

Above all, he neglects to describe the mechanism by which he seeks to realize his vision: force and coercion. In keeping with the countless other omissions, he avoids dealing with the question: why should any human being be held at gunpoint to perform any task at all just because he is believed to possess the *ability*? And why should anyone be entitled to hold another at gunpoint to meet a supposed *need*? Of course, Marx pays no mind to any of this because an honest assessment, from his point of view, would merely undermine his cause.

Whereas Marx operates from fantastical imaginings of what the world *could* (or *should*) be, the shrewd economist sets out to first understand how it naturally exists: how it *actually* works, how people *naturally* interact, operate, and behave, *not* how he'd *like* them to behave. The shrewd economist seeks to understand the natural state of things before calculating the risks, the tradeoffs and the externalities attending any intervention or any proposal which stands to disrupt or distort that natural state. This is starkly at odds with the Marxist, who proceeds with his experiments through trial and error in real time, administering "solutions" ad hoc without an adequate understanding of the problems, let alone the foreseeable effects and consequences of his proposals. The Marxist waxes rhetorical and poetic, whereas the shrewd economist favors reason, logic, evidence, and, by extension, maintains a profound appreciation for the individual.

Through his fantastical imaginings, his poetic pronouncements, and his overestimated intellect, and yet without any assessment of, or regard for, the purpose of life and the ambitions of man, Marx merely surmises that society can be feasibly restructured in accordance with these subjective *abilities* and *needs*; that the wisdom of millions can be replaced by a committee of self-serving actors; that society can be ordered in accordance with *his* vision and *his* ambitions, and that society will be better because of it. In their rush to reject free enterprise and assume control over society, Marx and his fellow collectivists appoint themselves or their representatives to replace the knowledge of business and industry, as well as the calculated wisdom of the *price system*.

Whereas Leftism seeks to redefine the purpose of each person's labor, to redistribute the fruits thereof, to bring the people into a form of slavery to the "common good", demanding that each work for the benefit of millions whom each will never know, the free market respects free association, freedom of contract, and the coordination of land, labor, and capital through natural incentives free of force and coercion. It appreciates the power of self-interest and that of profit, and it accepts the fixed and undeniable constant that people work for their own benefit and the benefit of the ones they love.

This is opposed to Leftism, which operates through force, coercion and the centralization of power and judgment, which thereby operates through mandates, flexing its power at will, not only behind the barrel of a gun, but with the benefit of an entire arsenal prepared to enforce its every edict; a system which effects the neutralization of its competition and, through each of these, the final solution for the end of the public liberty.

Indeed, if there are just two prime examples of the risks attending the centralization of power, those are the Milgram experiment and the Stanford prison experiment, each conducted in 1961 and 1971, respectively; two separate experiments just one decade apart demonstrating the risks posed by the inherent meekness of mankind, especially "civilized" types, in their subordination to "officials", and the dangers posed by agents enjoying absolute power.

Thus, with the benefit of the findings from these two experiments, there is no particular cause for surprise when faced with the horrors throughout history, in the present, and into the future. There is likewise no question as to the extent of the threat posed by any establishment wielding so much power as to have no use for ethics, no need for the individual; having, therefore, no particular reason to hesitate in its enforcement, nor any reason to tolerate noncompliance among the public.

It is therefore true that, as the British politician Lord Acton is believed to have put it in the nineteenth century, "Power tends to corrupt, and absolute power corrupts absolutely"; that the ultimate end of unchecked power is the unbridled abuse of the people, the scourge of cultural and physical genocide, and even the complicity of ordinary people in the administration of so much misery.

The antithesis to this suffering is found in freedom, and economically through the free market. Far from the denial and the wickedness which are indispensable to Leftism, the free market accepts the self-interest inherent in all of us; the fact of in-group preference and that we care more about the people around us than we do about others unrelated and far away;

the fact that competition has the power to produce optimal outcomes, to spur innovation, and to maintain accountability through the decentralization of influence.

The free market accepts and harnesses the power of the profit motive; all else equal, a motive powering continuous economic growth, and thus the most efficient and most ethical medium for coordinating resources, maintaining discipline, incentivizing intelligent investment, and discouraging waste in a world of impersonal exchange, a world of perfect strangers: in the modern economy, this is known as the *price system*, which (along with money itself) represents the single greatest achievement in the history of mankind. This introduces the final two defects of socialism: the *knowledge problem* and the absence of market prices. This brings us to the next and final point: the remedy.

CHAPTER XX

THE REMEDY

Finally, in freedom and capitalism we find the remedy to the contagion. By necessity we find our way toward progressively smaller and more local governance.

Some of the principal advantages of small and local governance are that it is better suited to the necessities of the people; it is inherently more accountable to them by proximity, by their ability to conspicuously and effectively withdraw their consent; it enables them to properly detect overreach and excessive political ambition, to deter and to snuff out even the slightest hint of tyranny. After all, it is the people who are the most dependable stewards and defenders of their own personal liberty, not through the institution of government but as represented through their own families and communities; whose interests cannot possibly be served by any arrangement which threatens or weakens those essential powers of the people.

So far as the people seek to secure for themselves and their heirs the blessings of liberty, they must never cease in representing that interest. Indeed, it is through their personal investment and their sacrifice that liberty endures, and so it survives only where proper governance is maintained, and thus only where any trusted representatives and servants are kept strictly accountable to that purpose; accountable not to the whims of the public, but to the defined terms of their arrangement; terms to be strictly enumerated and maintained by the people through their vigilance; terms to be inherited, defended and respected across generations, to be maintained always and unflinchingly for the defense of the people, for the defense of liberty and posterity against the timeless temptations of tyrants.

It is through honor, vigilance, and self-sacrifice for the sake of posterity that we stand to enjoy freedom; and it is through freedom that we stand to enjoy the fruits of our land, labor and capital. This is the essence of life, liberty, and the pursuit of happiness, as it is the essence of self-ownership and true self-determination; as it is the essence of private property and free enterprise.

Ultimately, it is through just this arrangement, otherwise known as *capitalism*, that the people finally take ownership over their own lives; whereby they own their property, the product of their labor, and ultimately themselves; whereby they are to be the free-willed possessors of their own destiny; whereby they are equally free to abstain from commerce as they are to engage in it; whereby they are free to associate or to disassociate to their liking; whereby they stand to resolve and to liberate themselves from the defects suffered under socialism.

Far from the alluring dream, socialism is a nightmare in theory and a living hell in practice. Contrary to liberty, the theories of socialism claim to give the power to the people; however, wherever it purports to give any power to the people, it is *in theory*, and it is in their *theoretical* power over government, not in any practical kind over their own lives. A far cry from liberty, it is an illusion imposed upon the public to convince them that they hold the power, that they can achieve fulfillment through government and their work for the ever-elusive and ill-defined "common good".

Socialism, as a theoretical model, stands at odds not only against nature, reason and reality but against the qualities that bring meaning and happiness to life. It is not only unethical and immoral but ignorant to its record in history and practice. It is too often appraised for its intentions in theory, rather than its results in fact; but its results are all too predictable.

Once understood, whether through critical thought or personal suffering, its defects invariably come to light. The key, however, is that the light keep shining on its failures, that the people never forget them, and that they reject every temptation to believe that this time is different.

Far from *progressive*, socialism is a parasite, sucking all of the value and virtue out of any society it infects. While socialism systematically destroys a civilization, capitalism prescribes the antidote: it operates from the protections of life, liberty and property, and while its advantages are in these and their soundness in reason and abundance in practice, socialism defies them and advocates to place the means of production in the hands of the public. In this manner, property and capital tend to land in the hands of self-serving bureaucrats and politicians, and voters *in theory*, who personally stand to incur none of the direct costs and risks, instead defraying them collectively in such a manner which altogether conceals them from the public and the people assumed responsible for their management.

Capitalism, on the other hand, advocates to place the means of production in the hands of their rightful owners. In this manner, property and capital tend to land in the hands of those who are most productive, who stand to personally incur the costs of their management, *and mismanagement*, who are thereby directly incentivized to proficiently manage their resources. As Scottish economist and moral philosopher Adam Smith, known colloquially as the father of modern economics, wrote in his 1776 magnum opus *The Wealth of Nations*, "It is not from the benevolence of the butcher, the brewer or the baker that we expect to eat our dinner, but from their regard to their own interest."

Wherever any society or movement seeks to disregard this veritable law of human action, wherever any such movement aims in futility to enforce equal economic outcomes, these incentives will assuredly vanish. While the socialists will have, by then, successfully obscured the costs attending their mismanagement, the people are sure to shoulder those costs and suffer those setbacks, while the elite, who rule over them and purportedly champion their cause, continue to enjoy the spoils of their political victory.

Under capitalism, the individual and his liberty are restored, as well as his ownership over his land, labor and capital. In this, we find that self-ownership is also restored. After all, can one claim to truly own himself where he doesn't even own his land or the product of his labor?

Through the ownership of his land, labor and capital, incentive is also restored for the individual to work for himself and his family, precisely where that incentive naturally exists and belongs. As the economist Milton Friedman put it, "Nobody spends somebody else's money as carefully as he spends his own. Nobody uses somebody else's resources as carefully as he uses his own. So if you want efficiency and effectiveness, if you want knowledge to be properly utilized, you have to do it through the means of private property."

Friedman also rightly described the market as a system guided not simply by the interests of individuals, but by those of families:

"The extent to which the market system has, in fact, encouraged people and enabled people to work hard and sacrifice, in what I must confess I often regard as an irrational way, [it is] for the benefit of their children."

Friedman continued:

"One of the most curious things to me... is that almost all people value the utility which their children will get from consumption higher than they value their own... and they scrimp and save in order to be able to leave something for their children."

This is precisely why it is essential that every civilization honor the institution of family and the freedom of each to provide for itself. Any policy which seeks to reconfigure the system or redistribute the gains will invariably destroy that most powerful and "irrational" incentive to save and produce. Ultimately, the market system, as described, has the effect of maximizing incentives and thereby output, the latter benefitting not only the families themselves but, incidentally, all of the people whose lives depend upon it.

What's more, this system specifically preserves the rights of man while promoting an ever wider range of *mobility*. After all, it is not *equality* but *mobility* which is characteristic of a free society. It is not *equality* but *mobility* which benefits the ambitious and truly encourages progress; and progress, in any free society, is everywhere the product of output and opportunity, each being indispensable to the other.

Put another way, higher output means that opportunity is always on the rise. In fact, Jean-Baptiste Say described this phenomenon in his 1803 work titled *A Treatise of Political Economy*: "A product is no sooner created, than it, from that instant, affords a market for other products to the full extent of its own value." Therefore, it may rightly be said that *mobility* and *opportunity* are as symptomatic as they are characteristic of *capitalism*, and that all three are synonymous with freedom.

Ultimately, the case for capitalism is found in ethics as well as utility. It is as efficient as it is honest. Capitalism not only accepts the forces which drive the individual to succeed, but it harnesses them.

Unlike socialism, which intends to change the reasons that people work, capitalism accepts their nature and the wisdom of the market. Through this, capitalism resolves the knowledge and calculation problems, all through the price system, as well as the inputs and decisions of countless numbers of businessmen and industries that no politician could even dream of replacing.

The beauty of capitalism is that the price system functions automatically, without any central authority requiring the knowledge or the wherewithal to coordinate land, labor and capital. Beyond the efficient coordination of resources, capitalism has expanded the reach and commerce of virtually all the countries of the world. Through prices and profits, it has succeeded in limiting waste, mitigating risk, reducing the influence of irrelevant factors, and alerting business to failures in order to inspire change and to redirect resources toward more efficient and profitable uses.

The purpose of the *price system* is not the elusive *common good*, but rather the coordination of resources at the consent of their owners. In this way, the *price system* advances the interests of the people while preserving their every right to their property and the product of their labor. While not its express objective, its fruits are plentiful in advancing what some might term the *common good*. The *price system*, however, achieves this end merely as a byproduct, not by express design, whereas the alternative system, predicated invariably on force, deception and coercion, pursues this end merely in theory, and at virtually unlimited expense.

Whether it is rising prices during an emergency or a natural disaster, alerting industry of some desperate need, or it is a failing, irrelevant or oversaturated industry, prices, profits and losses will afford workers and investors invaluable insight into the value and efficiency of their work. Under socialism, or any alternative system devoid of this benefit, the workers can only await judgment by the ruling class, who cannot possibly ever know enough about the changes that need to be made, and who can never match the responsiveness of those monitoring the price signals in real time.

On balance, the major differences between capitalism and socialism revolve around the role of government and the perceived nature of economics, which is to say the perceived nature and purpose of man. Capitalism promotes economic freedom, consumer choice, and economic growth. It is that social arrangement whereby all land, labor, and capital are privately owned and exchanged freely and voluntarily; whereby, through some credible arbiter or body of arbiters, contracts are enforced and property rights are respected. Anathema to freedom and irreverent to choice, socialism advertises *social welfare*, *equality*, *equity*, *inclusion*, and the *common good* through strict controls over social, personal, and business activities; ends sought only through the subversion of freedom and the continual enslavement of the public.

The advantages of capitalism include consumer choice and economic mobility, which afford individuals choices in consumption and occupation; choices inherently regulating the market, leading to more competition and better, more affordable products and services. Capitalism also affords workers the opportunity to save and invest, to hold a stake in life as in business, allowing them to enjoy the fruits of their labor while assuming the costs and the risks of their ventures.

This contrasts with socialism, which dictates to subjects what will be produced and consumed, regardless of consumer wants and needs; with this, the regime dictates the very purpose of their existence. As opposed to capitalism, socialism privatizes profits and socializes losses. It replaces market incentives with political priorities; whereas the first operates from mutual self-interest, the second operates from the preferences of the regime. Through capitalism, on the other hand, market incentives are restored, and with them the principle of self-ownership: profits are privatized along with the losses, and the individual is just as accountable to the risks as he is entitled to the rewards.

Of course, capitalism does not singlehandedly solve all of the world's problems; only individual people can aspire to do that. Capitalism is merely the most humane and practical means by which we can feasibly obtain the resources to solve as many of them as possible. What's more, capitalism achieves this end while preserving the individual, his rights, and his choice in determining his own purpose in life.

The single greatest deficiency among the tenets of socialism is that which rejects the individual and presupposes an infinite and unhesitating cooperation between people immune to their own self-interest. In this way, socialism seeks to achieve the most preposterous of outcomes, to radically transform the manner in which human beings operate, coexist and interact.

In their haste to regiment society, the proponents of the collective predicate their world order on expectations of cooperation among humans condemned, or otherwise expected, to work for the benefit of others whom they do not even know. This ignores the true reason that people work, save and invest the fruits of their labor: not for the many, but for the few who comprise their homes, their families, and the other associations they elect to keep. Of course, whereas the people are first *expected* to work for the benefit of people whom they do not even know, under socialism they are ultimately *condemned* to this expectation.

Socialism, often concealed by grandiose designs of "equality" and the "common good", defies the fact that people within society are naturally competitive and focused on personal gain; indeed, the people are rightly focused on their own wants and needs, and those of their own families. They are the ones inherently responsible for those wants and needs; they are the ones who can most effectively serve them; and they are the ones who can effectively maintain that responsibility.

Contrary to the thinking of the socialist, the greater the scale, the greater the suffering. The greater the scale, the more force is required to keep the people quiet and working, and the less gratification there is in their labor. After all, they find gratification in their work by developing their own property, by owning the product of their own labor, and by meeting the wants and needs of the people they know and love. As the

German philosopher Friedrich Nietzsche put it in his 1886 book *Beyond Good and Evil*, "Every select man instinctively aspires to have his own castle and hiding place where he can redeem himself from the crowd, from the many, from the majority." Ultimately, men cannot be made happy in service to the contrived *wants* or *needs* of *society* or any of the nebulous abstractions formulated atop the ivory tower.

The truth is that socialism not only rejects reality but, at the same time, denies the intangibles of love and happiness; it seeks to replace family and community with the dubious *wants* and *needs* of *society*. Through this arrangement, the state becomes not only the owner of all land, labor and capital, whether implicitly or explicitly, but the chief beneficiary of that system. It thereby condemns its unfortunate subjects to share in a misery justified superficially by the "greater good" of society.

Capitalism, on the other hand, harnesses the greed inherent in all of us for the betterment of society, while socialism pretends that it does not, or should not, exist; that it can be reformed or erased altogether from the human condition. In rejecting greed, self-ownership, and self-determination, the socialist supports yet another form of oppression aptly termed slavery, granting the benefits of greed exclusively to a select elite.

The modifying distinction between this form of slavery and the more familiar form is that socialism is shrouded by intellectual justifications and popular intentions, guilt trips and grand gestures, and voices shaming the people for just how good they have got it. As the Nazi Party's Hermann Göring once shouted from the rostrum during the Beer Hall Putsch in 1923, at the point of Hitler's *socialist revolution*, "There is nothing to fear. We have the friendliest of intentions. For that matter you've got no cause to grumble. You've got your beer."

Regardless of intentions — the "common good" or otherwise — the effect of Leftism is to make people work for and dependent on the establishment. Even the people depending upon the establishment are working on its behalf, actively as ambassadors or passively as statistics, convincing some fraction of the true laborers that they are morally obligated, and that there is some good that comes of the scheme. In still other cases, some of the laborers and industrialists even come to depend on the establishment because of preferential treatment (i.e. subsidies, grants, protections, et cetera).

Over time, the number of people not benefitting, not on net but in some particular way, is eventually so small as to be inconsequential. Put another way, as the establishment grows larger and more powerful, there are fewer and fewer in the ranks of the honest and the impartial, and progressively more who have been bought and paid for in one way or another. Let us not forget that this is the *true* nature of government: accountable in theory to the terms of its constitution, but in practice to interest groups, on the one hand, and, on the other, the few who aren't already compromised by a stake in the business of government; the latter, of course, generally being of little consequence.

These forces wreak irrevocable havoc upon civilization, and their casualties are incalculable beyond the countless tens of millions sacrificed at the altar of Leftism over the course of the past century. In this way, socialism, at first a populist movement appealing to the trends and fashions of the hour, is tantamount to a series of childish rants taken too seriously; so seriously that they eventually come to rule the roost.

This has been the arc of civilization, from honor to outrage; from realism to whining; from the primitive and honest demands of reality to a state dominated by outrage and emotion, problems all too often manufactured and imagined in the abstract with the benefit of ample idle time; for the fruits of somebody else's labor or for the temporary comforts afforded them by debt. In any event, the costs are ultimately paid by their heirs, who not only subsidize that idle time but stand to suffer through the society that they have inherited. As the economist Thomas Sowell once quipped, "Much of the social history of the Western world over the past three decades has involved replacing what worked with what sounded good." Unfortunately, much of this has been made possible by fiat currency and debt, tools used throughout history to fleece and manipulate the public. This is why the people are to remain always and everywhere alert to the impingements of government, however discreet and however well-intentioned. This is why it behooves the public to remain forever skeptical of *democracy*.

There's a popular misconception around the developed world, and even, to a lesser extent, among undeveloped nations: the misconception is that there is virtue in democracy. Whether political or economic, there is this notion that democracy, or democratic process, provides a positive good in and of itself. However, when pressed to support their claims, if they are even prepared to defend them, more often than not its proponents are full of trite, dogmatic, or euphemistic language. Of course, most of them believe that the merits of democracy are self-evident, but beneath the trite, dogmatic, and euphemistic language, we find the disturbing truth about democracy: between the lines of propaganda and deceit, the treasured myths and misconceptions, we find nothing more than another form of mob rule; every election serving, per Mencken, as "a sort of advance auction sale of stolen goods."

As a people, we are better off with whatever system succeeds in securing the jewel of the public liberty, not for a term or a dynasty, but for all of posterity. This was fundamentally the idea of the American experiment: not a system promising positive political privileges, but an America set on securing liberty and unalienable rights, and on securing those blessings for themselves, for their heirs, and for the rest of time.

In his treatise *The American Republic*, Orestes Brownson described the true American system as an idea of liberty, "but liberty with law, and law with liberty... which secures at once the authority of the public and the freedom of the individual — the sovereignty of the people without social despotism." Indeed, the cause of America has always been the cause of freedom, and through this the cause of all of mankind: freedom from government and freedom from despotism; indeed, freedom from despotism under any name and despotism of any kind — democracy included.

As opposed to the visions of "order" and "justice" through the lens of Leftism, "The American Mission," as essayist Russell Kirk put it, "is to reconcile the claims of order with the claims of freedom." This is especially urgent where that mission is threatened by the means capable of instantly menacing a civilization. It is a mission "to maintain in an age of ferocious ideologies and fantastic schemes a model of justice"; a model which serves to recognize and respect the individual, his life, his liberty, and his property. It is a great idea for, as Brownson put it, "the development and realization of the beautiful or the divine splendor in art, and of the true in science and philosophy; and... for the development [and maintenance] of the state, law, and jurisprudence" where, and *only* where, it continues to serve its total mission.

For the proponents of democracy, they are hypnotized by empty promises, the perception of participation, notions of *equality*, and so-called *social justice*. They often fancy themselves *the will of the people*, but in truth they are the angry mob laying siege to the towns and traditions of the silent majority; indoctrinating the youth and priming them to promote democracy for their own ends; hoping that their disease will metastasize to destroy every last cell of liberty, both at home and abroad.

Through a swelling population spanning an increasingly vast area, and with so many of them abandoning their hometowns and routinely relocating, they devolve into a society of transients whereby precious few among them maintain any spiritual ties to the lands on which they reside. Unlike a tribe honoring its land and its ancestors, and establishing its roots ever deeper with every subsequent generation, the socialists come to treat the land like a public restroom or roadway. Always littered with trash or falling into disrepair, it is the tragedy of the commons: overused and under-appreciated, their society gets stuck in a constant state of decay, which degrades their relationships, their quality of life, and the values that once brought peace, joy and meaning to their lives. Of course, all of this is quite predictable. After all, the people are just passing through, and so, as they see it, there is nothing worth defending.

Fortunately, the antidote is near, not through democracy or society, but through virtue, family, liberty and the free market. While democracy claims to promote the *public interest*, the latter four are proven in both theory and practice; they are as good as a means as they are in producing outcomes. In fact, the record shows that, while free markets do not independently solve every problem, they tend to solve important ones over time; while they do not *guarantee* a standard of living, they afford the greatest good for the greatest number. Oddly enough, this is specifically because free markets and families are *not* democracies.

Contrary to the myths and misconceptions, free markets are not as much a democracy as they are a meritocracy. Indeed, this is an invaluable feature for any productive and sustainable economic system. After all, one of the failings of democracy is that it operates from talk and the consensus of unaccountable actors. A free market, on the other hand, functions through visible productivity and the inputs of accountable owners, managers, stakeholders and investors. As the old adage goes, in the short run the markets are a voting machine; in the long run they're a weighing machine. As for talk, it doesn't even show up on the scale.

Apart from the good feelings often associated with the very mention of *democracy*, it is no match for a free market. A free market operates from and incentivizes the productive use of land, labor, and capital, and no form of unbridled democratic process will ever match the efficiency of a sound monetary system and a market economy that together coordinate those resources between owners accountable to profits and losses; who, in assuming the risk, have every natural incentive to properly assess the risk and the prospects of any venture; and who, in managing that risk, stand, on aggregate and over time, to do the most good with those resources. The latter is an incidental byproduct of the free market, a positive utilitarian outcome which operates from a more important premise: respect for life, liberty, and property.

On the subject of free markets, they are not a panacea but merely represent the most natural, honest and desirable of options, considering the alternatives. All economic and political affairs are a matter of tradeoffs; there are no solutions. The principal utilitarian advantage of a free market is that it inherently vets and regulates independent of any government body; it is regulated continuously in real time by countless inputs and eclectic economic preferences as expressed by the second.

Human action is interminable, happening all the time and all around us. The free market is constantly being shaped and reshaped by it, minute by minute, moment to moment, not by a defined interval of some arbitrary term of office, and not through a limited number of options at a ballot box; the latter kept so secret that it is less than credible. So long as life, liberty, and property are protected under the rule of law, a free market is self-regulating, and so long as the people share common values, among them faith, goodwill and respect for life, liberty, and property, the free market will generally, on aggregate and over time, produce the most optimal of outcomes: indeed, it will yield the most good for the most people.

For this reason, multiculturalism and so-called *social justice*, combined with legislation demanding *equal opportunity*, have compromised many of the essential features of the free market. In a true free market, where values are as important as prices, people are left free to associate and to transact with any person of their choosing. Where they are forced to serve people and accommodate ideas of which they disapprove, or which are incompatible with their values, they are forced to serve people and to advance ideas that are threatening to or incompatible with their tribe, community, society, et cetera. This is just one of the many ways that societies are reshaped; one of the many ways that certain people and cultures are targeted by the political machine, albeit discreetly. Indeed, this is just one of the many ways that cultures and customs are targeted for extermination: a subtle form of cultural genocide, becoming less subtle and more brazen over time.

A prime example of this is in housing, where landlords have declined applicants on the basis of credit and rental history, lifestyle preferences, and cultural incompatibility. Whether a member of the LGBTQIA+ cohort in a primarily-Christian community or even a white person in a primarily-black neighborhood — a noted experience in Greensboro, North Carolina — smart businessmen make decisions based on more than just price alone. However, in modern America, only certain people are afforded protections against this sort of *discrimination*: they are called the *protected class*.

Contrary to its politicization, it is worth noting that *discrimination* is not a bad word; that it is merely a form of discernment and pattern recognition indispensable to the continued survival of every species. While discrimination may err from time to time, while it can be faulty or exercised nefariously, people discriminate in virtually every aspect of life, every decision that they make. They do so naturally through inferences and out of necessity in serving their own interests and those of their loved ones. It is not only a matter of preferences but essential to survival, essential to progress and innovation, essential to distinguishing between *right* and *wrong*. As such, the members of society who so vehemently protest against discrimination are indeed protesting against a natural, essential, and indeed ineradicable behavior, and indeed are, in their own ways, doing the very same thing: discriminating against others and their points of view in favor of their own interests, at the exclusion of those which contradict them.

Conveniently for them, they are protestors who generally go unopposed, who are often successful with the aid of *political correctness*, the benefit of the doubt, and the protection afforded them by the state as the so-called *protected class*. This is a privilege enjoyed and guaranteed for their benefit and that of the politicians who depend upon it as part of their strategy, who extend and guarantee those protections for all affairs social, political, and economic, privileges which rear their head in both subtle and relatively conspicuous and measurable ways.

Indeed, the privileges enjoyed by the *protected class* may not appear to conflict with the price system, and yet they do. Now, this system whereby one particular class is protected at the exclusion of the others is just one means to the destruction of those other classes — and that destruction will come through the vestiges of a free market in a form of jujitsu that leverages the strength of the market against the *protected class's* political enemies, in this case the heirs of the very people who built it and sacrificed to defend it.

So, just as businessmen and consumers respond to prices, it is just as important that they promote virtue all the while. As

George Washington once wrote, "Human rights can only be assured among a virtuous people. The general government... can never be in danger of degenerating into a monarchy, an oligarchy, an aristocracy, or any despotic or oppressive form so long as there is any virtue in the body of the people." Now, in addition to human rights, this author adds the free market, the first being indispensable to the second. A free market can yield positive results, on aggregate and over time, only among a virtuous people.

Now, this does not mean that a free and virtuous people will not fail. Indeed, just as free people are free to commit mistakes or err in judgment, so too can any businessman, property owner, employee, or consumer. From a utilitarian perspective, the most important aspect of the free market is that it not only vets participants (or voters) on the basis of their value-add but automatically signals to business owners whether they are efficiently using and allocating resources. Industries and businesses will flourish and fail on this basis, yet, as odd as it may sound, that is an *advantage* of the free market. After all, if a business or industry is not efficiently using resources, or if, all else equal, a competitor has discovered or invented a better mousetrap, we are all better off in reallocating those resources where they are best utilized.

This is a feature of the free market, not just because it is right and just, but because it frees up resources to be used where they can offer the most value. This means that, as opposed to governments and managed economies determining *who gets what*, free markets empower the people to make that determination on their own merits. It is in this way that free markets are the purest form of *opportunity*: they are dynamic and adaptable, meaning that power is limited, decentralized and impermanent, and they are therefore always subject to correction, always subject to new buyers and sellers.

Indeed, the power of the market is strictly limited, reshaped time and again by the people who comprise it. In this way, accountability is supersonic, whereas government moves at a snail's pace to remedy its failures, if it even gets around to admitting them at all. One of the overlooked advantages of the free market is that its power is not of the coercive variety; it is more aptly termed *influence* or *pricing power*, as opposed to the case of government, whose powers are absolute. Just as essential, a free market respects private property, which, in the investment of one's labor and capital, is the entire essence of life and self-ownership. Indeed, insofar as any business fails to deliver value, the right to private property protects the individual's last resort and his ability to meet his needs and work for himself.

Ultimately, in a free market we have not a universal panacea, but rather the least threatening arrangement, and the most bountiful one to boot. After all, the most dangerous arrangement is that which confers power permanently and without question, or, in the more practical view, which systematically threatens life, liberty, property, and every last resort of the people in the defense and exercise of their rights.

In response to the threats, it is up to the people to swiftly and adamantly reassert their values, to maintain "virtue in the body of the people." Among their various forms, none of the threats is more insidious than those resulting from a collaboration between government and industry. It is through precisely this kind of relationship that a new kind of technology threatens life, liberty, and property; which threatens to substitute *the pursuit of happiness* with the demands of *the common good*. In other words, this technology stands to completely redefine life as we know it, and thereby the ends we serve. That technology is artificial intelligence.

CHAPTER XXI

TECHNOLOGY

As technology has evolved, mankind has benefitted handsomely from the many improved systems and labor-saving devices which have afforded them a higher standard of living. These devices have enabled workers to become more efficient and more productive, and they have afforded investors the capital to economize and expand operations, to develop technology, and to innovate for continued improvements. However, there are hidden costs and risks attending the evolution in technology, and more generally the further complexity of society, particularly where the state stands to inherit and to abuse the newfound powers, and to capitalize on the shortcomings in public understanding.

The insidiousness of the establishment is no clearer than in the way that it metamorphosizes along with the complexity of the civilization which it enslaves. Where enterprise has succeeded in developing the networks for utilities, transportation and the supply of goods, the political system soon succeeds in regulating or monopolizing it, albeit occasionally with sound intentions.

Where these networks become progressively more complex, so too will government assert its authority over each of the processes; with members of the state all the while claiming that their authority stands to prevent abuse or to otherwise enhance oversight for the "common good". Under the cover of complex systems, the state furthers its true interests through expanded claims on property and some fraction of its slaves' incomes; property which, whether implicitly or explicitly, the state claims as its own.

The added complexity of the establishment leaves the average slave, or *taxpayer*, bewildered; so bewildered that, even if he wished to challenge the establishment, he cannot possibly begin to imagine running a convincing case, let alone replacing it with his own designs. Therefore, instead of rejecting the impositions of the state, the ordinary man views them as the small sacrifices necessary to retain access to the complex networks that he cannot even dream of ever comprehending; to retain access to all of the business, commerce, and utilities administered or otherwise governed by the state.

Whereas simpler times witnessed more conspicuous forms of overreach, the modern subject must remain increasingly vigilant in order to stave off the forces of that malignant institution which thrives within the uncertain, the abstract, and the ambiguous. This ultimately becomes a generational affair, whereby the added complexity continually makes a case against the freedoms and the rights, the incomes and the resources, of the slaves who, becoming ever more specialized in their crafts, ever more indoctrinated and confused by the complexities, remain none the wiser to the scam; who in fact, in relative terms, know progressively less about the technologies of their time than their predecessors did in their own — the latter of whom also having committed the costly mistake of accepting or otherwise tolerating each of the previous impositions.

Despite the fact that private enterprise develops those networks, or in other cases enables the original investment for their creation, the private company is due to expire long before the establishment which will happily claim credit under the same seals and banners; happily claiming credit for having overseen, authorized, championed or merely associated with the projects of that departed organization. What's more, where the establishment has, in the past, failed to effect "internal improvements", its rhetoricians redirect the public's attention away from the failures toward newer projects; projects intended primarily to increase revenue and power to the state.

Politicians most often achieve these ends by charming their audiences with poetic proclamations, dazzling them with illusions of grandeur, and impressing them with lofty language, or what former Federal Reserve Chairman Alan Greenspan called *syntactical destruction*. Of course, the politician can always point to a list of achievements accompanying the trillions of dollars spent annually, while deliberately omitting the facts about the state's profligacy: the waste, the boondoggles, the projects that failed, the opportunity costs of its largesse. The political system benefits handsomely not only from the spoils of taxation, but also from all of the ways that its agents can claim to have *generously* distributed all of the loot: after all, they always manage to do *something* with such extremes of wealth.

In a classic case of *the seen versus the unseen*, the average citizen has no idea how to score the expenditures, as he simply has no way of measuring how things might have otherwise gone without them. So, while the state chalks up one victory after another, conveniently excusing the failures along the way, private enterprise is nowhere visibly represented unless it is conspicuously aligned with the state. Indeed, the state seldom hesitates to cast blame upon private enterprise. Whether in response to a genuine failure or the market's apparent inaction, from the perspective of the state each case serves as further "justification" for an expanded role of government; even in such cases when government expenditures are, in the first place, responsible for preventing private enterprise from effectively allocating those resources.

Where any political initiative has failed, the cunning politician faces little accountability from the unwitting public, tending to attribute each failure to some abstract combination of inadequate funds, insufficient authority, incomplete information, or inept leadership. In jockeying for political advantage, the politicians imbue the citizenry with false confidence in a "new" direction with "improved" methods that remain hampered by the very same fundamentals which ailed their predecessors; initiatives and methods as ambitiously pursued, as confidently voiced, and even sharing in many of the same details, albeit under different disguises.

Instead of gauging the merits of government by its track record, the citizenry all too often commits the error of measuring them by the apparent sincerity or conviction in their messaging, where the populace replaces logical evaluation with an assessment of agreeability, likability, and general presentation: this twisted system rewards con artists almost exclusively, who are arrogant enough to crave the authority and clever enough to beguile an audience.

It is simply impossible for any human being to know everything, but the state assumes enough power and resources to know a great deal, or to otherwise do a good job pretending. This deficit has yielded devastating results in the form of ceded authority to agencies and con artists employed twenty-four hours a day in the arts of deception and feigned intelligence, conning their uninformed and all-too-trusting constituents into believing in their scams.

Where this knowledge deficit guides ill-informed public opinion and unfortunate voting outcomes, and where it renders the public particularly vulnerable to rhetoric, it also grooms them to accept the prescriptions of state actors who have been entrusted with too much authority; who naturally have inside information about the inner workings of the state; who specialize in favorably representing their own departments, their own causes, and their own specific interests; who have every incentive to swindle the paying public into believing that the state is doing an excellent job; and who possess the vocabulary to run a convincing case. Here we find every cause for remaining vigilant and suspicious of government, its persuasive promises, and the actors who stand to benefit most from convincing their unsuspecting victims that they, the actors, are working for them instead of the other way around.

In a world of people desperate for promise, magic and sophistication, whether a more "presidential" political candidate, a more mysterious spouse, a more elegant religion, a more refined automobile, a more stylish wardrobe, a more powerful identity, a more dramatic motion picture, or a more adventurous lifestyle, people are, in the modern age, more susceptible than ever to the ever greater promises of utopia; even those which clearly defy truth and reality. For these reasons, the people are usually prepared to pay the fare to journey into the abstraction of empty promises. Unfortunately, this one-way trip offers no refunds, advertises first-class accommodations, and guarantees nothing short of a crash landing.

Whereas technology and economies of scale have enabled workers to boost their incomes and to enjoy more time in leisure, the people have, in the course of so much ease and convenience, lost sight of the risks attending technology, the risks of surrendering so much to systems, protocols and machines. Although occasionally innovative, people generally have such a tendency to be dumb and naive, lazy and complacent, that it becomes nearly impossible for them to prevent their own constructions, their own tools, from eventually ruling over them and their lives. Once built to make life easier, those machines and those systems threaten to define life altogether, indeed in many cases even coming to reign supreme. These risks are nowhere more apparent than in the technologies designed around artificial intelligence (AI).

Just as any scientific study demands a complete enumeration of assumptions, so too must any honest study account for risk. This is especially important in the field of economics, where the implications are as serious as the consequences can be irreversible. All proposals and enterprises introduce risks and tradeoffs, and the same is true for artificial intelligence.

In the case of AI, the risks and the tradeoffs are manifold: (1) among others, the minimization of humanity and spirituality; (2) the further severing of ties between man and nature; (3) the rate of change in excess of human ability (and consequently the ability of any society) to vet, audit and account for the implications — and, just as importantly, the ability to thoroughly scrutinize the inputs and operating assumptions underlying the outputs of this technology — failures stemming from a distinct inability (or general disinclination) to keep pace with such rapid change; (4) the calculated regimentation of society at the diminishment of individual liberty, discretion, and preference; (5) the development of unfounded trust between man and machine, at the expense of man's own ability to think and operate for himself; (6) the relinquishment of critical thought and critical decisions to elaborate systems, protocols and processes which, at some future date, may not present the same measure of fidelity, at which time most will lack the insight and prowess to identify the faults, let alone control the fallout of such an enormous, complex and thus incoherent system having usurped progressively more authority over the thinking, behavior and government of society; (7) the assertion, eventually established, that artificial intelligence has no bounds, that it presents a superior alternative in every case, and that man's creativity, compassion and judgment can be replaced with limited or no adverse effects on his quality of life; (8) the rejection of the subjective, the nuanced, the romantic, the poetic, the existential, the spiritual, and the artistic aspects of life which, for the aspirant, come to define life altogether; and (9) the eventual conclusion that, as Marx so dangerously promulgated, "Society does not consist of individuals, but expresses the sum of interrelations, the relations within which these individuals stand."

As with the views of Marx, the threats posed by AI are not merely in their acceptance or their use at the individual level. Indeed, one vital distinction not understood by most people is that it is not necessarily one person's opinion or point of view which is inherently dangerous; it is rather the universality of the idea which potentially poses a threat. The question is not whether AI offers utility. The question is whether civilization can tolerate its faults at the Nth degree; whether man can cede that much authority to such a system, one which can only simulate human intelligence, without placing the fate of civilization in its hands and eventually succumbing to its rule.

The question is, indeed, whether civilization can tolerate such faults without succumbing to the rule of a system which is entirely incapable of non-linear thinking; the kind of system which, as in the case of Chat GPT when asked how long it would take for nine towels to dry if it takes three hours for three towels to dry, reaches the following conclusion: "If it takes three hours for three towels to dry, then it would take nine hours for nine towels to dry. This is because the drying time is directly proportional to the number of towels. If you double the number of towels, you double the amount of time it takes for them to dry. Similarly, if you triple the number of towels, you triple the amount of time it takes for them to dry."

Of course, human judgment would conclude otherwise, that, given enough space to dry each towel, and assuming simultaneous drying for identical towels under identical conditions, it is to be expected that each will dry within the same amount of time. This is just one example of the error in judgment to be expected from artificial intelligence, just one of the irreconcilable defects of a system incapable of appreciating nuance, and thus incapable of appreciating the human element. This is precisely the threat posed by artificial intelligence where it threatens to assume any measure of authority over human beings.

Of course, this happens in subtle ways, not as one might imagine because of Hollywood. In the view of the author, AI appears to solve problems in the way that porn solves man's sexual frustrations; in the way that online encyclopedias displace actual research and original sources; in the way that online tutorials enable people to solve problems (or find workarounds) without an understanding of the problems themselves; in the way that social media has made people more connected but less meaningfully so; in the way that digital media improves upon print media but, in many cases, makes it more difficult (not less) to get to the truth. The principal issue with the latter, as with the whole, is the speed with which information spreads, and therefore the speed with which people and their minds are satisfied.

It is also true that information has come to spread more quickly than the pace of literacy, and that, with improved printing and distribution, people have become better informed without necessarily becoming more enlightened, without necessarily understanding what they are reading and repeating. Indeed, the chronology of our species supports this; the Age of Enlightenment having eventually given way to the so-called Age of Information, an age which explains why people have become so anxious and hostile, and why so many issues have become so polarizing. A far cry from the Age of Enlightenment, the Information Age has trained the people to look everywhere but internally for answers, to trust others and to doubt oneself, to kneel before the ideas provided to them, and to pass them off as their own and act like geniuses while harassing those who dare to disagree, to be curious, to cast doubt, or to simply think for themselves.

It is an age in which the people, particularly those of the Western world, feel the need to form or express an opinion on virtually every news item, on all social issues and current events; and to do so based on very limited knowledge, fearing that they might otherwise appear stupid. In the unending chase for information and cheap entertainment, people have become frantic and anxious, always searching for that next news item or their next thrill, and always ready to be brought into a frenzy. With the frequency of communication and the sheer volumes of information, the people have been effectively paralyzed.

As it turns out, if you throw enough information at people, they are left so busy just trying to keep up, just sorting through it and making sense of it all, that they will scarcely have the time or the energy to actually scrutinize it. By this time, of course, the people are conditioned to simply accept what they are told, to accept the opinions of the pundits and the conclusions of the *experts*. The people are then told to *trust the experts*, to *trust the science* and to *stay in their own lanes*. In other words, the people are expected to remain silent and to simply think, talk, and act in strict accordance with what they are told; they are instructed to leave the thinking and decision-making to the establishment, to place their absolute trust in its wisdom. Due to the alien nature of most of the subject matter, the people are generally unprepared to examine the material for themselves anyway, lacking the knowledge and the tools necessary to distinguish fact from fiction; thus, they are prepared, and in many cases more than willing, to oblige.

In the Information Age, news is constantly breaking, and another headline is always on the way. For this reason, the people are constantly stressed, bewildered and overwhelmed. For this reason, most of them retreat, resign, or otherwise latch onto pithy slogans in an effort to appear educated and better informed; with the latter, of course, consisting primarily of the dishonest and disingenuous.

Ultimately, people have not the energy, nor the desire, nor the time to scrutinize the details, as they are simply too lazy, too comfortable and complacent, or too busy trying to keep up. As a result, more often than not, we are left with three primary camps: the first setting the agenda, the second running with the headlines, and the third taking sedatives, finding a way to cope. Meanwhile, still another, albeit a strict minority, patiently examines the information and weighs the options. All the while the wheels keep turning, the world keeps moving faster, and the first of the camps continues its crusade.

As the British mathematician Bertrand Russell put it, "The whole problem with the world is that fools and fanatics are always so certain of themselves, and wiser people so full of doubts." Thus, it is the fools and the fanatics who are so quick to mobilize, and the wiser people so patient, careful, and averse to failure that they seldom react in time or take sufficient action to stem the tide.

The implications for communities and interpersonal relationships are just as serious: whereas mentorship once fostered relationships between people, online resources and applications, having staked their claim on all of the answers and all of the best entertainment, suggest that there is nothing left to learn or gain from our fellow man. Indeed, the advancements in technology have had the adverse effect of pulling the people away from their traditions and even their respect for humanity; pulling them away from humanity to view people as pawns or factors of production, at best, as nuisances, laughing stocks or parasites, at worst. In this way, one's fellow man comes to personify incompetence, to be regarded as nothing more than a nuisance, an imbecile, or the butt of a joke. So, as man has dispensed with mentorship, so too has he dispensed with the civility and respect which once defined civilization, and which once made it hospitable.

Besides the social risks posed by artificial intelligence, it is also a matter of whether mankind can exercise enough caution to respect and maintain its limits, to keep government, which always benefits disproportionately from technology, from abusing its powers. Indeed, with each innovation in industry and technology, the establishment enjoys the benefit of acquiring virtually as much of it as it wants, using it to its greatest effect, keeping it from the people and employing it without their knowledge. With the public largely unaware of (or uneducated on) the technology, or generally misunderstanding it, the establishment can get away with the most heinous of crimes, all while keeping the public out of the loop, puzzled and paralyzed with bewilderment.

The end result is a people so confused and frustrated that they resign to blissful ignorance, taking solace in conventional wisdom, supporting the status quo, accepting and parroting generally everything they are told to believe. They are left so frustrated and confused *Figure 1* that they become increasingly hostile toward each other or otherwise indifferent. Those who resign to indifference do so out of utter disgust, disinterest, exhaustion, or disillusionment, to avoid persecution, to preserve one's own sanity, or to simply avoid the morass altogether.

They default to the status quo or resign to indifference in an effort to comfort themselves, to maintain the illusion of normalcy, and to keep their peace of mind so they can continue to live in their fantasies and sleep soundly at night. This leaves the public bickering amongst themselves: the mainstreamers and the status quo supporters against the truth-seekers and the uncertain, with the former ignoring or endlessly seeking to humiliate and ostracize the latter; even scoffing at the ever-shrinking minority who have — in advance and afterwards — spoken the truth and sounded the alarm about the threats posed by that technology in the hands of government; technologies which serve not only to annihilate the enemy by force but to crush their spirits, to so envelop the enemy as to suffocate them before they have even begun to consider an attack.

In fact, the annals of history so consistently evidence these points, the veritable threats posed by any government so well-equipped, as to have appeared in the fifth-century BC Chinese military treatise *The Art of War* by military strategist Sun Tzu, the modern English interpretation expressing the belief that, "To subdue the enemy without fighting is the supreme excellence" in a war; that more comprehensive means, including political, diplomatic, economic, and technical resources, can be, and have indeed proven to be, far more effective in subduing and deterring the enemy. Therefore, this is a matter of a people not only conquered militarily but controlled by the intricate and inconspicuous forces around them; forces which alter the relationship not only between man and his government, not only between him and his fellow man, but between him and the unseen.

Indeed, with these advancements, it is a matter of whether people, brought directly into competition with AI, remaining disadvantaged by government through taxes and regulations, can live healthy and wholesome lives under conditions and demands of such rapid change and development; whether people possess the ability and the fortitude to rein in this technology when it becomes abusive of its ends; or whether that technology, over such a sprawling society ever short on virtue, will merely hasten its demise.

The 2022 blockbuster film *Top Gun: Maverick* offers a brilliant exposition of this theme: man vs machine, putting the heart back into the cockpit, where critical decisions are left to a sentient human being who, as opposed to any computer, experiences pain, regret, and guilt; who can likewise experience triumph and fulfillment, who can therefore offer relevant value judgments and exercise subjective discretion where appropriate, functions (by nature and definition) not possible through AI. As Russian Chess grandmaster Garry Kasparov one put it, "Our humanity is not defined by any skill, like swinging a hammer or even playing chess. Machines have calculations; we have understanding. Machines have instructions; we have purpose. Machines have objectivity; we have passion." Indeed, it is the human being, through his intuition, his compassion and his judgment, who creates and yet acknowledges the dangers and the limits of his creations; who, in sighting a fellow human being in the crosshairs, possesses the capacity to respect life and to spare the world the uncompromising wrath of systematic suffering; who, as former US Secretary of Defense Harold Brown once put it, maintains the "human safeguards" against such "irretrievable actions".

Through just this kind of human judgment we find the forces which connect people, which dignify the individual, his life and his labors. We arrive at the conclusion that fulfillment, as a human being, is ultimately a function of one's service, not in the abstract but through the tangible and visible fruits of his labor: service for the benefit and the defense of his fellow man; for the development of his own ideas and his own property, for the benefit of his own loved ones, namely his family and his heirs.

This is precisely why so many people are so anxious and depressed in the modern world, particularly in the West: they lack this kind of fulfillment, where they instead deal in the abstract or serve large, bureaucratic institutions whereby the product of their labor measures in dollars (contemporarily in digital terms, forms still more abstract) and the approval of their bosses; where they fill the void left by their unfulfilling work with mindless entertainment, if only to keep themselves distracted, preoccupied, or even driven to madness in order to pass the time.

As opposed to failing and learning for oneself in the development of his own ideas and his own property, instead of coming to depend on one's own judgment and intuition, and instead of being accountable to (and responsible for) oneself and his own family, the modern man has been made accountable to (and responsible for) people whom he neither knows, nor trusts, nor cares about; thereby serving as a pawn or a cog within a greater apparatus. This is manageable to an extent, but insofar as it begins to journey into the abstract, where the underlying factors, critical assumptions and related "justifications" become too remote or esoteric, it presents risks that will, in time, be met with progressively less scrutiny and understanding; factors that will keep the people from asking questions and probing for answers, as they (the people) seek to avoid failure and humiliation as measured against the "perfect" standard.

This means a diminished capacity and growing disinclination to scrutinize antecedents and properly assess the underlying value judgments, so far as they exist in the protocol preceding the outcomes. Indeed, such a standard can only silence or discourage the people, a people becoming so progressively specialized in their own fields, so reduced in their occupations, that they become utterly incompetent beyond them; so reduced in their own occupations that precious few among them will possess anything more than a shallow understanding of others, and thus hardly the means or the cause to question anything at all. In most cases they will be completely in the dark, completely ignorant to and disinterested in other fields, such that the honest person will simply defer to others who are more confident, thus leaving the people more vulnerable to opportunists and conmen who make a habit of lying, deceiving, and cheating their way through life.

Indeed, with the developments in artificial intelligence, just as with those in information technology, people have come to not only *relinquish* much of their ability and their desire to think for themselves personally; they have come to *fear* the consequences of thinking for themselves and, thus, running the risk of reaching an alternate or unpopular conclusion.

Indeed, with such developments in technology inevitably come more sophisticated modes of surveillance and policing, each broadly supported by the notion that, "If you've got nothing to hide, you've got nothing to fear." This is a notion which is particularly dangerous to the public. It threatens to systemically encroach ever further upon the rights of man, to uncover ever more "justifications" for ever further encroachments, to permanently violate the sanctity of privacy and private property, to criminalize the most innocuous and the most arbitrary of "offenses", and to, given enough surveillance, eventually suppress all controversial and meaningful expression, even that which occurs behind closed doors.

It is in this way that the state manages to accomplish near-perfect conformity, that it discourages independent thought, that it dehumanizes the people and transforms them into programmable robots in service to the establishment. It is in this way that it comes to control the very thinking of the public, not merely through endless propaganda but by discouraging the people from being honest and truly human, both in public and in private.

As a consequence, the people ultimately come to tolerate or to accept the conventions, to eventually erase themselves for fear of exposing themselves as human, for fear of exposing themselves as individuals out of accordance with society and the prevailing attitudes, conventions, and expectations. As evidenced by even recent history, they come to fear challenging the conventions, to fear expressing or even harboring any thoughts threatening to contradict the collective wisdom of the conventions and the technologies which rule over them.

Needless to say, despite their apparent sophistication, that wisdom, too, is fallible, often compromised by the unstated, the mistaken, the unexamined, the subjective, the convoluted, the unprovable, and the enigmatic.

Just as we observed in the wake of lockdowns (as in "two weeks to flatten the curve") beginning in 2020, a number of politically-connected so-called scientists erred in failing to account for the bigger picture, the unknowns, and the social consequences. Even where we might accept the efficacy of such measures as lockdowns, which we shouldn't (given the lack of positive proof in the face of contradictory evidence published well ahead of 2020), a thorough study must account for the assumptions, the unknowns and the foreseeable consequences on the whole.

If there is one thing that lockdowns proved about society, it is that it cannot tolerate them without serious ramifications; which is to say, on balance and in the long run, it cannot tolerate them at all. The same must be said about social media and technology such as smartphones and tablets, which have significantly degraded people's interpersonal relationships and their patience for meaningful research, insight and conversation, in favor of instant gratification through Google searches, short video clips, and short tidbits of information on their news feeds. Along with other factors, this has also had the effect of destroying our sense of community, our sense of family, our sense of the past, the present, and the future, and even our desire to figure things out for ourselves.

Indeed, where popular online search engines such as Google, and online video sharing and social media platforms such as YouTube (also owned by Google), are trusted to furnish the truth, they themselves ultimately decide what is history, what is present, and what will be in the future. After all, Google and Wikipedia appear to have all of the answers, but, in truth, they don't. For evidence of this, look no further than two separate Wikipedia pages which place Lee Harvey Oswald in two separate places at the same time on November 22nd, 1963; or another page which describes "an independent United States of America" in the singular, despite the original text from the Declaration of Independence regarding *these United Colonies*, in the plural, as *free and independent States*.

With the benefit of so much technology and influence, government has practically usurped all control over the matter of education, which has left parents woefully unprepared to reclaim that role, to truly educate their children and rescue them from the clenches of public indoctrination camps; camps where they are left learning *what* to think instead of *how* to think, how to conform instead of how to find the truth.

Whereas individuals, clergy, wisemen and parents, among others, were once heavily involved in children's education, even this has been outsourced to an abstract bureaucracy whose merits are dubious, and whose practical value is questionable in the view of so many students, partly because they cannot see how their lessons apply in real life; and part of that is due to the fact that their parents can no longer show them how they apply, because they too operate within a bureaucracy in service to the abstract. In this author's view, fulfillment in life is the result of a man's laboring to figure things out, to leave a legacy, and by that to leave an inheritance (both tangible and intangible) to be further developed by his heirs.

On the subject of learning, it is not just a matter of memorizing methods and protocols (or simply reciting what you have been told), but, in the case of innovations and novel discoveries, a matter of figuring out how to think for yourself. In the absence of this, we are not only stripped of the potential for personal fulfillment, but doomed to social ruin.

CHAPTER XXII

RESPONSIBILITY

While there are those who propose democracy as a solution, the preferred alternative ought rightly to be personal responsibility. Indeed, this is precisely how a people retrace their steps back to virtue, not through democracy or by relinquishing their responsibilities, but through self-ownership and the reinforcement of one's own values. Indeed, this is one of the features of the free market through its price system.

Contrary to the characterization of a free market as a democracy or an unregulated free-for-all, it is the price system whereby votes are expressed and the system is kept accountable. Whereas votes are expressed per capita in a democracy, they are expressed by stake in a free market; whereas government regulations are tied to political interests, market discipline is imposed through private property and the daily decisions (and preferences) of individual people in their assumption of the risk. The latter is a far more reliable and efficient mechanism.

Indeed, the price system is the single most efficient mechanism by which to coordinate land, labor, and capital, and it accomplishes this end without necessarily imposing upon the public liberty. Of course, this does not mean that businessmen will not make mistakes, but that they will personally suffer those losses and, all else equal, they will continue to accrue losses until they eventually run out of capital. The latter is especially prompt in an economy of market interest rates, as opposed to rates artificially set by a governing body with a monopoly over both the money supply and the instruments of force and coercion; a governing body, no less, compromised by its own conflicts of interest.

This also does not mean that businessmen will not engage in fraud, but that the free market, through improved vetting and information technology, will generally, over time, expose it. Ultimately, whether fraud, inferior goods or services, unethical business practices, or an inefficient allocation of resources, the price system will expose it. As the 1974 Nobel laureate Friedrich von Hayek put it, "The curious task of economics is to demonstrate to men how little they really know about what they imagine they can design."

That task is accomplished through the price system, and through the aggregation of data through a decentralized web of inputs by individual actors pursuing their own interest. In this way, the free market has the brains of countless innovators and entrepreneurs, whereas government has the brains of the select few who couldn't cut it, who prefer to exercise their power instead of creating value.

Hayek put it best:

"To the naive of mind that can conceive of order only as the product of deliberate arrangement, it may seem absurd that in complex conditions order, and adaptation to the unknown, can be achieved more effectively by decentralizing decisions and that a division of authority will actually extend the possibility of overall order. Yet that decentralization actually leads to more information being taken into account."

It sounds almost paradoxical to conceive of order absent deliberate arrangement, but this is indeed the case in nature through homeostasis, just as it is in the free market through prices. Indeed, this is supported not only by theoretical conjecture but by real results. Free markets are always changing and adapting to new information — new inputs, technologies, and incentives — and they consistently introduce innovations and efficiencies that, absent the price system, would be neither feasible nor sustainable. It is only because of the price system that the modern world enjoys such sophisticated economies of scale, and that the most consequential of business investments are even possible.

Now, the free market is viable over the long run only through the continued vigilance of the people, who must stay wary of the interference of government: because of this inherent weakness, and because people have the tendency to get comfortable and complacent, the price system has not kept governments from exploiting, manipulating, or interfering in the market. Indeed, the price system has often been employed by governments to cleverly conceal their influence, but wherever the government imposes upon or interferes in the free market, it causes distortions in both prices and incentives; and so, wherever government interferes in this way, we have progressively less of a free market and more of a controlled economy, the latter benefiting initially from the extant product of a beleaguered free market.

For example, the United States is, by virtually all accounts, less of a free market today than ever: it is driven not by capitalism, but by corporatism; so, if one measures the principles and the value of the free market, in theory, against the outcomes of the United States in practice, then he is sorely mistaken in this comparison.

It is important to note that, in the United States, the most important price in the economy is set unilaterally by one committee: the single most important price in any economy is the rate of interest, the prime rate. Every price, and virtually every business and consumer decision, is based on or influenced by the price of capital. For this reason alone, the whole economic structure of the United States, as it currently exists, is strictly incompatible with a free market. It is through the means of control, whether through public debt, monetary or fiscal policy, tariffs, taxes, sanctions, prohibitions, embargoes, price controls, affirmative action, artificial barriers to entry, or a managed economy, that political forces threaten the free market; so, whether democracy or any other despotism, it is opposed to liberty.

Only a state of liberty can sustain the life worth living, and only the free market can do the greatest good for the greatest number. Ultimately, a free market is a necessary but not sufficient condition for liberty, and liberty is a necessary but not sufficient condition for a free market. It is not democracy which shapes the free market, but rather, as Adam Smith once famously put it, one's regard for his own self-interest, and the interest of his family. It is not through a vote at the ballot box, but through one's own productivity that he shapes the free market and provides for his family. Democracy, on the other hand, is all talk and no action, a death sentence for liberty and any free market as soon as voters discover that they can, as one Alexander Fraser Tytler put it, vote themselves generous gifts from the public treasury.

So, while the free market functions from the premise that we need to produce before we consume, democracy operates from the premise that we can enjoy the same benefits by casting a vote. While we all seek to bring meaning to our lives, and to meet our wants and needs with as little work as possible, the free market enables the people to pursue that end through their work, whereas the proponents of democracy claim that we can do this with a pen, or worse the sword. In still other cases, they use *monetary policy*, or debt.

In all courses of life, debt is a curious yet dangerous instrument: it can serve a person well, but it can just as easily ruin him. Whereas personal debt serves a vital function to meet needs in times of great exigency, the public debt is a scourge to be avoided everywhere and at all costs.

Obscured by empty promises and delusions of grandeur, the public debt, as exercised historically and today, is little more than perpetual slavery: it is a debt-financed government powered exclusively by the exploits of theft, force and coercion. Where its promises are plenty, the costs to the public liberty are infinite.

Debt-financed government is insidious not only because it creates the illusion that the public can have something for nothing, but because it distorts the relationship between the public and their government. In this way, the government gets away with an expansion of its powers (or programs) without ever having to prove their viability; without ever having to prove that they can be maintained without significantly more control over the people, their resources, and their labor, or without war.

In this way, the government funded through debt is more disconnected from the public which it purports to represent. It is thereby less accountable to the limitations imposed and grievances expressed by the people as the state inflicts untold suffering on a public neither present in the negotiations nor represented by their government.

In this way, a government becomes progressively more audacious and undeterred, seemingly unstoppable because of the creditors who temporarily let them off the hook. It is in this way that government is rendered beholden not to the public and their compact, but to the lenders who expect their compensation. In other words, the state is limited by its power over its creditors, whether foreign or domestic, regardless of the foundations of its constitution.

Simply put, the more debt to the state, the more it can finance the development of its arsenal for use both domestically and internationally: it can leverage its arsenal to manage its debts, whether by forcing its citizens or others to foot the bill or by conquering or threatening its creditors in order to repudiate its debts. This is one of the main advantages enjoyed by the state through the public debt, whereby the state can expand its power and influence at the same time it manages to "justify" or secure further obedience from the people. Little do the people know that the outside investment and the issuance of debt are secured by their future labor; pledged by the coercive forces of government which stand to swoop in and steal from them, whether directly or discreetly, in order to repay its creditors, repudiate its debts, or justify more of the same.

It is in this way that government, through its issuance of debt, seeks to expand its powers over the people, to subjugate the masses to maintain "full faith and credit" in their unit of account, a currency they have been thoroughly conditioned or outright forced to use in all of their economic affairs.

Regrettably, in the course of ensuring repayment, government expands its powers to collect from the public, as well as its powers to intimidate them and quell any objections. So, in the course of carrying the public debt, government grows ever more tyrannical in order to service and repay it; and where it meets the faintest of objections against further debt, the institution is thoroughly prepared to overcome them.

And so the public debt rises alongside the powers of government, hand in hand as a necessary complement to one another, forming a vicious cycle of perpetual debt slavery. Just as insidious, the debt-financed society leverages future generations to support itself and humor their delusions, condemning their heirs to honor their debts. In this way, the debt-financed society willfully surrenders its freedoms for some temporary enjoyment, leaving its heirs to suffer the costs; leaving its principled and disapproving heirs as enemies of the state.

Those not privy to the mechanics of this exchange are untroubled by the implications; meanwhile, those who understand the mechanics are sufficiently encouraged to play along. It is in this way that generations are broadly bought and paid for, paving the road to serfdom for their heirs as they bask in the glory of their unearned riches.

By the time the public has been made abundantly aware of the scam, they have forfeited virtually all of the means to self-sufficiency and self-preservation. By this time, they too have become dependent on the structures built upon the precarious debt pyramid; they can hardly wait to forfeit every last measure of their freedom to even stand a chance of survival, a chance at the future they have been promised. After all, by this time their freedom will be all that they have got left to sell, lest they journey into almost certain death in the remotest hopes of revolution.

It is for these reasons, and still others, that the public debt is an abomination, a scourge to be avoided everywhere and at all costs, which in every case irrevocably plagues a people into utter ruin. Wherever any people are to allow for any measure of it, they ought to hasten to responsibly rid themselves of it in their time, so that their heirs may know peace, sovereignty and freedom in theirs.

It is essential that they never forget the sanctity of liberty, that they reject every proposal and proclamation which seeks to impinge upon it and alter the nature of their associations. Far from social, socialism has nothing to do with the "greater good" of society, yet everything to do with the power of the state. Its stated intentions always belie the truth, but this has hardly ever been an obstacle for them, as they have been just as apathetic to the record of history. Indeed, for those at the controls, the latter serves only to remind them of just how effective their scheme can be; that is, just how effectively they can bring the people under their control.

Through any number of means, socialism ultimately enslaves the public to the "common good"; it eliminates choice and, with it, quality; it fails to reward people for being entrepreneurial; and it denies people the unalienable rights with which Americans have long asserted that they are endowed. It struggles to innovate, as its subjects soon discover as they, like their counterparts of East Germany, inevitably flee to enjoy the enviable fruits of the freer and more innovative capitalistic society.

All else equal, the freest society will always be the most desirable, and the capitalist economy is not merely the only form compatible with that society, but they are mutual preconditions to one another: freedom is a necessary condition to capitalism, just as the principles of capitalism are necessary conditions to freedom.

As Henry Grady Weaver wrote in *The Mainspring of Human Progress*, "It is important to notice that trade — the exchange of material goods — is always an exercise of individual freedom. Production and trade are possible only to the extent that restraints upon personal freedom are absent."

Incidentally, the problem in socialism is not just that it seeks to limit freedom, but that it must succeed in limiting freedom in order to endure. Capitalism, on the other hand, operates exclusively from the protections of freedom, where one is free to enjoy freedom or otherwise free to leave. History shows that socialism, on the other hand, is a roach motel: once you have checked in, there is no checking out.

In this, the risk of socialism is found not only in the threats posed to freedom, but in the risk of having no alternative; the risk of living in a world where tyranny has no competition. The debate, then, is hardly academic, but rather one about whether any people anywhere should be free on this earth; not free from want or need, as the sophists might frame it, but free from government and oppression, free to choose, to associate, to enjoy the fruits of one's own labor, to define the terms of one's own life, and to bequeath upon one's heirs the same rights and freedoms which allow for the kinds of purpose, privilege, and pursuits that make life worth living.

EPILOGUE

Sold in books, it would be fairytales. Sold in art, it would be rainbows. Sold in blueprints, it would be resorts. Sold in maps, it would be paradise. Sold in fashion, it would be lab coats. Except appearances can be deceiving.

It is a nightmare, it is a siege; it is prison, it is captivity; it is men in camo, it is men with guns, it is the silencing of souls, it is bodies by the tons. It is persecution and execution, death, imprisonment and destitution; for man in the flesh, his civilization, the slicing of man, of soul, of creation. However defined, however mistaken, it is sold under banners as righteous and salvation. It is the death of principle, the death of a nation. It is the road to perdition, the state of damnation. It is the death of wisdom, the rule of a system. In all of its glory and as it's been written, it's worse than abuse at the hands of Great Britain. Some shy and some smitten, in the end all will be bitten; by the sword or the gavel, living as rats among rabble. Controlled by hand or by algorithm, it is death nonetheless: it is *Death by Socialism.*

INDEX

The greatest threat to liberty is the aspiration to define its terms.
It is up to you to keep them in its favor.

Ad libertas,